Nations, Markets, and War

Nations, Markets, and War

*Modern History and
the American Civil War*

Nicholas Onuf and Peter Onuf

University of Virginia Press · Charlottesville and London

University of Virginia Press

© 2006 by the Rector and Visitors of the University of Virginia

All rights reserved

Printed in the United States of America on acid-free paper

First published 2006

9 8 7 6 5 4 3 2 1

Library of Congress Cataloging-in-Publication Data

Onuf, Nicholas Greenwood.

   Nations, markets, and war : modern history and the American Civl War / Nicholas
Onuf and Peter Onuf.

        p.   cm.

   Includes bibliographical references and index.

   ISBN 0-8139-2502-9 (cloth : alk. paper)

   1. United States—History—Civil War, 1861–1865—Causes.   2. United States—
Politics and government—1849–1877.   3. United States—History—Civil War,
1861–1865—Economic aspects.   4. United States—Commerce—History—19th
century.   5. Southern States—Commerce—History—19th century.   6. Liberalism—
United States—History—19th century.   7. Liberalism—Southern States—
History—19th century.   8. Nationalism—United States—History—19th century.
9. Liberalism—Case studies.   10. Nationalism—Case studies.   11. Free enterprise—
Political aspects—Case studies.   I. Onuf, Peter S.   II. Title.

   E459.O58   2006

   973.7′1—dc22

                                                                    2005018028

Dedicated to our mother, Barbara Greenwood Onuf

Contents

Acknowledgments

Two brothers (hereinafter Nick and Peter) who happen to be scholars in allied disciplines are bound to have diverging perspectives, converging interests, and plenty to talk about. For more than three decades we have talked about our respective scholarly concerns—in Nick's case, political, legal, and social theory applied to international relations and, in Peter's case, the political and constitutional history of the early American republic—and we have talked a lot. Some twenty years ago, we realized that the largely unexplored question of the impact of the new republic on the liberal world order of the nineteenth century was something we could work on together, more or less as equals in ignorance. The earliest result of this collaboration was a paper we presented to the annual meeting of the Organization of American Historians in 1985, with encouragement from George Billias. This early effort duly appeared in his edited volume *American Constitutionalism Abroad: Selected Essays in Comparative Constitutional History* (1990).

On the belief that our subject warranted a book-length treatment, we ended up, rather serendipitously, writing a book-length prologue on the founding and early history of the federal union in a time of world war. When *Federal Union, Modern World: The Law of Nations in an Age of Revolutions, 1776–1814* appeared in 1993, we asserted that "*Federal Union, Modern World* is the general title for a pair of books," the second of which we planned to subtitle "International Law and the Rise of Liberalism, 1815–1848." Both of us distracted by other projects, we did little for several years to execute this plan, which we understood to give a conspicuous place to the diplomatic history of the United States. When we finally launched into action, we asked James E. Lewis Jr., a talented diplomatic historian, to join our collaborative undertaking. James was skeptical from the beginning that the project's emphasis on conceptual history, political economy, and the general features of modernity took advantage of his strengths. He was right, of course, and his graceful exit from the collaboration taught us a good deal about what we were not doing.

Collaboration at a distance is never easy. Writing this book became much easier when Peter spent the 2001 spring semester as a visiting professor in the history department at Florida International University—Nick's home institution. As Davidson Eminent Scholar Chair in the Humanities, Peter was able to bring James Lewis Jr. and David C. Hendrickson to campus for an intense two days of discussion. We also taught a seminar together, in which we were able to develop the book's central themes and arguments week after week. We are grateful to graduate students from the departments of history, international relations, and political science; to colleagues who sat in occasionally for responding so enthusiastically to our self-serving and no doubt puzzling preoccupations; and to the College of Arts and Sciences for making Peter's stay in Miami possible.

Nick was generally responsible for drafting material in part 1, a good deal of it when he was Visiting Scholar at the Center for International Studies, University of Southern California, during the 2001–2002 academic year. J. Ann Tickner, then the center's director, and the center's staff provided a hospitable working environment, and the center's colloquium series offered an opportunity to try out some large claims about "The Rise of the Modern World." Discussions with faculty members and graduate students at the Instituto de Relações Internationais, Pontifícia Universidade Católica do Rio de Janeiro, in summer 2002 also helped. For significant intervals thereafter, Nick's affiliation with the Department of Political Science at the University of California, Irvine, as a visiting researcher gave him access to needed resources and another opportunity to sketch the story of modernity in a faculty colloquium. On this occasion, Bernard Grofman offered some shrewd advice. Brown University's Watson Institute provided yet another valuable opportunity to present an overview of part 1; and in Miami, ongoing conversation with François Debrix, Harry D. Gould, and Mohiaddin Mesbahi clarified many matters.

Of the five chapters making up part 1, chapter 2 is closest in conception and content to the project we embarked on so long ago. Portions of this chapter were drafted some years back and reworked for presentation to the American Society of International Law at its annual meeting in 1998; again for presentation to the Faculty of Law, Tokyo University in 1999 (with particular thanks to Onuma Yasuaki); and yet again for publication (in Portuguese) as "Uma Reflexão sobre 'A Idade de Ouro do Dereito Internacional,'" *Contexto Internacional* 23 (2001): 223–44.

Chapter 3 benefited from discussions with David Blaney, Onuma Yasuaki, and Wayne Sandholtz. A few pages of this chapter appeared in somewhat different form as "Eurocentrism and Civilization," *Journal of the History of International Law* 6 (2004): 37–42. A few pages of chapter 4 were adapted from "Normative Frameworks for Humanitarian Intervention," in Anthony F. Lang Jr., ed., *Just Intervention* (Washington, D.C.: Georgetown University Press, 2003), 28–45; and a few others from "Parsing Personal Identity: Self, Other, Agent," in François Debrix, ed., *Language, Agency, and Politics in a Constructed World* (Armonk, N.Y.: M. E. Sharpe, 2003), 26–49. R. Ned Lebow read chapter 4 to good effect, and, at critical junctures, conversations with Ann Tickner shaped the drafting of chapter 5. Previously published material appears in this volume by permission.

Peter was responsible for drafting part 2, although chapter 6 was a joint production. Portions of this chapter were presented at a colloquium on the Atlantic Enlightenment at the University of Edinburgh in spring 2001. Thanks to the organizers Frank Cogliano and Susan Manning and to the Adam Smith experts Nicholas Phillipson and Emma Rothschild for a stimulating session.

Peter had hoped to take a break from his ongoing work on Thomas Jefferson, but an invitation to a conference on the Louisiana Purchase at the University of Texas Law School in February 2003 led to a preliminary version of chapter 7. Many thanks to Bat Sparrow and Sandy Levinson for their hospitality and helpful criticism. Peter also previewed chapter 8 at a conference on the U.S. Congress in the 1820s organized by Paul Finkelman for the Capital Historical Society, Washington D.C., in April 2003. Finally, Peter summarized the major themes of the two concluding chapters in lectures and colloquia during 2003 and 2004 at Siena College, hosted by Bruce Eelman; the University of Missouri at St. Louis, Louis Gerteis presiding; Oxford University, with Richard Carwardine and Rick Beeman doing the honors; Chico State University, where Alan Gibson was a most gracious host; and at the University of Calgary, where Jewel Spangler and Frank Towers offered warm hospitality.

Constantin Fasolt, David Hendrickson, Gary W. Gallagher, Michael F. Holt, Ned Lebow, and Brian Schoen read drafts of the text, raised important questions, and made detailed comments. Peter benefited enormously from conversations with Brian; the influence of his 2004 Virginia dissertation, "The Fragile Fabric of Union: The Cotton South, Federal Politics, and the Atlantic World, 1783–1861," will be apparent throughout part 2. We are especially indebted to the Virginia historians Edward L. Ayers, Ben Carp, Allan Megill, Melvyn P. Leffler, Johann Neem, Kate Pierce, and Leonard Sadosky, who along with Constantin Fasolt and Richard K. Holway, the latter our editor from the Press, assembled at the Robert H. Smith International Center for Jefferson Studies at Monticello in May 2004 with copies of the full draft in hand. A long day of spirited discussion helped us reorganize the text and give the book a more suitable title. On the advice of several participants, we added a prologue and epilogue; to Ed Ayers goes the credit for the thrust of the prologue. We are grateful to Andrew J. O'Shaughnessy, the director of the center, for making this extraordinary gathering possible. In a perfect world, all authors would have the opportunity to present their work in such propitious circumstances.

George Van Cleve of the University of Virginia reviewed the completed manuscript with extraordinary care. His sharp eye saved us from many errors.

Finally, we are indebted to our wives and children for all the usual reasons, and more: whatever the occasion for our families to get together, we would talk about the project as soon as we could and for as long as we could. Our wives, Sandra Keowen and Kristin Onuf, forbade us to talk about *it* at the dinner table, but otherwise they pretty much forgave us for our anti-social conduct. The reward for their patience and support is not just this book but our disinclination to write a third volume. There is, after all, quite a bit else to talk about.

We dedicated our first book to our parents, who made it all possible in more than the obvious way. Bronis Onuf died not many years later. We dedicate this book to Barbara Greenwood Onuf, whose spirit, energy, and caring make her the mother that the many of our friends and colleagues who know her wish they had.

Nations, Markets, and War

Prologue
"The Momentous Issue of Civil War"

When Abraham Lincoln was inaugurated as president of the no longer United States on March 4, 1861, the nation was on the brink of the most destructive war in its history. In the decades since the colonies had declared their independence from Britain in 1776, the United States had become a great and powerful nation. But as the contagion of secession spread from South Carolina through the cotton states, the grand experiment in republican self-government that the founders had launched seemed doomed to failure. The new president would not capitulate to the "slave power"; he would not preside over the union's collapse. "In contemplation of universal law, and of the Constitution," Lincoln told his fellow Americans, "the Union of these States is perpetual. . . . Continue to execute all the express provisions of our national Constitution, and the Union will endure forever." [1]

Lincoln saw the American Civil War as an epochal moment in world history, not just in the history of the United States. "This issue embraces more than the fate of these United States," Lincoln told Congress in July 1861. "It presents to the whole family of man, the question, whether a constitutional republic, or a democracy—a government of the people, by the same people—can, or cannot, maintain its territorial integrity, against its own domestic foes." [2] The American Declaration of Independence articulated universal

---

1. Lincoln, First Inaugural Address (final text), Mar. 4, 1861, in Roy Basler, ed., *The Collected Works of Abraham Lincoln,* 9 vols. (New Brunswick, N.J., 1953–55), 4:264–65. Our understanding of Lincoln is indebted to the recent biography by Richard J. Carwardine, *Lincoln: Profiles in Power* (Edinburgh, 2003) and Allen C. Guelzo's two insightful studies, *Abraham Lincoln: Redeemer President* (Grand Rapids, Mich., 1999) and *Lincoln's Emancipation Proclamation: The End of Slavery in America* (New York, 2004).
2. Lincoln, Message to Congress in Special Session, July 4, 1861, in Basler, ed., *Collected Works of Abraham Lincoln* 4:426.

principles of national independence and self-determination for all peoples, not just Americans. "All honor to [Thomas] Jefferson," Lincoln wrote during his presidential campaign, for "in the concrete pressure of a struggle for national independence by a single people," the Declaration's author "had the coolness, forecast, and capacity to introduce into a merely revolutionary document, an abstract truth, applicable to all men and all times, and so to embalm it there, that to-day, and in all coming days, it shall be a rebuke and a stumbling-block to the very harbingers of re-appearing tyran[n]y and oppression."[3] But the bold experiment in self-government the Revolutionaries of 1776 had launched would fail if the union could not be preserved. The progress of political civilization would then come to a sudden, bloody halt, and the exponents of "classification, caste, and legitimacy," the "van-guard— the miners, the sappers—of returning despotism . . . will subjugate us."[4]

The founders had warned of the dangers of disunion and the state of war that inevitably would ensue. "If a minority" should break away from the union, Lincoln thus lectured Southerners in his first inaugural, "they make a precedent which, in turn, will divide and ruin them."[5] But by Lincoln's day, the hackneyed threat of incipient anarchy was no longer compelling to most Americans. Southern secessionists were evidently all too willing to unleash the dogs of war, and Lincoln would rather fight than seek another compromise with the slave states that could only briefly protract the waning life of an increasingly moribund union. "In *your* hands, my dissatisfied fellow countrymen, and not in *mine,* is the momentous issue of civil war," the president told seceding Southerners: "The government will not assail *you.* You can have no conflict, without being yourselves the aggressors."[6]

The union Lincoln would fight to preserve was not the bundle of compromises that secured the vital interests of both slave states and free but was, rather, the *nation*—the single, united, free people—Jefferson and his fellow Revolutionaries supposedly had conceived and whose fundamental principles must never be compromised. Nor did Lincoln fear the onset of war. According to the founders, the constitutions of fragile republics were jeopardized by the exigencies of war as the need for concentrated power and strong executive authority inevitably paved the way for despotic rule. Such

---

3. Lincoln to Henry L. Pierce and Others, Springfield, Apr. 6, 1859, ibid., 3:376. On Lincoln and Jefferson, see Harry V. Jaffa, *Crisis of the House Divided: An Interpretation of the Issues in the Lincoln-Douglas Debates* (1959; Chicago, 1982).
4. Lincoln to Pierce et al., Apr. 6, 1859, in Basler, ed., *Collected Works of Abraham Lincoln* 3:375.
5. First Inaugural Address, Mar. 4, 1861, ibid., 4:267.
6. Ibid., 4:271, original emphasis.

concerns now seemed quaintly anachronistic. Great nations were made to make war, and the power they derived from the people gave them irresistible force. War might be "as exceptionable from the habits as it is revolting from the sentiments of the American people," as Lincoln's Secretary of State William H. Seward insisted. But if foreign powers should, from a mistaken conception of their own interests, choose to intervene in the American conflict, the United States was prepared to make war with "one, two, or even more European nations." After all, Seward concluded, "War in defence of national life is not immoral, and war in defence of independence is an inevitable part of the discipline of nations."[7]

The Civil War indeed proved to be a critical, defining moment in American national history.[8] The nation survived its great trial but, as Lincoln insisted at Gettysburg, was reborn in the process. A union that was finally redeemed at the cost of more than six hundred thousand lives would no longer be seen as an experiment. "These dead shall not have died in vain," Lincoln promised, and "this nation, under God, shall have a new birth of freedom." To properly honor those who "gave the last full measure of devotion," Americans must rededicate themselves to the proposition "that government of the people, by the people, for the people, shall not perish from the earth."[9]

The character of the American union was transformed between Jefferson's time and Lincoln's. Lincoln invoked Jefferson in order to establish a legitimating genealogy for the American nation and to define its world historical destiny. Lincoln's emphasis on the progress of liberty and free government was all the more important because the logic of nationhood minimized the distinctions among regimes—between Old World monarchy and New World republicanism—that were so important to the American founders. The battlefield, where conflicts among nations were adjudicated, was the great equalizer. Under the "discipline of nations," all nations must develop the capacity to make

---

7. Revision of William H. Seward to Charles Francis Adams, Washington, May 21, 1861, ibid., 4:380.
8. For a good narrative history of the war, see James M. McPherson, *Battle Cry of Freedom: The Civil War Era* (New York, 1988). For an insightful study of the impact of the war on similar Northern and Southern communities that emphasizes the central importance of slavery, see Edward L. Ayers, *In the Presence of Mine Enemies: War in the Heart of America, 1859–1863* (New York, 2003).
9. Lincoln, Gettysburg Address (final text), Nov. 19, 1863, in Basler, ed., *Collected Works of Abraham Lincoln* 7:23. The literature on the Gettysburg Address and the transformation of American politics is enormous. Notable works include James M. McPherson, *Abraham Lincoln and the Second American Revolution* (New York, 1991) and Garry Wills, *Lincoln at Gettysburg: The Words That Remade America* (New York, 1992).

war, efficiently mobilizing human and industrial resources in the name of defending "national life"; to seem legitimate, all national governments must plausibly claim to embody their peoples' collective identity and exercise their will. Nationalists such as Lincoln had to nationalize universal values; in appealing to the larger world, they had to universalize national values.

Lincoln's efforts to make sense out of the Civil War reflected a fundamental tension between the universal and the particular, the world and the nation, that characterizes the modern world. Our purpose in *Nations, Markets, and War* is to illuminate the critical conceptual developments in Western liberal thought that enabled Lincoln to see the crisis of the union as an epochal struggle for the new nation's soul. As the first part of this book will show, these developments were not peculiar to the United States, but American circumstances were propitious for their precocious elaboration. Not only was the United States the "first new nation" but the sectional crisis that threatened its survival gave rise to the first great conflict in the nineteenth century between modern nations that commanded the loyalties and lives of their peoples.

The novelty of nationhood claims, North and South, in the disintegrating union has been obscured by the war's outcome and the vindication of Lincoln's insistence that the Confederacy was not a legitimate nation, that the union was and remained the legitimate government of the whole nation, South included, and that the federal Constitution he was sworn to uphold was its "organic law." [10] Yet *union* and *nation* were not interchangeable terms for all Americans in 1861. The idea that Americans constituted a single people was traceable back to the American Revolution, but its implications for governance in the federal republic were always controversial, and controversies over the nature of the union led many Americans—North and South—to question the "nation's" existence. By 1861, the great intersectional conflict over slavery and its extension westward had fractured the union, undermining any sense that Americans shared a common identity.

The emergence of a self-proclaimed Confederate nation should have been the definitive refutation of Lincoln's fundamental premise. The new president thus faced a formidable challenge as his administration prepared to crush the slaveholders' rebellion and preempt intervention and recognition by foreign powers: he had to show that the Confederacy had no right to exist, that the loyalty of its people had no bearing on its legitimacy. Jefferson's Declaration was

---

10. "I did understand however, that my oath to preserve the constitution to the best of my ability, imposed on me the duty of preserving, by every indispensable means, that government—that nation—of which that constitution was the organic law" (Lincoln to Albert G. Hodges, Apr. 4, 1864, in Basler, ed., *Collected Works of Abraham Lincoln* 7:281).

not "a merely revolutionary document," and therefore it could not authorize any self-proclaimed people's bid for independence in defiance of the will of the majority. There was no analogy, Lincoln insisted, between the circumstances of American Revolutionaries who were not represented in the British Parliament and Southern secessionists who were not only represented in but who had long dominated the federal government.

Yet Lincoln's conception of the nation did not finally rely on the principle of majority rule. A majority of the present generation did not have the right to forfeit the sacred trust of nationhood, regardless of its ephemeral sentiments or interested calculations. Lincoln most fully articulated this transcendent conception of nationhood in the darkest days of the war. "A nation may be said to consist of its territory, its people, and its laws," he told Congress in December 1862, and "the territory is the only part which is of certain durability." "Our national strife springs not from our permanent part; not from the land we inhabit; not from the national homestead." A husband and wife might divorce, but the permanent separation of a great, continental nation was a physical impossibility. The nation "demands union, and abhors separation. In fact, it would, ere long, force reunion, however much of blood and treasure the separation might have cost." "Our strife pertains to ourselves—to the passing generations of men," Lincoln concluded, "and it can, without convulsion, be hushed forever with the passing of one generation." The "hush" that descended over the nation's battlefields marked the sudden, violent "passing" of its best young men, the present "generation," sacrifices to the unholy frenzy of rebels who violently assaulted the integrity and inviolability of the "national homestead."[11]

The deeper meanings of nationhood became clearer to Lincoln as battlefields were drenched in blood and he faced the horrific prospect of defeat. War represented both the negation—the literal destruction—of the nation and its apotheosis. The Civil War at once severed and reaffirmed the connections with the Revolutionary fathers that Lincoln so anxiously and repeatedly invoked, thus justifying the trope of rebirth. The powerful relationship between modern ideas of nationhood and the awful realities of war that were so conspicuous in Lincoln's eloquent rhetoric constitutes a central subject of this book. Warfare, the ultimate failure—or, perhaps, essential expression—of international politics, demonstrates that nations do not and cannot exist in isolation. Lincoln was obsessed with the judgment of posterity on the American role in world history, but he was also necessarily obsessed with the more immediate, interested judgments of other nations in

---

11. Annual Message to Congress, Dec. 1, 1862, ibid., 5:527, 529.

the ongoing conflict. "British recognition" of the Confederacy, Seward wrote, "would be British intervention to create within our territory a hostile State, by overthrowing this Republic itself." Recognition would be a constitutive act, giving the self-proclaimed new nation "body and independence by resisting our measures of suppression."[12]

The modern idea of the nation emerged in tandem with the modern idea of the world, or international society, that nations collectively constitute. Our book therefore is an essay in modern history, an effort to understand a mode of historical thinking that rationalized and authorized the nation-states making up the modern world. As Enlightenment historians argued, the "progress of opulence"—the expansion of markets—promoted the "wealth of nations" and their progressive civilization. Americans saw themselves as the leading beneficiaries of this progress, as "recipients of the choicest bounties of Heaven." In the midst of the war, Lincoln asserted that, thanks to the spread of market relations—and, of course, God—"we have grown in numbers, wealth and power, as no other nation has ever grown."[13] But what was the proper extent of the market? Americans reached conflicting conclusions, as we show in our concluding chapters, about whether the market was properly bounded by the nation or union, the "national household," or whether Americans should trade freely in a larger world market where national distinctions dissolved. Advanced commercial societies gave rise, simultaneously, to both the modern nation and the modern world. Union was inconceivable without trade: "commerce, brings us together, and makes us better friends," Lincoln insisted. The "mutual accommodations" of an intersectional division of labor "are the cements which bind together the different parts of this Union."[14] At the same time, however, conflicts of interest over commercial policy—like divisions over slavery—drove Americans apart.

Lincoln was a historical thinker, as his constant references to the American founding and its world historical significance attest. But he could hardly imagine that the United States in 1861 represented the fulfillment of the Revolutionaries' progressive intentions. To the contrary, the new nation stood at an epochal fork in the road: its future—and the future of the world—hung

12. Revision of William H. Seward to Charles Francis Adams, Washington, May 21, 1861, ibid., 4:379. For Lincoln's diplomacy, see the definitive works of Howard Jones, *Union in Peril: The Crisis over British Intervention in the Civil War* (Chapel Hill, N.C., 1992) and *Abraham Lincoln and a New Birth of Freedom: The Union and Slavery in the Diplomacy of the Civil War* (Lincoln, Neb., 1999).
13. Lincoln, Proclamation Appointing a National Fast Day, Mar. 30, 1863, Basler, ed., *Collected Works of Abraham Lincoln* 6:156.
14. Seventh Debate with Stephen Douglas, Alton, Oct. 15, 1858, ibid., 3:309.

in the balance. Was the institution of slavery, the only thing that "ever threatened . . . the dissolution of the Union," really "in the course of ultimate extinction"?[15] In view of the Supreme Court's *Dred Scott* decision of 1857, denying citizenship to free blacks, it was perhaps more plausible to predict that slavery "may be pushed forward until it shall become alike lawful in all the States, old as well as new, North as well as South." The nation might very well "go one way or the other."[16] Lincoln's conception of American nationhood thus came into sharp focus as he confronted the possibility that it might be dedicated not to freedom but rather to the perpetuation of slavery. A "house divided" on this fundamental issue could not long stand. The horrifying prospect was that the national "house" would be united on the foundation of slavery, that the American people—because of pervasive racial prejudice, selfish interest, or simple indifference—would fail to recognize that the American conflict over slavery represented "the eternal struggle between these two principles—right and wrong—throughout the world." These "two principles" have "stood face to face from the beginning of time," Lincoln asserted, and they "will ever continue to struggle. The one is the common right of humanity and the other the divine right of kings."[17]

Yet Lincoln understood that these principles—and their application to the slavery controversy—were not self-evident to most Northerners, much less to Southerners. Of course, "we all declare for liberty," he conceded in April 1864, "but in using the same *word* we do not at all mean the same *thing*." For advocates of free labor, "the word liberty may mean for each man to do as he pleases with himself, and the product of his labor," while for defenders of slavery "the same word may mean for some men to do as they please with other men, and the product of other men's labor."[18] The immorality of slavery and its incompatibility with cherished American principles might be clear to some Northerners, but Southerners hold "that Slavery is morally right, and socially elevating," and therefore "cannot cease to demand a full national recognition of it, as a legal right, and a social blessing. . . . If it is right, we cannot justly object to its nationality—its universality."[19] Massive bloodletting on Civil War battlefields did not clarify the issue, instead reinforcing Lincoln's doubts about the progress of civilization and God's inscrutable purposes. If devout Northerners believed God was on their side, so did devout

15. Fifth Debate with Douglas, Galesburg, Oct. 7, 1858; Seventh Debate, Alton, Oct. 15, 1858, ibid., 3:236, 306.
16. Ibid., 3:306.
17. Ibid., 3:315.
18. Address at Sanitary Fair, Baltimore, Md., Apr. 18, 1864, ibid., 7:301–2, original emphasis.
19. Speech at New Haven, Conn., Mar. 6, 1860, ibid., 4:29.

Southerners: Northerners and Southerners alike "read the same Bible, and pray to the same God," Lincoln acknowledged in his second inaugural address.[20] "The only difference between them and us," the Kentucky-born Lincoln concluded in 1858, "is the difference of circumstances."[21]

Perhaps "progress" was not inevitable after all, and a new era of darkness was descending on the world. Would the massive power that nations could now deploy necessarily serve higher, transcendent purposes? Nationalism— the faith that national self-determination would necessarily promote the progress of civilization—was the emergent faith of nineteenth-century liberals. But who could judge between nations when their claims conflicted—as did those of the two nations that made war on each other in North America from 1861 to 1865? Confronting the nation's possible negation and destruction, Lincoln had to justify coercion, the capacity to make war in order to sustain "national life," as the nation's ultimate foundational principle, even as secessionists plausibly invoked Revolutionary conceptions of consent and national self-determination on behalf of their own nation-making project. A "civilized," great, and powerful nation was in some sense its own justification, and war offered the broadest scope for the expression of national purpose. But Lincoln could never overcome doubts about his nation's destiny. What price should Americans pay to vindicate a national idea that so many Americans of good faith so conscientiously rejected? Lincoln's suspicion that God might not be on the union's side but meant to punish *all* Americans for their sins—"may we not justly fear that the awful calamity of civil war, which now desolates the land, may be but a punishment, inflicted upon us, for our presumptuous sins, to the needful end of our national reformation as a whole People?"—made the willful nationalist humble and circumspect, magnanimous in victory.[22] For it was manifestly *not* dedication to the principles of free government, as Lincoln defined them, that in fact bound Americans together. Perhaps the American founders had intended to destroy all forms of despotism, including racial slavery; perhaps future generations of Americans would fully redeem the founders' promise. But Lincoln's generation, in its plunge into the abyss of war, shared something more mundane and yet more profound, the massive suffering, destruction, and death that is the nation's negative—and most compelling—image of itself.

---

20. Second Inaugural Address, Mar. 4, 1865, ibid., 8:333.
21. Speech at Springfield (fragment), Oct. 30, 1858, ibid., 3:334.
22. Lincoln Proclamation Appointing a National Fast Day, Mar. 30, 1863, ibid., 6:156.

PART I

Modern History

This is an essay in modern history. To say this is to confirm that there is a condition, a distinctive state of affairs, we call modernity; that there is a place we know as the modern world; that there was a time when this condition began to exhibit its distinctive properties and perhaps a time when it will come to an end; that there are other times and places exhibiting different properties, to which we moderns give other names.

We often say that modernity got its start with the recovery of ancient learning. When Renaissance humanists began to celebrate what is modern (*modernus,* from the Latin adverb *modo:* just now, recently) instead of what they admired for its priority and enduring worth (*antiquus:* what is in front, preferable, important, venerable), they saw themselves standing on the shoulders of giants. That an ancient, glorious world had come to an end with the fall of Rome and a new world had begun with the Renaissance left a time between. In this middle age (*medium aevum*), the wisdom of the ancients had been lost, and the convergence of inertia and Christian dogma created an empty shell, a time out of time, a world denied. More modern thinkers came to see the Middle Ages not as the aftermath of antiquity's dreadful demise but as a world unto itself, a world whose distinctive properties set it apart from the heroic world of the ancients and the new world in the making. Even if the fall of Rome marked no more than the beginning of the end of the ancient world, no comparable event marked the end—even the beginning of the end—of the medieval world. Yet the arrival of Renaissance humanism signaled a momentous change in ways of thinking.

Modernity's inescapable creation story unfolds in three chapters: antiquity, the Middle Ages, and the modern world. Only in the last chapter does modernity rescue time from eternity, the living past from the oblivious present, the moving panorama of human history from the dead weight of custom.

Time becomes the metric for change, the past a stream of events charged with meaning only in relation to other events, history the record of a receding present that is no less a river into the future. As time, change, and history came together as modernity's single source and then locked together as modernity's relentless pump, a swelling, cascading deluge of events has swamped the planet.

Modern people have witnessed momentous changes: material prosperity once unimaginable; waves of technical innovation; the compounding of wealth deployed as capital and the transformation of "the productive powers of labour" (to use Adam Smith's words); the immiseration of millions of people; the crystallization of classes, class consciousness, and class conflict; the multiplication of sites of production, circuits of exchange, and opportunities for consumption; the accumulation of waste, the relentless decay of whatever people make and use, the fouling of the Earth; disenchantment, secularization, the disruption of time-honored ways of life—and their paradoxical persistence; the vast migrations, the proliferation of cities, triumphs of public health, crises in healthcare; the convergence of impersonal rule, legal personality, and territorial jurisdiction in the form of the state; the emergence of the nation as the embodiment of social life, the forging of nations in the crucible of war, the nation as catalyst for war; the symbiosis of nation and state, the burgeoning relations of nation-states; the organization of violence and the fear of war, the readiness to fight and the costs of war.

Our concern in this essay is not the torrent of events that made the modern world. Nor do we propose to look at a series of exemplary episodes that would make the rampaging flood of modernity an edifying story—or perhaps a not so edifying story. Instead, we take an extended episode in this story—the coming of the Civil War in the United States—and situate it in the larger context of conceptual change. We treat the antebellum United States as an early experiment in nation making that was driven by the logic of economic development and that, finally, gave rise to two separate and hostile nations. Radically different approaches to world markets and irreconcilable ways of life led to disunion and war. The world in which this experiment unfolded was rapidly and decisively changing in a recognizably liberal direction anticipated by two centuries of conjecture about the meaning of history and the moral implications of the human condition.

We are concerned with the dynamics of change that play out in the modalities of production and exchange. We consider the relation of modernity to a way of life that depended on, and defended, the institution of slavery. And we will have much to say about the distinctive political arrangements of the modern world—about the state, the nation, and international relations. Yet we do not pretend to offer either a comprehensive review of these developments or a detailed narrative of the events leading to the Civil War. Instead, we will focus on how people in the process of becoming modern thought about themselves and their world—a world changing before their eyes.

We change the world in innumerable ways when we change the way we think about it. Modernity began as a revolution in the conditions of knowledge. What we think we know depends on how we identify things and their relations to each other by reference to the identifiable properties of both. Things are wholes consisting of parts in relation; wholes are themselves parts whose relations constitute some larger whole. This is an Aristotelian formula deeply embedded in Western ways of thinking.

From an Aristotelian point of view, relations have priority because their functional properties tell us what purposes things serve in what must be, in the end, the whole of wholes, an inclusive system of relations. A modern point of view presupposes a notional space having no properties of its own, within which things are related. Form and matter combine in concrete things that have unique properties; yet every single thing is somehow related to, and affected by, everything else. The language of parts and wholes conveys this complex of ideas with maximal economy.

Medieval thinkers were certainly aware of Aristotle's conception of parts and wholes; Saint Thomas Aquinas used this language when writing about the common good, "the good of the whole."[1] Yet the more general tendency was to vitiate the Aristotelian formula by choosing Plato's doctrine of unchanging forms over Aristotle's world of functional relations and empirical properties. If Plato saw the perfect form in the sphere, some Christian Platonists saw God as a sphere with no center and no circumference—a God more awesome for the absence of earthly properties. The Ptolemaic universe consisted of concentric spheres, none related to any other. The Pope, the Holy Roman Emperor, and various kings ruled in their overlapping spheres as if their powers were exclusive, incontestable, and eternal. This was not the result of "confused thinking" but of a way of thinking quite unlike our own—or Aristotle's.[2]

---

1. Antony Black, "The Individual in Society," in J. H. Burns, ed., *The Cambridge History of Medieval Political Thought c. 350–c. 1450* (Cambridge, 1988), 588–606, at 600. And note Otto Gierke's influential claim that the "peculiar characteristic" of medieval thought is to see "every Being—whether a joint-Being (Community) or a Single-Being—as both a Part and a Whole" (*Political Theories of the Middle Age,* trans. F. W. Maitland [1900; Bristol, 1996], 5–10, at 7).
2. Gierke, *Political Theories of the Middle Age,* 97. See Constantin Fasolt, *The Limits of History* (Chicago, 2004), chap. 4, on how someone could think that the emperor was the ruler of the world but not France, for example, without being the slightest bit confused.

All such wholes are empty, unrelated forms. Whether matter or spirit, substance migrates from form to form. In such a world, things are substantially interchangeable; they come and go as if by magic (or so we moderns like to say); their presence is as real and as certain as it is inexplicable. To the medieval mind, the Eucharist brought forth the real presence of Christ. Transubstantiation is a mysterious process and not a powerful, imaginatively satisfying analogy, whatever modern Christians might want to think.

Ostensibly one world, a unity of spiritual and temporal realms, medieval Europe consisted of many and diverse social bodies having only the most limited need or use for each other. The static formalities and substantial anomalies of medieval thought suited a world of small worlds, a formal whole of more or less self-contained wholes, consisting in turn of individual human beings who, by virtue of their stations in life, had no trouble thinking of themselves as wholly individual. Insofar as we moderns see these wholes neatly nested, we exaggerate the functional relations and hierarchical properties of the arrangement. This was a world of forms and formalities, of spectacles and miracles, of many and diverse bodies, but it was not an ordered world: *order* is a term that lends itself too readily to anachronism.

With modernity came a renewed interest in matter (the stuff of experience), in the properties of things (and how they change), in predication (what we say things are). Just as advanced thinkers renounced Aristotle's physics and abandoned his ethics, they came back to his metaphysics. Only then could they search for the right balance between formal relations and material properties. And so they did, in a never-ending quest to control and direct this torrent of changes that we moderns insist on viewing as a whole and that we call modernity. Punctuating this quest was a series of epochal turns in the way we think about wholes and their parts.

Renaissance humanists shared with their medieval predecessors a preoccupation with wholes. For the latter, many wholes were essentially the same and thus interchangeable, but wholes in general were formally unrelated and thus not comparable. For the former, however, every whole shared at least some properties with other wholes, wholes in general were subject to comparison, and analogy offered an attractive method by which to draw comparisons. By the middle of the seventeenth century, attention had shifted to the relations of whole things and to the properties of parts. Looking back, this too was a time of giants: Galileo Galilei, Johannes Kepler, Hugo Grotius, Thomas Hobbes, Pierre Gassendi, and René Descartes (all born between 1564 and 1596), soon to be followed by Robert Boyle, John Locke, Samuel Pufendorf, Isaac Newton, and Gottfried Wilhelm Leibniz (born between 1627 and 1646). These figures of lasting importance populate the "early modern" period of European history, a label that signals a change in thinking at least as revolutionary as any in the Renaissance.

For early modern Europeans, the relations of whole things were causal and extensive. As in a world of Newtonian mechanics, these relations operate universally. The parts are subject to minute description and exhaustive cataloging in formal systems or tables of classification. The order of the world and the order the mind imposes on the world correspond in principle. Most Enlightenment thinkers accepted the premise that the mind could represent the order of the world with the help of such tables. David Hume's skeptical analysis of claims about causal relations and Immanuel Kant's demonstration that the mind imposes order on the world constituted a philosophical challenge to this way of thinking without ending our practical reliance on systems of classification.

The interval between James Watts's steam engine of 1769 and the first commercial railroad in 1825, between the partition of Poland and the Peace of Vienna, between the Declaration of Independence and the Missouri crisis, and between the publication of Adam Smith's *The Wealth of Nations* in 1776 and David Ricardo's *On the Principles of Political Economy and Taxation* in 1817 marked a second turn. Many moderns think that what follows the early modern period is our own time—a time in which we are, and continue to be, simply modern. While we have some sympathy for the view that modernity has taken, or at least is entering, yet another turn, warranting another name such as *late* modern or *postmodern,* we follow the simple expedient of using the term *modern* for the world that took form two centuries ago. Since we also use this term for the entire reach of modernity, we will make it clear whether we are talking about the past two centuries, or the past five, as the context requires.

Where early modern Europeans had focused on the relations of wholes and the properties of parts, their modern successors focused on the properties of wholes and the relations of parts. The similar properties of many wholes are subject to generalization: they become the statistical properties of a notional whole. When the relations of parts exhibit a significant degree of interdependence, the relations are functional and the whole is indubitably and concretely a thing in itself manifesting a unique ensemble of properties. Literally or metaphorically, the whole lives. Parts (themselves wholes) constitute wholes, in turn (and as parts) constituting yet greater wholes. To the extent that each set of relations operates on its own plane, we see that these planes are themselves ordered by level. Ever since Auguste Comte, this is the way we moderns have visualized the organization of human knowledge.

It would be a mistake to think that transformations in the conditions of knowledge have changed all of our ideas about the world. Most of us have familial statuses and personal qualities that we ascribe to God, nature, or fortune, as we always have. Religious faith links a rich premodern past to the fates that many of us foresee for ourselves. Greco-Roman antiquity endowed Christian Europe with an enduring preoccupation with powers, both human or superhuman. Humanists and Scholastics shared this preoccupation with *powers* (or *faculties:* we use these terms more or less interchangeably); there is no break between medieval and modern thinking on the subject. Our powers of mind and speech are nature's gift. As such, they are signs of God's favor, and they make us the instruments of God's will.

When these higher powers are combined with the sorts of bodily powers that animals also possess, the higher and lower powers together enable us to meet our needs as social animals. By developing our various powers, each of us as we can, we fulfill our God-given potential, and our skilled practices encourage the division of labor and the collective development of all things good. Already articulated by Aristotle, this way of thinking fostered the corporate arrangements characteristic of medieval law, economy, and society. It also inspired the functional language of organs and machines that early modern thinkers favored. Duly secularized, it underwrites the liberal worldview that only comes to the fore after the Enlightenment.

The liberal worldview is not merely an Enlightened ensemble of ideas about human powers. Liberalism is a kind of social practice. While we can only make sense of this practice by recalling ancient claims about human powers and noting the progressive refinement of these claims over the centuries, the practice itself is barely two centuries old. Liberalism presupposes a bounded setting within which a number of autonomous, self-directing entities interact freely within the limits imposed by their formal status as equals and the agreements they have made. If these conditions are met, liberals believe, self-interested conduct will *naturally* bring collective benefits otherwise impossible to achieve. Before the nineteenth century, such conditions were little more than an aspiration, even in the most modern societies. Only then did these societies, organized as states and embodied as nations, begin to take on recognizably "liberal" features. A liberal international society fostered the emergence of liberal societies.

Yet this development was only possible after the modern world had experienced an abrupt change in the way people who thought themselves modern thought about the world and, more particularly, the *nation*. Early modern writers identified the nation as one *kind* of social body. Nations are similar—or, more precisely, made similar—by virtue of their place in a classificatory scheme corresponding to the natural order of things. As a kind, nations are territorially bounded bodies that exist for the common good of their inhabitants. Each nation is under the control of its own head, and all are subject to a set of overarching rules—the law of nations—constituting them as members of a "natural society."

Like any other society, the society of nations exists for the common good of its members. Equally competent to carry on relations with each other, nations are also subject to rules—laws of nature—broadly regulating their relations. These rules only seem to change as writers investigate the natural order of things more deeply and articulate its laws more accurately. Within these rules, the relations of nations have whatever properties nations and their heads give them in the pursuit of their particular ends as nations *and* of their common ends as members of natural society.

Enlightenment savants continued to talk about the nation in very much the same terms. Many hewed to the notion of a natural order manifest in the society of nations, but some recognized that the nation, as an identifiable kind of social body, was unique to Europe and not a universal feature of the human experience. Moreover, progressive opinion held that Europe's nations were developing together as a civilization unlike any other. Older civilizations were built as despotic empires or devolved into despotism; by their nature, empires disregarded the common good and could not endure.

Independent but alike, the civilized nations of Europe were building an order based on common values and shared experience. The close relations of these nations promoted all kinds of innovations and improvements—in practical techniques, material goods, moral education, public administration—and prompted their dispersal within Europe and then to Europe's imperial dependencies and finally to the world at large. Such a civilization can master nature, shape its own future, and better the world. Or so it has seemed to the Enlightenment's most forward and cosmopolitan thinkers and their many modern successors.

If early modern writers viewed the nation as one kind of social body with a privileged place in the natural order of things, and if Enlightenment thinkers began to view the nations of Europe as a kind apart and Europe as a social body singularly privileged by history, later modern writers turned their attention to the nation. They saw each and every nation as a social body on which nature and history—or providence—had conferred a unique set of properties and for which history had promised a unique destiny. Nations had always been bodies, with organs whose functional relations permit them to operate as wholes in relation to other wholes. Yet no one had yet mistaken a nation for a living thing; as a kind, nations function for the good of some or all of their inhabitants.

By contrast, a completely modern nation exhibits a new vitality: it has a will, organic powers, and ends of its own. The nation must be organized to effectuate the nation's will, to act for its own good. Through the apparatus of the state, the nation exercises its powers. No nation can function without the state, even if other kinds of social bodies develop some of the organs that we identify with the state. Conversely, what is good for the nation gives the organs of state their specific ends, or functions, as interdependent parts of the whole.

The nation's members—its inhabitants—are themselves functional wholes, each one unique and autonomous, operating at a level below the nation. As such, they relate to each other within the regulative sphere of the state, in the process generating additional functional demands on the state's organs. In turn, organs of states use the nation's resources to meet their members' demands and conduct relations with other nations in order to assure the nation's well-being. The modern nation makes liberal society possible, but only because each such nation is a member of a liberal society.

The modern world paradigmatically operates at these two levels: within nations and among nations. The levels are themselves fixed by their relation to each other. Because people continue to form other kinds of social bodies, we can always identify other levels. Yet these levels are constantly waxing, waning, and shifting about as the social bodies composing them change their properties and their position in relation to the modern world as a functional whole. From this point of view, the American federal union was a transitional innovation (with an Aristotelian provenience) between the age of tables and the age of levels.[3]

Just as use of the term *nation* exemplifies the shift from an early modern way of thinking to a later one, so does use of the term *market*. In a concrete, historical sense, the market is a place, a specific site to which goods are brought, exchanged, and removed. With the rise of the modern world, the term acquired an additional sense of exchange dissociated from any given site. Now an abstraction, the market is defined not by properties intrinsic to it but by the properties of the goods—corn, cattle, cloth—subject to exchange.

This is how Smith used the term in *The Wealth of Nations,* to the extent that he used the term at all. At the same time, Smith had a great deal to say about *exchange,* which he stipulated to be a propensity of individual human beings and also considered a characteristic form of social relations: among people, between towns and countryside, among nations. At any given moment, nature imposes limits on these relations, as in the exchange of perishable goods. So do history and policy. Sorted by kind, all such relations form a table that is normatively ordered by reference to human needs and powers.

3. A point of view developed in our previous volume, *Federal Union, Modern World: The Law of Nations in an Age of Revolutions, 1776–1814* (Madison, Wisc., 1993).

Once modern thinking shifts from the relations of wholes and properties of parts to the properties of wholes and relations of parts, the market becomes a whole with properties of its own. The market's defining property for many liberal thinkers is its purportedly self-regulating character. While Smith's "invisible hand" anticipates this claim, and later many liberals offer it is as an article of faith, the convergence of nation, state, and market as coterminous wholes made this key liberal concept conceivable. As a bounded whole, the nation forms a container within which exchange has the blessing of history.

The national market encourages the development of existing vehicles and instruments of exchange (transportation, money, credit, insurance) within the scope of the nation, not to mention the development of tastes and needs peculiar to the nation. The presumed existence of a national market also creates functional demands on the organs of the state. These organs respond with policies variously designed to promote these developments. By doing so, they substantiate the existence of that which is already presumed to exist—the nation—and regulate that which is presumed to be self-regulating—the market.

At the same time, nations as undifferentiated wholes engage in exchange with other nations. The new way of thinking about markets, substantiated by association with nation and state, in turn substantiates the existence and self-regulating properties of an international market. The latter supposedly operates at one level and national markets at another. Underlying this scheme is an assumption that the development of an international market benefits all nations to the greatest possible degree.

Nation making works best when it makes nations that are also liberal market societies. As the world market expanded in the post-Napoleonic era, nation-states mobilized productive forces and promoted development of their own home markets in order to counter British domination. In the United States, Northern protectionists were precocious nationalists, recognizing that Britain's economic power represented as great a threat in peacetime as its military might did in war. Southerners only embraced this sort of nationalism when they recognized that neutralizing the North in an increasingly moribund union was not a sufficient guarantee of their vital interests. Separate nationhood was the essential vehicle for full participation in the liberal society that the modern world had become. But first Southern nationhood, and Southern honor, would have to be vindicated on the battlefield.

The modern world is strewn with battlefields old and new; some of the most spectacular technical improvements in modern life are inextricably linked to the systematic organization of violence. One might think that liberal values, the effective operation of markets, and material prosperity would dampen the all too human enthusiasm for bloodletting and diminish, even eliminate, the recourse to war. Indeed, many liberals have thought just this, and many still do. Yet modern history also confirms that war has an integral place in an international society whose members, as nations, often have incompatible ends and the resources to pursue those ends.

If civilized nations conduct war with each other because they are nations, they are presumed to do so within limits derived from a shared sense of what it means to be civilized. We suggest that a society of such nations is by definition a civil society, and therefore every war between nations is a civil war. Nevertheless, fully modern nations tend to push the conduct of war to the limit of what material prosperity and technical developments make feasible, at least when the leaders and populations of these nations conclude that incompatible ends leave them no choice. In other words, civil wars among fully modern nations threaten the very existence of the civil society defining the modern world as a civilization unlike any other.

The American Civil War was the first fully modern war; there would have been no war had the North and the South not been modern nations. In the same sense, World Wars I and II were civil wars fought by modern nations to the limits of civilized conduct—and beyond. Nations, markets, *and* war have made the modern world what it is—for better or for worse. The liberal imagination emphasizes the good in modern history. Even if national imperatives, market forces, and the risks of unlimited war threaten the modern world with moral and material catastrophes, and perhaps even with destruction, the liberal imagination can only look ahead. Modernity has burned all bridges and scorched the earth behind it; there is no going back.

Obviously this book differs from most histories to the extent to which we conjecture about matters that most historians generally avoid. The historian's craft makes the properties of wholes its primary focus. This calls for the systematic marshaling of evidence in support of thick description—is this what the nation really looked like?—and a compelling and coherent narrative of its development. At an earlier time, the discovery of the ordered relations of wholes gave philosophers, scientists, and historians a common calling.

Marking the Enlightenment transition from that time to our time is a shift in focus from the relations of wholes to their properties. Here the federal union comes to mind as an experiment in fixing the relations of wholes—the union and its member states—by specifying their complementary properties. Also marking this transition is a willingness to conjecture about the large patterns and general direction of social change, to generalize about whole societies and civilizations on the basis of sketchy historical records and with the help of judicious inference. Conjectural history is an innovation of the Enlightenment. With some exaggeration, we might say that part 1 of this essay is a conjectural history of conjectural history. Its five chapters focus attention on related aspects of modernity's remarkable career. Each chapter proceeds more or less chronologically, but the chapters are not themselves chronologically ordered.

The first chapter returns to history as an organizing feature of the modern imagination, as the key to interpreting the rise of the modern world. In most accounts, the dialectical relation of the individual and society motivates the story of modernity's rise. As the individual wins out, so does liberalism. At the same time, the state emerged as an organizational necessity and with it the state system. In this essay, we turn this familiar story on its head. Chapters 2 and 3 chart the development of a liberal international society of civilized nations. Early on, the nations of Europe exhibited the telltale features of a liberal society, and liberal societies emerged first in those nations on which liberal international society conferred the greatest advantages. We give this dimension of the story priority because we see it as the primary set of relations giving modernity its momentum.

Chapters 4 and 5 chart the complementary development of moral personality as a property of bodies—wholes that have the powers of agency. In medieval thought, the most important of these is the church, which is the mystical embodiment of Christ. In early modernity, social bodies of many kinds are moral persons, while individuals are moral persons only derivatively, by virtue of their relation to society. Nations finally emerge as the most vital of social bodies and markets as their source of sustenance. Nation making has world-shaking consequences because the modern world functions as a liberal society whose constituent members are nations, in form alike but each seeking its own destiny.

Throughout these pages, readers will discern the magisterial presence of Aristotle, whose philosophical concerns are always in the background of Western thought. Readers will also find us returning to Adam Smith again and again. An exemplary figure in a time of transition, Smith's conjectures about the four stages of societal development survived the transition to modernity to inform nineteenth-century political economy in its nationalist, socialist, and liberal cosmopolitan permutations. Smith's presence today is even more in evidence than Aristotle's but is no better understood. Because Smith's conjectures are integral to his work on ethics, law, and politics—work so thoroughly integrated to warrant calling him a moral historian—we devote the lead chapter in part 2 to the whole of his work. Such is Smith's impact on the political economy of North-South relations in antebellum America that his abiding presence binds the two parts of this essay into a whole. From Aristotle we learn that no whole is seamless, no part sufficient. From Smith we learn that history has a logic that sets the modern world apart from other worlds.

1
The Limits of History

Let us repeat: This book is an essay in modern history. Such a claim is ambiguous on its face—and doubly so. As an adjective, does the term *modern* refer to the manifold of events transpiring in a designated time and place (the subject of history), or does it refer to a particular ensemble of practices (the historian's craft) applicable to any time or place? If the former, what are the limits of time and place to which the term refers? If the latter, when and where did these practices arise? What makes them distinctive? Or does the term *modern* not even refer to time and place in the first instance but to some other limiting property of history as subject, or history as craft?

Historians today have no consistent answer to these questions. Nor does it seem to matter very much whether they are political, economic, social, cultural, or intellectual historians or historians of science, technology, or law. Philosophers, social theorists, and students of international relations are no better. Some scholars would take the story back to the first expressions of humanism in the fourteenth century. Others date the rise of the modern world from about 1500, as the Renaissance moved north from Italy, Muslims left Iberia, and European voyagers encountered distant peoples. Niccolò Machiavelli and Martin Luther spoke the languages we speak, and what they had to say stirs us still.

From that time commenced a "historical revolt," to use Constantin Fasolt's words, a challenge to the timeless unities of medieval life that did not fully succeed until the middle decades of the seventeenth century.[1] As the historical revolt took hold, science and philosophy changed the way literate Europeans saw themselves and their world, the Peace of Westphalia ended

---

1. Constantin Fasolt, *The Limits of History* (Chicago, 2004), 16–32.

Europe's religious wars, and states emerged as impersonally ruled territorial entities. Many scholars would date the turn to modernity from this juncture. Others would assign that date to the last decades of the eighteenth century, as the Enlightenment's celebration of reason gave way to revolutionary politics and national consciousness, industrial capitalism brought great changes in daily life, and Europeans translated technical and material triumphs into a vision of civilizational superiority.

Still other scholars use dates such as 1650 and 1800 to mark successive, more or less distinctive periods in a five-hundred-year span. As a further complication, many scholars in the arts and letters identify yet another period dating from about 1880 or perhaps 1900, styled modern or modernist. For historians and social scientists, this same period marks the professionalization of their disciplines. Modern historians of the Renaissance are likely to consider their subject to be modern history, if only because they know that what they study is *not* medieval history. Yet modern historians do not view their Renaissance predecessors as modern practitioners of the historical craft.

That Renaissance scholars began to see history in distinctive periods, and not as recurring cycles or eternal verities, hardly sufficed to make them modern historians. They sifted obscure sources, compiled lists, collected oddities, and noted signs and portents; their exhibitions of erudition rarely reveal a sense of discrimination, narrative continuity, or, behind these, an abiding authorial presence. Scriptural authority had its place, and with it the medieval belief in a divine plan. As an expression of God's will, providence bore no discernible relation to periodic change in the Christian era. After the Renaissance had run its course, early modern writers found providence, not in human history but in nature's lawful order. Still later, Enlightenment thinkers found providence exercised through our God-given capacities and manifest in human betterment. Not yet modern in the practice of the historical craft, they turned models of human nature into conjectures about human origins and the development of diverse societies through comparable periods.

Nineteenth-century historians moved away from the Enlightenment preoccupation with humanity's remote origins and common experiences—with human nature and universal history—and toward national histories characterized by distinct origins and distinctive experiences. Such histories called for documentation, the more systematic the better, in order to confirm the supposition that each nation's history is as unique as its providential destiny. More recent origins meant better factual records. Better trained historians meant more information was recovered and put to use. Gaps in the factual record diminished and so did the need to fill gaps with conjectures.

Even today, when historians are professionally trained and exceedingly conscious of their craft, most of them take the nation as an established context (American history, British imperial history, history of China). Their histories build on earlier ones by organizing vast amounts of information, some of it newly recovered, in a continuous stream of events, many of which are (implicitly conjectured to be) causally linked. In expository terms, such histories are free of gaps. Explicit conjectures are permitted to break the flow, but only if they are rhetorically framed. Some conjectures are imaginative projections of future developments or alternative pasts (What if?). Some are linked to the context in which the nation's history takes place, since this context is, at least from the national historian's point of view, less important and less well documented. Some use the appearance of discontinuities and ruptures in the record—points at which causal patterns in the flow of events shift abruptly—to mark off historical periods.

Modern historians know that periodization is as indispensable as it is indefensible. As we look more closely at the factual record, claimed discontinuities seem less distinct, and the conjectured properties of adjacent periods seem more contrived. The history of the modern practice of history admirably illustrates this common perception. While the professionalization of historical craft accelerated in the modern era of national histories, the idea of *craft* as an activity linking human powers (or faculties), acquired skills, and productive achievements goes back to Plato and Aristotle.

This idea informed the developing political economy of medieval society. It furnished early modern models of human nature with their central propositions. It inspired the (re)discovery of the division of labor. It gave Enlightenment thinkers a basis for their conjectures about human improvement and modern liberalism a basis for its distinctive claims about agents' choices and societal consequences. In other words, modern historians today practice a craft that, with a number of other crafts, including law, medicine, engineering, war making, and statecraft, only became modern as the world did, by fits and starts, over a period of many hundreds of years.

Conjectural History

A man of the Enlightenment, Adam Smith died in 1790. Two and a half years later, Dugald Stewart, the professor of moral philosophy at Edinburgh, read a long eulogy to the Royal Society of that city.[2] As Emma Rothschild

---

2. "Account of the Life and Writings of Adam Smith, L.L.D.," read by Dugald Stewart, Jan. 21, and Mar. 18, 1793, to the Royal Society of Edinburgh; rpt. in Adam Smith, *Essays on Philosophical Subjects*, ed. W. P. D. Wightman and J. C. Bryce (Oxford, 1980), 269–351.

has remarked, Stewart's memoir "is by far the most important biographical work about Smith, and an early source of Smith's subsequent conservative renown."[3] Indeed, Stewart concisely formulated the "fundamental doctrines" that made *The Wealth of Nations* (1776) a seminal text for those whom we now characterize as classical liberal economists. Nevertheless, Stewart directed most of his attention to Smith's lifelong commitment to "the improvement of society."[4]

This goal Smith thought he could contribute to by studying human nature and, more particularly, by studying "the political history of mankind."[5] Here we should interpret Stewart's use of the expression *political history* in the broadest possible sense. "In Mr Smith's writings, whatever be the nature of his subject, he seldom misses an opportunity of indulging his curiosity, in tracing from the principles of human nature, or from the circumstances of society, the origin of the opinions and the institutions which he describes."[6] Moreover, Smith knew that his inquiries into the "history of mankind" could never rely on the factual record, because large parts of the relevant record are lost to memory.

> When, in such a period of society as that in which we live, we compare our intellectual acquirements, our opinions, manners, and institutions, with those which prevail among rude tribes, it cannot fail to occur to us as an interesting question, by what gradual steps the transition has been made from the first simple efforts of uncultivated nature, to a state of things so wonderfully artificial and complicated. Whence has arisen that systematical beauty which we admire in the structure of a cultivated language; that analogy which runs

---

3. Emma Rothschild, *Economic Sentiments: Adam Smith, Condorcet, and the Enlightenment* (Cambridge, Mass., 2001), 57.
4. "The fundamental doctrines of Mr Smith's system are now so generally known, that it would have been tedious to offer any recapitulation of them in this place. . . . I shall content myself, therefore, with remarking, in general terms, that the great and leading object of his speculations is, to illustrate the provision made by nature in the principles of the human mind, and in the circumstances of man's external situation, for a gradual and progressive augmentation in the means of national wealth; and to demonstrate, that the most effectual plan for advancing a people to greatness, is to maintain that order of things which nature has pointed out; by allowing every man, as long as he observes the rules of justice, to pursue his own interest in his own way, and to bring both his industry and his capital into the freest competition with those of his fellow-citizens" (Stewart, "Account of the Life and Writings of Adam Smith, L.L.D.," 271, 315).
5. Ibid., 271.
6. Ibid., 295.

through the mixture of languages spoken by the most remote and uncon-
nected nations; and those peculiarities by which they are all distinguished
from each other? Whence the origin of the different sciences and of the
different arts; and by what chain has the mind been led from their first
rudiments to their last and most refined improvements? Whence the astonishing fabric of the political union; the fundamental principles which are
common to all governments; and the different forms which civilized society
has assumed in different ages of the world? On most of these subjects very
little information is to be expected from history; for long before that stage of
society when men begin to think of recording their transactions, many of the
most important steps of their progress have been made. A few insulated facts
may perhaps be collected from the casual observations of travellers, who have
viewed the arrangements of rude nations; but nothing, it is evident, can be
obtained in this way, which approaches to a regular and connected detail of
human improvement.

In this want of direct evidence, we are under a necessity of supplying the
place of fact by conjecture; and when we are unable to ascertain how men
have actually conducted themselves upon particular occasions, of considering
in what manner they are likely to have proceeded, from the principles of their
nature, and the circumstances of their external situation. In such inquiries,
the detached facts which travels and voyages afford us, may frequently serve
as land-marks to our speculations; and sometimes our conclusions *a priori,*
may tend to confirm the credibility of facts, which, on a superficial view,
appeared to be doubtful or incredible.

Nor are such theoretical views of human affairs subservient merely to the
gratification of curiosity. In examining the history of mankind, as well as in
examining the phenomena of the material world, when we cannot trace the
process by which an event *has been* produced, it is often of importance to be
able to show how it *may have been* produced by natural causes. Thus, in the
instance which has suggested these remarks, although it is impossible to
determine with certainty what the steps were by which any particular
language was formed, yet if we can shew, from the known principles of
human nature, how all its various parts might gradually have arisen, the mind
is not only to a certain degree satisfied, but a check is given to that indolent
philosophy, which refers to a miracle, whatever appearances, both in the
natural and moral worlds, it is unable to explain.

To this species of philosophical investigation, which has no appropriated name in our language, I shall take the liberty of giving the title
of *Theoretical* or *Conjectural History;* an expression which coincides
pretty nearly in its meaning with that of *Natural* History, as employed

by Mr Hume, and with what some French writers have called *Histoire Raisonnée.*[7]

Stewart may have been familiar with the Swiss mathematician Jakob Bernoulli's famous *Ars conjectandi* (1713). He did not, however, follow Bernoulli in linking conjecture to procedures for establishing the probability—or fixed degree of certainty—that some event will transpire.[8] Instead, Smith and Stewart started with a world of events that have already taken place, some of them known and others lost to history. As Thomas Hobbes had noticed, this too can inspire conjecture, not as a probability statement but as an imaginative act reconstructing any world of events, past or future. Hobbes had no clear sense that one might achieve a set degree of certainty about events to come (for example, sums on dice over many throws), but he was sure that conjecturing about a completed course of events (for example, a civil war) "has the same incertainty almost with the conjecture of the Future; both being grounded onely upon Experience."[9]

Events linked by causes are, in David Hume's account, not directly knowable. If, as a matter of experience, causal relations must be inferred from the sequence of events, they are nonetheless subject to generalization; those most reliably so are "natural causes." Always provisional and reliable in various degrees, causal inferences may be applied to an incomplete factual record of events in order to fill the gaps. The resulting conjectures are also provisional, of course, but we judge them as plausible—and this is itself a matter of degree. As more or less plausible assertions of that which cannot be directly known, conjecture falls between certain knowledge and Hobbes's "trayne of imaginations." As such, they are a legitimate undertaking, for which Stewart used the term theoretical in much the sense it is used today.

Smith was not alone in the practice of conjectural history. Jean-Jacques Rousseau's first and second discourses offer brilliant examples; the *Discourse*

7. Ibid., 292–93, deleting a reference to Hume's *The Natural History of Religion* (1757), original emphasis. According to Bertrand de Jouvenel, one J. L. Favier, "who in his time had an immense reputation as an expert on foreign policy," used the expression *histoire raisonnée* in a work written for Louis XV (*The Art of Conjecture*, trans. Nikita Lary [New York, 1967], 21 n. 20).

8. Basic ideas about probability date from about 1660, but it remained for Bernoulli to give the concept of probability "a self-conscious analysis" (Ian Hacking, *The Emergence of Probability: A Philosophical Study of Early Ideas about Probability, Induction and Statistical Inference* [Cambridge, U.K., 1975], quoting table of contents). On Bernoulli, see chap. 16.

9. Thomas Hobbes, *Leviathan* (1651), ed. Richard Tuck (Cambridge, U.K., 1991), pt. 1, chap. 3, "Of The Consequence or TRAYNE of Imaginations," 23.

on Inequality (second discourse, 1755) also offers an explicit rationale.[10] The term *conjectural history* fits many of Hume's essays dating from the mid-eighteenth century, not to mention the writings of other luminaries in the Scottish Enlightenment.[11] Anne-Robert-Jacques Turgot's discourses *On Universal History* (1752) are strikingly similar to some of Hume's best-known essays. Universal histories are conjectural, and conversely conjectural histories tend to be cast in universalizing terms.

Immanuel Kant is well known for an essay proposing an "Idea for a Universal History with a Cosmopolitan Purpose" (*Idee zu einer allgemeinen Geschichte in weltbürgerlicher Absicht, 1784*). He is less well known for a companion essay offering "Conjectures on the Beginning of Human History" (*Mutmaßlicher Anfang der Menschengeschichte, 1786*). The latter begins with remarks about conjecture that might have been Stewart's—or Smith's:

> To *introduce* conjectures at various points in the *course* of a historical account in order to fill gaps in the record is surely permissible; for what comes before and after these gaps—i.e. the remote cause and the effect respectively—can enable us to discover the intermediate causes, with reasonable certainty, thereby rendering the intervening process intelligible. But to *base* a historical account solely on conjectures would seem little better than drawing up a plan for a novel. Indeed, such an account could not be described as a *conjectural history* at all, but merely as a *work of fiction*.

Conjectures about the origins of human history have little support in the factual record. Yet they are defensible on the assumption that human nature has

---

10. "I admit that since the events I have to describe could have occurred in several ways, I can choose between them only on the basis of conjectures; but not only do such conjectures become reasons when they are the most probable that can be derived from the nature of things and the only means available to discover the truth, it also does not follow that the consequences I want to deduce from mine will therefore be conjectural since, on the principles I have just established [about our natural faculties], no other system could be formed that would not give me the same results and from which I could not draw the same conclusions" (Jean-Jacques Rousseau, *Discourse on the Origin and Foundations of Inequality among Men*, in Victor Gourevitch, ed., *Rousseau: The Discourses and Other Early Political Writings*, trans. Gourevitch [Cambridge, U.K., 1997], pt. 1, 159).

11. See chapter 3 in this essay on Hume and Turgot. And see Mary Poovey, *A History of the Modern Fact: Problems of Knowledge in the Sciences of Wealth and Society* (Chicago, 1998), chap. 5, and J. G. A. Pocock, *Barbarism and Religion*, vol. 2, *Narratives of Civil Government* (Cambridge, U.K., 1999), pt. 2.

timeless, universal properties—"an assumption which accords with the analogy of nature and which has nothing presumptuous about it."[12]

Kant's conjectural history begins with beings who could talk ("i.e. speak with the help of coherent concepts") and therefore think: this is our nature. By application of reason to the rest of nature, human beings went from the "savage life of the hunter" to domesticating and herding animals and from "the sporadic digging for roots or gathering of fruit" to sowing and planting crops. "*Pastoral life* is not only leisurely, but also the most reliable means of support"; by comparison, agriculture is "extremely laborious, subject to the vagaries of climate, and consequently insecure." At the same time, agriculture brings people together in permanent settlements and fosters exchange. "This inevitably gave rise to *culture* and the beginnings of *art* . . . ; but first and foremost, it also meant that certain steps were taken to establish a civil constitution and the public administration of justice."[13]

For Kant these are mixed blessings. "From these first crude beginnings, all human aptitudes could now gradually develop, the most beneficial of these being *sociability and civil security.*" Yet "human *inequality*" also begins in this epoch, as does the conflict between "the nations of nomadic herdsmen," who, "as declared enemies of all land ownership," "continued to swarm around the town-dwellers and farmers"; "the two sides were continually at war, or at least at constant risk of war," but they were also free. Ending the risk of war increased the likelihood of despotism, "soulless extravagance," and slavery. Despite setbacks, "the course of human affairs as a whole . . . develops gradually from the worse to the better," and each of us "is called upon by nature to contribute towards this progress to the best of his ability."[14]

In characterizing Smith's conjectural history, Stewart alluded to many of the same themes: unchanging human nature, rude beginnings, cultivation and culture, the rise of the arts and sciences, political union. Kant suggested that history proceeds in epochs marked by great changes in material practices. While Stewart was not explicit on this point, Smith had embraced just such a view and expressed it more systematically than had Kant. "There are," in Smith's account, "four distinct states which mankind pass thro:—1st, the

---

12. Immanuel Kant, "Conjectures on the Beginning of Human History," in Hans Reiss, ed., *Kant Political Writings,* 2nd ed., trans. H. B. Nisbet (Cambridge, U.K., 1991), 221, emphasis in translation. While "the analogy of nature" connects God's will, by way of human nature, to the realization of human freedom, Kant reassured his readers that the journey he was about to undertake "on the wings of imagination" would "follow precisely" the Bible story of human origins (Ibid., 222).

13. Ibid., 222, 229–30, emphasis in translation.

14. Ibid., 230–31, 234, emphasis in translation.

Age of Hunters; 2dly, the Age of Shepherds; 3dly, the Age of Agriculture; and 4^{thly}, the Age of Commerce."[15]

Kant considered pastoral life and agriculture as parallel developments. The endemic conflict between these ways of life makes for a darker reading of human history than Stewart attributed to Smith. Smith held that societies develop at different rates; encounters among peoples in different states of development (or stages, as we say today) are likely to produce conflict. Indeed, nomadic barbarians disrupted the development of Western Europe and then gave development novel features when it resumed.

Moreover, Smith had much to say about despotism, luxury, and slavery, as did Hume, Rousseau, and so many other Enlightenment thinkers. Stewart passed over these matters in order to emphasize Smith's commitment to the general improvement of societies. Hume thought them incurable features of the human experience. "Men," he said in a late essay, must "endeavour to palliate what they cannot cure."[16] Rousseau and Kant dwelled on them.

Rousseau held that "a few ambitious men" had "subjugated the whole of Mankind to labor, servitude and misery." Despite such "evils," Kant professed a deep faith in the inevitability of human progress. If this is nature's *"hidden plan,"* so is its slow and erratic pace.[17] Whenever conjectural history starts with nature, as conjectural history of the Enlightenment always did, we find a moral vision embedded in its claims about the human condition.

Modern Ways of Thinking

There are, of course, many scholars (few of them historians) who are greatly concerned about the defining properties of the modern period of history. Among them, perhaps the most celebrated, and reviled, is Michel Foucault. His difficult, sometimes baffling book *The Order of Things* (*Les mots et les choses*, 1966) is a conjectural history of modernity—of the changing conditions of knowledge defining successive periods in the Western world from

---

15. Adam Smith, *Lectures on Jurisprudence,* ed. R. L. Meek et al. (Oxford, 1978), Report of 1762–63, i, 27, 14. These are the detailed notes of a student not published for two centuries; there is no comparably succinct statement in *The Wealth of Nations.* Also see Ronald L. Meek, *Social Science and the Ignoble Savage* (Cambridge, 1976).
16. David Hume, "Of the Origin of Government" (1777), in Eugene F. Miller, ed., *Essays Moral, Political and Literary,* (Indianapolis, Ind., 1985), 38.
17. Rousseau, *Discourse on the Origin and Foundations of Inequality among Men,* pt. 2, 173; Immanuel Kant, "Idea for a Universal History with a Cosmopolitan Purpose," in Reiss, ed., *Kant Political Writings,* 41–53, at 45, 50.

1500, or thereabouts, to a moment now decades behind us.[18] Many modern historians have criticized Foucault for his methods (stating his conjectures in bold, even inflammatory terms, pulling texts out of a hat to support his conjectures), his prose style (running from refractory and pretentious to utterly unintelligible at important junctures), and his objectives (dismantling the established edifice of modernity, contributing to the impending erasure of "man"). Yet our project resembles Foucault's in important respects.

Foucault's boldest, highly suggestive conjecture holds that Western thinkers twice refigured the foundations on which they ordered knowledge of themselves and the world—once roughly in the middle of the seventeenth century and again at the beginning of the nineteenth century—and they may now be doing so a third time. The first of these discontinuities ends the Renaissance *episteme* (in French, *épistémè;* this is Foucault's term for the conditions of knowledge that Renaissance thinkers took for granted). The second ends the classical age (we call this *episteme* the early modern period) and begins the modern age. The modern *episteme* experienced a significant discontinuity at the turn of the twentieth century (a modernist turn not identified in Foucault's sketch) and perhaps another, late modern turn now underway, to which Foucault has contributed.

Foucault emphasized that the epistemic discontinuities he had identified transformed ways of thinking about some self-defining bodies of knowledge ("sciences," "fields of study," and more abstractly, "discursive formations") but not others. Least of all were they changes in the way that everyone in the modern world thought about everything.[19] Yet the three formations that he did study at some length—concerned respectively with life, labor, and language—underwent closely related changes to become the three "human sciences"—biology, political economy, and philology—organizing even today what we moderns think we know about ourselves and our circumstances. Given the centrality of these related formations to systematic inquiry more generally conceived, Foucault often referred to an *episteme* as if it were the defining property of an age. Forgoing an assessment of causes, which would necessarily require consideration of "non-discursive domains," may have spared him criticism for generalizing about an age, but it was at the cost of

18. Michel Foucault, *The Order of Things: An Archeology of the Human Sciences* (New York, 1973); trans. (Alan Sheridan) not identified in this edition. To our knowledge no one else has called Foucault a conjectural historian, although Gary Gutting's helpful assessment, *Michel Foucault's Archeology of Scientific Reason* (Cambridge, 1989), identifies *The Order of Things* as "constructive history" marked by "ambitious conjectures" (176).

19. Foucault, *Order of Things*, xii; idem, *The Archeology of Knowledge*, trans. A. M. Sheridan Smith (New York, 1972), 157–62.

criticism for ignoring the "institutions, political events, economic practices and processes" that give the rise of the modern world its momentum.[20] In this book, we share Foucault's predilection for discursive formations (and thus for textual analysis), but we tie our conclusions to other developments (which always exhibit a significant discursive dimension). Rarely, however, do we specify these relations extensively and concretely enough to warrant causal inferences of any generality (for example, the causes of the Civil War); in this respect, we follow Foucault and not the conjectural historians of an earlier time.

Foucault's account of the Renaissance *episteme* points to the central place assigned to the way that the things of the world strike the senses. If things are as they appear, then *resemblance* is the key to the organization of knowledge, and *repetition,* for example through analogies, is the key to the way that knowledge is conveyed. The classical *episteme* turns from the *appearance* of things, and thus their superficial similarities, to their fundamental *nature,* to be discovered by comparing the differences among things— differences to be determined by careful measurement.

The different properties of things allow us to sort those things into categories. Writ large, nature has *order;* indeed, nature *is* order. In this way of thinking, *classification* is the key to the organization of knowledge; *representation* is the key to the way knowledge is gained and conveyed. Representing the things of the world in our minds, we present them again to the world through speech and otherwise act on them, as things *in* the world. Classifying them reproduces a providential natural order in our minds and guides our actions in the world.

Regrettably, Foucault's clotted account of the modern *episteme* is as difficult to grasp as it is tantalizing. It is clear that History—"the fundamental mode of being of empiricities"—comes to the fore in the nineteenth century, displacing history as one way to represent the order among things. "History *gives place* to analogical organic structures, just as Order opened the way to *successive* identities and differences."[21]

It is tempting to interpret these conjectures as a banal affirmation of the shift from mechanical to organic metaphors commonly held to signal the end of the Enlightenment and the beginning of the romantic era. But this cannot be right, because the terms *empiricities* and *structure* are simply not discursive tokens for romantic sentiments. Nevertheless, the term *organic* is crucial

---

20. Foucault, *Archeology of Knowledge,* 162.
21. Foucault, *Order of Things,* 219, emphasis in translation. It is also clear that this development has little or nothing to do with the "historical revolt" that Fasolt, *Limits of History,* found beginning perhaps three centuries earlier.

to Foucault's account of the modern *episteme,* and his discussion of modern biology gives the clearest sense why this is so. According to Foucault, credit for introducing an entirely new way of thinking about living things belongs to Georges Cuvier, the zoologist, paleontologist, and Parisian fixture from 1795 until his death in 1832. Instead of classifying organs by reference to structure and function as necessary complements (for every function a structure, for every structure a function), Cuvier saw that life depends on the integrity of functional relations operating as a whole, "that 'organic structures' are contingent solutions" to functional needs, and that classification must proceed accordingly. "From Cuvier onward, function, defined . . . as an effect to be attained, is to serve as a constant middle term and to make it possible to relate together totalities of elements without the slightest visible identity."[22]

While the "totality of elements" is functionally interdependent, some functions are more important than others. The hierarchical ordering of functions "implies that the organism, in its visible arrangements, obeys a *plan.* Such a plan ensures the control of the essential functions and brings under that control . . . the organs that perform less vital functions."[23] All such plans must account for the environment within which the organism functions as a whole. In this way of thinking, every living thing faces unique challenges to its survival, even as it is a dispensable element in the functional relations making nature an integral whole. "Empiricities" matter: Cuvier was the first scientist to show that an entire living species had become extinct. By no means was Cuvier an evolutionary thinker. Yet the epistemic revolution in biology to which he contributed so much fostered just the kind of empirical studies that later made evolution a compelling explanation for the extinction and emergence of species—for unplanned changes that seem, at a higher level, to obey some universal plan of nature. Before the modern *episteme* emerged as a novel species of thought, such an explanation was not even imaginable.

In Foucault's view, Jean-Baptiste Lamarck was *not* an evolutionary thinker, despite his conjectures about the inheritance of acquired traits, because he "conceived of the transformation of species only on the basis of ontological continuity, which was that of Classical natural history."[24] Also not an evolutionary thinker was Lamarck's famous patron Georges-Louis Leclerc, Comte de Buffon, who took the history of the earth to be an "ontological continuity" and divided it into seven epochs, in the last of which we humans finally make our appearance. This is conjectural history on the grandest scale. Yet Buffon's

---

22. Foucault, *Order of Things,* 263–79, at 263, 265. Also see Toby A. Appel, *The Cuvier-Geoffroy Debate: French Biology in the Decades before Darwin* (New York, 1987).
23. Foucault, *Order of Things,* 266–67.
24. Ibid., 275. Also see 150–57.

massive *Histoire naturelle* (1749–88) favors a methodical approach to nature in all its empirical richness, whatever the effect on established classificatory procedures. Because Buffon anticipated "a certain *modern* manner of knowing empiricities" while still believing in a providential nature, we take him to be a transitional figure.[25]

It would seem that Foucault's conjectural history of the rise of the modern world pays too little attention to the transitional moments between successive ages, and it makes less room than ours does for transitional figures. In chapter 4, we locate Hobbes in the transition from the Renaissance to the early modern period, the better to understand the lasting significance of his way of thinking. And here we place Smith with Buffon in the transition from early modern and midmodern ways of thinking. Foucault saw Smith still stuck in "the Classical analysis of wealth," and David Ricardo the apostle of modern political economy. For Smith labor has "a fixed and constant value exchangeable as such in all places and all times," while for Ricardo "any value, whatever it may be, has its origin in labour."[26]

Smith's way of thinking hinges on classification and representation. Ricardo, by contrast, dissociated "the creation of value from its representivity," and this "made possible the articulation of economics upon history." Wealth constitutes "a system of equivalences" for Smith, while it "is organized and accumulated in a temporal sequence" for Ricardo.[27] Accepting Foucault's claim that the analysis of labor and value put Smith and Ricardo on two sides of an epistemic divide, we show in chapter 6 how important the organization and accumulation of wealth is for Smith's conjectural history and its moral underpinnings. By making the "annual supply" of produce and "the productive powers of labour" into Foucault's equivalences, Smith could identify a temporal sequence of societal development, or "improvement" both in material benefits accruing to society and in the productive powers of labor.[28] Viewing wealth in this general way reflects the moment of epistemic transition *and* the way we think about the modern world even today.

Smith might have thought one way about labor and wealth and Ricardo quite another way. Yet both focused their attention on commerce, which they saw as a phenomenon so unprecedented in scale, in Britain and across

---

25. Ibid., 250.

26. Ibid., 253–63, at 255, 254.

27. Ibid., 255.

28. Adam Smith, *An Inquiry into the Nature and Causes of the Wealth of Nations*, ed. R. H. Campbell and A. S. Skinner (Indianapolis, Ind., 1981), intro. and plan of the work, §§ 1–5, vol. 1, 10. Since the two volumes of this edition are continuously paginated, we henceforth omit the volume number.

the world, that the functional relations giving rise to it—the division of labor—explain *"the natural Progress of Opulence."* [29] In Foucault's account, the modern *episteme* brings the "empiricities" of functional relations to the fore. Indubitably modern, Foucault's model of social change starts with empiricities of an exceedingly limited sort, functional relations that are never specified, and commerce that is quite modest in scale. The engine of change is the exchange of ideas—evidently the kinds of ideas that make philosophy and the sciences different from other activities.

Foucault's model stipulates a sudden change of mind about the way that our minds work. René Descartes meditates on what he knows for certain, Kant awakens from his dogmatic slumber: these events had a direct effect on discursive formations where the status of knowledge depends on rules of inquiry that are subject to change as inquiry proceeds, questions arise, and answers accumulate. As Europeans talked about life, labor, and language (first as matters of philosophy and then science), they kept changing their mind about these matters because they drastically revised their most basic ideas about knowledge. We could add law to Foucault's list of discursive formations and find the same pattern.

Human Powers

Obviously we agree with Foucault that epistemic change is important. Indeed, a conjectural history of conjectural history must take into account the fundamental shifts in ways we talk about thinking—about the art of conjecture. Yet it is only half the story. The other half of the story must account for the way in which we talk about doing useful things for ourselves and each other—about functional relations and instrumental activities. The way we talk about these activities exhibits a striking continuity; it changes, shall we say, organically, and it matches more or less the rise of the modern world as a material phenomenon, to which the metaphor *growth* is almost inevitably applied.

Both halves of the story have ancient lineages. We need to go back to Aristotle, and we need to do so *twice*, in order to expose the assumptions that make the two halves of the story distinct *and* to form the halves—roughly speaking, thinking and doing—into an intelligible whole. It hardly needs saying that the Greeks talked a great deal about thinking. With the translation of Aristotle's major works into Latin, this disposition found new life. Saint Thomas Aquinas

---

29. Ibid., III, i, chapter title, 376.

adapted Aristotle's views on the mind to the needs of Christian theology, and Scholasticism emerged as medieval Europe's most sophisticated way of thinking about the world. Aristotle's *De anima* (*On the Soul*) was the key text, and the claim that "the study of the soul [in Greek, *psuchē*] . . . must fall within the science of nature" was the text's guiding principle.[30]

In nature, the soul gives life to living things; even plants exhibit movement from within. Animals have additional faculties of discrimination and coordinated movement. Guided by the senses, animals move because they have appetites or desires. Animals are capable of thinking, but only in a limited sense of being able to process images in order to be able to move as needed to satisfy their appetites. Human beings have something more: a "calculative faculty" (or will) in aid of bodily movement and the satisfaction of appetites.[31]

In addition to willpower and self-control, human beings have the faculty of "deliberative imagination"—of thinking for its own sake.[32] We alone are capable of thinking about the world and its purposes, without some immediate purpose in mind that would require us to act. In effect, Aristotle ordered living things into three categories: plants, animals, and human beings—the first passive, the second active, and the third reflective. With our sensory faculties, we apprehend "individuals," as indeed animals do, while reflection enables us to apprehend "universals."[33] Even if we are active in the same ways that animals are, emphasizing how we differ from other animals has the effect of putting soul over body, reason over desire, faith's inner knowledge over the corrigible evidence of the senses—and thus of supporting the neo-Platonic tendencies within Christianity.

In keeping with these tendencies, the Scholastics devoted much attention to the higher faculties that make us human and bring us closer to God. Following Aristotle, they conjectured that imagination and judgment are thinking's constitutive faculties.[34] Aristotle's *On Memory* added the "faculty of remembering" to the mix.[35] Yet they were unsure how these faculties related

---

30. Aristotle, *On the Soul,* I, iii (403a29), trans. J. A. Smith, in Jonathan Barnes, ed., *The Complete Works of Aristotle,* Revised Oxford Translation (Princeton, N.J., 1984), 1:643. Since the two volumes of this edition are continuously paginated, we henceforth omit the volume number.

31. See Ibid., III, ix–xi, 687–90, at 432b26.

32. Ibid., III, xi (434a6-7), 690.

33. Ibid., II, v (417b22-23), 664–65.

34. "Thinking is different from perceiving and is held to be in part imagination, in part judgement: we must first mark off the sphere of imagination and then speak of judgement" (Ibid., III, iii [427b28-428a1], 680).

35. Aristotle, *On Memory,* i (449b22-3), trans. J. I. Beare, in Barnes, ed., *Complete Works of Aristotle,* 714.

to each other, to will, and to perception. Most of all, they wondered how a soul described in Aristotle's physicalist terms, as an ensemble of bodily organs, could grasp metaphysical universals, the will of an immaterial God, or its own immortality.[36]

During the Renaissance, the discussion of the cognitive faculties—or faculty psychology, as it is generally called—continued unabated, and not just among Scholastics. For example, the humanist Francis Bacon rejected Aristotle's view of the world as a whole, but not his view of the way the mind works, in order to affirm the "league of mind and body."[37] Humanists, alchemists, seers, and reform-minded priests all kept the body in the picture. As Foucault might have said, if there are no bodies, no things, no appearances and resemblances, there is no picture, no world—and no Renaissance *episteme*.

Descartes ushered in the classical *episteme* by declaring that appearances are deceiving. Only one thing is certain to him, or to me: that he exists, that I exist. "But what then am I? A thing which thinks. . . . It is a thing which doubts, understands, affirms, denies, wills, refuses, which also imagines and feels." It is hard to imagine a more striking reaffirmation of the Scholastic emphasis on the higher faculties and, among them, on the faculty of thinking (*facultas cognoscitiva*).[38]

Descartes' ruminations disembodied the mind—thanks to Greek philosophy and Christian theology, a familiar and persistent condition. By squeezing all signs of life from the higher faculties, Descartes and his successors reduced them to capacities. The classical *episteme* requires the mind to be ordered as nature is. In a favored metaphor of the time, the mind is a container with a number of compartments. What the mind knows depends on the properties and relations of the boxes, and their contents, whether sensed, imagined, or remembered.[39]

---

36. Here see Gary Hatfield, "The Cognitive Faculties," in Daniel Garber and Michael Ayers, eds., *The Cambridge History of Seventeenth-Century Philosophy* (Cambridge, U.K., 1998), II, 953–1002, at 954–61.

37. Francis Bacon, *The Two Bookes of the Proficience and Advancement of Learning* (London, 1605; New York, 1970, photo-reproducing 1605 ed.), bk. 2, 37. Also see Karl R. Wallace, *Francis Bacon on the Nature of Man: The Faculties of Man's Soul: Understanding, Reason, Imagination, Memory, Will, and Appetite* (Urbana, Ill., 1967).

38. René Descartes, *Meditations on First Philosophy,* ed. Stanley Tweyman, trans. Elizabeth S. Haldane and G. R. T. Ross (London, 1993), Meditation II, 54. Also see Hatfield, "Cognitive Faculties," 965–72.

39. See George Lakoff and Mark Johnson, *Philosophy in the Flesh: The Embodied Mind and Its Challenge to Western Thought* (New York, 1999), 400–404, on Descartes and the "disembodied mind"; 337–40, on the mind as a container; and 409–14, on faculty psychology.

Once the higher faculties are rendered inert, they are easily reduced to a single faculty of understanding. The senses produce ideas, which are mental representations of the contents of the world; by a process of association (and dissociation), the mind discovers the possible combinations and relations of ideas that correspond to the natural order of things in the world. This is John Locke's general argument in *An Essay Concerning Human Understanding* (1690).[40] A consummate expression of classical thinking, the *Essay* led almost inevitably to Hume's skeptical assessment of what we can possibly know about causal relations in nature and Kant's last-ditch effort to undo the damage that Locke and Hume had done by explaining how the mind employs the faculties of sense, imagination, and apperception to create order from sensory chaos.[41] With the advent of the modern *episteme,* the faculties of mind disappeared from view. In their place we find a single, physical property of mind called intelligence, which each of us has in greater or lesser degree, making us more or less normal.[42]

The early modern Locke could hardly ignore the question of free will: "*liberty* cannot be, where there is no thought, no volition, no will." Along with understanding, he granted the mind a second "power": "we find in ourselves a *power* to begin or forbear, continue or end several actions of our minds, and motions of our bodies." Understanding follows from perceiving, will from preferring. Between preference and action is choice, and the act of choosing must not be confused with the satisfaction of natural desires, since this is something over which we often have no choice.[43] By association with liberty, Aristotle's calculative faculty found its place in Locke's theory of mind.

When Locke defined will in terms of preferences and choices, he brought body and soul, world and mind, back together. Human beings have ends not limited to the satisfaction of needs, and we choose courses of action based on what we know about ourselves and our world. We know what aptitudes and abilities we have, what the world makes available for our use, how to change ourselves and the world the better to achieve our ends, how to deal with each

---

40. John Locke, *An Essay Concerning Human Understanding,* ed. Peter H. Nidditch (Oxford, 1975), bk. 2.

41. Immanuel Kant, *Critique of Pure Reason* (1781; 2nd ed. 1787), trans. Norman Kemp Smith (New York, 1965), 127–28 (A94-5, B127-9; A is 1st ed., B is 2nd ed.). Roughly speaking, apperception makes whole what imagination bundles together, in the process producing what we experience as the "unity of consciousness" (135 [A108]).

42. See Jerry Fodor, *The Modularity of Mind: An Essay on Faculty Psychology* (Cambridge, Mass., 1983), 23–29.

43. Locke, *An Essay Concerning Human Understanding,* II, xxi, §§ 5–30, 222–33, at § 8, 223, § 5, 222, original emphasis.

other. What is implicit in Locke's conception of will he made explicit in the *Two Treatises of Government* (1690). Whether talking about the capacities and contents of the mind or the aptitudes and activities of human beings, Locke used the term *faculties*—with reservations, it must be said, and perhaps for rhetorical purposes.[44] For one's mental capacities, he preferred the term *powers*. For the exercise of one's aptitudes and abilities, he preferred the term *rights*.

Both the terms *power* and *right* have juridical connotations, Latin antecedents, Aristotelian resonances. A power involves potential (*potentia*) and its actualization (*potestas*): this relation is central to Aristotle's metaphysics. A right (*jus*) gives formal standing to any given faculty (*facultas*) in Scholastic jurisprudence: this relation gave Hugo Grotius a platform from which to launch the early modern discussion of rights. Grotius followed his Scholastic predecessors by drawing directly on Aristotle's *Nicomachean Ethics*.

Named or not, this text figures in every early modern discussion of human ends and the means to achieve them. Its first words signal its relevance: "Every art and every inquiry, and similarly every action and choice, is thought to aim at some good; and for this reason the good has rightly been declared to be that at which all things aim."[45] Not only do these words give priority to the calculative faculty and instrumental action. They also acknowledge that diverse ends have a common property. We aim for what (we think) is good, and so we should.

Moreover, we should try to be good at what we do. Just as our eyes, hands, and other parts function for us, our activities constitute functions for society, this being the whole of which we are parts. By implication, we cultivate certain of our faculties, and we become skilled at certain activities because it is good for society and rewarding to us. Yet we need to exercise all of our faculties (hands, eyes, judgment, will) to be whole ourselves. The functional integrity of the whole (society, ourselves) depends on the complementarity of many well-functioning parts and well-performed activities.

Aristotle's ontology of parts, wholes, and functional relations comported with developments in the medieval world. The emergence of towns, arts and crafts, guilds and corporations, and circuits of exchange all validated an Aristotelian concern with useful things, skilled practices, complementary

---

44. Ibid., § 17, 226–27. Locke used the term *faculty* only twice in *The Second Treatise of Government,* and only in characterizing the state of nature, ii, §§ 4, 6 (John Locke, *Two Treatises of Government,* ed. Peter Laslett [Cambridge, U.K., 1988], 269, 271).

45. Aristotle, *Nicomachean Ethics,* I, i (1094a1-3), trans. W. D. Ross and J. O. Urmson, in Barnes, ed., *Complete Works of Aristotle,* 1729.

activities, and good results. Neither Scholastic nor humanist ways of thinking vitiated these developments and their practical significance. Religious and political turmoil may have aided as much as hindered them. Early modern writers made constant metaphorical references to machines, mechanisms, and organisms, all of which are functioning wholes *and* parts in the functional relations of some larger whole.

Whatever the whole, its functional integrity depends on the adaptation and distribution of things for use. Tools, techniques, faculties, and organs are the functionally specialized parts suited to adaptive activity: to use Smith's words, these are the productive powers of labor. So are human beings. Labor is what we are and what we do. And so are the various enterprises that our labor produces.

The movement of useful things affects the parts, not always for the better. Often the movement of things prompts the alteration of activities in useful ways. When human beings make things specifically for use, we call the movement of these things *commerce*. The term applies to exchanges or interactions within any system of functional relations. Early modern thinkers such as G. W. Leibniz and Isaac Newton often wrote each other to discuss their findings, methods, and conjectures and to air their disagreements; when published, this correspondence was called a *commercium epistolicum*. Kant held that apperception—the faculty of sensing wholes—turns any "chain of empirical representations" into a "thorough-going community of mutual interaction," or *"commercium."*[46] Underlying the commerce in objects, ideas, or perceptions is the relation of faculties, minds, and bodies that makes us human.

As we shall see, early modern writers paid a good deal of attention to commerce in the most common sense of the term, because commerce was in fact rapidly changing their world—and because they saw the world of human activity very much as Aristotle did. The epistemic shift from order to history, from the classification of objects to the tracing of functional relations, reinforced the long-standing concern with aptitudes and activities, tools and techniques, utility and exchange. As commerce became even more important in the nineteenth century, so did functional specialization, and not just in the production of goods. Medical practices, the organization of the workplace, education, and jurisprudence all became recognizably *modern*.

Once Foucault turned his attention to these kinds of activities (which he misleadingly described as non-discursive), he brilliantly documented

---

46. Kant, *Critique of Pure Reason*, 235 (A213-4, B260).

the cumulative effects of changes in technique. What is intriguing about Foucault's investigation of these practices is their focus on functional specialization in relation to the production of social control.[47] Following Karl Marx, most discussions of production focus on the use of wealth and labor in the production of things for use. Marx's conjectural history of the modes of production minimizes the development and deployment of human faculties as the engine of social change—neither big shifts in thinking about life and labor nor the incremental learning of more specialized skills made capitalism a transforming force in the relations of production. By contrast, conjectural histories of a sort that Smith and his contemporaries proposed assign a particular significance to practical skills.

As we saw, Smith's reconstruction of human history identifies four ages: hunting and gathering, herding, farming, and commerce. Large, long-term shifts in the way people apply practical skills to the problem of meeting their needs are responsible for the rise of herding and then farming. Transitions take place over generations, if at all. The fourth age presupposes such a degree of specialization in productive activities that circuits of exchange become its most prominent feature. In principle, the four ages follow in a necessary order because they require progressively greater functional specialization. Falling back from one age to an earlier one is always possible, and it can be sudden, even catastrophic, if social disruption translates into a massive loss of skills.

In general terms, conjectural histories of this sort are *liberal.* At the heart of the empirical claims and normative dispositions about the human condition that might be called liberal are five ambiguously related, deeply Aristotelian judgments about human aptitudes, human beings, and human collectivities.[48] First, they should all have a degree of autonomy sufficient for their *whole* development—by *right.* Second, they should all contribute to the development of the whole of which they are a part—according to *need.* Third, development is a matter of choice, calculation, and instrumental action—of *will.* Fourth, development is only potential. Its actualization depends on the production and use of ideas, skills, and "the necessaries and conveniences of life"—of *good* things.[49] These processes depend in turn on the circulation of good things—on *commerce.* Fifth, parts as wholes

47. See, for example, Michel Foucault, *Discipline and Punish: The Birth of the Prison,* trans. Alan Sheridan (New York, 1979).
48. For an exposition along similar lines by a leading contemporary liberal, see Amartya Sen, *Development as Freedom* (New York, 1999), chaps. 3–4.
49. Smith, *Wealth of Nations,* intro. and plan of the work, § 1, 10.

need a framework—or *constitution*—within which to function as parts of wholes.[50]

Such a framework separates autonomous, interacting wholes into sets identified by some property common to every member of the set and visualized in ascending *levels*. At each level, wholes are equals in their capacity to choose and execute courses of action. Yet the consequences of their chosen activities need not be equal. Nor are they likely to be. Since aptitudes tend to be normally distributed, so will the benefits of productive activity and exchange. Insofar as like cases are treated alike (comparable wholes are treated as equals), a normal distribution of such outcomes is *just*—for contemporary liberals as it was for Aristotle. Liberals also worry about the safety of human beings, the protection of property, and integrity of exchange. People institute more or less adequate responses to these concerns, and in the process such responses also become matters of justice.

The liberal conception of the human condition starts not with the human individual but with *society*, and thus with commerce in the largest sense. Our many faculties constitute a society of mind *and* body as a functional whole, and not just a "society of mind."[51] We might just as well speak of the commerce of the faculties. By nature, individual human beings live in society, and they cannot be whole unless they do so: Aristotle insisted on this, and so did the early modern writers from whom liberal claims and dispositions directly derive. With society comes exchange; with development, commerce blossoms; with commerce comes collaboration, competition, and conflict in every conceivable combination.

Society is an abstraction, a general testament to human need and will. When people come together to exercise their faculties and meet their needs, they form social bodies that have various features, functions, and connections to other social bodies. As a whole, these bodies are a great deal more varied than are people and their faculties. Certainly medieval Europe consisted of diverse social bodies, thoroughly different in purpose, scale, and development and weakly linked by circuits of exchange. A whole in name perhaps but not in practice, Europe only became a society as it swept the world.

For convenience, we can date this development from around 1500. The rise of the modern world meant the progressive elimination of social bodies

---

50. We develop the Aristotelian logic of parts and wholes with particular reference to the U.S. Constitution in *Federal Union, Modern World: The Law of Nations in an Age of Revolutions, 1776–1814* (Madison, Wisc., 1993), pt. 1.
51. Marvin Minsky, *The Society of Mind* (New York, 1986); Lakoff and Johnson, *Philosophy in the Flesh*, 410–14.

to which the term *nation* could not be applied. Nations began to deal with each other in what we can only describe as liberal terms. Organized as states, they acted much the way that human individuals do when they have the opportunity. They guarded their autonomy yet saw themselves an ordered whole, engaged in commerce for instrumental reasons, competed strenuously across the world, waged war and made peace as equals.

By the first decades of the nineteenth century, the jumble of diverse social bodies had become a homogeneous set of comparable wholes—a liberal society whose members were, and still are, nations. Liberal international society fostered the development of liberal societies in those nations where commerce prevailed. Some nations changed convulsively; revolution spilled across Europe and the Americas. All nations began to assert their differences—as "living beings"—even though they continued to become more alike. The more they were connected by commerce, the more strident they became. Liberal ideas coexisted uneasily with traditional values; the development of societies in a rapidly changing world was far more complex than the conjectural historians had assumed. The machinery of industrial capitalism began to roar, and with it the machinery of war.

National Histories

Conjectural historians' hypotheses about the stages of historical development provided a universal template for articulating the particularities—or "empiricities"—of national histories. The differences that an expanding regime of commercial relations brought to the fore could only be comprehended by invoking a common standard of measurement. For enlightened environmentalists, the "nation" and its distinctive "character" provided the most sensitive register of "natural" differences in climate and productions. Yet natural variations across space could not adequately account for how particular peoples improved their natural advantages (or overcame their natural disadvantages) across time. National history mediated between whole and part, situating a particular people at a distinctive location in the spatial and temporal matrix of universal history. Discrepancies among nations could thus be explained historically: Britain and the other advanced commercial societies of Western Europe were rapidly progressing through the stages of historical development, leaving the barbarous peoples of the New World far behind and even beginning to overtake the highly civilized, but stationary societies of the East. A closer look at the civilized nations of the West revealed wide variations as well, variations that could only be explained by understanding the ways in which their particular constitutions fostered or retarded progress.

National histories chronicled the quasi-mythic origins of particular peoples, giving the emerging nation-states of the early modern world a legitimating pedigree. These conjectural origin stories focused on the reciprocal constitution of people and regime, tracing the evolution of a distinctive national character back into the mists of time. In England, the genius of the people was expressed in the gradual, organic development of the common law that was codified in modern times in the great treatises of the common lawyers. The translation of custom into precedent drew the "people" into historical time, giving the modern English an "ancient constitution" that shaped their ongoing struggles to secure and promote liberty. The lawyers thus portrayed liberty-loving ancestors as "founders," reducing the many histories of a highly decentralized feudal polity into a single story line that ultimately culminated in modern nationhood.[52]

National history fostered a homogenizing collective identity—subsuming differences by eliminating or subordinating corporate bodies that jeopardized national unity—even while exaggerating differences with other, "foreign" nations. Historians thus played a vital role in nation building, making conceptual space for the national idea by suppressing alternative pathways to the present. While nations became alike, taking on the common form of the modern nation-state, they cherished essential differences in "character"—that is, in their distinctive historical experiences. In other words, the obstacles that the nation had to overcome to fulfill its destiny—the internal as well as external challenges to national self-determination and territorial integrity that constituted its history—defined the nation apart from, if not in opposition to the other nations it increasingly resembled. National historians thus elaborated (or "invented") the paradox of identity in difference—of national particularity in the context of universal human nature—that characterizes the modern world.[53] The same paradox is also reflected in the modern law of nations: nations can "recognize" and therefore deal with

52. We are here indebted to the work of J. G. A. Pocock, notably his *The Ancient Constitution and the Feudal Law: English Historical Thought in the Seventeenth Century* (Cambridge, U.K., 1957). See also David C. Douglas, *English Scholars, 1660–1730*, 2nd ed. (London, 1951). On the importance of Whig history to American patriots, see H. Trevor Colbourn, *The Lamp of Experience: Whig History and the Intellectual Origins of the American Revolution* (Chapel Hill, N.C., 1965).

53. For further development of this argument, see Peter S. Onuf, "Nations, Revolutions, and the End of History," in Michael A. Morrison and Melinda Zook, eds., *Revolutionary Currents: Nation Building in the Transatlantic World* (Lanham, Md., 2004), 173–88. On the historicizing inventiveness of nation makers, see Eric Hobsbawm and Terence Ranger, eds., *The Invention of Tradition* (Cambridge, U.K., 1983) and E. J. Hobsbawm, *Nations and Nationalism since 1780* (Cambridge, U.K., 1990).

each other peacefully because they are similar and have common interests (nations collectively constitute a society), but those dealings are also potentially belligerent because nations in pursuit of their own distinctive interests are so prone to overlook and thus fail to recognize the rights of other nations.

Historical writing was crucial to the precocious development of English national identity.[54] But the extension of English rule through the British Isles and beyond made the boundaries of the nation problematic. The emerging conception of a greater "British" nationality appealed to many provincials on the margins of empire. Others, chafing at metropolitan challenges to local authority, articulated claims to separate nationhood. Locke's friend William Molyneux offers a pertinent example.

In *The Case of Ireland* (1698), Molyneux claimed that Ireland was a "*Separate and Distinct Kingdom* by it self from the Kingdom of *England.*"[55] The Anglo-Irish did not constitute a separate people because of ethnic or religious differences from the English. To the contrary, their parallel experience over the previous five hundred years as free Englishmen—their independent relation to the crown through their own parliament—constituted them a nation. Long before Anglo-American colonists began to articulate the idea of a federal empire, Molyneux advocated a constitutional settlement among separate kingdoms, united by their fealty to a common king. Like the colonists, Molyneux invoked the principle of consent set forth in Locke's *Second Treatise of Government.*[56] He also invoked "the Universal Agreement of all Civilians"—including Grotius and Samuel Pufendorf—on the rights of distinct civil societies under the *"Law of Nations."* If the nationhood claim was the "Birth-right of every Free-born English Subject," it was also the common

---

54. For the precocity—and exemplary character—of British nationalism, see Liah Greenfeld, *Nationalism: Five Roads to Modernity* (Cambridge, Mass., 1992), 27–87. On British identity in the eighteenth century—and tensions between English and greater British patriotism—see Linda Colley, *Britons: Forging the Nation, 1707–1837* (New Haven, Conn., 1992).

55. William Molyneux, *The Case of Ireland Being Bound by Acts of Parliament in England, Stated* (Dublin, 1698), 40, original emphasis.

56. "Reason being plain on our side, that Men are naturally free, and the Examples of History shewing, that the *Governments* of the World, that were begun in Peace, had their foundations laid on that foundation, and were *made by the consent of the People;* There can be little room for doubt" (Locke, *Second Treatise of Government,* viii, § 104, 336, original emphasis). Less clear are the circumstances under which the people are free to withdraw their consent to be governed; established property rights and settled social relations necessarily limit the people's right to resist all but the most tyrannical governments. See John Marshall, *John Locke: Resistance, Religion and Responsibility* (Cambridge, V. K., 1994), chap. 6.

right of "the whole *Race of Mankind*" and was equally applicable to the French, Poles, and Turks.[57]

Molyneux's "case" for the Anglo-Irish shows how claims to separate nationhood grew out of the assertion of identity—as "Free-born" Englishmen or as any group of men organized in civil societies, those "*Immortal . . . Corporations*" whose rights were secured by the law of nations—and the historical experience of invidious and oppressive treatment, the "long train of abuses" invoked by Locke and fully elaborated by Thomas Jefferson for his fellow Americans. History was the nation-making experience that transformed identity into difference. "We might have been a free and a great people together," Jefferson wrote in his draft of the Declaration of Independence, but English unwillingness to recognize Americans' equal rights "denounces our eternal separation."[58]

Creole nationalists such as Jefferson formulated rights claims for communities of Englishmen on the margins of empire that simultaneously asserted identity—a greater Britishness that obliterated distance from the metropolis—and the integrity and autonomy of their provincial constitutions.[59] The invention of colonial corporate identity was an act of the historicizing imagination, made manifest in colonial constitutionalism generally as well as in the efflorescence of new provincial and incipiently "national" histories throughout the Anglo-American world.[60] The British empire proved to be an incubator for nationalist thought because English (and British) nationalism served as both the source and model for the aspirations of overseas expatriates. As a result, conceptions of "empire" were correspondingly impoverished

57. Molyneux, *Case of Ireland Being Bound by Acts of Parliament in England,* 153–54, original emphasis. Molyneux's arguments once attracted considerable attention from constitutional historians, sympathetic in the case of Charles Howard McIlwain, *The American Revolution: A Constitutional Interpretation* (paper ed.; Ithaca, N.Y., 1966), and hostile in the case of R. L. Schuyler, *Parliament and the British Empire* (New York, 1929).

58. Molyneux, *Case of Ireland Being Bound by Acts of Parliament in England,* 152, original emphasis; Jefferson, Declaration of Independence, in Merrill D. Peterson, ed., *Thomas Jefferson Writings* (New York, 1984), 19, 23.

59. The best general study of colonial constitutionalism in the imperial context is Jack P. Greene, *Peripheries and Center: Constitutional Development in the Extended Polities of the British Empire and the United States, 1607–1788* (Athens, Ga., 1986).

60. On provincial historiography, see the essays collected in Jack P. Greene, *Imperatives, Behaviors, and Identities: Essays in Early American Cultural History* (Charlottesville, Va., 1992); idem, "The Intellectual Construction of Virginia," in Peter S. Onuf, ed., *Jeffersonian Legacies* (Charlottesville, Va., 1993), 225–53; idem, *The Intellectual Construction of America: Exceptionalism and Identity from 1492 to 1800* (Chapel Hill, N.C., 1993); and idem, "Empire and Identity," in P. J. Marshall, ed., *The Eighteenth Century,* vol. 2 of William Roger Louis, ed., *The Oxford History of the British Empire* (Oxford, 1998), 208–30.

and attenuated, subject to divergent, ultimately incompatible formulations. Even while Molyneux and other provincial Britons imagined the empire as a community of "separate kingdoms" under the law of nations, imperial reformers projected the power of the British nation across—and over— subordinate, dependent colonial jurisdictions.[61]

Anglo-American provincial patriots began writing national histories long before they acknowledged and declared an intention to make a new nation, or rather—for most of them—a federation of independent republics. The idea of separate colony constitutions was the ultimate product of provincial historicism, providing a conceptual framework for understanding and justifying the ongoing struggle to vindicate provincial rights. But the emphasis on separateness, difference, and distance from the metropolis came at a heavy price for anxious provincials, insecure about their status as civilized Englishmen.[62] The great challenge for provincial historians was to refute the metropolitan presumption of creole degeneracy. Provincials might acknowledge that the primitive conditions of the first settlements and their proximity to, and dependence on barbarous natives entailed a temporary regression from metropolitan standards. But they insisted that the histories of their provinces—the remarkable transformation of a benign natural environment by successive generations of enterprising, liberty-loving Englishmen who in the process transformed themselves into distinctive provincial peoples— demonstrated a natural, nation-making capacity to move rapidly through the stages of historical development outlined in the conjectural histories of the Enlightenment.

Anglo-American constitutionalism converged with the conjectural model of developmental stages to precipitate the precocious elaboration of the national idea on the western side of the Atlantic. Rights-conscious, extra-European Britons replicated metropolitan legal and political forms in a mimetic process that buttressed claims to provincial autonomy, while their adaptation to the New World's bountiful environment affirmed their genius

---

61. The best general study of the problem is still Richard Koebner, *Empire* (Cambridge, U.K., 1961). See also excellent recent works by Eliga H. Gould, *The Persistence of Empire: British Political Culture in the Age of the American Revolution* (Chapel Hill, N.C., 2000) and David Armitage, *The Ideological Origins of the British Empire* (Cambridge, U.K., 2000).

62. For suggestive recent discussions of the civility problem in America, see Joyce E. Chaplin, *An Anxious Pursuit: Agricultural Innovation and Modernity in the Lower South, 1730–1815* (Chapel Hill, N.C., 1993), chap. 2, and Leonard J. Sadosky, "Revolutionary Negotiations: An Intellectual and Cultural History of American Diplomacy in the Age of Franklin and Jefferson" (Ph.D. diss., University of Virginia, 2003), chap. 1.

for achieving progressively higher levels of civilization. The simplicity of provincial societies—the notable absence of a well-articulated, legally entrenched social hierarchy—could be celebrated by provincials and their enlightened admirers as a tremendous advantage in moving rapidly to the highest levels of economic and political development. In *The Wealth of Nations,* Smith thus envisioned a process of reform and improvement—clearing away the thicket of mercantilist regulation and corporate privilege—that would refashion the British metropolis along American provincial lines. The fulfillment of the national idea depended on the freedom of subjects (or citizens) to pursue their own interests while thus promoting the wealth and welfare of the larger community. An expanding ambit of market freedom characterized the most advanced commercial societies and was critical to their ongoing progress.

Americans naturally found such thinking congenial, linking it with the parallel narrative of constitutional progress culminating in their new republican regimes. Both developments pointed toward the modern idea of the nation, the homogenous and homogenizing space that *makes* all men equal and most efficiently mobilizes human and natural resources. The outbreak of war, the result of mobilizations over the previous decade of the imperial crisis and the threshold for further mobilization of a scale and scope unprecedented in provincial Anglo-America, marked the culminating phase of Revolutionary American nation making. The Revolutionary experience would in turn become the touchstone for a new national historiography that built on, but never fully transcended, the provincial histories that had inspired Patriots to overthrow the yoke of British tyranny.

The Revolutionaries' great achievement was to articulate and implement the idea of popular sovereignty.[63] Because of terminological confusion surrounding federalism—the conventional association of *federal* and *national* and the anomalous situation of semisovereign *states*—the connections among claims to provincial autonomy, popular sovereignty, and developing conceptions of nationhood have remained elusive. Historians and theorists have been enamored with the idea that the Federalists' supposed invention of a continent-wide American "people" during the debates over the ratification of the federal Constitution somehow resolved and rationalized a complex division of authority in the "extended" American republic. But the linkage among province, state, and people remained powerful in America and was

---

63. Edmund S. Morgan, *Inventing the People: The Rise of Popular Sovereignty in England and America* (New York, 1988).

reinforced by the constitutive role of state ratifying conventions—the "peoples" of the separate states—in launching the new regime.[64]

If the British Empire fostered proliferating nationhood claims, the new federal regime, a "peace pact" among the new American republics, was designed to perpetuate and secure those *"Immortal . . . Corporations."*[65] The Constitution's framers would not repeat the failed effort of British imperial reformers to demolish provincial liberties and create a unitary, consolidated nation-state. In America, the national idea always could be turned against a domineering central government. Ultimately the national idea was turned against a union that Southerners believed jeopardized their fundamental rights and interests.

Everywhere in the enlightened world, conjectural history enabled nationalists to conceptualize new national histories that celebrated, legitimized, and embodied the "people." Drawing on their experience in the British Empire, the great incubator of "nations," Americans took the lead in refining and implementing the national idea in the age of revolutions. The Civil War that marked the ultimate collapse of their federal republic and gave rise to a consolidated nation-state did not belatedly bring Americans into step with European developments. To the contrary, the precocious development of nationalist thinking in America led to the coalescence of two great nations in the place of one and a great war between them that would transform their world. Subsequent crises within the liberal international system—great wars among nations—would follow the Americans' script. Modern history, still largely written as national history, has chronicled the impact of these crises and conflicts on rulers and ruled alike. But historians rarely acknowledge that "history," by inventing, confirming, or simply assuming the existence of nations, played a crucial role in creating the modern, war-torn world.

---

64. The most influential argument for the role of "popular sovereignty" in justifying a more energetic central government is in Gordon S. Wood, *The Creation of the American Republic, 1776–1787* (Chapel Hill, N.C., 1969), 344–89. For a corrective, emphasizing the continuing salience of states' rights, see Forrest McDonald, *States' Rights and the Union: Imperium in Imperio, 1776–1876* (Lawrence, Kans., 2000).

65. See David C. Hendrickson, *Peace Pact: The Lost World of the American Founding* (Lawrence, Kans., 2003).

2
Liberal Society

Purportedly a liberal thinker, Adam Smith assumed that human beings had always lived in civil society. Proprietors work out ways of improving their lives through their labors; the division of labor is integral to the human condition. Without exchange, people could not deploy their faculties to advantage, or even survive in a world of animals that have no need for such behavior. Where there is exchange, we find markets. Smith simply stipulated that the limits of exchange determine the extent of any given market.

If Smith's markets have natural boundaries, then it is the nature of the goods exchanged that mark these boundaries. Trade in corn constitutes a market. Otherwise, a bounded set of social relations, such as those that constitute the nation, will always include exchange relations among them. Nations have markets in this nearly nominal sense. For Smith the nation is a given—a place marker and thus a market marker. The nation is more than this only insofar as nations are states that have governments. Smith's view is typical of his time. Governments protect nations as sites of exchange, and nations participate in exchange with other nations.

On this view, the nation is a given because the law of nations gives nations their common properties. The idea that nations are corporate entities seemed utterly natural to early modern Europeans. As "moral persons," nations are bound by just rules (*juris*) in their relations with other such moral persons. Roman law offered an inventory of rules whose relevance rested on the assumption that all kinds of corporate entities are proper subjects of law, and on a series of analogies. By analogy with the Roman law of peoples (jus gentium), nations have a prominent place in natural law. Roman civil law fostered an analogy between property and territory as a basis for jurisdiction—for deciding which persons are subject to given rules in what circumstances. Yet the practice of drawing analogies so broadly suggests that the law of nations developed before anyone had a clear sense that nations constitute a category of moral persons exercising exclusive territorial jurisdiction.

When Hugo Grotius published his great treatise *De jure belli ac pacis* in 1628, he understood the law of nature to apply to all moral persons. A century and a half later, writers conventionally associated the law of nature and the law of nations, but they did so without ever having given up the inclusive logic of a natural law to which all moral persons are subject. Emmerich de Vattel's *Le droit des gens* (1758) is illustrative. While this accessible yet authoritative exposition more or less limits itself to the law applicable exclusively to nations in their relations with each other (there is some discussion of general constitutional law), its full title points to its inclusive premises: *Le droit des gens ou principes de la loi naturelle, appliqués à la conduite & aux affaires des nations & des souverains.*

Henry Wheaton's *Elements of International Law* (1836) succeeded Vattel's treatise as the primary reference work on the substantive rules of what had by this time come to be called international law. Wheaton couched this exposition in a conjectural history of the European moral universe. Looking back on the unfolding of legal doctrine from Grotius to Vattel, Wheaton gave Vattel credit for definitively establishing the conceptual autonomy of the law of nations, whereas Wheaton was the one to do so by attributing this development to Vattel. The lasting effect of this conceptual clarification was to separate the relations of nations from those of other moral persons into levels that seem ontologically necessary, morally imperative, and historically confirmed.

A constitutional lawyer and diplomat from the United States, Wheaton followed Vattel in arguing that European nations constituted a society, and thus a moral world, within which nations are equally free to pursue their interests within the limits set by international law. In keeping with state practice, Wheaton itemized the specific sources of this law. He confirmed that states become members of international society by virtue of recognition by other states. He took for granted that the rules of international law confer rights and duties on states. In doing so, he made it clear that international society is not only autonomous but that it is, as we would say today, a liberal society—perhaps the first liberal society in the modern world.

Markets and Nations

In *The Wealth of Nations* (1776), Adam Smith had almost nothing to say about nature as a state of affairs or source of analogy about persons and their relations. His earlier work makes it clear why. In *The Theory of Moral Sentiments* (1759), Smith affirmed the sentiment, common to Aristotle and the Stoics, "that man, who can only subsist in society, was fitted by nature to that situation for which he was made. All the members of human society stand in need of each others assistance, and are likewise exposed to mutual injuries. Where the necessary assistance is reciprocally afforded from love, from gratitude, from friendship, and esteem, the society flourishes and is happy."[1] Nature and society are inextricable; human nature can only express itself in social terms.

Smith could have made these claims by way of analogy, as did so many of his early modern predecessors. Indeed, he did so in his lectures on jurisprudence at Glasgow University in 1762. "If we should suppose 10 or 12 persons of different sexes settled in an uninhabited island, the first method they would fall upon for their sustenance would be to support themselves by the wild fruits and animals which the country afforded."[2] When "their numbers multiplied," Smith's islanders would devise a better method for providing for their needs by taming and caring for wild animals who would also "multiply their kind."[3] With this analogy, Smith introduced his conception of the four ages of society. Nevertheless, his island is a contrived and dispensable setting, little more than a rhetorical gesture.

By contrast, *The Wealth of Nations* starts abruptly with this striking claim: "The greatest improvement in the productive powers of labour, and the greater part of the skill, dexterity, and judgment with which it is any where directed, or applied, seem to have been the effects of the division of labour."[4] Locke earlier had made human labor a central concern, conceptualizing it by reference to human aptitudes such as dexterity and judgment. Yet Locke had nothing to say about skills, a concern that presumably would emerge only after the proprietors of productive powers constituted a civil society. For Smith human society is always civil, proprietors are always thinking of ways of improving their lives through their labors, and the division of labor is inevitable. The concept of a division of labor

---

1. Adam Smith, *The Theory of Moral Sentiments,* ed. D. D. Raphael and A. L. Macfie (Indianapolis, Ind., 1981), II, II, iii, § 1, 85. See chapter 6 in this essay on the classical sources of Smith's thought.
2. Adam Smith, *Lectures on Jurisprudence,* ed. R. L. Meek et al. (Oxford, 1978), Report of 1762–63, i, 27, 14.
3. Ibid., i, 28, 14–15.
4. Adam Smith, *An Inquiry into the Nature and Causes of the Wealth of Nations,* ed. R. H. Campbell and A. S. Skinner (Indianapolis, Ind., 1981), I, chap. i, § 1, 13.

neatly ties classical and Lockean assumptions into a compelling point of departure.[5]

The division of labor depends on an empirical generalization that liberal thinkers always accept but rarely articulate. Those faculties that make labor productive are not equally distributed in any human population, nor are they equally applicable to every natural setting. Broadly speaking, any useful faculty is normally distributed; few proprietors of these faculties have them all in equal measure. Everyone has an incentive to specialize in any given setting according to their markedly divergent but interdependent faculties.

Smith left all this unspoken.[6] He simply stipulated that the division of labor arose "through very slow and gradual consequence of a certain propensity in human nature . . . to truck, barter, and exchange one thing for another."[7] Smith guessed that this propensity was not "one of those original principles of human nature" but instead was "the necessary consequence of the faculties of reason and speech." In support of this conjecture, Smith argued that the propensity to engage in exchange "is found in no other race of animals, which seem to know neither this nor any other species of contract," and he proceeded to offer a counteranalogy from nature to make the point. "Two greyhounds, in running down the same hare, have sometimes the appearance of acting in some sort of concert. Each turns her towards his companion, or endeavours to intercept her when his companion turns her towards himself. This, however, is not the effect of any contract but of the accidental concurrence of their passions in the same object at that particular time."[8]

---

5. Plato remarked on the division of labor in *The Republic,* a text that Smith discussed with some care in *Theory of Moral Sentiments,* VII, II, i, 267–70. On Plato's thinking and its relation to Smith's, see Gloria Vivenza, *Adam Smith and the Classics: The Classical Heritage in Adam Smith's Thought,* trans. Clive Cheesman and Nicola Gelder (Oxford, 2001), 126–37. The modern discussion of a division of labor dates back to Locke's time. William Petty seems to have initiated it in 1683, but not to have coined this turn of phrase; Henry Martyn spelled out its implications for trade between England and the East Indies in 1701. See Smith, *Wealth of Nations,* I, I, ed. note 1, 13–14, and Douglas A. Irwin, *Against the Tide: An Intellectual History of Free Trade* (Princeton, N.J., 1996), 56–59.

6. Smith did say that the division of labor results in "the increase of dexterity in every particular workman" (*Wealth of Nations,* I, i, § 5, 17). We might infer that workers will choose the sort of work at which they are most dextrous, but, as a practical matter, Smith did not make this inference. While an investment in labor and time could increase any worker's dexterity, he recognized that most workers have little choice in acquiring skills or finding work (Ibid., I, x.b, §§ 6–8, 118–19).

7. Ibid., I, ii, § 1, 25.

8. Ibid., § 2, 25–26.

Human society differs from nature because animals do not think the way that people do even when animals and people behave the same way: animals cannot make promises with the intention of keeping them, and therefore they cannot engage in commerce of any kind. David Hume might have questioned Smith's assumption that every exchange is predicated on a contract, or exchange of promises, but he certainly believed that human society is a normative condition and that commerce of every kind depends on conventional support to succeed. For Smith an exchange of promises is not merely the source of civil society. Exchanging useful things is characteristic social behavior, without which people could not deploy their faculties to advantage, or even survive.

Smith saw no socially imposed limit to exchange driven by human labor. "As it is the power of exchanging that gives occasion to the division of labour, so the extent of this division must always be limited by the extent of that power, or, in other words, by the extent of the market."[9] The term *market* is defined nowhere in *The Wealth of Nations*. While Smith rarely had occasion to use the term, there is no great mystery about its meaning. The *market* is an abstract representation of some network of exchange limited only by material conditions.

The most obvious material limit is the nature of the commodity undergoing exchange. Various goods have distinctive properties inducing a division of labor. In turn, the specialization of labor makes these goods even more distinctive. Differentiation affects the conditions of exchange. Corn and cattle are so different as goods that their exchange involves specialized activities in different places and at different times. Judging the quality of cattle and corn requires different skills; transporting corn and cattle are drastically different undertakings. If Smith supposed that corn and cattle have their own markets, we make the same sort of supposition about various commodities, not to mention the factors of production (land, labor, and capital), for the same sort of reasons.[10]

Obviously, people have occasion to exchange commodities that are very different by nature. Corn and cattle can be exchanged. If the division of labor expedites these transactions, then they too constitute a market for the commodities in question. New markets lap over old ones; improvements in transportation extend markets; standardized media of exchange, such as precious metals, facilitate transactions within and across markets; material limits fall

---

9. Ibid., I, iii, § 1, 31.
10. Smith's extended discussion of corn trade is the clearest instance of this supposition at work in *Wealth of Nations* (Ibid., IV, v.b, 524–43 [added to 1778 ed.]).

away. The water's edge becomes progressively less important as a barrier to commerce; shipping "opens the whole world for a market to the produce of every sort of labour."[11]

Smith's "market" is a summary description of natural human behavior in the aggregate. We might, however, bring the market back to social reality by considering it as a *place*. For his part, Smith clearly did *not* construe markets as the particular places in towns or ports where people exchange goods, any more than he thought that all commerce is predicated on actual contracts.[12] Nevertheless, he fell back on the idea of place in a less concretely, immediately social sense. We see it in his discussion of the "invisible hand."[13]

Smith offered an illustration to make his point clear. "The taylor does not make his own shoes, but buys them of the shoemaker. The shoemaker does not attempt to make his own cloathes, but employs a taylor." The same is true for all producers: everybody benefits from a division of labor.[14] Then comes the more general claim. "What is prudence in the conduct of every private family, can scarce be folly in that of a great kingdom. If a foreign country can supply us with a commodity cheaper than we ourselves can make it, better buy it of them with some part of the produce of our own industry, employed in a way in which we have some advantage."[15]

The normal exchanges of tailors and shoemakers, butchers and bakers, constitute a market largely local, or perhaps regional, in extent.[16] Yet markets, considered by reference to commerce and the division of labor, have no

---

11. Ibid., I, iii, § 4, 34. On the origin of money, which "has become in all civilized nations the universal instrument of commerce," see Ibid., I, iv, 37–47, at § 11, 44.

12. See Jean-Christophe Agnew, *Worlds Apart: The Market and the Theater in Anglo-American Thought, 1550–1750* (Cambridge, U.K., 1986), 40–46, on the shifting meanings of the term *market* before Smith's time:

    The medieval "market" suggests a more or less sharply delineated sphere of commerce, an experienced physical and social space. . . . By the sixteenth century, however, the meanings of "market" had multiplied and grown more abstract. . . . "Market" now referred to the acts of both buying and selling, regardless of locale, and to the price or exchange value of goods and services. A culturally confined site was no longer the precondition of a market so-called. . . . As a matter of customary usage, the process of commodity exchange had spilled over the boundaries that had once defined it. By the end of the eighteenth century, "market" had come to imply, especially in literate circles, a boundless and timeless phenomenon—so much so, in fact, that legal thinkers felt constrained to set off the original, situated meaning of the term as a "market overt." (at 41)

13. Smith, *Wealth of Nations*, IV, ii, § 9, 456.

14. Ibid., § 11, 456–57.

15. Ibid., § 12, 457.

16. Nicholas Phillipson has argued that Smith equated markets with regions informally defined by town-country relations, but that he was "studiously vague in his choice of

natural limit. Smith took for granted that home markets coincide with national boundaries, that many countries benefit from access to more extensive foreign markets, and that material conditions impede the movement of goods within some countries' home markets.[17] What makes any such market *home* is its situation within a nation's boundaries and subject to the control of its government, as in the case of the grant of a national monopoly to inefficient domestic producers.[18] Whether nations are conventional or contractual in origin, just or unjust, prudent or not, they function for Smith as place markers. It is, after all, the wealth of nations—corporate persons—to which his great treatise attends, not the wealth of individual human beings or families, even royal families.

As Karl Polanyi has insisted, there is nothing necessary or inevitable about the nation as the defining criterion for the presence of a market. "So-called nations were merely political units, and very loose ones at that, consisting economically of innumerable smaller and bigger self-sufficing households and insignificant local markets in the villages. Trade was limited . . . either locally as neighborhood trade or as long-distance trade—the two were strictly separated, and neither was allowed to infiltrate the countryside indiscriminately."[19] Polanyi claimed that "state intervention" produced specifically national markets in an era of mercantilist competition.[20] Polanyi might better have said that competition among crowns and courts, conducted by war and the manipulation of commerce, jointly produced the early modern state and the national market, and at the same time made them inseparable.[21] Less cause than consequence, state intervention depended on these earlier developments, which competition alone cannot fully explain.

---

terminology to describe this regional structure" ("Adam Smith as Civic Moralist," in Istvan Hont and Michael Ignatieff, eds., *Wealth and Virtue: The Shaping of Political Economy in the Scottish Enlightenment* (Cambridge, U.K., 1983), 179–202, at 194).

17. "In countries . . . less extensive and less favourably circumstanced for interior commerce than China, they [manufactures] generally require the support of foreign trade. Without an extensive foreign market, they could not well flourish, either in countries so moderately extensive as to afford but a narrow home market; or in countries where the communication between one province and another was so difficult, as to render it impossible for the goods of any particular place to enjoy the whole of that home market which the country could afford" (*Wealth of Nations,* IV, ix, § 41, 680).

18. Ibid., § 11, 456.

19. Karl Polanyi, *The Great Transformation: The Political and Economic Origins of Our Time* (Boston, 1957), 63.

20. Ibid., 63–67.

21. Kurt Burch, *"Property" and the Making of the International System* (Boulder, Colo., 1997).

The title of Smith's book suggests an unacknowledged inspiration for his point of view and a fuller explanation for the development of specifically national markets. That there are nations at all, that they possess among their attributes greater and lesser wealth, that authorized agents represent nations in their relations, and that these agents are capable of deploying their nations' wealth to advantage is due to the *law of nations,* a development to which early modern Europeans attached great significance. Had there been nothing more to the development of this body of law than the accretion of customary rules, the status distinctions inherited from feudal Europe would have sufficed to determine its emerging form. Yet something altogether different took place.

By analogy, Roman law gave Europeans everything they needed to organize and explain their rapidly changing world. Thanks in good measure to Grotius, jus gentium provided the framing analogy, within which all other analogies found their place and new rules grew like crystals. As Rome absorbed whole peoples, the Romans devised the jus gentium as a system of rules separate from but similar to their own civil law, by which to regulate relations with foreigners in their midst.[22] Although *not* a system of law above and apart from individuals, a *jus inter gentes,* Grotius and his many followers loosely construed jus gentium as both a law for people and of peoples. In so doing, they made whole peoples, or nations, conceptually central and legally primary but without making other, secondary categories of persons conceptually or legally irrelevant.

Early modern writers assimilated elements of Roman public law to jus gentium in ways that gave the nation additional salience.[23] In Rome, the law authorized public officers, and no one else, to enforce the law outside the household. By analogy, the king's officers alone had the powers to enforce the law. With this in mind, Alexis de Tocqueville would later call the Roman law "the work of a very civilized and subordinated people. The kings therefore enthusiastically adopted it" in their campaigns against "the old liberties of Europe" claimed by fractious lords.[24] By yet another analogy, of kings with the *fetiales,* a small and august body that could conduct negotiations and

---

22. Wolfgang Kunkel, *An Introduction to Roman Legal and Constitutional History,* 2nd ed., trans. J. M. Kelly (Oxford, 1973), chap. 5.
23. At least those with humanist sympathies seem to have done so. Richard Tuck, *The Rights of War and Peace: Political Thought and the International Order from Grotius to Kant* (Oxford, 1999), 9–12. Grotius so thoroughly mixed humanist and scholastic elements in his analysis of public powers that it is difficult to generalize about him. But see Ibid., 81–82, and Furukawa Terumi, "Punishment," in Onuma Yasuaki, ed., *A Normative Approach to War: Peace, War, and Justice in Hugo Grotius* (Oxford, 1993), 221–36.
24. Alexis de Tocqueville, *The Old Regime and the Revolution* (4th ed., 1857), trans. Alan S. Kahan (Chicago, 1998), 258.

declare war on Rome's behalf, kings alone could declare war on behalf of their nations. Since the Roman law treated war and peace as entirely separate legal conditions, the relations of nations came to be differentiated no less strictly. Private wars had no place in this scheme.

Influenced by Stoic thought, a few Roman writers linked jus gentium and natural law, and Grotius and many other early modern thinkers followed their lead.[25] Since all peoples were presumed to order their affairs according to the same natural and transcendent principles, these principles gave the jus gentium universal applicability. While this association powerfully reinforced the idea that nations were, by nature, the primary category by which to order human relations on any scale, it did not eliminate the messy multiplicity of legal subjects. This was equally true of Roman civil law, which never reduces persons to individual human beings.

After its revival in the twelfth century, Roman civil law provided an array of specific analogies by which to guide the peaceful relations of early modern nations. National territory was directly analogous to private property, and specific rules for the acquisition of territory in the age of discovery were derived from the Roman law for acquiring a title to property.[26] The Roman law of contract enabled Grotius to conceive of a properly conducted treaty as an exchange of promises and not as a complex of merely conventional assurances. Smith's conception of contracts probably derived from Grotius, Samuel Pufendorf, and the other writers on the law of nations and not from common law.[27]

Behind all such analogies are three primary points of reference ordering Roman legal thought: *persons, things,* and *actions,* the who, what, and how of the law. For some purposes, these points of reference serve as categories corresponding to subjects, objects, and verbs as parts of speech. For other purposes, they refer to the properties of any society's most important institutions, including *imperium* and *dominium*—the enduring institutions of

---

25. Henry Sumner Maine, *Ancient Law* (New Brunswick, N.J., 2002, photo-reproducing 3rd ed., 1866), 52–61; P. E. Corbett, *Law and Society in the Relations of States* (New York, 1951), 4–7, 17–26.

26. See, for example, Corbett, *Law and Society,* 91–98, and Yanagihara Masaharu, "*Dominium* and *Imperium,*" in Yasuaki, ed., *Normative Approach to War,* 147–73.

27. As a teacher of jurisprudence in a Scottish university, Smith was steeped in Roman law. "From the sixteenth century onwards English society evinces signs of a natural-law approach in areas of economic activity. Free commerce was man's natural right, and like its corollary, the right to property, one tending to promote the general good. Roman law, however, was not received into the system at all. In this, Scotland was very different. . . . Areas of particular influence include the wardship of minors, property, succession, and contract" (Vivenza, *Adam Smith and the Classics,* 94–95).

rule and ownership.[28] Subject to endless discussion among medieval specialists in both civil and canon law, the relation between these institutions contributed to the conceptualization of the state as an agent empowered to rule on the nation's behalf, and as the protector of the people's rights and object of their loyalty. Taken as a whole, Roman law analogies made nations, their agents, and their practices into an operative whole consisting of whole nations and their relations.

Wheaton's World

When Smith published *The Wealth of Nations*, the law of nations was an important feature of European public life. Its development correlated with an era in which civil government progressively displaced governance based on status distinctions, and governments engaged each other in strenuous competition. The law of nations suited mercantilist competition in peace, just as it rationalized the conduct of wars. Vattel's *Le droit des gens* offered the most accessible and influential statement of that law for its time.[29] Because of the importance of the law of nations for both European corporate identity and the progressively republican spirit that Vattel imparted to his text, the Europe of this period was in some significant sense "Vattel's World."[30] Looking back, we can see in Vattel the complement of dispositions and assumptions that made Smith something of a liberal thinker in a world still mercantilist and hardly republican—a world that would soon change, dramatically and irrevocably.

Revolution and war shattered the world of Vattel. Nevertheless, the years after 1815 favored the Atlantic world with rapidly increasing prosperity and growing pressure to liberalize the European system and its member states. Even as the Atlantic world turned liberal, the law of nations continued to give nations the freedom to choose their own domestic arrangements and

---

28. Kenneth Pennington, *The Prince and the Law, 1200–1600: Sovereignty and Rights in the Western Legal Tradition* (Berkeley and Los Angeles, 1993), chap. 1; Brian Tierney, *The Idea of Natural Rights: Studies on Natural Rights, Natural Law, and Church Law, 1150–1625* (1997; Grand Rapids, Mich., 2001), chaps. 6–7; Constantin Fasolt, *The Limits of History* (Chicago, 2004), chap. 4.

29. [Emmerich] de Vattel, *Le droit des gens ou principes de la loi naturelle, appliqués à la conduite & aux affaires des nations & des souverains* (Washington, 1916, photo-reproducing London ed., 1758); [Emmerich] de Vattel, *The Law of Nations or the Principles of International Law Applied to the Conduct of Nations and of Sovereigns*, trans. Charles G. Fenwick (Washington, 1916).

30. Peter Onuf and Nicholas Onuf, *Federal Union, Modern World: The Law of Nations in an Age of Revolutions, 1776–1814* (Madison, Wisc., 1993), 10–11.

commercial policies. Over the long term, liberal international society fostered domestic liberalization; in the short term, government gained significant benefits by establishing and perfecting national markets at home and pursuing mercantilist strategies abroad.

In the meantime, expanding state capabilities in the early decades of the nineteenth century prompted doctrinal developments in international law that decisively shaped liberal international society *before* it took on global proportions. The term *liberal* in this instance refers to any society whose members, whether individual human beings or corporate persons such as states, can safely put their interests before society's. Just as Vattel provided the late decades of the eighteenth century with a defining text, Wheaton's *Elements of International Law* did the same for the world of the nineteenth century.[31] Its appearance in 1836 conveniently dates the world of liberal international relations as a conceptually coherent although hardly complete project.

Martti Koskenniemi has suggested that the liberal era in international law did not begin for another thirty years. In 1869, a small group of lawyers launched it with publication of the *Revue de droit internationale et de législation* "as a professional forum for liberal legislative reform in Europe."[32] By *professional,* Koskenniemi seems to have in mind the practices that give the members of a scientific discipline, including law (and history), a sense of corporate identity, organizational capacity, and societal voice. Diplomats are barely professional in this sense because their identity and voice are assured by their positions in governments as agents of states in relations with other states. In this respect, Wheaton warrants attention because he was both a constitutional lawyer (as reporter for the Supreme Court of the United States from 1816 to 1827, he was significantly involved in the Court's institutional development) and a diplomat, representing his government in Copenhagen and then Berlin from 1827 to 1847.[33]

Rather dismissively, Koskenniemi identified Wheaton as a diplomat whose "professional sensibility" resembled that of Grotius, Vattel, and "old-fashioned" German writers for whom international law was an aspect of public law. Until the *Revue*'s publication, "international law had been an affair of professors and philosophers, diplomats with an inclination to reflect on the

---

31. Henry Wheaton, *Elements of International Law with a Sketch of the History of the Science,* 1st ed. (Philadelphia, Pa., 1836).
32. Martti Koskenniemi, *The Gentle Civilizer of Nations: The Rise and Fall of International Law, 1870–1960* (Cambridge, U.K., 2001), chap. 1, at 14.
33. On Wheaton's tenure as Supreme Court reporter, see G. Edward White, *History of the Supreme Court of the United States,* Vols. 3–4, *The Marshall Court and Cultural Change, 1815–35* (New York, 1988), chap. 6. On Wheaton's diplomatic career, see Elizabeth Feaster Baker, *Henry Wheaton, 1785–1848* (Philadelphia, Pa., 1937).

history and procedure of their craft."[34] Yet in Koskenniemi's account, what gave the *Revue's* founders a different sensibility had very little to do with disciplinary practices then emerging in the sciences. These lawyers came together because of their reformist liberal sentiments—*liberalism* in a much more limited sense than we have used the term—coupled with a distrust of diplomacy. If Wheaton the lawyer and diplomat displayed little interest in the progressive social legislation that citizen activists sought to have their governments adopt, his silence would seem to reflect the professional way in which he sought to bring law to bear on the relations of states. Indeed, the reformers seem like dilettantes, not professionals, even if they did contribute to the long process of making international law into the discipline it has since become.

There are good reasons for treating Wheaton the professional lawyer-diplomat and treatise writer as an exemplary figure. First, no one writing about international law exceeded him in influence for at least three decades. His book went through several editions, including a French edition in 1848—the year of his death—and a Chinese edition in 1864. The latter is famous for being the first translation of any international legal treatise into a non-European language. The eighth edition, which Richard Henry Dana Jr. edited for publication in 1866, assured a continuing wide influence for Wheaton's *Elements* during the later decades of the century.[35] Second, Wheaton recapitulated the long, messy, and uncertain process by which writers came to separate legal relations among states from legal relations within states. In doing so, he helped make liberal international society a conceptually distinct domain.

We often exaggerate the extent to which liberal ideas represent a sharp break with the past. Transparently liberal, Wheaton nevertheless emphasized doctrinal continuity. When he held that the state is an "independent moral being," he invoked a way of thinking that Grotius had canonically established two centuries before.[36] States are moral because their corporate character implicates them in human society, independent only by virtue of rights that confer duties on other, equally independent states. Obviously, the society that states constitute among themselves is a legal order, and thus a moral

---

34. Koskenniemi, *Gentle Civilizer of Nations,* 11–24, at 4, 23, 17.
35. Henry Wheaton, *Elements of International Law,* 8th ed., ed. Richard Henry Dana Jr. (1866; Oxford, 1936).
36. Wheaton, *Elements of International Law,* 1st ed., II, ii, § 1, 95. Grotius had relied on medieval sources to a degree disguised by his humanist preference for ancient materials. Political considerations may also have been involved (Tierney, *Idea of Natural Rights,* chap. 13).

condition. Within that society, states are no less clearly free to pursue their interests individually and collectively. Indeed, the world became liberal, in just these terms, before Britain and the United States, the paradigmatically liberal societies, became liberal. But this world needed an appropriate doctrinal accommodation before it could become liberal. The same is true for those societies that we most closely associate with liberalism.

Petty commercial activity, rights in common law, constitutional development, and social contract theorizing had not turned Britain and its North American colonies into liberal societies during the eighteenth century, and perhaps could never have done so. Republican ideas and practices pulled in a different direction, and so did the vestiges of feudal life. But once states found themselves relating to each other in liberal terms, societies where conditions were most propitious changed rapidly and reaped material advantages accordingly. Liberal international society fostered liberal societies, and not the other way around. If states moved to institute or rationalize internal markets, for example, they did so in response to pressures from the larger world beyond their borders more than from internal developments.

The key element in Wheaton's construction of the modern world is a conjectural history of legal doctrine tracing the separation of international and domestic law. Wheaton gave Grotius credit for the "new science of natural jurisprudence"—"a mixed science of the law of nature and nations."[37] In the great succession of "scientific writers," Christian Wolff, following on Pufendorf, "entitled himself to the credit of first separating the law which prevails or ought to prevail, between nations, from that part of the science which teaches the duties of individuals; and of reducing the law of nations to a full and systematic form."[38] These claims on Wolff's behalf are apparently plausible, since Wolff's systematic, multivolume treatise on natural law concludes with a separate volume devoted to the law of nations, the first such to appear. Yet there is little evidence in Wolff's volume that he clearly distinguished domestic and international law on conceptual grounds.[39]

Wheaton gave the unfolding of doctrine far more attention in his subsequent *History of the Law of Nations* (1845). There he repeated his claim that Wolff was first to consider the law of nations on its own, but with a significant difference: "To Wolf [*sic*] belongs, according to his elegant abridger Vattel, the credit of separating the law of nations from that part of natural jurisprudence

37. Wheaton, *Elements of International Law,* 1st ed., "Sketch of the History of International Law," 30.
38. Ibid., 31.
39. See Nicholas Greenwood Onuf, *The Republican Legacy in International Thought* (Cambridge, U.K., 1998), chaps. 3–4.

which treats the duties of individuals."[40] To substantiate this new, more subtle claim, Wheaton reviewed Wolff's system and Vattel's reaction to it. As Koskenniemi has argued, Vattel "is logically led to making a boundary between international and municipal law."[41] Wolff had, for his part, resisted the logic in question—the logic of territorial sovereignty—and drew no such conclusion.

While Wheaton's discussion of Vattel shows how inescapable this conclusion is, nowhere did Wheaton quote Vattel as having come to it in such straightforward terms. Indeed, in paraphrasing Vattel (very closely, it should be noted), Wheaton made it clear that Vattel never really came to terms with the logic of territorial sovereignty.

> According to Vattel, that law of nations, in its origin, is nothing but *the law of nature applied to nations.*
>
> Having laid down this axiom, he qualifies it in the same manner, and almost in the identical terms of Wolf [*sic*], by stating that the nature of the subject to which it is applied being different, the law which regulates the conduct of individuals must necessarily be modified in its application to the collective societies of men called nations or states. A state is a very different subject from a human individual, from which result, in many cases, obligations and rights very different.[42]

For Vattel to have acknowledged the logical implications of territorial sovereignty, he would have had to reconsider the "axiom" that the law of nations derives from natural law.

The same implicit logic drives Pufendorf's incisive critique of irregular political systems.[43] Nevertheless, as Wheaton remarked, Pufendorf was content to lay down "the general principles of natural law, leaving it to the reader to apply it as he might find it necessary to private individuals or to independent societies."[44] Later writers, up to and including Vattel, were no less content to compile the rules applicable to states, leaving the reader to decide whether nature made these rules necessary, presumably within states as well

---

40. Henry Wheaton, *History of the Law of Nations in Europe and America; From the Earliest Times to the Treaty of Washington, 1842* (New York, 1845), 177. Also see 183.
41. Martti Koskenniemi, *From Apology to Utopia: The Structure of International Legal Argument* (Helsinki, 1989), 92. Also see Onuf, *Republican Legacy in International Thought,* 163.
42. Wheaton, *History of the Law of Nations,* 186, original emphasis.
43. Here see Onuf and Onuf, *Federal Union, Modern World,* 65–68.
44. Wheaton, *Elements of International Law,* 1st ed., I, i, § 5, 38.

as among them. In short, all of these writers lacked a clear understanding that legal rules must have sources specific to the legal orders within which they are found.[45]

Wheaton possessed just such an understanding, largely due to James Madison, which he fully articulated in *Elements*.[46] Wheaton viewed the separation of international and domestic orders as obvious, and not only to himself. On logical grounds, he thought it must have been equally obvious to Wolff and Vattel, although it could not have been when they wrote. Wheaton's error in this respect led to an anachronistic reading of his predecessors and an imaginative reconstruction of doctrinal developments specific to liberal international society. Notice that the line of descent leading to Wheaton (Grotius to Pufendorf to Wolff and Vattel) parallels the familiar line of descent for liberal thought leading eventually to John Stuart Mill (Hobbes to Locke to Montesquieu, Hume, Rousseau, Smith et al.).

Fully separate from standard histories of political thought, Wheaton's conjectural history leads the other by a few years at every interval. Moreover, his sequence of developments moves toward conceptual coherence while its domestic counterpart moves in the other direction. Once a coherent division between domestic and international law is finally, firmly established, the story ends in a recitation of the sources of international law. Thereupon Wheaton proceeded to catalogue the entirety of international law then known to him, rule by rule, along with the evidence needed to convince any reader that these rules had the force of law in the relations of states. The bulk of the book is a manual written by an experienced diplomat for the use of other diplomats and their legal advisers. As such, it has been the enduring model for the professional practice of international law in a liberal world—Wheaton's world, and ours.

European International Society

Wheaton's conjectural history of legal doctrine demanded a show of respect for natural law. Yet he gave practical primacy to *positive law*—a term he clarified by reference to Jeremy Bentham's and John Austin's claim that the rules of international law could not "with strict propriety be called *laws*" because there exists no single sovereign will to proclaim and enforce

---

45. Onuf, *Republican Legacy in International Thought*, 81–82.
46. For details, see Onuf and Onuf, *Federal Union, Modern World*, 197–211.

them.[47] For Wheaton such rules qualify as law because they do the work of legal rules: the issue is a practical, not a conceptual one. "What has commonly been called the practical or positive law of nations may also be inferred from treaties," even though "the binding force of express compacts may not depend on positive law."[48] Instead, treaties have the force they do because like-minded sovereigns acting on behalf of states—for example, by concluding treaties—together constitute a society. This is not a universal society, such as might be claimed if most rules were based on customary practices. On the contrary, Wheaton took international law to be grounded in legal practices specific to Europe.

Wheaton was hardly alone in working out the properties of such a society. It might better be said that he completed a conceptual development that Wolff had initiated and Vattel advanced. In the process, Wheaton helped to eliminate a long history of confusion over natural law and how it relates to positive law. For Wolff natural law came in two forms—necessary law and voluntary law—the latter inferred from the former to suit particular circumstances. Vattel defended this distinction and reinforced it by making the former "the inner law of conscience"[49] and the latter truly voluntary. At the same time and somewhat contradictorily, Vattel gave the voluntary law, now indistinguishable from positive law, the ascendant position in the practical affairs of states even as he continued to profess natural law principles.

Wolff held that there was a "natural society" ordained by the necessary law and, beyond that, a *civitas maxima,* or great republic, comporting with voluntary law. Vattel repudiated the latter but not the former. With natural law confined to conscience, it would be easy to conclude that Vattel's natural society is strictly notional.[50] Yet Vattel had no doubt that an actual international society existed in his time and that it had existed for some time. Curiously, he never troubled to provide a basis for it in positive law, perhaps because the development of such a society bore out the conjectured properties of a universal history reflecting nature's purpose. In other words, the actual and the natural converged in time. Vattel implied as much when he evoked the time-honored practices of Europe's many sovereigns and their agents,

47. Wheaton, *Elements of International Law,* 1st ed., I, i, § 12, 47, citing Bentham, *An Introduction to the Principles of Morals and Legislation,* 1823 ed., and glossing the definition of *laws* "properly so called" that Austin put forward in *The Province of Jurisprudence Determined,* Lecture V (1832; London, 1955), 133.
48. Wheaton, *Elements of International Law,* 1st ed., I, i, § 14, 50, 49.
49. Vattel, *Law of Nations or the Principles of International Law Applied to the Conduct of Nations and of Sovereigns,* pref., 11a.
50. See, for example, Andrew Carty, *The Decay of International Law? A Reappraisal of the Limits of Legal Imagination in International Affairs* (Manchester, U.K., 1986), 16–17, 68.

who, by fostering a balance of power, gradually brought stability and prosperity to the "Republic of Europe."[51]

True to Vattel, Wheaton honored natural law as one of international law's "two branches," and he limited it by making the positive law the other branch.[52] Notwithstanding the convulsions that France had brought upon Europe in the intervening years, Wheaton adopted Vattel's position that Europe constituted an actual international society.[53] He also took a step that neither Vattel nor, as far as we have been able to determine, anyone else before him had taken. In his preface to the third edition of *Elements* (the first revised edition, 1846), he spelled out a specifically juridical basis for a distinctively European international law.

In Wheaton's account, the law of nations had its origins in the Middle Ages, thanks to two developments. First, the "Christian states of Europe" were drawn together by the moral authority of the Latin church. Codified in the thirteenth century, canon law enhanced that authority by guiding "decisions of the Church in public as well as private controversies." The second development was the "revival of the study of Roman law, and the adoption of this system of jurisprudence by nearly all the nations of Christendom, either as the basis of their municipal codes, or as subsidiary to the local legislation in each country." Wheaton could not have made his point more clearly: "The origin of the law of nations may thus be traced to these two principal sources,—the canon law and the Roman civil law."[54]

After the Reformation "undermined one of the bases of this universal jurisprudence," namely, canon law, jurists "continued to appeal to the Roman civil law, as constituting the general code of civilized nations."[55] The idea of "universal jurisprudence" has less significance than it might seem in this context. For Wheaton, European international law is universal only to the extent that its sources reflect an ancient tradition of universalizing discourse. Roman civil law did not supply universally valid rules so much as it supplied

---

51. See further in Onuf, *Republican Legacy in International Thought,* 83–84, 101–3.
52. Wheaton, *Elements of International Law,* 1st ed., I, i, § 13, 47.
53. Nor was Wheaton alone. As Onuma Yasuaki has pointed out, many writers in the late eighteenth and nineteenth centuries took Europe as the frame of reference for their treatments of international law. "When Was the Law of International Society Born? An Inquiry of the History of International Law as Seen from an Intercivilizational Perspective" (*Journal of the History of International Law* 2 [2000]: 38–39).
54. Preface to the third edition (1846), rpt. in Henry Wheaton, *Elements of International Law,* 8th ed. Wheaton's account is prefigured in "Sketch of the History of International Law" (*Elements of International Law,* 1st ed., 22–23).
55. Ibid., xiv.

analogies that, by informing practice among European nations, contributed to the emergence of customary rules of European international law.

The phrase *civilized nations* dates from the mid-eighteenth century; Vattel used it, and so did Smith. In Wheaton's case, the use of terms such as *Christian* and *civilized* is, at least in some measure, an incidental effect of the way he corroborated the specifically European ancestry and reach of international law.[56] His main concern was eminently secular and practical. He wanted to provide European international society with a solid foundation in law, not as a substitute for Vattel's balance of power to which Vattel had granted such importance but as a complementary source of stability.

Of course, Wheaton was not entirely free of Eurocentric pretensions. Consider the following: "If the international intercourse of Europe, and the nations of European descent, has been since [Grotius] marked by superior humanity, justice, and liberality, in comparison with the usages of the other branches of the human family, they are mainly indebted for this glorious superiority to these private teachers of justice [such as Grotius], to whose moral authority sovereigns and states are often compelled to bow."[57] Yet even here, the claim of superiority is incidental to the claim that the jurists whose line of descent Wheaton was so careful to document, and who drew so resourcefully on Roman law and ancient authority, had made European international law into an effective system of order over the preceding two centuries.

Practically speaking, Wheaton considered natural law less a repository of specific, universally valid rules than a conditioning presence, one shared by canon and Roman and international law and shaping successive generations of juridical craft. Thus his definition of international law almost makes a virtue of ambiguity: "The law of nations, or international law, as understood among civilized, Christian nations, may be defined as consisting of those rules of conduct which reason deduces, as consonant to justice, from the nature of the society existing among independent nations; with such definitions and modifications as may be established by general consent."[58] Once defining international law in such process-oriented terms, Wheaton introduced Austin's

---

56. "The ordinary *jus gentium* is only a particular law, applicable to a distinct set or family of nations, varying at different times with the change in religion, manners, government, and other institutions, among every class of nations. Hence the international law of the civilized, Christian nations of Europe and America, is one thing; and that which governs the Mohammedan nations . . . is another and very different thing" (Wheaton, *Elements of International Law,* 1st ed., I, i, § 9, 44–45).

57. Ibid., "Sketch of the History of International Law," 30–31. Also see Wheaton, *Elements of International Law,* pref., 3rd ed., xx, for a close paraphrase.

58. Ibid., 1st ed., I, i, § 11, 46. Wheaton took this definition, almost word for word, from James Madison, who penned it while secretary of state of the United States.

rule-oriented objection that international law, backed as it is by "moral sanctions," is law only "by an analogical extension of the term."[59] Faced with the opportunity to reject this claim, Wheaton simply ignored it.

Austin's view that analogy does not suffice to make international law truly law reflects the epistemic shift that Michel Foucault identified as taking place at the end of the eighteenth century. If nature and society are no longer linked by analogy, then society must be a natural condition, and a disordered one at that. This was an understanding of nature that David Hume presaged and Thomas Malthus endorsed. Reflecting the influence of Enlightenment natural philosophy, Wheaton was ambivalent about nature's relation to society—his definition of international law makes this all too clear. Just as clearly, Bentham and Austin aligned themselves with the Malthusian conception of nature as a dynamic and thus disordered material condition. If societies were ordered, it was only because human beings adopted rules to order their relations and appointed sovereign authorities to enforce them. Analogies might be suggestive but never constitutive; the positive law is not to be confused with nature's order, such as it is; rules are legal when sanctions are both legal (as rules) and effective (as instruments of social control); systems of rules are unambiguously legal—or not.

Never a positivist in this sense, Wheaton agreed with Austin that both branches of international law depend on moral sanctions to work.[60] Conceived as an integral development over many centuries, the rules of international law and the sanctions backing them up are specific to European international society. Wheaton failed to see why anyone should be bothered by the claim that international law qualifies as law only by analogy. In itemizing the sources of international law, he observed that treaties embody rules that "are familiarly called *laws* by analogy to the proper use of the term."[61] One of Wheaton's contemporaries, Jean Louis Klüber, went so far as to list analogies as a source of international law.[62] Clearly, these writers saw the use of analogy not as a threat to the integrity of international law but a mark of its distinctive status. Reciting the sources of international law has the same effect.

State recognition is yet another mechanism for insuring the independence, and perhaps the primacy, of international society as a legal order.

---

59. Ibid., § 12, 47, quoting Austin, *Province of Jurisprudence Determined*, Lecture V, 157, also see 141. On the perils of analogical reasoning, see 119–22.

60. Also see Wheaton, *Elements of International Law*, 1st ed., I, i, § 9, 44, where he affirmed "amicable or vindictive retaliation" in support of international law.

61. Ibid., § 14, 49, original emphasis.

62. Jean Louis Klüber, *Droit des gens moderne de l'Europe* (Stuttgart, 1819), 17–18. Koskenniemi has usefully situated Klüber in the cultural and political context of early nineteenth-century Germany (*Gentle Civilizer of Nations*, 19–28).

Neither Klüber nor, at least initially, Wheaton conceived of it as such.[63] Citing Klüber, Wheaton observed in 1836 that a state acquires sovereignty when "it separates itself lawfully from the community of which it previously formed a part, and on which it was dependent."[64] Lawful separation here means a grant of independence, and not self-determination. Wheaton's discussion of the new Latin American states suggests as much: "where a revolted province or colony has declared, and shown its ability to maintain its independence, the recognition of its sovereignty by other foreign states is a question of policy and prudence only."[65]

For Wheaton, as a citizen of the United States, this is a surprisingly conservative position.[66] A decade later, he developed a new position on recognition better suited to the modern world on conceptual as well as policy grounds. The revised edition of *Elements* (1846) invokes the now familiar distinction between internal and external sovereignty before turning to recognition.[67] Internal sovereignty is a matter of constitutional law and external sovereignty of international law. "The internal sovereignty of a State does not, in any degree, depend on its recognition by other States."[68] Wheaton then concluded that the United States obtained internal sovereignty by declaring independence in 1776.

"The external sovereignty of any State, on the other hand, may require recognition by other States to render it perfect and complete." It is through recognition that a new state enters the "great society of nations," which has now clearly become Wheaton's frame of reference. Nevertheless, other

---

63. See C. H. Alexandrowicz, "The Theory of Recognition *in Fieri*," *British Year Book of International Law*, Vol. 34 (1958), 176, on the early history of recognition, with particular attention to Klüber (187–89) and Wheaton (192–95).

64. Wheaton, *Elements of International Law*, 1st ed., I, i, § 15, 70.

65. Ibid., § 19, 74. For Klüber state practice led him to view recognition as a "declaratory act dictated by the requirements of political expediency" (quoting Alexandrowicz, "Theory of Recognition *in Fieri*," 188).

66. Alexandrowicz called it a "legitimist" position consistent with Old World practice ("Theory of Recognition *in Fieri*," 194). On the political complexities of recognizing new republics in the Americas, see James E. Lewis Jr., *The American Union and the Problem of Neighborhood: The United States and the Collapse of the Spanish Empire, 1783–1829* (Chapel Hill, N.C., 1998), chaps. 4–6.

67. Wolff had no clear conception of external sovereignty. While Vattel possessed just such a conception, he did not specifically distinguish between internal and external sovereignty (Onuf, *Republican Legacy in International Thought*, 75–76, 164–66). Writing in 1819, Klüber drew no such distinction. G. W. F. Hegel did so in 1821 but with little elaboration (*Elements of the Philosophy of Right*, trans. H. B. Nisbet [Cambridge, U.K., 1991], § 278, 315, § 321, 359).

68. Wheaton, *Elements of International Law*, 3rd ed., I, i, § 6, 56, and Wheaton, *Elements of International Law*, 8th ed., I, ii, § 21, 28.

states are "at liberty to grant, or refuse, this recognition" as they see fit, and recognition is not perfect until it has become "universal."[69] Wheaton's concise exposition definitively captures the tension between recognition's declaratory and constitutive properties. In a fully liberal international society, no membership rule could be otherwise.[70]

Rights and Duties

Wheaton's treatise rendered the entire body of international law—natural and positive—in the language of rights and thus the only language that makes liberal ideas intelligible in practice. Born in the United States and seasoned in constitutional law, Wheaton undoubtedly found the language of rights especially congenial. Yet he was not the only, or even the first, writer in his time to use this language in making international law uniformly available for liberal needs and uses. Indeed, Wheaton's expository format closely resembles the format that Klüber used in his treatise some years earlier. If neither writer developed a systematic doctrine or theory of rights, it is no doubt because they already had one at hand.

A theory of rights is one of the great achievements of the writers whose doctrinal lineage Wheaton had so carefully established. The concept of a right has a distinguished heritage as *jus,* a term the early Romans used for "something objectively right and discoverable, and in this sense it remained as a kind of synonym for 'law' throughout the history of Latin as an effective language."[71] Nevertheless, it is unlikely that the Romans ever thought of *jus*

---

69. Wheaton, *Elements of International Law,* 3rd ed., I, ii, § 6, 57, and Wheaton, *Elements of International Law,* 8th ed., I, i, § 21, 28.

70. Alexandrowicz suggested that Hegel may have influenced the development of Wheaton's position on recognition ("Theory of Recognition *in Fieri,*" 195–96). While Wheaton was steeped in German intellectual developments, any influence specifically due to Hegel seems unlikely. The latter said in his brief remarks on international law that the "state has an absolute and primary entitlement to be a sovereign *in the eyes of others,* i.e., *to be recognized* by them." Hegel conceded that this entitlement is "purely formal" and "abstract"; actual recognition "depends on the perception and will of the other state." Hegel granted recognition a declaratory role but not the constitutive one that Wheaton also provided for. As "the absolute power on *earth,*" Hegel's state makes itself. Nothing could be further from Wheaton's assumptions about the society of states (G. W. F. Hegel, *Elements of the Philosophy of Right,* trans. H. B. Nisbet [Cambridge, U.K., 1991], § 331, 366–67, emphasis in translation).

71. Richard Tuck, *Natural Rights Theories: Their Origin and Development* (Cambridge, U.K., 1979), 8. *Law,* as in a legal rule or body of legal rules, is the standard term by which to translate the Latin term *lex.* Recall our discussion earlier in this chapter of the jus gentium as a body of legal rules.

subjectively, as a benefit that people might consider their due or a state of affairs subject to their control—by *right*. Richard Tuck has persuasively argued
that the Romans had no such conception because there was nothing normative in the way that they saw themselves in relation to the world. Either one
had "independent and total control" over one's world (subject to agreements
limiting one's control in favor of someone else) or one did not. If not, then
someone else did. Increasingly that someone else was the emperor, whose
laws objectively limited everyone else's control over their circumstances.[72]

Nor did the ancient Greeks think about rights in any subjective sense.
Like the practical-minded Romans, most Sophists saw the world as normative insofar as people make it so, whether by coercion, consent, or customary practice. Alternatively, Aristotelians and Stoics held that nature endows
us with faculties uniquely suiting us to our place in the world as a whole. If
everything has a purpose, as Aristotle believed, then no human faculty is
normatively distinguishable from any other. Conduct in relation to position
is the basis for judging worth; virtuous conduct fulfills a teleological mandate
that makes the world normative by definition. As one of the republic's would-
be saviors, Cicero adapted Stoic premises to Roman conditions. Again, virtue, not right, is the measure of one's control over circumstances.

Two events transformed the way that literate Europeans of the Middle
Ages looked at the world. One was the recovery of Roman law as a body of
rules potentially adaptable or analogically relevant to any civil society, and
the other was the recovery of Aristotle's major works. Both events challenged Christians to rethink the meaning of human striving in a God-given
world. Reconciling ancient wisdom with Christian theology resulted in variously formulated claims about *jus naturale*. No doubt the most famous of
these formulations is to be found in Saint Thomas Aquinas's *Summa Theo-
logica* (1265–1273). According to Tuck, Aquinas probably did not have the
concept of a subjective right clearly in mind; at least, "he does not often (if
at all) talk about *iura* as other than objective moral rules."[73]

Nevertheless, canon lawyers had written about *jus* in an evidently subjective sense for a hundred years before Aquinas. Only gradually did they dis-
criminate between objective and subjective senses of the term.[74] In the first
half of the fourteenth century, controversies over the use of things and the
right to property help to clarify the distinction. When the French theologian
Jean Gerson expressly defined *jus* as a human faculty in 1402, he drew on

---

72. Ibid., 9–13, at 10.
73. Ibid., 19.
74. Tierney, *Idea of Natural Rights,* chaps. 2–7.

familiar resources.[75] That we speak enables us to formulate rules for our conduct, but it also grants us an ability to reason about our conduct normatively even when we have no rules to guide us.

In other words, human beings possess a specifically moral faculty. God gave us the ability to decide what *should* be ours to control by having us think through what nature makes available for anyone to control. Renaissance writers argued over the analogy between God's intentions and human powers, with the effect of diverting attention from *jus* as a moral faculty. At the same time, the conquest of the Americas raised moral issues for Iberian Scholastics, who revived the discussion of *jus* to address them. It remained for the Spanish priest Francisco Suárez to situate *jus* as *facultas* in a Thomistic framework of natural law and, finally, for Grotius, a Protestant and humanist nevertheless greatly indebted to his Scholastic predecessors, to make it a central feature of early modern thought.[76]

Grotius emphatically asserted that human beings are sociable by nature. According to Grotius, law (*jus*) is "a rule of action." Without rules, no society can exist, and nature is thwarted. Furthermore, law is "nothing else than what is just"; justice depends on the existence of objectively discernible rules reflecting the nature of society as an association for common good. There are two kinds of law thus defined: law as between "brothers, or citizens, or friends, or allies" and law as between "father and children, master and slave, king and subjects, God and men"—rules applicable to those who are equals and rules "applying to him who rules and him who is ruled."[77]

Law has another meaning, "different from the one just defined but growing out of it, which has reference to the person. In this sense a right [*jus*] becomes a moral quality of a person, making it possible to have or do something lawfully."[78] The objective and subjective senses of *jus* are brought together as alternative points of reference to the same state of affairs: in an objective sense, the person is the subject of, or subject to, certain rules; in a

---

75. "*Ius* is a dispositional *facultas* or power, appropriate to someone and in accordance with the dictates of right reason" (Jean Gerson, *Vita spirituale animae,* quoted in Tuck, *Natural Rights Theories,* 25, Tuck's translation). Tuck's claim that Gerson "really created" the first rights theory (25) is utterly groundless, as Tierney has shown at great length (Tierney, *Idea of Natural Rights,* chap. 9).

76. Tuck, *Natural Rights Theories,* chap. 2; Knud Haakonssen, *Natural Law and Moral Philosophy: From Grotius to the Scottish Enlightenment* (Cambridge, U.K., 1996), 15–30; Annabel S. Brett, *Liberty, Right, and Nature: Individual Rights in Later Scholastic Thought* (Cambridge, U.K., 1997); Tierney, *Idea of Natural Rights,* chaps. 11–13.

77. Hugo Grotius, *De jure belli ac pacis libri tres,* 1646 ed. trans. Francis W. Kelsey (Oxford, 1925), I, I, ii, at section title, §§ 1–2, 33–34.

78. Ibid., iv, 35. For the Latin, see Grotius, *De jure belli ac pacis libri tres,* photo-reproducing 1646 ed.

subjective sense, the person is free to act as that person wishes, as long as such acts accord with the relevant rules. Grotius did not align the subjective sense of law with rules for equals or the objective sense of law with rules applying to unequal relations. In his conception, rules of both kinds distribute rights to persons.[79]

Grotius went on to distinguish between rights that are "perfect" because their existence is manifest in actual conduct and those that are imperfect because they have the potential to affect conduct. There is an elusively Aristotelian character to an imperfect right, which Grotius called an *aptitude* (*aptitudo*) and to which he gave a distinctly teleological interpretation. A perfect right is a faculty, and this is "a legal right properly or strictly so called." As against an aptitude, a faculty is specifically normative and not generally teleological. "Under it are included power, now over oneself, which is called freedom, now over others, as that of the father and that of the master over slaves; ownership [*dominium*] . . . ; and contractual rights, to which on the opposite side contractual obligations correspond."[80]

Grotius failed to make clear what it is in or about nature that makes rights specifically normative and enables them to function as rules in human societies. If human beings are to survive in a world that includes others of their kind, then they must exercise their freedom to their own advantage. There is nothing in Grotius's brief account to prevent any or all of us from seeking advantage at the expense of others. Reiterating Cicero's claim that such behavior "is contrary to nature" does not save Grotius from having to explain our natural faculty for predatory conduct toward each other.[81] Having jettisoned Aristotle's teleological worldview, Grotius had to show how the moral faculty takes precedence over other faculties and how its common use makes society morally and functionally different from the rest of nature. Otherwise, Grotius's natural society is indistinguishable from the state of nature that Thomas Hobbes imaginatively derived from the Grotian view of the faculties.

Hobbes elaborated the position Grotius had formulated in a way that exposed the Grotian person as only nominally moral. Even though Grotius had read Hobbes's *De cive* "with discernible sympathy" a few years before his death, he made no attempt in his late work to address the conceptual implications of Hobbes's formulation.[82] While any number of Hobbes's contemporaries raged against him, it remained for Pufendorf to give moral persons

---

79. For further discussion of Grotius on *jus*, see Tanaka Tadashi, "Grotius's Concept of Law," in Yasuaki, ed., *Normative Approach to War*, 32–38.
80. Grotius, *De jure belli ac pacis*, I, II, v, 35–36, two footnotes omitted.
81. Ibid., ii, § 1, 33.
82. Richard Tuck, *Philosophy and Government, 1572–1651* (Cambridge, U.K., 1993), 200.

a genuinely social existence in a lawful nature. Pufendorf did so by returning to the concept of *jus* as faculty and insisting on the difference between natural faculties in general and the moral faculty in particular.

> Now we admit that man has by nature a faculty to take for his use all inanimate objects and animals. But that faculty, thus exactly defined, cannot properly be called a right, both because such things are under no obligation to present themselves for man's use, and because, by virtue of the natural equality of all men, one man cannot rightfully exclude the rest from such things, unless their consent, expressed or presumed, has let him have them as his very own. Only when this has been done, can he say that he has a proper right to the thing. To state it more concisely: A right to all things, previous to every human deed, must be understood not exclusively, but only indefinitely, that is, . . . nature does not define what particular things belong to one man, and what to another, before they agree among themselves on their division and allocation. And even less does the same equality of men allow one man to claim that he has by nature a right over every other man.[83]

Pufendorf's position hinges on his strong claim that human beings are naturally equal. "Now since human nature belongs equally to all men, and no one can live a social life with a person by whom he is not rated as at least a fellow man, it follows, as a precept of natural law, that 'Every Man should esteem and treat another man as his equal by nature, or as much a man as he is himself.'"[84] Pufendorf contrasted this notion of equality to Hobbes's, which is confined "to a parity of strength and other human faculties." Pufendorf called his own conception "an equality of *right,* which has its origin in the fact that an obligation to cultivate a social life is equally binding on all men, since it is an integral part of human nature as such."[85]

By virtue of natural equality, no one can claim an exclusive control over anything at the expense of anyone else or exercise control over anyone else "previous to every human deed." Since natural society is a world of deeds, equality of right means that all rights are *civil* rights, even in natural society. Every right implies some procedure or process, itself lawful, by which rights

---

83. Samuel Pufendorf, *De jure naturae et gentium libri octo* (1671), trans. C. H. Oldfather and W. A. Oldfather (Oxford, 1934), III, v, § 3, 391–92. On Pufendorf and his treatment of *jus,* also see Tuck, *Natural Rights Theories,* 156–62, Stephen Buckle, *Natural Law and the Theory of Property* (Oxford, 1991), 62–86, and Haakonssen, *Natural Law and Moral Philosophy,* 37–43.

84. Pufendorf, *De jure naturae et gentium,* III, ii, 330–45, at § 1, 330.

85. Ibid., § 2, 330, citing Thomas Hobbes, *De cive,* I, i, § 3, 333, emphasis in translation.

are conferred on moral persons. Any such right is conferred only when some other person accepts a corresponding duty. With an impeccable chain of reasoning, Pufendorf came to the general proposition that rights and duties are necessary correlates: for every right, there is a corresponding duty.[86]

While we exercise our natural faculties in putting things to use, these faculties are not rights, Pufendorf observed, "because such things are under no obligation to present themselves for man's use." When we exercise our rights as moral persons, only others of our kind have corresponding obligations. "It is a perfect promise when a man not only declares his will for a future time to perform something for another, but also shows that he gives him a right, whereby the other is fully entitled to demand of him the thing promised."[87] People obligate themselves by making perfect promises for the same reason that they accept duties on themselves corresponding to others' rights: everyone benefits from generalized reciprocity.

Often reciprocity is specific, because promises come in matched pairs. The model situation of reciprocal promising is the contract. As we saw in the Grotian account of *jus*, a contract produces rights, "to which on the opposite side contractual obligations correspond," and it does so for *both* sides. For Pufendorf rights and duties arise from a process that is generically similar to that in which formally equal parties engage in a contract. Nothing in this process suggests general agreement, even notionally, as a constitutive event. Society is a world of moral persons with the faculty of making and keeping promises. Society is a world of deeds, many with lasting normative effects, subjectively described as rights and duties and objectively as rules distributing rights and duties. These rules have the force of law—*natural law*, in Pufendorf's terms—because it is human nature to accept the burden of many obligations in order to enjoy the benefits of a social life.

The correspondence of rights and duties among moral persons follows from an analogy with the mutual exchange of promises and an analysis of the normative implications of promising. Drawing on the Roman law of contracts, Grotius gave this analogy its central place in early modern thought,

---

86. This conclusion is central to the modern discussion of rights. Bentham stated it concisely: "For every right which the law confers on one party, whether that party be an individual, a subordinate class of individuals, or the public, it thereby imposes on some other party a *duty* or *obligation*" (Jeremy Bentham, *An Introduction to the Principles of Morals and Legislation* [1823; New York, 1948], 224–25 n., original emphasis).

87. Pufendorf, *De jure naturae et gentium*, III, v, § 7, 395. An imperfect promise involves "a willingness to be obligated, yet in such a way that no right is given the other man to require the thing of him" (§ 6, 393). Expressed intentions may suffice to create moral obligations but not legal duties. Grotius had made the same distinction in the same terms (Yasuaki, "Agreement," in Yasuaki, ed., *Normative Approach to War*, 187–90).

along with the conviction, not warranted by Roman law, that promises are binding by virtue of natural law.[88] The deficiency in the Grotian conception of natural law was not its claims about the source of obligation but its disregard for equality as the foundation for reciprocity in obligations. Pufendorf remedied this deficiency, but the contract model of obligation favored the assessment of rights and duties arising from the relations of moral equals, and not those that arise from the control that moral persons have over the things that they need and use. After all, things do not have duties, and Pufendorf, following Grotius, called *dominium* a power, not a right.[89]

Locke redressed the balance by focusing attention on the human faculties associated with control over things, or property rights. For Locke these are natural rights in the first instance, not civil rights deriving from the contract model. In nature and before society, human beings exist in "a *State of perfect Freedom*," which makes them equals and gives them the right to those things that are under their control: themselves and their powers, the results of their labors, and whatever they take from nature to provide for themselves and their families. The *right of ownership* implies an additional right to defend what others might take away. That "all Men may be restrained from invading others Rights, . . . the *Execution* of the Law of Nature [is] put into every Mans hands, whereby everyone has a Right to punish the transgressors of that Law."[90]

By favoring rights over duties and self-help over reciprocities among equals, Locke's conceptualization of natural law justified revolution in British North America. The king and parliament had abused the rights of the people, and the people had a right to execute the law of nature and resist the invasion of their rights. While the revolutionary appropriation of the Lockean scheme gave liberal thinking a normative foundation for limited government within nations, Pufendorf's argument for the correspondence of rights and duties gave eighteenth-century writers, and especially Vattel, a coherent way to represent the liberal society that had emerged among nations. *"The Law of Nations"*—here Vattel was echoing Wolff—"is *the science of the rights which exist between Nations or States, and of the obligations corresponding to these rights.*"[91]

---

88. Not to mention biblical authority. For explication and citations, see Yasuaki, "Agreement," in Yasuaki, ed., *Normative Approach to War,* 190–98.

89. Pufendorf, *De jure naturae et gentium,* IV, iii, "On the Power of Mankind over Things," 524–31.

90. See John Locke, *The Second Treatise of Government,* in Peter Laslett, ed., *Two Treatises of Government* (Cambridge, U.K., 1988), at ii, § 4, 269, § 7, 271, original emphasis.

91. Vattel, *Law of Nations,* intro., § 3, 3, original emphasis. The classical *episteme* then reigning fully warranted the presumption that the law of nations exists in practice only insofar as it is subject to systematic exposition (science).

Because nations are moral persons subject to the law of nature, they "must be regarded as so many free persons living together in the state of nature." Nations have the same duties that human individuals have to contribute to the common good, but only insofar as doing so is consistent with every nation's duty to advance the interests of its own members. Otherwise, the nation "should be left to the peaceable enjoyment of that liberty that belongs to it by nature." Furthermore, independent nations, like individuals, "are by nature equal and hold from nature the same obligations and the same rights." Some rights are perfect, and they "carry with them the right of compelling the fulfillment of the corresponding obligations"; "all Nations may put down by force the open violation of the laws of the society which nature has established among them, or any direct attacks upon its welfare."[92] This is, of course, the natural right of self-help that Locke had defended.[93]

In Vattel's authoritative depiction of the law of nations, the multiple reciprocities of enforceable rights and corresponding duties lock independent nations together in a naturally liberal society. Vattel's nineteenth-century successors progressively dropped Vattel's many references to natural law but kept the rest of the argument substantially intact. Thus Klüber and Wheaton both organized their expositions of the law by reference to the rights and duties of nations. Gone from both is the language of perfect and imperfect rights, with its Aristotelian resonance and long history from Grotius to Vattel, but not the underlying claim that legal rights are rightfully subject to enforcement by those nations whose rights have been violated.

Instead, we have absolute and conditional rights.[94] Klüber and Wheaton agreed that self-preservation, independence, and equality are absolute rights, and each presented them in this order. Klüber thought that property is a conditional right, but Wheaton classified it as absolute. For both writers the rights and duties of states that constitute the bulk of the positive law are conditional. As Wheaton put it, states are entitled to these rights "under particular circumstances"; they "arise from international relations existing either in peace or war."[95]

---

92. Ibid., 3–8, at §§ 4, 15, 18, 17, 22.
93. Grotius had made the argument for self-help in natural law in "De Indis," an early unpublished work that neither Locke nor Vattel could have seen (Tuck, *Rights of War and Peace*, 81–82).
94. But see Wheaton, *Elements of International Law*, 1st ed., II, iv, § 12, at 151. Positive law can modify an absolute right in respect to the "mode of its exercise"; on the authority of Grotius, Pufendorf, and Vattel, such a right is imperfect.
95. Ibid., II, i, § 2, 81.

The way that Wheaton defined international law, presented its sources, and then ordered rights from absolute to conditional creates a firm structure of two levels. In recognition of Wheaton's vocation as a constitutional lawyer, we might call the upper level higher law in the sense that a constitution is.[96] In effect, natural law grants international society a liberal constitution. Within the broad reach and permissive terms of that constitution, states' agents are free to conduct themselves as they see fit except insofar as they collectively agree to limit their conduct. They interpret those limits subjectively as rights and regard them objectively as binding rules, for which the term *law* seems entirely appropriate.

Anybody possessing legal rights and duties is a subject of the legal order enumerating those rights and duties; anybody not in possession of rights and duties is an object of the law. Wheaton stipulated that "the subjects of international law are separate political societies of men living independently of each other, and especially those called Sovereign States."[97] In principle, states are "completely sovereign, and independent, acknowledging no superior"; in practice, the sovereignty of many states "is limited and qualified in various degrees."[98] Although he gave no further consideration to the term *subject,* the way he organized the four parts and twelve chapters of *Elements* confirms its importance. The first part, "Source and Subjects of International Law," consists of two chapters, the first devoted to conceptual preliminaries and the sources of international law and the second devoted to sovereignty and statehood. The second part is devoted to the "Absolute Rights of States," and the last two parts present the conditional rights of states in their "pacific relations" and then their "hostile relations."[99]

None of this changed for at least a century. After World War II, the leading treatise for scholars and diplomats—Lassa Oppenheim's *International Law,* Volume 1, *Peace,* 8th edition, edited by Hersch Lauterpacht— followed Wheaton closely. The introduction's first chapter avers that the international law is indeed law, Austin's objection notwithstanding, that states are the subjects of the law, that customary practices and treaties are the principal sources of the law, that international and domestic law differ as to the kind of relations to which they refer, and that international law is "a product

---

96. For further see Onuf, *Republican Legacy in International Thought,* chap. 7. On levels, see chap. 8.
97. Wheaton, *Elements of International Law,* 1st ed., I, ii, § 1, 51.
98. Ibid., § 2, 51.
99. Ibid., 33, 35, 51, 79, 165, 207. The table of contents, v, mistakenly omits the title for the first part and uses it instead for the title of the first chapter.

of Christian civilisation."[100] The introduction's second chapter recounts "The Development and Science of International Law." Part 1 begins the systematic exposition of the law, rule by rule, and its subject is "The Subjects of the Law of Nations."

"As a rule," the introduction declares, "the subjects of the rights and duties arising from the Law of Nations are States solely and exclusively."[101] Rejected, however, are the two grades of rights that Klüber and Wheaton took for granted. "Until the last two decades of the nineteenth century there was general agreement that membership of the international community bestowed so-called fundamental rights on States" and (a footnote tells us) "the corresponding duty to respect the rights of international personality." Yet disagreement on the content of these rights "has led to a searching criticism of the whole matter, and many have urged, rightly it is believed, that the notion of the fundamental rights of States should totally disappear from the exposition of the Law of Nations."[102] So it has in the years since, with no effect at all on the more general claim that states, as legal persons, are subjects of international law.

As "the normal subjects of International Law," states may nevertheless "treat individuals and other persons as endowed directly with international rights and duties and constitute them to that extent subjects of International Law."[103] Indeed, states have long conferred duties directly on individuals that, if ignored, make them pirates or war criminals. More recently, the movement to confer a wide range of international human rights on individuals and correlative duties on "sovereign governments" may indicate a genuine departure from Wheaton's way of thinking. Even more revolutionary is the claim that certain human rights are fundamental, a claim normally supported by invoking natural law doctrine *and* constitutive instruments such as the Charter of the United Nations.[104] Whether presented in the language of natural law or positive law, or both, any such claim points to a transformation in the conceptual underpinnings of the liberal world.

---

100. Lassa Oppenheim, *International Law: A Treatise*, Vol. 1, *Peace*, 8th ed. by Hersch Lauterpacht (New York, 1955), 3–70, at §§ 26–27, 48.

101. Ibid., § 13, 19. States are presumably sovereign to qualify as subjects. Nevertheless, as Wheaton had suggested, sovereignty is a matter of degree. "Full sovereign States are perfect, not-full sovereign States are imperfect, International persons, for not-full sovereign States are only in some respects subjects of International Law" (§ 63, 118).

102. Ibid., § 112, 259–61.

103. Ibid., § 13a, 20.

104. Ibid., § 340k, 736–38. It should be noted that Hersch Lauterpacht was one of the earliest exponents of what has become the prevailing point of view in legal and diplomatic practice.

3
Civilized
Nations

Civilized nations is one of the nineteenth century's most familiar turns of phrase. For example, Auguste Comte introduced his plan for the scientific reorganization of society (1824) as an inducement to "civilized nations" to respond to the threat of anarchy.[1] Postrevolutionary France struck Comte as a dangerous time, but most writers emphasized the success of civilized nations in ordering their collective affairs. War and revolution were at worst temporary setbacks, both brought on and mitigated by the fact of many nations in close conjunction and constant interaction. At best, they were learning experiences. Civilized nations had become civilized together; their changing customs had become rules for better relations among them.

The emphasis on rules was pervasive. Henry Wheaton advertised the first edition of *Elements of International Law* (1836) as setting out "the general principles which may fairly be considered to have received the assent of most civilized and Christian nations, if not as invariable rules of conduct, at least as rules which they cannot disregard without general obloquy and the hazard of provoking the hostility of other communities who may be injured by their violation."[2] John Stuart Mill's influential essay on nonintervention (1859) held it a "grave error" to "suppose that the same international customs, and the same rules of international morality, can obtain between one civilized nation and another, and between civilized nations and barbarians."[3]

1. Auguste Comte, "Plan of the Scientific Work Necessary for the Reorganization of Society," in *Early Political Writings,* ed. and trans. H. S. Jones (Cambridge, U.K., 1998), 49.
2. Henry Wheaton, Advertisement, *Elements of International Law with a Sketch of the History of the Science,* 1st ed. (Philadelphia, Pa., 1836), iii–lv.
3. John Stuart Mill, "A Few Words on Non-Intervention," in *Dissertations and Discussions: Political, Philosophical, and Historical* (Boston, 1864), III, 252.

General Orders No. 100, issued by the United States Secretary of War in 1863, defines military necessity, "as understood by modern civilized nations," as "those measures which are indispensable for securing the ends of war, and which are lawful to the modern law and usages of war."[4] Francis Lieber drafted these "Instructions for the Government of Armies of the United States in the Field"; other "civilized nations" used them as a model for their own codes of military conduct. The last decades of the nineteenth century produced constant references to *civilized nations*, and the Statute of the International Court of Justice keeps the expression alive even today.[5]

What it means to be civilized had been a leading question for Enlightenment thinkers. Of course, modern civilization had predecessors, most of them empires not nations and certainly not an ensemble of diverse yet civilized nations. What made modern civilization different was an ancestry reflecting successive worlds of experience specific to Europe. Writing in the 1850s, Lieber catalogued these worlds and their distinctive contributions: "Grecian culture and civilization" and with it "intellectuality and æsthetics," "christian morality, Roman legality and Teutonic individuality and independence"; together these elements form "the great phenomenon we designate by the term modern civilization."[6] This is a civilization like no other. It is a whole greater than the worlds from which it has sprung, an ensemble of parts politically organized to achieve their own ways of being modern, separately and collectively.

These distinctive parts are nations organized as states. Nations have histories; states have agents, interests, ruled relations. "We must have national states," Lieber declaimed; "we must have national broadcast liberty (and not narrowly chartered liberty;) we must have increasing wealth, for civilization is expensive; we must have liberty, and our states must endure long, to perform their great duties."[7] As Lieber made clear, nations are a defining feature of modern civilization; their members choose national destinies for themselves. Yet they do so within the limits set by law and morality.

---

4. General Orders, No. 100 ("Instructions for the Government of Armies of the United States in the Field"), War Department, Washington, Apr. 24, 1863, Section I, § 14, rpt. in Richard Shelly Hartigan, *Lieber's Code and the Law of War* (Chicago, 1983), 48.

5. Controversially, Article 38 makes "general principles of law recognized by civilized nations" one of several sources of international law. On the period after 1870, see Gerrit W. Gong, *The Standard of "Civilization" in International Society* (Oxford, 1984) and Martti Koskenniemi, *The Gentle Civilizer of Nations: The Rise and Fall of International Law, 1870–1960* (Cambridge, U.K., 2001).

6. Francis Lieber, *On Civil Liberty and Self-Government*, enlarged ed. (Philadelphia, Pa., 1859), 369.

7. Ibid., 368.

These limits would seem to preclude the holding of slaves. Lieber's emphasis on liberty leads to the same conclusion. Nevertheless, Lieber's adopted homeland, the self-proclaimed land of liberty, made slavery lawful, and the world economy made plantation slavery a way of life much too successful for its beneficiaries to give it up without a fight. As a federal union, the United States was composed of less than fully sovereign states, but it could not contain two nations. Yet two nations developed because of slavery. One defined itself as civilized because slavery gave it a prosperous economy, a genteel ruling elite, and a secure place in the liberal world. The other defined itself as civilized because commercial and industrial prowess secured its place in that same world.

Mores

The term *civilization* and the related idea of "becoming civilized" date from the mid-eighteenth century. The French statesman Anne-Robert-Jacques Turgot may have referred to such a process in 1752 in the first of his two discourses *On Universal History:* "agricultural peoples who were up to a point civilised" conquered the "barbarous peoples" surrounding them, and the latter "adopted the civilisation of the conquered."[8] Whether Turgot deserves credit for this usage, it was familiar to English writers by the 1770s.[9] Thus Adam Smith made passing reference to "civilization" and its "extension" in *The Wealth of Nations* (1776).[10] German writers had other ideas. In preference, or even opposition, to *Zivilisation,*

---

8. Anne-Robert-Jacques Turgot, *On Universal History,* in Ronald L. Meek, ed., *Turgot on Progress, Sociology and Economics* (Cambridge, U.K., 1973), 75. These discourses were long unpublished and then edited rather freely.
9. Following convention, Fernand Braudel gave credit to Turgot (*A History of Civilizations,* trans. Richard Mayne [New York, 1994], 3). For Lucien Febvre and Norbert Elias, the evidence suggests that the term is a later embellishment (Febvre, "*Civilisation:* Evolution of a Word and a Group of Ideas," in Peter Burke, ed., *A New Kind of History: From the Writings of Febvre,* trans. K. Folca [London, 1973], 221–22; Elias, *The Civilizing Process,* Vol. 1, *The History of Manners,* trans. Edmund Jephcott [New York, 1978], 291–92 n. 25). According to the *Oxford English Dictionary,* James Boswell's diary records in 1772 that Samuel Johnson, in revising his dictionary, "would not admit *civilization* but only *civility*"; Boswell thought "*civilization,* from *to civilize,* better in the sense opposed to *barbarity*" (3: 257).
10. Adam Smith, *An Inquiry into the Nature and Causes of the Wealth of Nations,* ed. R. H. Campbell and A. S. Skinner (Indianapolis, Ind., 1981), V, i.a, §§ 39, 42, 44, 706–8.

they typically used the term *Kultur,* also traceable to the mid-eighteenth century.[11]

The phrase *civilized nations* preceded the neologism *civilization.* David Hume used it in 1748: "Treachery is the usual concomitant of ignorance and barbarism; and if civilised nations ever embrace subtle and crooked politics, it is from an excess of refinement, which makes them disdain the plain direct path to power and glory."[12] In *The Theory of Moral Sentiments* (1759), Smith also contrasted "civilized nations" and "rude and barbarous nations."[13] *The Wealth of Nations* refers repeatedly to "civilized countries," "civilized societies," and "civilized nations." Smith's concern that an "opulent and civilized nation" needs to be able to defend itself from "the invasion of a poor and barbarous neighbour" resonates with Hume's warning about the dangers of excessive refinement.[14]

Writers in French were less likely to apply the participle *civilisé* to nations.[15] There are references to "barbarous peoples" and "barbarian nations" in Montesquieu's enormously influential treatise *The Spirit of the Laws* (1748) but not to "civilized nations." Instead, *politesse* stands in contrast to barbarian *mœurs.*[16] There is no exact English equivalent to *poli:* "polished nations" is awkward at best. *Policé* presents an even bigger problem.[17]

The problem arises in translating one of Jean-Jacques Rousseau's most ringing passages, written in 1750: "While the Government and the Laws see to the safety and well-being of men assembled, the Sciences, Letters, and Arts, less despotic and perhaps more powerful, spread garlands of flowers over the iron chains with which they are laden, throttle in them the

---

11. See Elias, *Civilizing Process,* 8–10; Wilhelm G. Grewe, *The Epochs of International Law,* trans. Michael Byers (Berlin, 2000), 446–50. For a critical evaluation of the opposition between French *Zivilisation* and German *Kultur* as "a construct in German intellectual history," see Daniel Gordon, *Citizens without Sovereignty: Equality and Sociability in French Thought, 1670–1789* (Princeton, N.J., 1994), 88–94, at 91.

12. David Hume, "Of National Characters," *Essays Moral, Political and Literary,* ed. Eugene F. Miller (Indianapolis, Ind., 1985), 211.

13. Adam Smith, *The Theory of Moral Sentiments,* ed. D. D. Raphael and A. L. Macfie (Indianapolis, Ind., 1981), V, ii, § 8, 204–5. Smith made passing reference to the "state of civilization" in material added to the 6th edition (1790) (Ibid., VI, ii, i, § 13, 223).

14. Smith, *Wealth of Nations,* V, i.a, § 39, 706.

15. Febvre found that the term *civilisé* had been used "from time to time" for the preceding century, but always, it seems, in reference to people, not peoples (Febvre, "*Civilisation,*" 224–29).

16. Montesquieu, *The Spirit of the Laws,* trans. Anne M. Cohler et al. (Cambridge, U.K., 1989), bk. 19, chap. 27, 331, bk. 20, chap. 5, 341.

17. Peter France, *Politeness and Its Discontents: Problems in French Classical Culture* (Cambridge, U.K., 1992), chap. 4; Gordon, *Citizens without Sovereignty,* 18–24.

sentiment of that original freedom for which they seemed born, make them love their slavery, and fashion them into what is called civilized Peoples." These *peuples* are *policés* not *civilés*.[18] In Voltaire's *Essai sur les mœurs et esprit des nations* (1756), *civilisé* appears in a sentence where *nations polies* are beset by *sauvages*.[19] Emmerich de Vattel used the terms *civilisé* and *policé* frequently and interchangeably in reference to nations, peoples, and states in his influential treatise *Le droit des gens* (1758).[20]

The idea that European international society consists of civilized nations, and that relations among these nations must be set apart normatively from their relations with all other nations, is a distinguishing feature of Vattel's work and a fair reflection of the time. When Wheaton ratified Vattel's conception of an international society in *Elements of International Law*, he gave Grotius credit for drawing attention to the normative practices of "civilized nations" more than a century before Vattel. "There are two ways of investigating the law of nature," according to Wheaton's loose translation of Grotius: "we ascertain this law, either by arguing from the nature and circumstances of mankind, or by observing what has generally been approved, by all nations, or at least by all civilized nations."[21] Grotius's Latin refers to *"gentes moratiores."*[22]

---

18. Jean-Jacques Rousseau, *Discourse on the Sciences and the Arts* (first discourse), in Victor Gourevitch, ed., *Rousseau: The Discourses and Other Early Political Writings*, trans. Gourevitch (Cambridge, U.K., 1997), pt. 1, 6; Rousseau, *Discours sur les sciences et les arts*, ed. George R. Havens (New York, 1946), 102. Cf. [Anne-Robert-Jacques] Turgot, *Réflexions sur la formation and la distribution des richesses* (1770), § xxiv, in *Oeuvres de Turgot, édition 1844* (Osnabrück, 1966), 19, where *"les nations se policent"* reads "nations become civilized" (Turgot, *The Formation and Distribution of Riches*, trans. unknown [New York, 1963], 20).

19. For a full quotation and translation of this passage, see J. G. A. Pocock, *Barbarism and Religion*, Vol. 2, *Narratives of Civil Government* (Cambridge, U.K., 1999), 118. The context is Asia, of which Voltaire said: *"Enfin, de quelque peuple policé de l'Asie que nous parlions, nous pouvons dire delui: Il nous a precédé, nos l'avons surpassé"* (Ibid., 119); Pocock's translation: "In short, of any civilized people in Asia whom we consider, we may say: It preceded us, and we have surpassed it" (118). Also see Febvre, *"Civilisation,"* 228–29.

20. Illustratively, *"dans les siécles polis & chez les Nations les mieux civilisées"* ([Emmerich] de Vattel, *Le droit des gens. Ou principés de la lois naturelle, appliqués à la conduite & aux affaires des Nations & des Soverains* [Washington, D.C., 1916, photo-reproducing London ed., 1758], II, III, iii, § 34, 27). Vattel referred more often to *Peuples civilisés*. See, for example, I, II, i, § 20, 273; II, iii, § 41, 286; II, III, iv, § 62, 52; II, III, viii, § 155, 128; II, III, viii, § 156, 129. Vattel also referred to *Nations policées* (I, *Preliminaires*, § 26, 14; II, III, viii, § 109, 83; IV, ix, § 117, 365), not to mention *Etats civilisés* and *Etats policés* (I, II, viii, § 108, 333; II, xiv, § 213, 428).

21. Wheaton, *Elements of International Law*, 1st ed., I, I, § 6, 39.

22. Hugo Grotius, *De jure belli ac pacis libri tres* (Oxford, 1925, photo-reproducing 1646 ed.), I, I, xii, 6.

The adjective *mōrātus* has two meanings: "Endowed with character or manners of a specific kind" and "Well-mannered, gentle, civilized." *Mōrātus* derives from *mos*, which means, in the first instance, an "established practice, custom or usage." The plural (*mores*) is familiar in English and means pretty much the same in both languages: "Habits (of a community, generation, etc.) in respect of right and wrong, morals, etc."[23] The modifier *civilized*, deriving from the term *civility* (*civilitas*) and thus from the Latin terms for *city* (*civitas*) and *citizen* (*cive*), has familiar associations only tangentially related to the family of words deriving from *mos*.

Nothing prevents terms from each family from being combined. In 1530, Desiderius Erasmus authored an instructional handbook for children, *De civilitate morum puerillum*, which went through 130 printings in the next two centuries and spawned an entire genre of manuals on good manners, or *civilité*.[24] Nevertheless, the two sets of terms point in different directions. *Civility* suggests a more limited sphere of practices and institutions representing the universal, normatively compelling features of the human experience. *Mores* suggest a particular but fully realized way of life whose normative implications are entirely self-contained.

Grotius kept these two quite different ways of conceptualizing normativity, the universal and the local and particular, clearly separated. The passage Wheaton paraphrased points to what Grotius had in mind. There are two methods available for ascertaining the contents of natural law. One is deductive, proceeding from the powers of reason and a priori truths about nature, including the fact of human sociability, and ending up with universal rules of human conduct. The other method is inductive, proceeding from widely distributed practices and inferring from them, a posteriori, rules that accord with nature's requirements. As Grotius explained, "an effect that is universal demands a universal cause."[25]

---

23. *Oxford Latin Dictionary,* ed. G. W. Glare (Oxford, 1982), 1133, 1136–37. The French term is, of course, *mœurs,* as in Voltaire's *Essai.* Montesquieu often used *mœurs* and *manières* in close conjunction, as in "the general spirit, the mores, and the manners of a nation" (*Spirit of the Laws,* bk. 19, title, 308). "Under the influence of Montesquieu one studied *mœurs* as an aspect of historical relativism, affected by climate and geography. Under the influence of Voltaire one studied *mœurs* as an example of cultural history as well as in a context of historical relativism" (Arthur M. Wilson, "The Concept of *Mœurs* is Diderot's Social and Political Thought," in W. H. Barber et al., eds., *The Age of the Enlightenment: Studies Presented to Theodore Besterman* [Edinburgh, 1967], 189).

24. Elias, *Civilizing Process,* 53–54.

25. Hugo Grotius, *De jure belli ac pacis libri tres,* 1646 ed. trans. Francis W. Kelsey (Oxford, 1925), I, I, xii, 42. Also see Stephen Buckle, *Natural Law and the Theory of Property: Grotius to Hume* (Oxford, 1991), 4–6; Tanaka Tadashi, "Grotius's Concept of Law," in Onuma Yasuaki, ed., *A Normative Approach to War: Peace, War, and Justice in Hugo*

Grotius's methodology follows Aristotle's *Organon,* where one book deals with *Prior Analytics* and another with *Posterior Analytics.* Different methods point to different conceptions of "nature" conveyed by the terms *physis* (nature ordered by purpose and always normative) and *nomos* (natural contingency rendered normative by convention). Against the standard Greek view, Aristotle took these conceptions of nature, and the methods for elucidating them, to be complementary.[26] So did Grotius. The two methods may not produce perfectly matched sets of rules, but they tend to converge as societies learn from their experiences and from each other. Insofar as the *mores* of any society more closely approximate the deductive axioms of natural law, that society could be considered more advanced or, in the language of Vattel, Smith, and Wheaton, more "civilized."

Thomas Hobbes wrote that "[i]gnorance of the causes, and originall constitution of Right, Equity, Law, and Justice, disposeth a man to make Custome and Example the rule of his actions."[27] Grotius accepted the possibility that customary practices could move away from the requirements of the law of nature, although he was unwilling to "draw a conclusion unfavourable to human nature."[28] Where there is no convergence, a priori judgments take precedence over a posteriori inferences. When Grotius invoked a posteriori method, he took the ultimate convergence of these sets of rules for granted, just as Hobbes assumed their divergence.

For Grotius the most important set of rules that followed from a posteriori reasoning exempted ambassadors from the jurisdiction of their hosts. "Everywhere, in fact, we find mention" of these rules; they are ancient, inviolable, even sacred.[29] The rule exempting ambassadors from the jurisdiction of their hosts is an exception to a more general rule (*communis mos*) making foreigners subject to local territorial jurisdiction (*loci territorio subjicit*).[30] No general rule better exemplified the law of nations as an enduring set of practical arrangements sanctified by the passage of time and inferred consent, and no rule could be more crucial to the idea that nations, as

---

Grotius (Oxford, 1993), 41–43. *A priori* and *a posteriori* are Grotius's terms. Wheaton simply omitted them in paraphrasing the passage in question.

26. Also see Nicholas Greenwood Onuf, *The Republican Legacy in International Thought* (Cambridge, U.K., 1998), 32–39.
27. Thomas Hobbes, *Leviathan,* ed. Richard Tuck (Cambridge, U.K., 1991), I, xi, "Of the difference of MANNERS," 73.
28. Grotius, *De jure belli ac pacis,* I, I, xii, trans., 43.
29. Ibid., II, XVIII, 438–49, at II, XVIII, i, 438. Illustratively, Grotius called the rule permitting nations to refuse permanent legations "ancient custom" (*mos antiquus*) (iii, trans., 441; Latin text, 296).
30. Ibid., II, XVIII, iv, trans., 443; Latin text, 297.

corporate persons, are what they are—in time and space—*only* in relation to each other. Because nations are moral persons by nature, then ambassadors, "as if by a kind of fiction," stand in for those who, by the same sort of fiction, act on behalf of their nations.[31]

Wheaton proceeded from his free and anachronistic translation of Grotius to quote from Cornelius van Bynkershoek's famous monograph *De foro legatorum* (1739): "the law of nations is that which is observed, in accordance with the light of reason, between nations, if not among all, *at least certainly among the greater part, and those the most civilized.*" Here again, the nations in question are, in Bynkershoek's Latin, *moratiores.*[32] Elsewhere in the text, Bynkershoek quoted Grotius on general custom and fictive persons, just as Wheaton had. More generally, he emphasized the importance of customary rules—interchangeably *jus gentium consuetudo* and *mores gentium.*[33]

Bynkershoek wrote a few years before the phrase *civilized nations* was first used. Yet his exposition of the *mores* controlling the status of ambassadors under the law of nations reflects the importance of diplomacy in the century after Westphalia. During these years, Europe had become, in Vattel's words, "a single body" (*un Corps*)—a conceptual whole—its parts "bound together by a common interest" expressed in diplomatic practice and by rules all the more elaborate for their long history as custom. Vattel captured the conventional sentiments of his time: "The constant attention of sovereigns to all that goes on, the custom of resident ministers, the continual negotiations that take place make modern Europe a sort of Republic."[34] Diplomats now had handbooks, and none was more influential than François de Callières's *De la manière de negociér avec les Souverains* (1716).[35] In Maurice Keens-Soper's apposite summary, "the civility and corporate sense of the *corps diplomatique* was a visible embodiment of

31. Ibid. As we show in the next chapter, this is Hobbes's conception of agency, for which the term *representation* might have suited Grotius had his Latin made it available to him.

32. Wheaton, *Elements of International Law*, 1st ed., I, i, § 8, 43, original emphasis. Cornelius van Bynkershoek, *De foro legatorum liber singularis: A Monograph on the Jurisdiction over Ambassadors in Both Civil and Criminal Cases*, trans. Gordon J. Laing (Oxford, 1946), photo-reproducing 1744 ed., chap. 3, 442. The translation reads "nations . . . with the highest standards of morals" (18).

33. Bynkershoek, *De foro legatorum*, VIII, trans., 43; XXIV, 567.

34. [Emmerich] de Vattel, *The Law of Nations or the Principles of International Law Applied to the Conduct of Nations and of Sovereigns*, trans. Charles G. Fenwick (Washington, D.C., 1916), III, iii, § 47, 251.

35. François de Callières, *The Art of Diplomacy*, trans. unknown, ed. H. M. A. Keens-Soper and Karl W. Schweizer (Leicester, 1983).

the *raison de système* of Europe."[36] It remained so for another century and a half.[37]

Standing in for princes, kings, and emperors, ambassadors were typically involved in the daily routines and ceremonies of royal courts.[38] A dominating feature of court life was a preoccupation with good manners, taking into due account distinctions of rank and ancestry, expectations of deference, and sensitivity to breaches of etiquette. "The preoccupation with issues of precedence and protocol . . . was typical of the social manners of the *ancien régime* and not only of its diplomacy. Moreover the 'compound of formalities, decencies and circumspections' was not always irrelevant to an activity whose *raison d'être* was to be a civilised and civilising force among states frequently inclined to violent remedies."[39]

Weaned from their warrior ways, courtiers had little but their status, and all the rules attaching to status, to keep them busy. This was obviously a historical development. However little life may have changed for most people, life at court had prompted the progressive improvement of manners.[40] The concern with refinement focused first on "decency of Behaviour," in Hobbes's formulation, on "how one man should salute another, or a man should wash his mouth, or pick his teeth before company, and such other points of the *Small Moralls.*"[41] Handbooks on decent behavior had appeared long before Hobbes's time, although their audience only very gradually extended beyond court society. Early modern readers were also drawn to Cicero's *De officiis*

---

36. Maurice Keens-Soper, "The Practice of a States-System," in Michael Donelan, ed., *The Reason of States: A Study in International Political Theory* (London, 1978), 36, footnote omitted. Also see Jens Bartelson, *A Genealogy of Sovereignty* (Cambridge, U.K., 1995), 181–85.

37. Harold Nicolson, *Diplomacy* (Oxford, 1939), chap. 3.

38. See Callières, *Art of Diplomacy,* chap. 3, "the qualifications and conduct of the minister." "An ambassador resembles in some respect a comedian, exposed upon the theatre to the eyes of the world, to act there the parts of great personages. As his employment elevates him above his condition, and puts him in some measure upon a level with Kings and Princes, by the right of representation that is annexed to his employment, and by the particular commerce which he is supposed to have with them, he must pass for a very bad actor if he knows not how to support the dignity of that rank" (77–78).

39. Abraham de Wicquefort, *The Embassador and his Functions* (Digby's trans., 1716), chap. 21, in Keens-Soper, "Practice of a States-System," in Donelan, ed., *Reason of States,* 36.

40. "If the superiority in politeness should be allowed to modern times, the modern notions of *gallantry,* the natural produce of courts and monarchies, will probably be assigned as the causes of this refinement" (David Hume, "Of the Rise and Progress of the Arts and Sciences," *Essays,* 131, original emphasis). On life at court as a vehicle for royal subordination of the nobility, see generally Norbert Elias, *The Civilizing Process,* Vol. 2, *Power and Civility,* trans. Edmund Jephcott (New York, 1982).

41. Hobbes, *Leviathan,* I, xi, 69, original emphasis. Also see Elias, *Civilizing Process,* Vol. 1.

(*On Duties*) (c. 44 BCE), a handbook in the form of Cicero's advice to his son on the duties attending his station. "Everything that is honourable in a life depends on its cultivation," Cicero had said, "and everything dishonourable on its neglect."[42]

In court society, men were induced to change their ways in such matters of comportment and hygiene because they spent so much time in the company of women, who were accounted the gentler and more sensitive of the sexes.[43] While good manners may have produced gentler men, they also reinforced sensitivity to slights and insults that these same gentlemen so skillfully delivered. Honor stood above all other concerns; issues of honor compelled gentlemen to settle their scores through carefully calibrated rituals of violence. Polished ways—the elaborate *mores* of polite society—undoubtedly lessened casual violence. At the same time, the obsession with honor multiplied the occasions of violence, glorifying the resort to arms even while regulating it and giving it a civilized veneer.

Court society was hardly unique in its preoccupation with honor. "In order to live comfortably in the world," Smith observed near the end of his life, "it is, upon all occasions, as necessary to defend our dignity and rank, as it is to defend our life or our fortune."[44] Indeed, Smith viewed the duel as a *modern* institution. "Modern manners," according to Smith, favored "the practice of duelling" as a technique for controlling anger through fear, although he thought that fear such as this is "contemptible" because it "takes away all the nobleness of the restraint."[45]

Smith's preference for self-control fit with his Ciceronian view of ranks and duties. His defense of anger calls for noble motives and warrants his sense of "just indignation" (see chap. 6 below). Smith's world was not yet modern and his moral universe still transitional. In time, any society so evidently based on status distinctions—on "Custome and Example"—would come to be seen as traditional, the antithesis of a modern society. When moderns finally abolished dueling in the 1830s, they took a last step in substituting positive law and social control for natural jurisprudence and self-control. Such a step makes a virtue of the kind of fear that Smith found so undignified and appalling.

---

42. Cicero, *On Duties*, trans. Margaret Atkins (Cambridge, U.K., 1991), I, § 4, 3.
43. "What better school for manners than the company of virtuous women, where the mutual endeavour to please must polish the mind, where the example of the female softness and modesty must communicate itself to their admirers, and where the delicacy of that sex must put every one on his guard, lest he give offence by any breach of decency" (Hume, "Of the Rise and Progress of the Arts and Sciences," *Essays*, 134).
44. Smith, *Theory of Moral Sentiments*, VI, iii, § 16, 244.
45. Ibid., § 9, 240.

Arts and Sciences

Many honor-bound societies develop rules for status competition that do not involve physical violence, however ritualized. By this measure, eighteenth-century polite society was never as advanced as its enlightened members liked to think. In some respects, however, Europe had developed as no other society had ever done before. Europeans were well aware—and generally proud—of their accomplishments. In Montesquieu's *Persian Letters* (1721), imaginary outsiders remarked on "the development of the arts, science and technology in the West" and debated the consequences: utility or abuse, industry or idleness.[46] Hume's essay "Of the Rise and Progress of the Arts and Sciences" (1742) extolled the benefits of these developments, while Rousseau burst on the scene in 1751 by damning them in his prize-winning *Discourse on the Sciences and the Arts*. Very much in the spirit of the time was the *Encyclopedia—L'encyclopédie ou dictionnaire raisonné des sciences, des arts et des métiers*. The first volume of this magisterial work also appeared in 1751.

Informed observers drew distinctions. Hume pointed to the gap between refined manners and the progress of knowledge when he claimed that "*a republic is most favourable to the growth of the sciences, a civilized monarchy to that of the polite arts.*"[47] Turgot called the subject of his second discourse on universal history "The Progress of the Human Mind," and he too discriminated between the arts and sciences.[48] Kant put the arts and sciences together in order to pit them against manners (Hume's "polite arts")—*Kultur* against *Zivilisation*. "We are *cultivated* to a high degree by art and science. We are *civilised* to the point of excess in all kinds of social courtesies and proprieties."[49]

For all three writers, progress implied the possibility of perfection. "Through alternate periods of rest and unrest, of weal and woe," Turgot proclaimed, "the human race as a whole has advanced ceaselessly toward its perfection."[50] In Aristotle's account, it is nature's purpose to achieve perfection.

---

46. Montesquieu, *Persian Letters,* trans. C. J. Betts (Harmondsworth, Middlesex, 1973), Letters 105, 106, 192–96, at 192.
47. Hume, "Of the Rise and Progress of the Arts and Sciences," *Essays,* 124, original emphasis. This passage is also quoted by Pocock, *Barbarism and Religion* 2:188. On Hume's *Essays* "as contemporary history," see generally chap. 12.
48. Turgot, *On Universal History,* 84.
49. Immanuel Kant, "Idea for a Universal History with a Cosmopolitan Purpose" (1784), in Hans Reiss, ed., *Kant Political Writings,* 2nd ed., trans. H. B. Nisbet (Cambridge, U.K., 1999), 49, emphasis in translation.
50. Turgot, first discourse, *On Universal History,* 72.

For Hume, Turgot, and Kant it is science's purpose to discover perfection in nature. "In all cases, it must be advantageous to know what is most perfect in the kind," Hume asserted, "that we may be able to bring any real constitution or form of government as near it as possible, by such gentle alterations and innovations as may not give too great disturbance to society."[51] Society is a natural phenomenon, and science will aid in its improvement.

In the manner of science in the a posteriori style, both Hume and Turgot offered an empirical generalization about the human condition. According to Hume, "as observation reaches, there is no universal difference discernible in the human species."[52] Turgot's position is exactly the same. "The original aptitudes are distributed equally among barbarous peoples and among civilised peoples; they are probably the same in all places and at all times." Therefore, the arts develop variously depending on "the different states of mankind," while science develops only after people shake off the yoke of authority and try to "work out the way in which our senses deceive us."[53] Turgot thus echoes Aristotle, Grotius, and Hobbes: the arts produce the *mores* that make science possible but not inevitable; the sciences use a priori and a posteriori methods together, and artfully, to discover the laws of nature and cast aside the *mores* that hold us down. "The sciences . . . are as boundless as nature. The arts, which are only relations to ourselves, are as limited as we are."[54]

We hear something else in these claims. "The arts and sciences," according to Hume, "have flourished in one period, and have decayed in another: But we may observe, that, at the time when they rose to greatest perfection among one people, they were perhaps totally unknown to all the neighbouring nations; and though universally decayed in one age, yet in a succeeding generation they again revived, and diffused themselves over the

---

51. David Hume, "Idea of a Perfect Commonwealth" (1752), *Essays*, 513–14. Cf. Kant on *"the problem of establishing a perfect civil constitution";* "Idea for a Universal History with a Cosmopolitan Purpose" (47, emphasis in translation). On purpose and perfection from Aristotle to Kant and the drafters of the Constitution of the United States, see Peter Onuf and Nicholas Onuf, *Federal Union, Modern World: The Law of Nations in an Age of Revolutions, 1776–1814* (Madison, Wisc., 1993), chap. 1.

52. David Hume, "Of the Populousness of Ancient Nations" (1752), *Essays*, 378. In revising the *Essays* for a 1777 edition, Hume seems to have changed his mind. "I am apt to suspect the negroes, and in general all the other species of men (for there are four or five different kinds) to be naturally inferior to the whites. There never was a civilized nation of any other complexion than white, nor even any individual eminent either in action or speculation. No ingenious manufactures amongst them, no arts, no sciences" (Variant Readings, "Of National Characters," *Essays*, 629). Also see David Brion Davis, *The Problem of Slavery in Western Culture* (Ithaca, N.Y., 1966), 457–58.

53. Turgot, second discourse, *On Universal History*, 88, 93, 95.

54. Ibid., 113.

world."[55] This was also Turgot's view: "Progress, although inevitable, is intermingled with frequent periods of decline as a result of the occurrences and revolutions that come to interrupt it. Thus progress has been very different among different peoples."[56]

Generalizing about the progress of different peoples, Turgot identified three states of humanity by their ways of life, characterized in turn by "hunters, shepherds, or husbandmen."[57] Montesquieu's *Spirit of the Laws* elaborates the same tripartite division of "plowmen, hunters, or herders," but not with the sense that these states are progressive.[58] In Montesquieu, their order is scrambled, because they are, like geography and climate, contingent features of particular nations. They are *mores*, and nothing more. In Turgot, their order registers "the successive advances of the human race"—indeed, its "main epochs"—and thereby are the proper subject of universal history.[59]

Turgot's different states of humanity are stages—or so we say today. Indeed, Turgot may be the proximate author of the conjecture that historical development proceeds, however fitfully, as a necessary sequence of stages.[60] In Smith's canonical version, there are four stages (in his words, "ages"): hunting and gathering, herding, farming, and commerce.[61] John Millar, who had been Smith's student and then associate at Glasgow, used the same scheme.[62] Turgot's earlier, simpler scheme apparently consisted of three stages. His contemporaries readily identified the first stage with hunters and gatherers in the New World. If they were *savages,* then the nomadic people, or *barbarians,* who first populated Europe and then, as warrior hordes brought down the Roman Empire, exemplified the second. The third stage saw the arrival of permanent settlements, cultivation of the soil, rights to

---

55. Hume, "Of the Populousness of Ancient Nations," *Essays,* 378.
56. Turgot, second discourse, *On Universal History,* 88.
57. Ibid., 93.
58. Montesquieu, *Spirit of the Laws,* bk. 1, chaps. 3, 9. Also see Meek, intro., *Turgot on Progress, Sociology and Economics,* 5–6.
59. Turgot, plan of the discourses on universal history, *On Universal History,* 64.
60. So Meek has claimed; see his intro., *Turgot on Progress, Sociology and Economics,* 5–12, and Ronald L. Meek, *Social Science and the Ignoble Savage* (Cambridge, U.K., 1976), 68–76.
61. Adam Smith, *Lectures on Jurisprudence,* ed. R. L. Meek et al. (Oxford, 1978), Report of 1762–63, i, 27, 14. According to Meek, "it seems *probable* that Smith was already using a version of it . . . in 1752–3; and it seems *possible* that he used a version of it in the course of lectures which he gave in . . . 1750–1" (*Social Science and the Ignoble Savage,* 99, original emphasis).
62. Indeed, Millar took the "different ages" as a frame of reference needing no further explication (William C. Lehmann, *John Millar of Glasgow, 1735–1801* [New York, 1960; rpt. *The Origin of the Distinction of Ranks*], 173–322; see esp. table of contents, chap. 1, 173).

property, and burgeoning arts and crafts accompanying the division of labor—in others words, the beginning of civilization.

Nevertheless, Turgot clearly implied that the rise of science constituted a fourth stage. The effects of science on commerce are mostly indirect, and it is not obvious that Smith's "Age of Commerce" is qualitatively different from the age preceding it.[63] "As soon as men quit their savage state," Hume argued, "they must fall" into two classes: *"husbandmen* and *manufacturers."*[64] Thus begins the systematic functional specialization of universal human aptitudes.

Over time, those who are engaged in "the mechanical arts" and trade will increase in numbers. Improvements in the quality of life will encourage additional arts and further improvements in "the refined arts," as well as in "the more vulgar arts . . . of commerce and manufacture" and in science broadly conceived to include government.[65] From Hume and Turgot to Comte, science is the application of technical skills to the production and distribution of useful things to meet human needs. More and better science is the mark of a civilized society. It is science applied to commerce, industry, and government, and not commerce as such, that sets Smith's fourth stage apart from the earlier stages of historical development.

If, in Hume's account, commerce promotes progress in a civilized society, then foreign commerce has an even more powerful effect: "commerce with strangers . . . rouses men from their indolence" by awakening a taste for new goods and providing an incentive to make them cheaper and better.[66] *"Nothing is more favourable to the rise of politeness and learning,"* Hume concluded, *"than a number of neighbouring and independent states, connected*

---

63. "The age of commerce followed on that of agriculture only in a purely quantitative sense" (Istvan Hont, "The Language of Sociability and Commerce: Samuel Pufendorf and the Theoretical Foundations of the 'Four Stages Theory,'" in Anthony Pagden, ed., *The Languages of Political Theory in Early-Modern Europe* [Cambridge, U.K., 1987], 254, commenting on Smith's scheme).
64. David Hume, "Of Commerce" (1752), *Essays,* 256, original emphasis.
65. "Laws, order, police, discipline; these can never be carried to any degree of perfection, before human reason has refined itself by exercise, and by an application to the more vulgar arts, at least, of commerce and manufacture. Can we expect, that a government will be well modelled by a people, who know not how to make a spinning-wheel, or to employ a loom to advantage?" (David Hume, "Of Refinement in the Arts" [1752], *Essays,* 273; see generally 270–73; "Of Commerce," *Essays,* 255–56, 260–63).
66. Hume, "Of Commerce," *Essays,* 264. And conversely: "The encrease of domestic industry lays the foundation of foreign commerce" (David Hume, "Of the Jealousy of Trade" [1758], *Essays,* 329). On the benefits of foreign commerce, see Montesquieu, *Spirit of the Laws,* bk. 20, chap. 1, 338, and Vattel, *Law of Nations,* I, viii, § 83, 39.

together by commerce and policy."[67] Hume thought geography favored Europe in this respect. "EUROPE, of all the four parts of the world, is the most broken by seas, rivers, and mountains," and "the divisions into small states are favourable to learning, by stopping the progress of *authority* as well as that of *power.*"[68] Science can flourish anywhere and spread everywhere in such a situation.

Hume could have used history as well as geography to make his case.[69] The great barbarian incursions disrupted Roman imperial authority and eventuated in a Europe of many nations. Turgot saw the point. "The kingdoms of Europe conquered by the northern barbarians . . . were saved from despotism, because these barbarians were free before the conquest, which was carried out in the name of the people and not in that of the king. The Roman way of life which was established, and the religion which the barbarians embraced, also contributed to protect them from despotism."[70] As each nation emerged, it combined Gothic liberties, the Roman inheritance, and Christian religion in a distinctive way.[71]

The barbarian disruptions shattered imperial authority and, as Smith emphasized, foreclosed the possibility of a future empire on the same scale. Instead, the many nations of Europe had no choice but to organize themselves individually to protect property, administer justice, and expedite

---

67. Hume, "Of the Rise and Progress of the Arts and Sciences," *Essays*, 119, original emphasis.
68. Ibid., 122–23, 120, original emphasis. Montesquieu also related the political organization of Europe to its distinctive geography. "In Europe, the natural divisions form many medium-sized states in which the government of laws is not incompatible with the maintenance of the state" (*Spirit of the Laws*, bk. 17, chap. 6, 283).
69. Hume hinted at a more abstract formulation, pointing to the conjoined effects of history and geography on the development of modern Europe: "I have sometimes been inclined to think, that interruptions in the periods of learning, were they not attended with such a destruction of ancient books, and the records of history, would be rather favourable to the arts and sciences, by breaking the progress of authority, and dethroning the tyrannical usurpers over human reason. In this particular, they have the same influence, as interruptions in political governments and societies" ("Of the Rise and Progress of the Arts and Sciences," *Essays*, 123).
70. Turgot, first discourse, *On Universal History*, 79.
71. David Gress has called these three elements together "the old Western synthesis" (*From Plato to NATO: The Idea of the West and Its Opponents* [New York, 1998], chap. 5). Invoking Tacitus, Montesquieu had argued that the "Germanic nations who conquered the Roman Empire were very free," and he saw in this "the origin of Gothic government among us" (*Spirit of the Laws*, bk. 11, chap. 8, 167). Also see Colin Kidd, *British Identities before Nationalism: Ethnicity and Nationhood in the Atlantic World, 1600–1800* (Cambridge, U.K., 1999), chap. 3, "Mapping a Gothic Europe." Among these liberties were all sorts of feudal privileges and immunities hardly compatible with equal rights and duties under natural law.

commerce through public works. While hunters have no property and shepherds need only concern themselves with the security of their herds, the development of agriculture and commerce require the consolidation of authority in the hand of a "sovereign."[72] Sovereigns have duties corresponding to societal needs. "The first duty of the sovereign, that of protecting the society from the violence and invasion of other independent societies," Smith declared, "can be performed only by means of a military force."[73] At each stage of development, societies protect themselves from outside threats in a characteristic way. "Among nations of hunters, . . . every man is a warrior as well as a hunter."[74] The same is true of shepherds, who are able to assemble larger numbers of warriors than hunters preoccupied with their subsistence. "A nation of hunters can never be formidable to the civilized nations in their neighbourhood. A nation of shepherds may."[75]

In an age of agriculture, most people must stay at home to work the land. They protect themselves, as needed, with volunteers organized for the occasion. As societies advance, so does the art of war, which becomes "a very intricate and complicated science."[76] In the age of science, commerce, and the arts, the militia is no longer adequate to the needs of society. "A well-regulated standing army is superior to every militia. Such an army, as it can best be maintained by an opulent and civilized nation, so it can alone defend such a nation against the invasion of a poor and barbarous neighbour."[77]

Even if standing armies are a potential threat to republican liberties, they allow the sovereign to defend "society from the violence and injustice of other independent societies," a responsibility that "grows gradually more and more expensive, as the society advances in civilization."[78] Smith thought the invention of firearms "a great revolution in the art of war" and a "great expence" for sovereigns and their societies. "In modern times the poor and barbarous find it difficult to defend themselves against the opulent and civilized. The invention of fire-arms, an invention which at first sight appears to be so pernicious, is certainly favourable both to the permanency and to the extension of civilization."[79]

Smith took a less benign view than many of his contemporaries of the impact of the barbarian hordes on Europe's development, leaving him with

---

72. Smith, *Wealth of Nations*, V, I, i.b–c, 708–23.
73. Ibid., § 1, 689.
74. Ibid., § 2, 689–90.
75. Ibid., § 5, 691.
76. Ibid., § 10, 695.
77. Ibid., § 39, 705–6.
78. Ibid., § 42, 707.
79. Ibid., §§ 42, 43, 708.

a lasting fear of the uncivilized world, particularly the nomadic societies of Asia. That geographical and historical contingencies resulted in a host of independent societies, as Hume and Turgot emphasized, was for Smith an incidental matter. The more "opulent" of these societies supported sovereigns with splendid courts and standing armies, and they went to war with their neighbors for the usual reasons of fear, greed, and honor. Nevertheless, Smith implicitly believed that *commerce and policy*, to use Hume's phrase, would foster "politeness and learning," that the balance of power would contain ambition, and that wars would be limited by custom and law.

Another Scot, Adam Ferguson, made these assumptions explicit in *An Essay on the History of Civil Society* (1767): "When a number of independent communities have been frequently involved in wars, and have their stated alliances and oppositions, they adopt customs which they make the foundation of rules, or of laws, to be observed, or alledged, in all their mutual transactions. Even in war itself, they would follow a system, and plead for the observance of forms in their very operations of mutual destruction."[80] From Grotius onward, Europeans told themselves that engaging in commerce and war had made their nations more advanced—more *civilized*—than any the world had known, but only because they pursued these activities in their own unique framework of law, applied science, and the arts. It was possible to see the development of this framework only in the larger, largely conjectural context of universal history.

Oriental Despotism

Every attempt to explain the course of European history took the fall of Rome and return of barbarism to be decisive events.[81] Smith's interpretation was darker than most. "The rapine and violence" of the barbarians "interrupted the commerce between the towns and the country" and left great tracts of uncultivated land in the hands of indifferent and irresponsible proprietors.[82] Europe was unable to recover until the Italian cities took up long-distance trade. "The inhabitants of trading cities, by importing the improved manufactures and expensive luxuries of richer countries, afforded some food to the vanity of the great proprietors, who eagerly purchased them with great quantities of the rude produce of their own lands. The commerce of a great part of

---

80. Adam Ferguson, *An Essay on the History of Civil Society*, ed. Duncan Forbes (Edinburgh, 1966), IV, iv, 193.
81. As J. G. A. Pocock has so extensively documented in the two volumes of *Barbarism and Religion*.
82. Smith, *Wealth of Nations*, III, ii, at § 1, 381.

Europe in those times accordingly, consisted chiefly in the exchange of their own rude, for the manufactured produce of more civilized nations."[83]

As towns throughout Europe prospered, agriculture returned to the countryside, and with it commerce between town and country within the nations of Europe. According to Smith, this was an inversion of "the natural order of things," in which agriculture comes first, followed by manufactures, and, finally, by foreign commerce. The development of an "unnatural and retrograde order" in Europe was the result of "manners and customs" dating back to the barbarian disruptions and culminating in the court societies of early modern Europe.[84] In the natural order of things, Europe should have entered the age of commerce on its own, its prosperity and its manners more appropriately reflecting the dynamics of internal development. Instead, the civilized nations of Europe depended on luxury goods imported from "richer countries" and "more civilized nations." As Smith pointed out, "China is a much richer country than any part of Europe."[85] Any such concession threatened the presumption that related developments in commerce, arts, and sciences (including the art of war and the science of government) had enabled the civilized nations of Europe to advance beyond all others. China offered an explanatory challenge, and not just to Smith.

The challenge was to explain Chinese wealth and devalue Chinese civilization at the same time. Smith undertook both tasks by observing that China was rich, fertile, cultivated, industrious, and populous, and yet in all respects it "seems . . . to have been long stationary."[86] This was a commonplace; Hume had remarked on it. "In CHINA, there seems to be a pretty considerable stock of politeness and science, which, in the course of so many centuries, might naturally be expected to ripen into something more perfect and finished than what had yet arisen from them."[87] Turgot was more succinct: "The Chinese were stabilised too soon."[88]

Hume provided an elegant explanation for this state of affairs. "CHINA is one vast empire, speaking one language, governed by one law, and sympathizing in the same manners. The authority of any teacher, such as CONFUCIUS, was propagated easily from one corner of the empire to the other."[89] Montesquieu concluded that "manners govern the Chinese"; "manners, mores, laws, and religion are but the same thing there, one cannot change all

---

83. Ibid., iii, at § 15, 406–7.
84. Ibid., i, § 9, 380.
85. Ibid., I, xi, § 34, 208.
86. Ibid., viii, § 24, 89.
87. Hume, "Of the Rise and Progress of the Arts and Sciences," *Essays,* 122.
88. Turgot, second discourse, *On Universal History,* 111.
89. Hume, "Of the Rise and Progress of the Arts and Sciences," *Essays,* 122.

of that at once."[90] According to Turgot, "the protection given to the sciences in the kingdoms of the Orient is what has caused their ruin: by burdening them with rites and transforming them into dogmas, it has restricted their progress and even caused them to move backwards."[91] Smith joined the refrain. China had "acquired that full complement of riches which the nature of its laws and institutions" had permitted it to acquire.[92] Chinese society did not change, and could not grow richer, because it had reached an advanced stage of status differentiation. As a society of manners, its *mores* fully developed, there was no way for China to change.

Enlightenment observers condemned two constants in Chinese civilization. Despotic rule insured extraordinary luxury for an indolent few. Meanwhile, the great multitudes of China lived in the meanest possible circumstances. Although willing to work, there was no work for them to do. As Smith saw, the emperor had the finest of clothes, but most people had few clothes, proper shelter, or enough to eat. "The poverty of the lower ranks of people in China far surpasses that of the most beggarly nations in Europe."[93]

In Montesquieu's view, despotic rule is "corrupt by its nature."[94] A romantic preoccupation of the rationalist Enlightenment, oriental despotism is not just a corruption of monarchy, to be expected in the natural rhythms in forms of rule. Oriental despotism reproduces itself, in China for twenty-two dynasties in succession.[95] Despotic rule had permanently distorted life for everyone, undermining the relation between labor and its normal rewards and disrupting normal family arrangements. Poor men could not provide for their families, while wealthy men had many wives and concubines. The Chinese were civilized perhaps, but their mannered ways offended nature.

---

90. Montesquieu, *Spirit of the Laws,* bk. 19, chap. 4, 17, 310, 318.
91. Turgot, second discourse, *On Universal History,* 111.
92. Smith, *Wealth of Nations,* I, viii, § 24, 89. Also see I, ix, § 15, 111, for a close paraphrase.
93. Ibid. Smith may have been unduly generous in his assessment of European conditions.
94. Montesquieu, *Spirit of the Laws,* bk. 8, chap. 10, 119.
95. Ibid., bk. 7, chap. 7, "A fatal consequence of luxury in China," 103. Indicatively, Montesquieu consistently treated despotism as a fourth form of rule; bks. 2, 3, 5, 7, 8, passim. For treatments of oriental despotism rather different than ours, see Franco Venturi, "Oriental Despotism," *Journal of the History of Ideas* 35 (1963): 133–42, and Lawrence Krader, *The Asiatic Mode of Production: Sources, Development and Critiques in the Writings of Karl Marx* (Assen, Netherlands, 1975), 19–43. Karl Wittfogel's *Oriental Despotism: A Comparative Study of Total Power* (New Haven, Conn., 1957) is chiefly responsible for recent, highly polemical discussions of political arrangements in "hydraulic societies." While Wittfogel's views resemble Montesquieu's at least in some obvious respects, his reference point is not Montesquieu, whom he failed to mention, but Karl Marx, whose conception of an unchanging mode of production in Asia he severely criticized. See chap. 9 in this essay. And for a careful discussion of Marx on this subject, see Krader, *Asiatic Mode of Production,* chaps. 2–3.

Oriental despotism produced household slavery on a grand scale. In the "rich and voluptuous nations," as Montesquieu put it, polygamy meant that rich and powerful men were able to keep "a very great number of wives."[96] Eunuchs, concubines, even wives were slaves. Seventeenth-century travelers had returned from the East with reports of harems with hundreds, perhaps thousands of cloistered women, most of them slaves, entrusted to the care of equally large numbers of slaves who had been emasculated for the task. Paradoxically, the harem's inhabitants had preferential access to the rulers and other wealthy men who possessed them, and thus a corresponding influence on public life. Many eunuchs rose from slavery to high office and great wealth in their own right. Moreover, the management of the harem, with its restrictive rules, restless residents, and endless intrigues, distracted their masters' attention from their public duties and reinforced their despotic tendencies.

From the Topkapi Seraglio to the Forbidden City, Europeans could see the same pattern of practices repeated across the great arc of the Orient.[97] Montesquieu's *Persian Letters* described them memorably. Montesquieu presented Uzbek, a Persian traveler whose letters home describe the peculiar customs of his European hosts, with a crisis of insubordination in his own seraglio. The letters sent back and forth chronicling the crisis form a morality tale on their own. "You are a thousand leagues away from me, and you judge me guilty," writes one of Uzbek's wives. "If a brutal eunuch raises his disgusting hand to me, he does so on your orders. It is by the tyrant that the outrage is committed, not by the man who carries out his tyranny."[98]

The dire consequences of polygamy and household slavery were a constant refrain. "Those who pass the early part of life among slaves, are only qualified to be, themselves, slaves and tyrants," Hume remarked in his indictment of polygamy.[99] "Having multiple wives," according to Montesquieu, "leads to the love that nature disavows; this is because one sort of dissoluteness always entails another."[100] Turgot expatiated on "slavery, polygamy, and

96. Montesquieu, *Spirit of the Laws*, bk. 16, chap. 8, 269.
97. For some sense of the origins, features, scale, and persistence of these practices, see Piotr O. Scholz, *Eunuchs and Castrati: A Cultural History*, trans. John A. Broadwin and Shelley L. Frisch (Princeton, N.J., 2001), chaps. 3–7.
98. Montesquieu, *Persian Letters*, Letter 158, 278.
99. David Hume, "Of Polygamy and Divorces" (1742), *Essays*, 185.
100. Montesquieu, *Spirit of the Laws*, bk. 16, chap. 6, 268.

the softness which is their consequence," and so did Smith to his no doubt impressionable students at Glasgow University.

> We see accordingly that all the countries where polygamy is received are under the most despotic and arbitrary government. Persia, Turky, the Mogulls country, and China are allso. They have no way of making any opposition, so that the government soon oppresses them and they can never again recover. And as the government is arbitrary so the heads of families are entrusted with the most absolute and arbitrary authority that possibly can be. The whole of the family is at their disposall, both their wives and their eunuchs, as it would be impossible otherwise to preserve order in the state.—By this method of living it necessarily happens that a great number of persons must be intirely incapacitated to have wives and families.[101]

Montesquieu had gone further. After explaining "how the pleasure of one may monopolize so many citizens of both sexes," Uzbek concluded that "they are dead as far as the State is concerned, and useless for the propagation of the species." Montesquieu's anxiety on Uzbek's behalf is palpable. "What a decline in population must result!"[102] Of course, Uzbek was mistaken. China "is the most populous country we know of," as Hume observed.[103] Nevertheless, slaves do not reproduce themselves adequately and their numbers must be continuously replenished. "CONSTANTINOPLE, at present, requires the same recruits from all the provinces, that ROME did of old; and these provinces are of consequence far from being populous."[104]

According to Montesquieu, despotism is "political slavery," a condition that is distinguishable from "civil slavery" in principle, if not in the practice of oriental despotism. Montesquieu's abhorrence of despotism led him to

---

101. Turgot, first discourse, *On Universal History,* 80; Smith, *Lectures on Jurisprudence,* Report of 1762–63, iii, 33–34, 154. Millar held a similar view:
> The voluptuousness of the Eastern nations, arising from a degree of advancement in the arts, joined perhaps to the effect of their climate, and the facility with which they are able to procure subsistence, has introduced the practice of polygamy; by which the women are reduced into a state of slavery and confinement, and the great proportion of the inhabitants are employed in such offices as render them incapable of contributing, either to the population, or to the useful improvements of the country." (*Origin of the Distinction of Ranks,* I, vi, 225–26)

102. Montesquieu, *Persian Letters,* Letter 114, 207.
103. Hume, "Of the Populousness of Ancient Nations," *Essays,* 399.
104. Ibid., 397–98.

treat civil slavery as a secondary symptom of a more general pathology. "In despotic countries, where one is already in political slavery, civil slavery is more bearable than elsewhere. . . . Thus, the condition of the slave is scarcely more burdensome than the condition of the subject."[105] If Montesquieu indeed thought civil slavery to be less "bearable" in nations that are not despotic, the unfortunate implication of his fixation on despotism was to make civil slavery by itself less visible and less morally offensive.

Contributing to this impression is Montesquieu's large claim that climate determines character. "There are countries where the heat enervates the body and weakens the courage so much that men come to perform an arduous duty only from fear of chastisement; slavery there runs less counter to reason, and as the master is as cowardly before his prince as his slave is before him, civil slavery there is again accompanied by political slavery." Slavery follows not from some defect of human nature—"as all men are born equal, one must say that slavery is against nature"—but from circumstances. "Therefore, natural slavery must be limited to certain particular countries in the world. In all others, it seems to me that everything can be done by freemen, however arduous the work that society requires."[106] In other words, slavery is a prime correlate of despotism, endemic in some places and useless in others.

Occidental Slavery

Enlightenment writers were convinced that conditions in Europe made slavery unnatural. Emerging from the long shadow of Rome and the barbarian past, European nations had "abolished" slavery as they became civilized in their own distinctive way. "The chief difference between the *domestic* œconomy of the ancients and that of the moderns," according to Hume, "consists in the practice of slavery, which prevailed among the former, and which had been abolished for some centuries throughout the greater part of EUROPE."[107] In Montesquieu's view, "Christianity had abolished civil servitude in Europe" without noticeable difficulty.[108] Millar asked: "By what happy concurrence of events has the practice of slavery been so generally abolished in Europe? By what powerful motives were our forefathers in-

---

105. Montesquieu, *Spirit of the Laws,* bk. 15, chap. 1, 246. Also see chap. 6, 251, and chap. 13, 256.
106. Ibid., bk. 15, chaps. 7–8, 251–52; and see bk. 17, chap. 2, 278.
107. Hume, "Of the Populousness of Ancient Nations," *Essays,* 383, original emphasis.
108. Montesquieu, *Spirit of the Laws,* bk. 15, chap. 8, 252.

duced to deviate from the maxims of other nations, and to abandon a
custom so generally retained in other parts of the world?"[109] Millar
doubted that Christianity deserved full credit: "it does not seem to have
been the intention of Christianity to alter the civil rights of mankind, or to
abolish those distinctions of rank which were already established." He was
also willing to give some credit to "civil government." Monarchs made subjects of the lords "by withdrawing the submission of their immediate
dependents."[110]

Yet these were secondary factors in ending feudal bonds. No *one* had
abolished slavery and bondage in Europe; no institution, movement, or
figure had expressed moral indignation, mobilized opinion, or otherwise
taken action. Instead, energetic, inventive Europeans worked hard, found
ways to make work easier, and prospered. "With the convenience of machines invented or applied by art, one can replace the forced labor that elsewhere is done by slaves."[111] Although Montesquieu was not entirely consistent in drawing this conclusion, Millar made the shift from agriculture
to commerce and the rise of the arts the driving force behind the disappearance of servitude in modern Europe.

Turgot had given slavery an important place in his scheme for a universal
history, but he failed to consider the demise of bondage, quite possibly because it so little resembled the slavery that develops when great empires
emerge and "general degeneracy" sets in.[112] Millar paid a great deal of attention to developments in Europe after the barbarian invasions ended the
degenerate Roman Empire and foreclosed the return of another such empire. As European agricultural practices improved, proprietors recognized
that sharing their profits with tenants created incentives for the latter to
work harder. Gradually the proprietors and tenants "entered into a sort of
co-partnership" with demonstrable benefits to them both. Free labor displaced bonded labor because it was more efficient, and the rise of commerce
and the arts accelerated the process.[113]

By contrast, Smith felt that the age of agriculture, in Europe as elsewhere, depended on treating labor as property under the protection of civil
government. Because commerce depends on free labor and thus the recon-
ceptualization of property, the progressive abolition of serfdom signaled for

109. Millar, *Origin of the Distinction of Ranks*, VI, iii, 305.
110. Ibid., 310–14, at 311, 313.
111. Montesquieu, *Spirit of the Laws*, bk. 15, chap. 8, 252.
112. Turgot, first discourse, *On Universal History*, 81–83.
113. Millar, *Origin of the Distinction of Ranks*, VI, iii, 308–10. And see Davis, *Problem of Slavery in Western Culture*, 435–38.

Smith the onset of the age of commerce. Where the age of agriculture persists, so does servitude. "This species of slavery still subsists in Russia, Poland, Hungary, Bohemia, Moravia, and other parts of Germany. It is only in the western and southwestern provinces of Europe, that it has gradually been abolished altogether."[114] Millar had remarked on the persistence of slavery in northern and eastern Europe, but he had no explanation for it.

Turgot and many other Enlightenment writers were obsessed with oriental despotism, but none of them paid much attention to servitude on the great estates of their continent. Where the age of agriculture is protracted and civil government turns despotic, Smith took a position like Montesquieu's: "That the condition of a slave is better under an arbitrary than under a free government, is, I believe, supported by the history of all ages and nations."[115] Smith offered this generalization in the context of colonial slavery in an age of commerce and general improvement. Evidently, colonial slavery is more pernicious than serfdom and serfdom more pernicious than the household slavery of oriental despots. Yet by enslaving whole nations and corrupting whole civilizations, oriental despots were subject to moral opprobrium far beyond what the other forms of slavery could provoke from enlightened Europeans.

One might think that the age of commerce was simply incompatible with slavery in any form. Montesquieu perfunctorily accepted natural equality on a priori grounds and then went on to generalize a posteriori about conditions that would naturally produce despotism and decadent manners in some places but not others. No less perfunctorily, Smith argued that the "love to domineer" and a distaste for dealing with one's inferiors as equals inclined property owners to use slaves in preference to free labor whenever they have a choice. Smith failed to consider how this propensity can be reconciled with his claim that human beings have a propensity to engage in exchange, and how both of these a priori claims play out in successive ages. Instead, he offered yet another broad empirical generalization: "The experience of all ages and nations, I believe, demonstrates that the work done by slaves, though it appears to cost only their maintenance, is in the end the dearest of any."[116]

Slavery is inefficient, not least because it "is very detrimentall to population."[117] Even if slaves do manage to reproduce themselves, they and their progeny will "labour as little as possible," and then only when proprietors pay

---

114. Smith, *Wealth of Nations*, III, ii, § 8, 387. On property and civil government, see Smith, *Wealth of Nations*, V, i.b, §§ 1–16, 708–16.
115. Ibid., IV, vii.b, § 55, 587.
116. Ibid., III, ii, § 10, 388, § 9, 387. On the inconsistencies in Smith's position, see Davis, *Problem of Slavery in Western Culture*, 433–36.
117. Smith, *Lectures on Jurisprudence*, Report of 1762–63, iii, 133, 192–93.

the cost of forcing them to.[118] Colonial planters always need new slaves. Slaves are costly to keep and new *recruits* (Hume's term) costlier still, making the slave trade a lucrative enterprise. The preference for slaves would continue until masters recognized the false economy of enslaved labor—and were ready to deal with free laborers as their equals.

Smith's a priori claims about exchange and domination would seem to warrant an empirical generalization about the slave trade. So would a consideration of plantation agriculture in an age of commerce. Yet he had almost nothing to say about slavery in the course of an extensive discussion of Britain's colonial trade.[119] As with Smith, so it was with other writers more concerned with oriental despotism.

When confronted with the horrifying spectacle of Africans being enslaved and then shipped to the New World, many Europeans looked the other way. Or they concluded that blacks were inferior to whites, ill suited to freedom, and morally incorrigible. Still hunters and gatherers, they were demonstrably incapable of becoming civilized. Or, in the face of irrefutable evidence of settled agriculture, social organization on an impressive scale and effective participation in the slave trade, Europeans could judge Africans despotic in the oriental manner. Reports from travelers to West Africa confirmed as much: the King of Dahomey had two thousand wives.[120] Either way, slavery was the way of life *outside* Europe. That European nations condoned slavery in their overseas colonies, that some Europeans enslaved Africans for sale and others bought them to work their plantations, that Europe as a whole benefited from a world economy based on slavery, that slavery might not be natural anywhere or as efficient as free labor—all this was beside the point.

Only in Europe could one find civilized nations. There were few slaves in civilized nations, no harems, and no despots. Beyond those few nations, there were a great many slaves and more than a few despots. Modern civilization was thought to be different because of the value it placed on liberty. Organized as sovereign states, civilized nations were free. Yet states were free within the limits set by a common system of law and morality, one that had progressively resolved the contradiction between liberty and slavery in liberty's favor.

The United States presented a peculiar problem from this point of view. Once widespread in British North America, slavery declined wherever family farms and commercial centers created work for large numbers of free migrants. As the economic benefits of slavery diminished, antislavery

---

118. Smith, *Wealth of Nations,* III, ii, § 9, 387.
119. Ibid., IV, vii.b, 564–90, passim.
120. For a detailed discussion, see Davis, *Problem of Slavery in Western Culture,* chap. 15.

sentiments increased sufficiently to allow abolition in northern states soon after independence. At the same time, plantation agriculture developed rapidly in large areas of the Deep South. Cotton emerged as the region's economic engine, free trade its economic ideology. Where cotton was king, property was paramount—property as large tracts of land under cultivation *and* large numbers of laborers to cultivate the land.

In *The Federalist* James Madison, a reluctant slave owner, acknowledged that a slave is a member of society "by the law" and thus "a moral person" and not "a mere article of property." Yet the slave *is* property, without choice or compensation as a laborer, subject to corporal discipline, breeding, and exchange. Perhaps ingenuously, Madison argued that the federal Constitution *therefore* construed slaves as having "the mixt character of persons and of property."[121] If slaves were property under the Constitution, then slave owners could view themselves as rightfully partaking of nature's abundance, and they could do so with little concern for the conceptual muddle enshrined in the Constitution.

Under constitutional protection, the slave system grew to an awesome size in the ensuing decades. Slaves numbered in the millions; as assets, they were worth billions of dollars; adequate compensation to their owners for giving them freedom was out of the question. Any number of secondary productive and commercial activities depended on plantation production. If slavery yielded benefits for people living outside of the South, such benefits were easier to overlook, or to contemplate forgoing, than in the South. Slave owners thought that they understood plantation economics better than Enlightenment thinkers commenting on distant colonies could ever hope to. Freed slaves would not work for wages. Abolition would destroy the plantations, and with them an entire regional economy larger than the economies of many European states.

As the slave system expanded, its direct beneficiaries developed an unshakable conviction that slavery was a just institution and that its abolition would be impossible. When outsiders raised questions about the natural, moral, or religious warrant for slavery, slave owners and their supporters responded that nature, history, and the Bible authorized slavery—it was not at all a peculiar institution, and least of all was it indefensible. Furthermore, slave owners understood themselves to be highly civilized, precisely because they lived in a society marked by stratified social relations. No society is more sharply stratified than one with slaves; no society has more striking status markers.

---

121. Federalist No. 54 (1788), in Jacob E. Cooke, ed., *The Federalist* (Middletown, Conn., 1961), 367–68.

Virginia planters knew they were English gentlemen, and they had the manners to prove it. By adopting refined manners, anyone possessing land and slaves could join the club. Preoccupied with appearances, wealthy owners built grand houses, staffed them with enslaved servants, equipped them with elegant furnishings, and pursued the endless reciprocities of a social life predicated on abundant leisure. As in court societies of the seventeenth and eighteenth centuries, honor stood above all other concerns. "Southern gentlemen expected men of honor to wear masks, to display a crafted version of themselves through their voices, faces, noses, and a thousand other projections into the world." Everyone whose station mattered paid the strictest attention to the proprieties of station. Everyone understood the pleasures and dangers of insulting or demeaning others, and many welcomed the almost theatrical occasions for violence and vindication.[122]

Matters of honor were by no means the exclusive province of well-born, well-bred, or well-heeled Southerners. Large numbers of immigrants from the Anglo-Scottish borderlands had settled the hilly, relatively infertile and inaccessible backcountry from Maryland to Georgia and west to the Mississippi River and beyond. They had few illusions about their lowly rank in society; they left behind an inhospitable material environment and centuries of chronic cross-border predation; they brought with them a pastoral way of life, a reliance on clans for self-protection, and a culture of honor. It is a plausible conjecture that the pastoral stage in the history of societies fosters a culture based on an ethics of honor. Terrain limits population density, animals are vulnerable to theft, people must rely on themselves and their families in emergencies, respect is protection, skill in violence brings respect and violence in any number of volatile combinations.[123] Even when

---

122. Kenneth S. Greenberg, *Honor and Slavery* (Princeton, N.J., 1996), chaps. 1–2, at 25, footnote omitted. On rank, manners, and honor in the slaveholding South, see John Hope Franklin, *The Militant South, 1800–1861* (Cambridge, Mass., 1956), chaps. 3–4; Bertram Wyatt-Brown, *Southern Honor: Ethics and Behavior in the Old South* (New York, 1982), chap. 4; Orlando Patterson, *Slavery and Social Death: A Comparative Study* (Cambridge, Mass., 1982), 94–97; Edward L. Ayers, *Vengeance and Justice: Crime and Punishment in the 19th Century American South* (New York, 1984), 14–21; and David Hackett Fischer, *Albion's Seed: Four British Folkways in America* (New York, 1989), 382–89.

123. Smith and his contemporaries seem not to have made the connection between pastoralism and honor. In a contemporary attempt to explain why Southerners are more likely than Northerners to commit murder, Richard E. Nisbett and Dov Cohen advanced this conjectured universal (without specifically mentioning stages of socioeconomic development) rather more boldly than the ethnographic materials on pastoral societies—at least the materials that they have cited—might warrant (*Culture of Honor: The Psychology of Violence in the South* [Boulder, Colo., 1996], 5–7).

backcountry settlers were farmers or craftsmen, they lived in unforgiving circumstances, and they too lived by stringent requirements of the herder's code.[124]

As Bertram Wyatt-Brown has emphasized, "primal honor" demands bravery, danger gives bravery its reason for being, and, in the absence of danger, bravery inspires truculence. The measure of one's worth is the opinion of others, which others form first from someone's physical appearance and then from the way that someone acts. As a test of courage, anyone can expect to be provoked. Slights and insults, real or imagined, to oneself or one's family, compel a response that will almost always lead to violence. Score must be kept, scores must be settled, revenge is a family affair. If these are the "archaic forms" of honor found the world over, they ruled social relations in the antebellum South.[125]

Plantation owners and backcountry families were separated by rank and the status markers of material success and good manners, but both groups brought the premises of the old regime to the New World. Their common appreciation of a world, old or new, defined by well-marked status differences and by honor's fierce demands gave them four substantial reasons to join forces. First, the imperative correlation of race and slavery meant that freedom was not a right but a status marker fixed by the color of one's skin and other physical attributes. Aside from gender, race was more important than any other status marker, and like gender, it was assumed to be natural. By separating whites and blacks so unequivocally, the subjection of blacks invited whites to see themselves as superior to blacks in every respect, to think that blacks deserved to be slaves, and to fear blacks indiscriminately for being resentful, insolent, indolent, servile, inscrutable, unreliable, given to childlike violence, or simply too numerous.

Second, white Southerners construed threats to property—slaves and plantations, herds and homesteads—as threats to a distinctive way of life. Third, the primacy of family meant that families experienced such threats together, and they responded as if like units were responsible for the peril, and not idiosyncratically motivated individuals acting alone. Challenges to the

---

124. See generally Wyatt-Brown, *Southern Honor,* chaps. 2–3; Grady McWhiney, *Cracker Culture: Celtic Ways in the Old South* (Tuscaloosa, Ala., 1988), chaps. 6–7; and Fischer, *Albion's Seed,* 605–782. On herding and honor in the backcountry South, see Wyatt-Brown, *Southern Honor,* 36–37; McWhiney, *Cracker Culture,* chap. 3; Fischer, *Albion's Seed,* 639, 756; and Nisbett and Cohen, *Culture of Honor,* 7–9.

125. Wyatt-Brown, *Southern Honor,* 34–59, at 34; also see idem, *The Shaping of Southern Culture: Honor, Grace, and War, 1760s–1890s* (Chapel Hill, N.C., 2001), app., on the "Recent Historiography on Honor." On the close connection between honor and slavery in many cultures, see Patterson, *Slavery and Social Death,* chap. 5.

Southern way of life made it easy for people in all ranks (excepting slaves) to come together as a great family in peril and to identify the North, and not just abolitionists, as the great source of peril. Through this logic of collective action, the South became a nation. In some measure, however, the prophecy of threatened honor and collective peril was self-fulfilling: the South became a nation to combat the very peril—the forcible ending of slavery—that its emergence as a nation brought into being.

The culture of honor gave white Southerners a fourth reason to join ranks. They responded to every criticism of slavery as if it were a brazen attempt to tear off the mask of gentility and tear down the facade of common purpose. They heard in every call to conscience an insult that could not be forgotten or forgiven, an indictment of the civilized South, an affront to their Christian faith. Every challenge to Southern honor was an occasion for truculence. Northerners were willing to trade insults, invoke honor, and welcome the prospect of war. In 1844, John Quincy Adams told the House of Representatives that ending slavery could cost thousands, even millions, of lives—and that it would be worth the cost.[126]

Conjectures about a universal history that proceeds in stages from hunting and gathering to pastoral barbarism to the cultivation of land and manners to commercial civilization might suggest that honor is a thing of the past. Not so. In most social situations defined by face-to-face interaction, issues of honor are central to the normative practices that arise from such interaction.[127] Despite the familiar story of rights, revolution, and the rule of law, the culture of honor persisted in all sections of the United States and in all sectors of the civilized world. As Joanne B. Freeman has suggested, "the code of honor was a way of life" among politicians from all over the new nation, and not just the South. "Particularly in a nation lacking an

---

126. William Lee Miller, *Arguing about Slavery: The Great Battle in the United States Congress* (New York, 1996), 469, 538–39. Edward Ayers has argued that North and South shared in a culture of honor until the 1830s, after which Northerners adopted "the gospel of dignity" (*Vengeance and Justice,* 23–26, at 24). Whether this was a shift from rank and manners to rights and duties, or from self-indulgence to discipline, or both, it was even more a shift from external, collectively applied standards of conduct to internalized standards. Such a shift may also encourage individuals to internalize and perhaps sublimate considerations of "worldly honor" (ibid., 23)—as the term *dignity* suggests. Self-sacrifice is an honorable calling. The great value placed on self-reliance during this period, especially in the North, also points to a revised understanding of what honorable conduct requires.

127. See Erving Goffman, *Interaction Ritual: Essays on Face-to-Face Behavior* (Garden City, N.Y., 1967). And for a formal treatment, see Barry O'Neill, *Honor, Symbols, and War* (Ann Arbor, Mich., 1999), pt. 2.

established aristocracy, this culture of honor was a crucial proving ground for the elite."[128]

A conspicuous feature of the concern for "personal honor" in the national politics of the United States was the link between reputation and violence. Gentlemen dueled, and so did ambitious politicians. In Freeman's account, the requirements of honorable conduct lent structure to an otherwise "unstructured national political stage," and preoccupation with honor declined when organized party competition displaced face-to-face interaction in national politics.[129] If this process placed factional interests over individual reputations and discouraged politicians from taking slights personally, partisans are nevertheless likely to see issues of honor in party relations.

Feuds among backcountry clans are not so very different from duels between gentlemen. Bravery confers honor in one's group, bravery is risking one's life for the group, an honorable life and an honorable death go hand in hand. That the United States was spared factional violence over matters of honor in an era of national expansion, economic growth, and political democratization suggests that the benefits of national growth outweighed the temptations for glorious combat and honorable death. When sectional economic interests and partisan concerns over honor converged during that era, the balance shifted. As civilized nations, North and South had good and honorable reasons to go to war, the one to save the union and the other to save itself.

---

128. Joanne B. Freeman, *Affairs of Honor: National Politics in the New Republic* (New Haven, Conn., 2001), xv.
129. Ibid., xvi–xvii.

4
Moral
Persons

The earliest conceptual manifestations of what we now call liberalism produced rival versions of human agency broadly attributable to Thomas Hobbes, John Locke, and David Hume, weak inferences about social structure, and little agreement on empirical fit in a changing world. Ever since, liberal-minded observers commonly start with individual human beings, bog down in paradoxes about individual rights, rational choice, and social goods, and fail to account for very many features of modern society. Yet if we are to be precise about conceptual developments, it must be said that Hobbes, Locke, and Hume did not start with individual human beings. They instead started with stylized representations of social relations and used them to point to changing conditions in their early modern world.

This is demonstration by analogy. Aristotle authorized analogical reasoning and linked it to his teleological worldview. Early modern writers continued this deeply normative practice, in the process helping to shape the form of modern liberal society. Thus the large purpose of this chapter is to give some sense of the effect that drawing on analogies has had on the development of liberalism as a whole, and not simply on the constituent units—the individuals with their characteristic impulses, interests, and rights—who dominate the modern liberal imagination.

Early modern thinkers gave a great deal of attention to human nature and the human condition. Among them, Hugo Grotius set the terms of reference by assembling a mass of material, going back to the ancients, into a comprehensive jurisprudence of war and peace, published in 1625. "Man is, to be sure, an animal," Grotius observed, "but an animal of a superior kind." One trait "peculiar to the human species . . . is an impelling desire for society, that is, for the social life." As Grotius forthrightly acknowledged, there is nothing novel in this claim: "this social trend the Stoics called 'sociability.'" [1]

We find this same emphasis in Aristotle, whose importance for Scholastic thought gave Grotius and his early modern contemporaries a way of thinking against which, at least rhetorically, to position themselves. Conveniently, Stoic thought exemplified by Cicero enabled these thinkers to combat Aristotelian Scholasticism while adopting a key component of Aristotle's system. For Hobbes even to introduce the "state of nature" to illustrate his claims about the human condition prompted Samuel Pufendorf's rejoinder that "the man described by Hobbes in such a state is still subject to the rule of natural laws and right reason," just as Grotius had said. When Pufendorf observed "that a state of nature actually never existed," he articulated a truism that Hobbes would not have challenged. Society, Pufendorf wrote, is the "natural state of man." [2] Fellowship entails fellow feeling—"a phrase of this present time" Hobbes called it in *Leviathan* (1651)—and fellow feeling, or sympathy, is a natural feature of the human experience. [3] A century later, Adam Smith put this sociability at the center of his moral theory.

We should be clear on what natural sociability entails. We *need* each other to flourish—to be able to act on our plans and achieve our goals individually. This is as much Hobbes's view as it is Grotius's, Pufendorf's, and Smith's. A Stoic goes on to say that we should strive for self-sufficiency, even if we can never achieve it fully. An Aristotelian insists that we must orient ourselves to the *common good* in order to achieve collective self-sufficiency: our plans and goals can never be simply our own.

In other words, society is a moral condition, and our natural sociability makes us *moral persons*. Grotius's moral person is a social being, perhaps an individual human being, perhaps a corporate being such as a nation or guild. Grotius followed his Stoic claim of natural sociability with an analysis of *jus* (the justness of an act or, more familiarly, *right*). *Jus* is a property of any moral person (*qualitas moralis personae*) formed into aptitudes and faculties. [4] An emphasis respectively on rights and needs supports divergent conceptions of moral self-realization, but neither requires the individual to be the sole

---

1. Hugo Grotius, *De jure belli ac pacis libri tres,* 1646 ed. trans. Francis W. Kelsey (Oxford, 1925), prolegomena, § 6, 11. In the Kelsey translation, *affectus socialis* is rendered "sociableness"; "sociality" is also often used.

2. Samuel Pufendorf, *De jure naturae et gentium libri octo* (1671), trans. C. H. Oldfather and W. A. Oldfather (Oxford, 1934), I, ii (*On the Natural State of Man*), 154–78, at §§ 3, 4, 158, 163. Also see Grotius, *De jure belli ac pacis,* I, I, xi, 38.

3. Thomas Hobbes, *Leviathan,* ed. Richard Tuck (Cambridge, U.K., 1991), pt. 1, chap. vi, 43.

4. Grotius, *De jure belli ac pacis,* I, I, iv–v, 35–36.

possessor of moral personality. To see in early modern writers the individual as a being whose autonomy, defined as such by right, took precedence over the encumbrances of society is to read them anachronistically—not through Smith's eyes but through the eyes of his nineteenth-century successors.

Liberalism by Analogy

Reasoning by analogy is a pervasive human activity. "Comparing novel situations to familiar ones and finding correspondences between them, and then using these correspondences to generate inferences about the new cases, is integral to human thinking." This process depends on "the construction of similarities."[5] In order to compare two situations, we must place them side by side in the mind's eye, or one after the other as a figure of speech. This is an imaginative act—we must *see* similarities and we then *make* something new, at least for ourselves, out of what we see.

In the first instance, the Greek term *analogia* means *proportion.* So it was for Aristotle.[6] This usage would seem to imply that (some) objects or events have (at least some) properties subject to quantifiable expression, and therefore relations of properties subject to expression as ratios in the form, A is to B as C is to D. In any field of objects and events, identical ratios in the relations of properties make similarities easy to see. As it is with the quantifiable properties of things, so it is with their qualitative properties, even if the similarities do not come so readily to mind. Furthermore, things imaginatively constructed from whatever properties we select for comparison are wholes capable of being substituted for one another. $A:B$ and $C:D$ are interchangeable things.

According to Aristotle, all such things exist potentially. They become actual when they take on substance, or we give them substance. The relation of actuality to potentiality is something best grasped by analogy. Consider this series of relations:

as that which is building to that which is capable of building, so is the waking to the sleeping, and that which is seeing to that which has its eyes shut but has sight, that which is shaped out of the matter to the matter, and that which has been wrought to the unwrought. Let actuality be defined as one member of

5. For an accessible introduction to the subject, see Keith J. Holyoak and Paul Thagard, *Mental Leaps: Analogies in Creative Thought* (Cambridge, Mass., 1995), at 262, 221.
6. Here see David Burrell, *Analogy and Philosophical Language* (New Haven, Conn., 1973), 75–77. For a good guide to Aristotle on analogy, see Ibid., chap. 4.

this antithesis, and the potential by the other. But all things are not said in the *same sense* to exist actually, but only by analogy—as *A* is in *B* or to *B*, *C* is in *D* or to *D*.[7]

For Aristotle all things are potentially related, and all relations are capable of realization in a perfect whole. Reasoning by analogy implicitly acknowledges the purposive nature of any thing, both as a part in functional relation to some whole and as a whole for which many parts stand in functional relation. The point of such reasoning is to uncover the structural similarities that functional relations produce or, to switch metaphors, to open ourselves to the harmonies of nature. Aristotle said that metaphors should bring "something fresh" to mind.[8] Yet they only work as figures of speech if they "fairly correspond to the thing signified: failing this, their inappropriateness will be conspicuous: the want of harmony between two things is emphasized by their being placed side by side."[9] Metaphors succeed only when they suggest plausible similes. Together reasoning *and* rhetoric make the potential actual and to help the actual fulfill its potential, in the process actualizing our potential in the whole, natural order of things.

Renaissance humanism emphasized rhetoric over reason, and thus the great Roman exponents of eloquence, such as Cicero and Quintillian, over Aristotle and his *Rhetoric*—even though the Romans were "deep students of Aristotle's text." As Quentin Skinner has further observed, "Aristotle begins by declaring that, if there is a genuine 'art' of rhetoric, it cannot simply consist of a series of devices for enabling us to improve the elegance and persuasiveness of our speech; it must on the contrary consist of a distinctive art of reasoning."[10] No doubt, the humanist disinclination to make the connection, so typical of Aristotle, between reason and rhetoric is part of a larger movement against an Aristotelian worldview that had been appropriated, developed, and promulgated by Scholastic thinkers over several centuries. Underlying this movement were some incontrovertible assumptions about the conditions of knowledge, or *epistēmē* (a term Aristotle favored, often rather inadequately

7. Aristotle, *Metaphysics,* IX, vi (1048a36-b7), in Jonathan Barnes, ed., *The Complete Works of Aristotle,* Revised Oxford Translation (Princeton, N.J., 1984), 1655. Also see Ibid., XII, v (1071a4-7), 1692.
8. Aristotle, *Rhetoric,* III, x (1410b13), trans. W. Rhys Roberts, in Barnes, ed., *Complete Works of Aristotle,* 2250.
9. Ibid., III, ii (1405a11-3), 2240.
10. Quentin Skinner, *Reason and Rhetoric in the Philosophy of Hobbes* (Cambridge, U.K., 1996), 36.

translated as *science*), that set the Renaissance apart from medieval ways of thinking on the one hand and early modern ways of thinking on the other.

As Michel Foucault has conjectured, the latter shift in ways of thinking—an *epistemic* shift—took place rather abruptly in the early decades of the seventeenth century. Towering figures such as Grotius, René Descartes, and Hobbes turned on their humanist educations and overturned not just the Renaissance preoccupation with rhetoric but the presumption that the resemblances on which rhetoric plays constitute the stuff of knowledge. Foucault has given us a vivid characterization of the Renaissance *episteme*.

> Up to the end of the sixteenth century, resemblance played a constructive role in the knowledge of Western culture. It was resemblance that largely guided exegesis and the interpretation of texts; it was resemblance that organized the play of symbols, made possible knowledge of things visible and invisible, and controlled the art of representing them. . . . And representation—whether in the service of pleasure or of knowledge—was posited as a form of repetition: the theatre of life or the mirror of nature.[11]

In Foucault's account, resemblances come in many forms, but in Renaissance discourse, four forms of "similitude" dominate. First is "adjacency," or juxtaposition, as "the sign of a relationship, obscure though it may be." Then there is emulation, as in "reflection and the mirror: it is the means whereby things scattered throughout the universe can answer one another." Analogy is third; it conveys "the more subtle resemblance of relations." Because these relations are proportionate, they are reversible and therefore universal. Nevertheless, we are on one side or the other in most analogies. "Man's body is always the possible half of a universal atlas." Finally, there is sympathy, which "has the dangerous power of *assimilating*, of rendering things identical to another, of mingling them, of causing their individuality to disappear."[12]

Similitudes make their appearance in and as signs. More than this, signs are things and things signs. "The world of similarity can only be a world of signs."

---

11. Michel Foucault, *The Order of Things: An Archeology of the Human Sciences* (New York, 1973), 17. Foucault had nothing to say about the shift from medieval to Renaissance ways of thinking, although we might plausibly assume that, in his view, it was no less abrupt than the shift from Renaissance preoccupations. Indeed, the change may have been as gradual as it was momentous. Recall our remarks on modernity's origins in the introduction to this part of this essay, and see William Egginton, *How the World Became a Stage: Presence, Theatricality, and the Question of Modernity* (Albany, N.Y., 2003), chap. 2.
12. Foucault, *Order of Things*, 17–19, 21–24, emphasis in translation.

All things are exchangeable with their signifiers, and all significations are interchangeable. Everything is a representation of something else; by repetition everything is in the end a representation of everything else. There is no ordered whole, no purpose in the end. "Nature, like the interplay of signs and resemblances, is closed in upon itself with the duplicated form of the cosmos."[13]

The Renaissance *episteme* ended with the realization that the worth of comparison was its yield of truth. No longer could we say that "some similarity between two things" made one "to be true of the other, even in that respect in which the two are different." If, as Descartes also claimed, "it is only by comparison that we recognize the truth precisely," then comparison must follow rigorous rules for the selection and representation of the properties and relations of things to be compared.[14] In Foucault's words, "every resemblance must be subjected to truth by comparison, that is, it will not be accepted until its identity and the series of its differences have been discovered by means of measurement with a common unit, or, more radically, its position in a common order."[15]

The methodical pursuit of truth will present us with many truths, which then must be enumerated in some order. A "well-instituted order" is the best possible arrangement of what we know to be true.[16] Everything finds its place in a class of things; all classes are ordered; we can find everything in its place. Comparison aims for "perfect certainty," while "the old system of similitudes," as Foucault has said, "was never certain."[17] Taxonomy represents the order of the world, perhaps approximating it, but the one does not repeat or replace the other. In the end, we may have a table of the world, but the world is no longer a table of itself.

The key to this great change in the conditions of knowledge is, at least for Foucault, *representation*. "It is through representation that resemblance can be known, that is, compared with other representations that may be similar to it, analyzed into elements (elements common to it and other representations), combined with those representations that may present partial identities, and

---

13. Ibid., 26, 31.
14. René Descartes, *Regulae ad directionem ingenii, Rules for the Direction of the Natural Intelligence: A Bilingual Edition of the Cartesian Treatise on Method,* ed. and trans. George Hefferman (Amsterdam, 1998), Rule 1, § 1, 65, Rule 14, § 2, 179. Written in 1628, the *Regulae* was not published until after Descartes' death in 1650, first in a Dutch translation (1682) and then in Latin (1701).
15. Foucault, *Order of Things,* 55.
16. Descartes, *Rules for the Direction of the Natural Intelligence,* Rule 7, § 8, 113.
17. Foucault, *Order of Things,* 55. On the "Quest for Certainty" and its relation to the turmoil of the Thirty Years' War, see Stephen Toulmin, *Cosmopolis: The Hidden Agenda of Modernity* (New York, 1990), chap. 2.

finally laid out in an ordered table."[18] It is not entirely clear why the Renaissance shift from real presence, as in Christ's presence in the host, to resemblance ought not mark (or perhaps we should say, represent) the (re)discovery of representation. Ordinary usage would seem to confirm that things resembling each other can also be said, by analogy, to represent each other. Foucault's concern seems rather to have been with what we *do* with our representations.

In Foucault's view, representation depends most of all on language; we even use language to represent language as a medium of representation. In the process, language withdraws "from the midst of beings themselves" by having ascribed to it the properties of "transparency and neutrality."[19] If language is neutral and transparent, a messageless medium, representation through language forms a bounded, gated space between us-in-our-heads and the objects of the world, including the heads-on-our-bodies and the things that we use language to represent. This is, of course, nothing other than Cartesian dualism, on which the whole of modern epistemology is predicated. By implication, the sensory effects of the world pass into our imaginations as representations of things. Conversely, things that we imagine, resemblances that we notice, we pass into the world when we use language to formulate them. Yet these two sets of things are no longer interchangeable, these processes no longer reversible.

Perhaps Foucault has overstated the importance of *representation*—of the change from endless repetition to sequential order—in bringing forth what he called the classical *episteme* and we call the early modern world. In the *Regulae,* for example, Descartes' headings for rules 13, 14, and 15 mention *representation* successively in relation to imagination, sense, and memory, but he otherwise used this term and its cognates only in passing—and less often than he used the term *signification*. Hobbes's *Leviathan* offers another pertinent example. The second sentence speaks of "representation or apparance," but the ensuing discussion of sense, imagination, and memory (chapters 1 and 2) makes no use of the former term.[20] Chapter 4, "Of Speech," uses *signification* repeatedly and not *representation* at all. Here Hobbes's primary concern was naming, for this is what speech consists of. As with "apparences," names are signs, always exchangeable with what they represent.

There is nothing emblematically modern in this way of thinking; naming has no system. Hobbes's relation to great changes then underway is ambiguous. Skinner has argued that "as soon as Hobbes addressed himself to the

18. Foucault, *Order of Things,* 68.
19. Ibid., 56.
20. Hobbes, *Leviathan,* I, i, 13.

topic of *scientia civilis* in the late 1630s he proceeded to pull up his own humanist roots." His aim in *The Elements of Law* (privately circulated in 1640) and *De cive* (1642) was to discredit the Renaissance association of "science and eloquence" and to replace it with "the methods of *recta ratio,* and hence the procedures of all of the genuine sciences"—procedures that produce self-evident truths about the nature of things.[21] Following Foucault, we might say that Hobbes had hoped to replace a collage of similitudes and significations with a system of representations corresponding to the actual nature of civil society.

When we turn, however, to *Leviathan,* we see that by 1651 Hobbes had changed his mind, not so much on the methods and findings of science as to the manner of its exposition. Indeed, Hobbes adopted the humanist emphasis on the rhetorical arts he had earlier repudiated. In particular, he followed the Roman rhetoricians who deployed figures of speech as ornaments, the effect of which would be to help the listener to "create novel visions in the mind's eye."[22] What makes *Leviathan* so different from Hobbes's earlier efforts is "the technique of using the figures and tropes—especially the master tropes of simile and metaphor—to supplement the findings of reason by 'preferring' or 'holding forth' the truth in such a way as to enable it, so to speak, to be visually inspected."[23]

In 1637, Hobbes had published in English an anonymous precis of Aristotle's *Rhetoric.* Hobbes's version of a passage we quoted earlier holds that "a Metaphor ought not to be so farre fetcht as that the Similitude may not easily appeare."[24] Consider Hobbes's first words in *Leviathan:* "NATURE (the Art whereby God hath made and governes the world), is by the *Art* of man, as in many other things, so in this also imitated, that it can make an Artificial animal"—an engine that moves itself. "For what is the *Heart,* but a *Spring;* and the *Nerves,* but so many *Strings;* and the *Joynts,* but so many *Wheeles,* giving motion to the whole Body, such as was intended by the Artificer?" Nature's art is to human art as an animal is to a machine; animals are to machines as the functional relations that constitute living beings are to the functional relations that make machines like living beings. "Art goes yet further, imitating that Rationall and most excellent worke of Nature, *Man,*"

---

21. Skinner, *Reason and Rhetoric in the Philosophy of Hobbes,* 3.
22. Ibid., 183.
23. Ibid., 383.
24. Thomas Hobbes, *A Briefe of the Art of Rhetorique,* quoted ibid., 190. "The most revealing tropes will be unproportionable," as Skinner commented, "but they must never be disproportionate." For background on this minor work of Hobbes's, see ibid., 38.

who has created civil society, "which is but an Artificiall Man, . . . and in which the *Soveraignty* is an Artificiall *Soul*, as giving life and motion to the whole body."[25]

All of these similitudes (and there are many more in this long passage) suggest that human intentions resemble God's intentions, or nature's purposes, and not by accident. They also support the conclusion that those functional relations making society analogous to nature also make the rules for reasoning about nature and society one and the same. "*Wisedome* is acquired, not by reading of *Books*, but of *Men*."[26] Hobbes might have added, wisdom also comes from reading the signs of life: by seeing the heart as spring, joints as wheels, sovereign as soul. For rhetorical purposes, these are arresting metaphors that jolt an "audience into seeing things in a new way."[27] Novelty stimulates the imagination, but what we see—the similarity in two situations—is an aid to judgment, an invitation to put reason to work, as if it too were a machine. In context, however, these metaphors are plausible similes. Despite what many commentators think, they are not a sign that Hobbes was at this moment authorizing a shift from organic to mechanical metaphors.

Hobbes's similitudes are fully interchangeable; any sequence of them is reversible. If art imitates life (which is nature's art), then the signs of life (the heart as a spring, joints as wheels) imitate art imitating life. Lodged in this ever-duplicating ensemble of similitudes is the "state of nature," to which Hobbes applied his considerable rhetorical power later in *Leviathan*. Because nature and society exhibit the same sorts of functional relations (life is/as artifice), they are interchangeable states. Because nature and society are similar in important respects, and because of the rhetorical effects that come from pointing up these similarities, Hobbes compelled the members of his early modern audience to reason more rigorously about the human condition and to sharpen their conventional, typically Stoic judgments about human sociability.

After Hobbes, many other writers summoned up the state of nature as a suggestive analogy by which to represent human society. We can see the development of liberal ideas about human possibilities in these conjectures; they tell a liberal story about the origins of liberalism. We propose to tell this story yet again—this time as conjectural history. The episodes in the standard version of the story seem to hinge on the changing terms of the Hobbesian

---

25. Hobbes, *Leviathan*, intro., 9, original emphasis.
26. Ibid., 10, original emphasis.
27. Skinner, *Reason and Rhetoric in the Philosophy of Hobbes*, 188.

analogy. In our telling, there is more than this going on. The function of the analogy has changed—not just once but twice—each time in keeping with an epistemic shift of epochal proportions.

With Hobbes, the analogy puts nature onstage (nature is artifice), in order for us to imagine society stripped of its trappings. For Locke the state of nature is homologous with an actual set of conditions—"in the beginning all the World was *America*"—from which society emerged and to which it may revert. Representing that world *as if* it were a naturally harmonious state of affairs allows us to compare actual societies with "the state of Peace, Good Will, Mutual Assistance, and Preservation" that they have the potential of becoming.[28] Reversing the analogy does not work; idealized representations of society can say nothing, even metaphorically, about nature as an actual condition. Most analogies are one-way streets.[29]

For Hume, the state of nature is even more stylized as a representation than it was for Locke, and it leads to a paradoxical conclusion. There never was, or need have been, a state of nature: we are social beings because we have always lived—by habit and not design—in actual societies. Or, there is nothing distinctive about the human condition: we are natural beings because society *is* a natural condition, but not one that is necessarily harmonious, even potentially. Hume gave his successors two ways to proceed, a metaphorical fork. Later writers were obliged to take one or the other. Either way, analogy lost its epistemic relevance in the modern quest for self-understanding.

Hobbesian Masks

Richard Tuck has suggested that Hobbes concocted the state of nature by analogy with the "real and imaginatively vivid . . . domain of international relations."[30] While Hobbes was obviously influenced by the spectacle of war among sovereigns, it is not at all certain that Hobbes or any of his contemporaries conceptualized international relations as a "domain," or distinctively whole set of relations that might be subject to comparison with any other domain. In chapter 3, we argued to the contrary. International relations came

28. Locke, *Second Treatise of Government*, v, § 49, iii, § 19, in idem, *Two Treatises of Government*, ed. Peter Laslett (Cambridge, U.K., 1988), 301, 280; A. John Simmons, *On the Edge of Anarchy: Locke, Consent, and the Limits of Society* (Princeton, N.J., 1993), chap. 1.
29. Holyoak and Thagard, *Mental Leaps*, 196.
30. Richard Tuck, *The Rights of War and Peace: Political Thought and the International Order from Grotius to Kant* (Oxford, 1999), 8–9.

to be conceptualized as a domain only gradually over the course of another two centuries. Tuck's assessment of the state of nature starts with an anachronism: "We can conceive of ourselves as natural individuals behaving like sovereign states, and a conception of this kind is a very powerful way of getting a sense of what it might feel like to be a liberal agent."[31] This is a striking and powerful claim, yet it is misplaced.

That we can indeed conceive of ourselves in this way in our own time, and have been doing so for quite some time, is in some part due to Hobbes. Yet Hobbes did not conceive of sovereigns as "natural individuals" in a domain of their own, to be clarified by analogy with the state of nature. Nor, conversely, do Hobbes's natural individuals bear even a "far-fetched" resemblance to those awesome beings who held sovereign authority in Hobbes's world.[32] Nevertheless, Hobbes introduced the state of nature, as an imaginative ploy, to make us see something important about civil society in all its possible manifestations.

Before claiming that Hobbes effectively invented liberal society by analogy with international relations, Tuck dismissed the alternative view that the "state of nature is simply a rather dramatic fictional device for making a point about the minimal character of the law of nature: strip away from agents all that is culturally specific, and one is left with merely the bare natural rights and duties which seem to be universal."[33] It is a mistake to dismiss the state of nature as a dramatic device. Hobbes's intention may be inferred from his campaign, before *Leviathan,* to strip from the language of civil science its conventional rhetorical embellishments. To understand the nature of civil society, it is necessary to strip away any and all of the cultural specifics of civil societies wherever known. In *Leviathan,* Hobbes did just this by taking rhetorical advantage of a familiar metaphor: *theatrum mundi,* the world is but a stage.[34]

In the world of the Renaissance, theater represents the world because the world presents itself as theater. The similitude is reversible. There is no one

31. Ibid., 9.
32. On the properties of sovereignty in early modern thinking, see Jens Bartelson, *A Genealogy of Sovereignty* (Cambridge, U.K., 1995), 150–54; Nicholas Greenwood Onuf, *The Republican Legacy in International Thought* (Cambridge, U.K., 1998), 124–33; and Edward Keene, *Beyond the Anarchical Society: Grotius, Colonialism and Order in World Politics* (Cambridge, U.K., 2002), 42–52.
33. Tuck, *Rights of War and Peace,* 6–7.
34. On this metaphor and its place in the English Renaissance, see Frances A. Yates, *Theatre of the World* (Chicago, 1969), chap. 9. Also see Jean-Christophe Agnew, *Worlds Apart: The Market and the Theater in Anglo-American Thought, 1550–1750* (Cambridge, U.K., 1986), 14–16, and his citations, 206 n. 24.

"reference world" that we live in; all worlds resemble all other worlds by virtue of the signs by which we choose to represent them. A conspicuous feature of Elizabethan London, public theaters playing to thousands of people
resembled Roman theaters that had been designed to reproduce the acousti-
cal harmony and visual geometry of the cosmos.[35] If stars in the heaven yield
the signs of the zodiac, a theater ceiling painted with these signs becomes the
heavens, while the circle of the zodiac gave the theater its floor plan as a
circle of triangles together resembling the human figure with limbs extended, the five points of a star, "the possible half of a universal atlas."

At the same time, the monarch sponsored lavish theatrical productions
for the court's entertainment. Court theater took place on sets designed for
the occasion and equipped with painted landscapes and mechanical con-
trivances.[36] Meticulous attention to perspective and sight lines, first for the
monarch's benefit and then for the rest of a small, splendid audience ordered
by rank, created the illusion of being somewhere mythical but real, and
affirmed for all present the rightness of their world. By the early seventeenth
century, costumed allegories called masques had become the court's premier theatrical events. Played by members of the court, including the queen,
masques confirmed the prerogatives of the crown: "the truth of the royal
productions was the truth of appearances. Power was asserted only through
analogies, faith affirmed only through symbols."[37]

The mounting excesses of royal rule angered puritans in parliament. So
did the relaxed public morals of Renaissance London, exemplified by players who were marginal members of Renaissance society yet public fa-
vorites.[38] Theaters were shut down in 1642 with the onset of civil war, and
the king lost his head in 1649. Both monarchy and theater returned to

---

35. Yates, *Theatre of the World,* chap. 7. The first public theater in England, and perhaps the
first in Europe after the fall of Rome, dates from 1576. "Before this moment, the concept of theater had included no sense of *place.* A theater was not a building, it was a
group of actors and an audience; the theater was any place in which they chose to perform" (Stephen Orgel, *The Illusion of Power: Political Theater in the English Renaissance* [Berkeley and Los Angeles, 1975], 2, original emphasis).

36. John H. Astington, *English Court Theater, 1558–1642* (Cambridge, U.K., 1999). On the
conceptual history of landscape as a Renaissance development, see Kenneth Robert
Olwig's illuminating account, *Landscape, Nature, and the Body Politic: From Britain's
Renaissance to America's New World* (Madison, Wisc., 2002), chap. 1.

37. Orgel, *Illusion of Power,* 88. On masques, their use of landscape, impact on theater, and
political significance, see ibid., chaps. 2–3; Yates, *Theatre of the World,* chap. 10; and
Olwig, *Landscape, Nature, and the Body Politic,* chaps. 3–4.

38. On "the long and bitter debate over the English stage," see Agnew, *Worlds Apart,*
104–43. "It was the player, not the play, who aroused the Puritans' greatest hostility"
(125, footnote omitted).

England in 1660. After the Restoration, court theater, not the public theater, became the standing model for theatrical productions.

Restoration theaters offered their audiences stage settings carefully conceived to create a world unlike any other staged world, within but apart from the theater itself. So it is even today. As the curtain rises, the theater darkens, a stage set with "natural scenery" fixes our attention, and players artfully sweep us into a particular place and time. We become parties to a private analogy: the player is to the world that I see onstage as I am to *my* world. Any such world is torn from nature. It is a world of particulars real only in their relation to each other, not an ensemble of exchangeable signs.

Hobbes's *Leviathan* marks the time in which theater lost its epistemic value as the world's double but gained the power to define reality uniquely for each member of the audience. Thanks in some measure to Hobbes, nature assumed theater's epistemic place in the early modern world. This is nature writ large, nature as a source of order and meaning, but not nature as we have come to experience it onstage. When Hobbes harked back to the Renaissance and made the world a stage, his players cannot have been "natural individuals"—this is Tuck's language, not Hobbes's. We know Hobbes's players by the signs that mark their place onstage and in the world. He called them *persons,* not individuals.

> A person, is he, *whose words or actions are considered, either as his own, or as representing the words or actions of another man, or of any other thing to whom they are attributed, whether Truly or by Fiction.*
> When they are considered as his owne, then he is called a *Naturall Person:* And when they are considered as representing the words and actions of an other, then he is a *Feigned or Artificiall person.*[39]

In the state of nature, human beings are "Naturall Persons" by definition. Acting individually on their own behalf, they agree to create an "Artificiall person," the *commonwealth* as holder of "soveraigne Power," whom they have authorized to act for them, individually and collectively, in a broad range of situations. Only insofar as human beings continue to act freely for themselves do they remain natural persons. Hobbes's definition of the term *person* makes this conclusion irresistible.

---

39. Hobbes, *Leviathan,* I, xvi, 111, original emphasis. Also see Hanna Pitkin, *The Concept of Representation* (Berkeley and Los Angeles, 1967), chaps. 2, 6, Agnew, *Worlds Apart,* 98–103, Skinner, *Reason and Rhetoric in the Philosophy of Hobbes,* 336–38, David Runciman, *Pluralism and the Personality of the State* (Cambridge, U.K., 1997), chaps. 2, 11, and Egginton, *How the World Became a Stage,* 146–48.

Persona in latine signifies the *disguise,* or *outward appearance* of a man, counterfeited on the Stage; and sometimes more particularly that part of it, which disguiseth the face, as a Mask . . . : And from the Stage, hath been translated to any Representer of speech and action, as well in Tribunalls, as Theaters. So that a *Person,* is the same as an *Actor* is, both on the Stage and in common Conversation; and to *Personate,* is to *Act,* or *Represent* himselfe, or another; and he that acteth another, is said to beare his Person, or act in his name. . . .

Of Persons Artificiall, some have their words and actions *Owned* by those whom they represent. And then the Person is the *Actor;* and he that owneth his words and actions, is the AUTHOR: In which case the Actor acteth by Authority.[40]

In tracing the term *person* back to its Roman roots, Hobbes made it clear that the distinction between natural and artificial persons is artificial. Nature *is* artifice, as we said earlier; all persons are similar because they are artificial in the same way—even holders of sovereign power to whom we grant authority in order to escape the state of nature. Whenever we grant others more limited powers to act on our behalf, those others are also artificial persons. In this same sense, natural persons are actors who share the artificial but indispensable property of acting on behalf, and in the name, either of oneself or someone else.

Onstage, all is artifice. Onstage, Hobbes placed singularly artificial persons, players ironically styled "natural persons," who could enter into agreements and otherwise act for themselves. The stage and civil society are doubles, each representing the other in the Renaissance manner. Yet civil society is a *civil person* in its own right because it acts on behalf of many persons in common. As such, it represents their interests, but it is not interchangeable with them: the commonwealth and the players massed onstage are not doubles. In one decisive move, Hobbes jumped from the Renaissance to the early modern world.

Onstage, there are other kinds of civil persons. "For it may happen that several persons will, with the permission of their commonwealth, unite as one person for the purpose of transacting business. These will now be *civil persons,* and companies of merchants are, and any other of other groups, but they

---

40. Hobbes, *Leviathan,* I, xvi, 112, original emphasis. On "the notion of the Latin *persona:* a mask, a tragic mask, a ritual mask, and the ancestral mask," see Marcel Mauss, "A Category of the Human Mind: the Notion of Person; the Notion of Self," trans. W. D. Halls, in Michael Carrithers et al., eds., *The Category of the Person: Anthropology, Philosophy, History* (Cambridge, U.K., 1985), 1–25, at 13–19, at 13.

are not *commonwealths*, because they have not subjected themselves to the will of the group simply and in all things."[41] Citizens subject themselves to the sovereign will in the same way: "Each of the *citizens*, and every *subordinate civil person*, is called a SUBJECT of him who holds the sovereign power."[42]

In Hobbes's logic of civil relations, citizens *are* civil persons insofar as they are subjects and thus members of civil society. Persons *are* what persons *do;* they may have bodies, but only incidentally. To use a term Hobbes favored in *Leviathan*, the *body politic* is a person consisting of many persons, for whom somebody (a representative) or some body (a representative assembly) acts as "the person of the Body Politique."[43] All such relations are artificial, as are the relations among civil persons lacking the properties of the body politic. The central feature of these relations is personality.

If every person has a body, it is because a body is social and thus a normative condition. Only by convention is it a natural condition. Persons exist because other persons act to make them so: some person must personate them. What persons do—*all* that they do—is act on behalf of others, chiefly by speaking for them. When we speak for ourselves, we are civil persons who also happen to be natural persons. Hobbes's particular concerns led him to single out the powers that persons hold by right, defining natural power as "the eminence of the Faculties of Body, or Mind: as extraordinary Strength, Forme, Prudence, Arts, Eloquence, Liberality, Nobility."[44] The powers of civil persons compound the power of natural persons; conversely, the powers of natural persons require civil society to be effective. Hobbes has ordered his list of powers from least dependent on civil society to most, but all of them are enhanced by reputation or assigned value in an existing social context.

According to Hobbes, we assign value to the use of powers and, by doing so, status to those persons whose powers we value. Hobbes did not use the term *status* in this context. Yet we need look no further than Pufendorf to find its relevance confirmed. Drawing inspiration from Grotius and Hobbes, Pufendorf sought in his early work (1660) to build a closed system of definitions and axioms by which to assess human action, which is voluntary, or willful, and therefore moral.[45] "Status," wrote Pufendorf, "is a suppositive entity" or fiction. As such, it provides a framework for moral action in the

---

41. Thomas Hobbes, *On the Citizen,* ed. and trans. Richard Tuck and Michael Silverthorne (Cambridge, 1998), V, § 10, 73, original emphasis.
42. Ibid., § 11, 74, original emphasis.
43. Hobbes, *Leviathan,* II, xxii, 157. On Hobbes's importance in the conceptual history of *representation,* see Pitkin, *Concept of Representation,* 14–37.
44. Hobbes, *Leviathan,* I, x, 62.
45. Samuel Pufendorf, *Elementorum jurisprudentiae universalis libri duo,* trans. William Abbott Oldfather (Oxford, 1931), Definition I, 3.

same way that space locates "physical motions."[46] Peace and war head
Pufendorf's brief survey of statuses, followed by liberty and servitude, and
then public and private spheres of action. As for the last, "one meets a number
of particular statuses," all of which may be denominated as "either *honorable* or *less so.*" Three other statuses round out this initial list: alien, resident, and sojourner; seniority; and majority, or the age after which one has
no "need of a tutor or guardian."[47]

Persons find their place in this system of statuses. Pufendorf's Definition
IV stipulates that a *"moral person is a person considered under that status
which he has in communal life."*[48] Thus there are public persons, and among
them political persons. *Representatives* are a "special kind of political persons" because *"principal* political persons" have granted them "power and
authority to act" for their principals, just as guardians and trustees do for private persons.[49] What applies to individual human beings applies no less to
collectives. "We can divide societies or moral persons, furthermore, like individual persons, into *public* and *private.*"[50] The former include ecclesiastical and political societies, the latter families and guilds. According to Definition VI, a *"title is a moral attribute by which distinctions are marked among
persons in communal life according to their esteem and status."*[51] Definitions
VII and VIII classify *right* and *authority* as active moral powers. Definitions
IX and X deal with *esteem* as the comparative value placed on persons, and
worth as the comparable value of things.

Pufendorf's discussion of statuses shows what Hobbes had in mind when
he spoke of honor at such great length in *Leviathan*. "To Value a man at a
high rate, is to *Honour* him; at a low rate, is to *Dishonour* him."[52] Hobbes
went on to enumerate literally dozens of acts that serve either to honor or
dishonor others. Taken together, these estimations of worthiness capture the
distribution of statuses in societies such as Hobbes's England, but *not* in all
societies at all times. Hobbes did not bother to note that the society he was
describing is stratified, or that it assigns women generally to a status beneath
that of men. Statuses are as particular as the conventions creating them.
If statuses seem to be natural, at least for those inside any particular
society, this is because nature manifests itself in the particularities of human

---

46. Ibid., Definition III, 7.
47. Ibid., 16–17, emphasis in translation.
48. Ibid., 18, emphasis in translation.
49. Ibid., 18–19, emphasis in translation.
50. Ibid., 20.
51. Ibid., 61, emphasis in translation.
52. Hobbes, *Leviathan*, I, x, 63–69, at 63, original emphasis.

experience. In any world in which honor is paramount, agency consists in the aggregate of statuses affording particular opportunities to act. In such a world, each person's statuses constitute his or her personal identity.

In a world of statuses, social relations depend on distinctions that speakers, as agents, *assert* (or affirm, or deny) to be true of themselves and others, as persons. Speakers, as agents, therefore have some fixed, more or less formal relation to other moral persons. Obviously, their assertions have social effects, although not always those that speakers intend. The constant repetition and interplay of assertive speech acts give rise to social rules that instruct persons in appropriate ways to act. To the extent that statuses constitute personal identity, internalized rules of this sort dictate moral action. In a world of status, acting honorably depends on knowing the rules that define one's station.

The world Hobbes described is the one he actually lived in—a world consisting of civil persons, identifiable by reference to their location in a labyrinthine system of statuses. In this light, it is clear why Hobbes posited a state of nature. The inhabitants of Hobbes's imagined world have been stripped of their statuses; they cease to be civil persons whose identity and agency are specified by their particular social positions. They are left with a slender repertory of faculties, of *naked* powers: strength, form, prudence.

Once shorn of statuses too thick for generalization, these few remaining powers lend themselves to general description. "Nature hath made men so equall, in the faculties of body, and mind; as that though there bee found one man sometimes manifestly stronger in body, or of quicker mind then another; yet when all is reckoned together, the difference between man, and man, is not so considerable, as that one man can claim thereupon to himselfe any benefit, to which another may not pretend, as well as he."[53] This condition is not, for Hobbes, an early stage in human development, in nature but before society. Rather, as we suggested above, Hobbes's state of nature is doubly artificial—if the theater is a stylized double of the world, its stage is stripped of artifice. On this stage, the players find themselves roughly equal because they have no props, costumes, or lines to speak.

When Hobbes's actors exercise their few remaining powers, they quickly discover that *any* act is futile because *all* of their acts cancel each other out. Stasis, not status, dominates the stage, as the actors find that their powers fail to assure their survival, much less the benefits inherent in their personal identities. In this dire situation, Hobbes permitted his actors two social powers that do not directly confer or deploy status. First is the power to enter into a contract with another person with the expectation that the terms of the

---

53. Ibid., xiii, 86–87.

contract would be fulfilled. Second is the power to give commands and expect to have them obeyed. These two powers are always embedded in any world of status. By stripping status away, Hobbes could emphasize what he took to be their importance in the orderly functioning of any society.

Neither the power to enter into contracts nor the power to give commands depends on drawing and defending social distinctions. Hobbes followed Grotius back to Roman law in asserting that contracts depend on reciprocal promises. Promises and guarantees stem from the commissive speech acts that define personal rights and duties. These rules constitute the many roles that we, as agents, assume in our reciprocal relations by extending and accepting promises. In like fashion, the power to give commands and have them followed depends on directive speech acts that function as standing orders subject to enforcement.[54]

Hobbes signaled the importance of promising by having his actors alienate their natural right to self-preservation and agree to a contract obligatory in its own terms, and not because of any collateral oaths.[55] He disallowed oaths (mere assertions, after all) because their power depends on statuses not available to actors in his notional state of nature. In civil society, persons have remedies if others break their promises or fail in their duties. On Hobbes's stage, however, the actors are bound by their contract because they feign to believe his offstage directive that this is a "law of nature."

However implausible this *deus ex machina* may be as a plot device, it reassures the actors and encourages them to enter into the social contract. In turn, this contract constitutes the "Civill Power" needed to warrant status and enforce contracts, including the contract constituting such a power in the first place.[56] The performance comes to an end with Hobbes admitting in his offstage voice that he tricked his actors with talk of nature's laws: "Covenants, without the Sword, are but Words, and of no strength to secure a man at all."[57] Yet this closing speech is not as duplicitous as it seems. Hobbes firmly believed that "Right, Equity, Law, and Justice" reside in the natural order of things, and that it is the task of civil science—*his* task—to discover it.[58]

---

54. For a fuller account of assertive, directive, and commissive speech acts and their relation to the statuses, offices, and roles constituting agency, and to networks, organizations, and associations as the institutional forms within which agents exercise their powers, see Nicholas Onuf, "Constructivism: A User's Manual," in Vendulka Kubálková et al., eds., *International Relations in a Constructed World* (Armonk N.Y., 1998), 58–78.
55. Hobbes, *Leviathan*, I, xiv, 91–100.
56. Ibid., xv, 100–103.
57. Ibid., II, xvii, 117.
58. Ibid., I, xi, 73, and see Skinner, *Reason and Rhetoric in the Philosophy of Hobbes*, chaps. 8–9.

Hobbes, of course, is remembered less for his views on nature and science than for his invocation of swords and covenants, which functions for his audience as a counterpoint to his vivid description of the state of nature. In one world, people kill each other with bare hands, in the other with swords. If we hear Hobbes saying that speech acts matter little in either world, we have missed the point. For Hobbes a world of talk is a world brimming with statuses. If we imagine a world without statuses, we still have talk. By making promises to each other, speakers constitute civil society as a partnership or association—a *polis* in Aristotle's sense.

Yet this is not the whole story. Someone has to be able to make these arrangements work, and this person must have sovereign power. Where there is sovereign power, there must be an *office*—"OFFICE *of the Soveraign Representative.*"[59] What makes an office sovereign is its relation to other offices.[60] There is no higher office. An unbroken chain of command descends from the sovereign, constituting political society as an arrangement of offices. Aristotle held that every *polis* must have an arrangement of offices, a *politeia,* in order to be wholly self-sufficient and therefore whole. Whenever there are officers in any organized relation, we hear these officers giving orders and delegating powers, thus spawning other organizations and more directive talk.

In effect, Hobbes used his actors to reproduce an Aristotelian world by bringing association and organization together in a form that we now instantly recognize as the state. Under the cover of sovereign power, roles and offices proliferate. So do statuses. In any world of talk, including our own, the proliferation of statuses will always make civil society more like the world that Aristotle or Hobbes lived in than the bare world that Hobbes's actors create with nothing more than fear and speech.

Lockean Bodies

Hobbes's person is entirely social, altogether artificial. Such a conception resembles the contemporary notion of agency, but not of person. In ordinary language today, a person is a human individual who is conscious of being a

---

59. Hobbes, *Leviathan,* II, xxx, 231, original emphasis.
60. But see Pufendorf's claim that the term *office* describes an honorable status (*Elementorum jurisprudentiae universalis,* Definition III, 16). Thus the sovereign, as the most honored person in a society, would hold the highest office. In Pufendorf's time, practical sovereignty combined the properties of exalted status and high office for mutual reinforcement, and so it does today (See Onuf, *Republican Legacy in International Thought,* 116–31).

singular and continuous presence in the world. Locke gave a striking and still influential formulation of this conception of person in *An Essay Concerning Human Understanding* (1690).[61] When, in *The Second Treatise of Government* (1690), Locke invoked the state of nature, it was *not* to make the human individual a person. Locke's individual is already a competent person, and Locke's state of nature hardly resembles Hobbes's. Nature confers on Locke's person the power—the needed faculties—both to stand apart from the world and, while taking its measure and using its fruits, remain within it.

In the *Essay,* Locke framed his conceptualization of "personal identity" with a discussion of ideas and substances.

> We have the *Ideas* but of three sorts of Substances; 1. God. 2. Finite Intelligences. 3. *Bodies.* First, God is without beginning, eternal, unalterable, and every where; and therefore concerning his Identity, there can be no doubt. Secondly, Finite Spirits having had each its determinate time and place of beginning to exist, the relation to that time and place will always determine to each of them its Identity as long as it exists.
>
> Thirdly, the same will hold of every Particle of Matter, to which no Addition or Subtraction of Matter being made, it is the same.[62]

For any substance to have an identity, we must have a clear conception of what it is. The identities of inert objects depend on our perception of the regular conditions of their existence. The same is true for machines and animals, both being the sort of objects that consist of "a fit Organization, or Constructions of Parts, to a certain end, which, when a sufficient force is added to it, it is capable to attain."[63] Finally, the same principle applies to human minds because the bodies containing them provide the conditions for their existence. Thus the identity of a human being consists "in nothing but a participation of the same continued Life, by constantly fleeting Particles of Matter, in succession vitally united to the same organized Body."[64]

---

61. John Locke, *An Essay Concerning Human Understanding,* ed. Peter H. Nidditch (Oxford, 1975), II, xxvii, 328–48.

62. Ibid., § 2, 329, original emphasis. Locke's view that bodies consist of particles of matter (corpuscles) culminated the philosophical movement in the seventeenth century to ground mechanistic thinking—a movement in which Hobbes also figured (Daniel Garber et al., "New Doctrines of Body and Its Powers, Place, and Space," in Garber and Michael Ayers, eds., *The Cambridge History of Seventeenth-Century Philosophy* [Cambridge, U.K., 1998], I, 553–623. On Hobbes, see 581–84, and on Locke, 608–10).

63. Locke, *Essay Concerning Human Understanding,* II, xxvii, § 5, 331.

64. Ibid., 331–32. And see Udo Thiel, "Individuation," in Garber and Ayers, eds., *Cambridge History of Seventeenth-Century Philosophy,* 212–62, at 233–41.

The identity of a human being depends, as a necessary condition, on having a body of one's own. Self-consciousness is another requirement. In Locke's account, "to find wherein *personal Identity* consists, we must consider what *Person* stands for; which, I think, is a thinking, intelligent Being, that has reason and reflection, and can consider it self as it self, the same thinking thing in different times and places; which it does by that consciousness, which is inseparable from thinking, and as it seems to me essential to it."[65] To engage in thinking in different times and places, one must occupy the same body all the time and everywhere. Thus embodied, consciousness is singular and continuous. This is "*personal Identity, i.e.* the sameness of a rational Being: And as far as this consciousness can be extended backwards to any past Action or Thought, so far reaches the Identity of that *Person;* it is the same *self* now it was then."[66]

As a singular, continuous self, a person experiences the world through perception. "*Self* is that conscious thinking thing . . . which is sensible, or conscious of Pleasure and Pain, capable of Happiness or Misery, as far as that consciousness extends."[67] This consciousness extends only as far as the body. If severed from the body, the "little Finger" ceases to play a part in a person's conscious life.[68] It is this integral relation of mind and body, not the operations of a disembodied mind, that accounts for the self as a singular and continuous consciousness.

For Locke any body (and not just the human body) is a sensible reality. When we touch a body, it offers resistance and brings forth in our minds the idea of solidity.[69] Solidity makes a body whole by excluding other bodies from "the space it possesses"; hardness is a relative property of a body describing "a firm Cohesion of the parts" such that "the whole does not easily change its Figure."[70] Sensing solidity and hardness are forms of perception, and perception gives rise to thinking in its many forms—reflection, remembrance, discernment, reasoning, judgment—or, more generally, understanding.[71]

---

65. Locke, *Essay Concerning Human Understanding,* II, xvii, § 9, 335, original emphasis.
66. Ibid., original emphasis.
67. Ibid., § 17, 341, original emphasis.
68. Ibid.
69. Ibid., II, iv, § 1, 122–23. By contrast, Descartes argued that extension alone is the defining property of a body, that space is an indefinitely extended body, that any body is infinitely capable of division but, by implication, incapable of any action (Garber et al., "New Doctrines of Body and Its Powers, Place, and Space," in Garber and Ayers, eds., *Cambridge History of Seventeenth-Century Philosophy,* 574–80, 592–94).
70. Locke, *Essay Concerning Human Understanding,* II, iv, § 4, 125. On whole and part as "an *idea* of a Relation," see ibid., I, iv, § 6, 87, original emphasis.
71. Ibid., vi, § 2, 128.

Complementing the "Power of Thinking" is the "Power of Volition," or will. As *"Faculties,"* "these two Powers or Abilities in the Mind" link mind and body.[72] While these powers enable human individuals to act on the world, Locke's large concern in the *Essay* is to document the world's effects on the mind. As bodies, Locke's individuals *"fill space."*[73] As minds, they exercise their powers in order to situate themselves in space, among other bodies. Yet Locke has them doing so incidentally, when the mind, by an act of will, directs "its thought to the production of any Action, . . . thereby exerting its power to produce it."[74]

Throughout the *Essay,* Locke's human individuals think and will in empty space; they are neither operative wholes nor the operating parts of a larger whole. Nature exists only as an index of cognitive development. As *"the inferior parts of Nature,"* plants do not perceive and beasts do not compare ideas.[75] At the beginning of *The Second Treatise of Government,* Locke made all living things into whole beings by situating them, as integral parts, in the state of nature. Because human individuals are "furnished with like Faculties, sharing all in one Community of Nature," we are not "made for one anothers use, as the inferior ranks of Creatures are for ours."[76] Instead, we are free and equal among ourselves: free to act as our faculties would have us act, free from "Subordination or Subjection" to the will of others.[77]

Hobbes granted considerable attention to "the LIBERTY of Subjects."[78] Sovereign power limits the extent to which subjects are free "by regulating their actions"; conversely, "nothing the Soveraigne Representative can doe to a Subject, on what pretence soever, can properly be called Injustice or Injury; because every subject is Author of every act the Soveraign doth."[79] However fictive, popular sovereignty saves Hobbes's subject from subjection. By contrast, Locke had subjection very much on his mind.

In rejecting the prevailing view that *"Every one is born a Subject to his Father, or his Prince, and is therefore under the perpetual tye of Subjection and Allegiance,"* Locke held that when people "submitted to the Government

---

72. Ibid., original emphasis. Also see xxi, § 5, 222.
73. Ibid., iv, § 2, 123, original emphasis.
74. Ibid., xxi, § 28, 248. On "power," see generally chap. xxi, 233–87.
75. Ibid., ix, § 11, 147, II, xi, § 5, 157–58.
76. Locke, *Second Treatise of Government,* ii, § 6, 271.
77. Ibid., § 4, 269.
78. Hobbes, *Leviathan,* II, xx, 145. "The freedom of man accordingly consists in nothing more than the fact that his body is not hindered from acting according to its powers" (Quentin Skinner, *Liberty before Liberalism* [Cambridge, U.K., 1998], 6–7). On the political context for this claim and its source in Roman law, see Ibid., 4–10.
79. Hobbes, *Leviathan,* II, xx, 148.

of their Father, or united together, out of different Families to make a Government," they did so by choice.[80] We find no such preoccupation with parental power in Hobbes. Subjection to the sovereign as head of the body politic is analogous to head in relation to the human body. With no head, there is no one to speak for the body as a whole. To resist this relation is to deny the life of the whole.

Locke's body politic does not exhibit the same tight interdependence of parts. Instead, it resembles the family, which ordinarily has a head among its several members. Relations between the family head and other family members start with subjection but do not preclude negotiation, resistance, and exit. Locke foreshadowed the anxiety over paternal power that Sigmund Freud brought to consciousness, and Locke's preoccupation with the personal identity of individual human beings takes on additional resonance when we think of them as family members, and members of bodies politic, struggling with demands for submission.

The Hobbesian claim that civil society depends on sovereign power, just as the living human body depends on its head, leaves us with just two kinds of actors monopolizing the action. Natural persons, now more simply known as *persons,* constitute civil societies in which they participate as subjects; sovereign persons, now better known as *states,* constitute a society in which they too participate as subjects. Here, of course, we encounter a familiar paradox: how can states be subjects when they have no head to which they are subject? For Hobbesians, a headless body is no answer; states are condemned to a state of war from which there is no escape.

Lockeans accept the Hobbesian claim that persons, as subjects, sort into two levels. Yet the paradox of subjects as members of a headless body is less dire if we bear in mind that the body in question is social. After all, headless families can survive, even flourish, with the help of its members, not to mention the help and hospitality of other families. Lockeans who favor the choice of a weak sovereign with limited powers would seem to agree. Headless social bodies are no doubt anomalous in Lockean terms, but hardly disallowed. The civil society of states, as subjects, has many heads acting on their own behalf, on behalf of other subjects, and on behalf of the whole body. These heads are bodies with heads speaking for them. Hobbesian civil relations permit all such arrangements, and many more.

Hobbes had stipulated that human beings are much the same in their faculties, with consequences in a state of nature far more brutal than the state of war among sovereigns. Locke observed that "all *Princes* and Rulers of

---

80. Locke, *Second Treatise of Government,* viii, § 114, 345, original emphasis, § 112, 343.

Independent Governments all through the World, are in a State of Nature."[81] Locke may seem to be suggesting here that the relations of sovereigns constitute the "vivid domain" of Tuck's imagination, but we have our doubts. Up to this point, Locke had been preoccupied with his central claim, that "The *State of Nature* has a Law of Nature to govern it, which obliges every one."[82] As Grotius taught, the law of nature is obligatory even on those sovereigns most inclined to engage in war. That sovereigns actually manage to have peaceful relations much of the time makes them a useful example of the state of nature as a lawful condition.

The crucial point in this exposition is Locke's "strange Doctrine, *viz*. That *in the State of Nature, every one has the Executive Power* of the Law of Nature." Such a claim is just as "strange" when applied to sovereigns, since their executive power extends ordinarily to their subjects, and not to other sovereigns. At its strangest, or at least most radical, the claim authorizes anyone to dispatch "*Absolute Monarchs,*" who "are but Men," when they disregard natural law.[83] Yet Locke seems to have had a more general point in mind.

Human individuals retain their executive power even after they organize "*Civil Government*" as "the proper Remedy for the Inconveniences of the State of Nature."[84] In Locke's lawful nature, the faculties that human individuals normally have in their possession take the form of natural rights possessed by them all equally. Writing at much the same time, Pufendorf made it clear that one's rights imply duties for others, and vice versa. Locke forcefully addressed the impact of rights on conduct but not duties. People are free to use their executive power to restrain others from "invading" their rights.[85] The recourse to self-help has desirable effects on relations among equals, which civil government in turn reinforces.

If faculties translate into rights in the relations of equals, they translate into property when considered on their own in relation to everything else in nature. "Though the Earth, and all inferior Creatures be common to all Men, yet every Man has a *Property* in his own *Person.* This no Body has any Right to but himself. The *Labour* of his Body, and the *Work* of his Hands, we may say, are properly his."[86] As always with Locke, the human individual is a body first, and faculties are the physical and cognitive aptitudes that any *body* must possess to survive. By nature, the individual is "Proprietor," or rightful owner,

81. Ibid., ii, § 14, 276, original emphasis.
82. Ibid., § 6, 271, original emphasis.
83. Ibid., § 13, 275–76, original emphasis. Also see § 9, 272.
84. Ibid., 276, original emphasis.
85. Ibid., § 7, 271. Also see § 8: "*every Man hath a Right to punish the Offender, and be Executioner of the Law of Nature*" (272, original emphasis).
86. Ibid., v, § 27, 287–88, original emphasis.

of these faculties and, derivatively, of anything "removed from the common state" and altered for use.[87] All that "the spontaneous hand of Nature" makes available—"all the Fruits it naturally produces, and Beasts it feeds"—"is given to Men for the Support and Comfort of their being."[88] If appropriated and then used, this largesse remains in nature, the many parts of which use each other as they must to flourish, so replenishing the whole. By the same reasoning, that which is removed from the common state *must* be used, if it is not to be removed from nature and lost to the whole. Possession for its own sake violates the law of nature as an expression of God's intentions.[89]

In the context of personal relations, the proprietor continues to be executor of all those rights the possession of faculties entails. No such power apparently applied to possessions removed from nature. In his discussion of property, Locke implied—but did not say expressly—that rights to things possessed must be civil rights. Insofar as their use affects the rights of others, civil government is responsible for deciding on the balance of rights and for executing its decisions. For civil society to improve on nature, it must adopt the natural principle of appropriation for use, not accumulation, and determine rightful possession accordingly. The "measure of Property" should confine possession "to a very moderate Proportion."[90]

When in the *Second Treatise* Locke finally turned to the institution of *civil* or *political society*—he used these terms interchangeably—he argued forcefully that rights to land were transferred from its natural proprietors to the government the majority had decided to form.[91] Again his argument hinges on the body as a whole. Civil society and its government constitute a *"Body Politick."*[92] Since it is "one Body, with a power to Act as one Body," it has the rights that any human body, possessed of normal faculties, has in nature, and it gains these rights by transfer from its constituent members, to whom it then has the power to reallocate rights. Proprietors thus manage to secure *"the Preservation of their Property."*[93]

87. Ibid., 288. See Locke, *First Treatise of Government*, ix, § 92, in idem, *Two Treatises of Government*, 209, and *Second Treatise of Government*, v, § 44, 298, for the term *proprietor*. Also see C. B. Macpherson's much cited discussion of its implications (*The Political Theory of Possessive Individualism* [Oxford, 1962]).
88. Locke, *Second Treatise of Government*, v, § 26, 286.
89. Ibid., §§ 31–34, 290–91.
90. Ibid., § 36, 292–93. On medieval adumbrations of Locke's position, see Brian Tierney, *The Idea of Natural Rights: Studies on Natural Rights, Natural Law, and Church Law, 1150–1625* (1997; Grand Rapids, Mich., 2001), chap. 6.
91. Locke, *Second Treatise of Government*, viii, § 120, 348.
92. Ibid., § 95, 331, original emphasis.
93. Ibid., § 96, 331; ix, § 124, 350–51.

The body politic also had the executive power to enforce its rights, through its government, in relations with other governments representing other such bodies. Yet Locke said nothing of this. Nor did he say anything about the normal distribution of aptitudes and abilities, or endowments, among any collection of persons that divided their labors and exchanged their possessions for mutual advantage. Nevertheless, by giving substance to agency, Locke's analysis of persons as bodies with diverse capabilities at their command, and as rightful owners in nature and society, pointed in just these directions.

Memory and Mute Nature

In Locke's analysis of human powers, "retention" comes immediately after perception. Without memory, "all the rest of our Faculties are in a great measure useless."[94] Yet memory is an unreliable adjunct to reasoning, and animals appear to have powerful memories but no capacity for reason. Memory has little importance in Locke's analysis of personal identity. Were it the key to self-consciousness, he could not have said that "a Man Drunk and Sober" is "the same Person" and therefore responsible for acts that he cannot remember.[95] Yet most interpretations of Locke make personal identity dependent on the "memory relation."[96] Perhaps they do so because Locke's analysis is too starkly unsocial not to undergo tacit revision, perhaps because they have mixed Locke's analysis with David Hume's in *A Treatise of Human Nature* (1739–40).[97]

Hume started where Locke did. Thanks to our sensory faculties, we experience a flood of perceptions. "The mind is a kind of theatre, where several perceptions successively make their appearance; pass, re-pass, glide away, and mingle in an infinite variety of postures and situations."[98] Not only does Hume's simile locate the familiar analogy of world and stage inside our heads, it suggests that we need something beyond bodily consciousness to locate our selves in the world. After our perceptions have glided away, we need to be able to bring at least some of them back to mind.

---

94. Locke, *An Essay Concerning Human Understanding*, II, x, § 8, 153.
95. Ibid., xxvii, § 22, 343.
96. Carol Rovane, *The Bounds of Agency: An Essay in Revisionary Metaphysics* (Princeton, N.J., 1998), 14. For conspicuous examples, see John Perry, ed., *Personal Identity* (Berkeley and Los Angeles, 1975), 12–15, and Anthony Paul Kerby, *Narrative and Self* (Bloomington, Ind., 1991), 24–27.
97. David Hume, *A Treatise of Human Nature*, ed. H. Nidditch (Oxford, 1978), I, iv, vi, 251–63.
98. Ibid., 253.

For Hume the faculty of memory is the key to personal identity because it gives meaning to the many disconnected perceptions that our senses shower on us.

> As memory alone acquaints us with the continuance and extent of this succession of perceptions, 'tis to be consider'd, upon that account chiefly, as the source of personal identity. Had we no memory, we never shou'd have any notion of causation, nor consequently of that chain of causes and effects, which constitute our self or person. But having once acquir'd this notion of causation from the memory, we can extend the same chain of causes, and consequently the identity of our persons beyond our memory, and can comprehend times, and circumstances, and actions, which we have entirely forgot, but suppose in general to have existed.[99]

The meaning that memory confers on perception Hume took to be one sort of relation, that of cause and effect, by which the mind gives order to the world.[100] Memory alone cannot account for our sense of singular and continuous consciousness because all of us, and not just Locke's drunkard, forget or misremember. By supplementing and correcting memory with causal inference, we can fill in the gaps. Furthermore, this is a collective activity. We share memories and draw inferences from our shared habits, or customs.[101] Hume's self-conscious beings are creatures like none other: they are creatures of convention.

Hume's elegant analysis takes memory beyond the recall of events and the exchange of reports. Memory is inextricable from the construction of a coherent past and the projection of a plausible future. Such acts are characteristically social and yet they eventuate in personal identity—a strictly personal identity at that. This is because each self can vouch for its own existence in the past and project itself into the future. While any *one* can perform these operations at any given moment of consciousness, with coaching from others as needed, *one* must do so within *one's* own body. After Hume, no one could safely disregard the social content of personal identity. Singular human beings share memories, tell stories, synchronize their habits, preferences, and expectations, and otherwise engage each other in an amazing variety of social practices. Their identities are shaped accordingly. Hume called the state of nature a "philosophical fiction" because "'tis utterly impossible for

---

99. Ibid., 261–62.
100. Ibid., I, i, v, 15.
101. Ibid., I, iii, xvi, 176–79.

men to remain in that savage condition, which precedes society." [102] Nor does society depend on any such contrivance as a social contract.

Instead, the human condition must have been social from the beginning, although oddly so, for in the beginning human beings had no language, no sense of what it meant to make a promise, and no concepts of property, right, and obligation.[103] If this is, in Hume's account, a historical and not an imagined state of affairs, Hume conveyed its nature with a striking analogy: "Two men, who pull the oars of a boat do it by agreement or convention, though they have never given promises to each other." They learn from shared experience, and not by speaking, to coordinate their efforts, and a convention—a rule instructing them to dip their oars in unison—"arises gradually, and acquires force by a slow progression, and by . . . repeated experience of the inconveniences of transgressing it." [104] According to Hume, just such conventions gave rise to language. We may infer that the presence of language will expedite the emergence of conventions without changing the fundamental, always social properties of the process.

Hume's claim that singular, competent persons are caught up, and actively participate, in a social process that has neither beginning nor end lends itself to two distinct readings. One is that human beings live in a vast midden of conventions, many eventuating in material artifacts, reflecting an extraordinary amount of social experience in getting along in the world. In effect, Hume explained where all the rules that Hobbes stripped away had come from, and why they could never be displaced entirely by other kinds of rules, such as those predicated on demands or promises. Such a world depends on talk; conversation is its most basic form of commerce. Smith saw the implications of this most human of conditions: Conversation and the exchange of useful things are inseparable; unrestricted conversation, commercial activity, and moral improvement reinforce each other in a virtuous circle.[105]

---

102. Ibid., III, II, ii, 493.
103. Ibid., 490–91.
104. Ibid., 490.
105. Nicholas Phillipson, "Adam Smith as Civic Moralist," in Istvan Hont and Michael Ignatieff, eds., *Wealth and Virtue: The Shaping of Political Economy in the Scottish Enlightenment* (Cambridge, U.K., 1983), 188–90; Emma Rothschild, *Economic Sentiments: Adam Smith, Condorcet, and the Enlightenment* (Cambridge, Mass., 2001), 243–44; and Andreas Kalyvas and Ira Katznelson, "The Rhetoric of the Market: Adam Smith on Recognition, Speech, and Exchange," *Review of Politics* 63 (2001): 549–79, at 568–70.

Alternatively, Hume's persons are social only in the most nominal sense, the self is "in reality nothing."[106] A social reality that does not depend on language is closer to nature, at least as we think of it today, than anything Hobbes or Locke imagined. In responding to stimuli, human individuals form habits that are social only insofar as other beings form the same or complementary habits. Animals actively participate in habit-driven routines that human beings initiate, and in so doing these "inferior creatures" join human society. Consciousness is beside the point, and consequences, not intentions, are the basis for judgment.

Once we begin to think of human behavior in these terms, human beings cease to be a distinguishable, privileged part of nature—the whole beings who fulfill their potential by finding meaning in, and giving voice to, the whole of nature—that Aristotle and even Locke took them to be. Only then can we think that Smith's "invisible hand" is not the "spontaneous hand of Nature" to which human individuals reach out with their own hands but merely a summary description of natural human behavior in the aggregate. From there it is only a short step to analogies in which mute animals take the place of human beings who might just as well be mute. Joseph Townsend, an English physician, preacher, traveler, and geologist of some reputation, took just this step soon after Hume and Smith published their great works.

While Townsend's name is largely forgotten, his vigorous polemic against public relief, *A Dissertation on the Poor Laws* (1786), stirred considerable interest in its own time and directly influenced Thomas Malthus and, through Malthus, Charles Darwin.[107] Hardly an egalitarian, Townsend argued that "pride, honour, and ambition" motivate the "higher ranks." As for the poor, "it is only hunger which can spur and goad them on to labour." Townsend had no wish to interfere with "distinctions which exist in nature."[108] Nevertheless, the stability of status distinctions in England had long depended on subsidies to the poor, who paid their betters back with indolence.

---

106. "Ourself, independent of the perception of every other object, is in reality nothing: For which reason we must turn our view to external objects" (Hume, *Treatise of Human Nature,* II, ɪɪ, ii, 340). Hume's concern here was sympathy, which proceeds from the fact, as Hume saw it, that "the minds of men are mirrors to one another" (v, 365). As we show in chapter 6, Smith's moral theory departs from Hume's most markedly on this point.

107. Joseph Townsend, *A Dissertation on the Poor Laws by a Well-Wisher to Mankind* (Berkeley and Los Angeles, 1971). On Townsend's influence on Malthus and Darwin, see Ashley Montagu, "Foreword," ibid., 9–13, and Karl Polanyi, *The Great Transformation: The Political and Economic Origins of Our Time* (Boston, 1957), 113.

108. Townsend, *Dissertation on the Poor Laws,* Sect. III, 23, IV, 26.

In Townsend's opinion, it would be better to let people go hungry. At least some of them would make an effort to insure their well-being. Those who would not, or could not, would die. To make his point, Townsend described an uninhabited island on which sailors had left a pair of goats, which multiplied until they had exhausted their food supply. "In this situation the weakest first gave way, and plenty was again restored. Thus they fluctuated between happiness and misery, and either suffered want or rejoiced in abundance, according as their numbers were diminished or increased; never at a stay, nearly balancing at all times their quantity of food."[109]

Later visitors introduced a pair of dogs to the island. The dogs flourished by feeding on the goats, who thereupon "retired to the craggy rocks, where the dogs could never follow them, descending only for short intervals to feed with fear and circumspection." In these circumstances, "none but the most watchful, strong, and active of the dogs could get a sufficiency of food. Thus a new kind of balance was established. The weakest of both species were among the first to pay the debt of nature; the most active and vigorous preserved their lives."[110]

Townsend's island functions as an analogy for any closed set of relations and not as analogy for a generalized state of nature. Once the analogy draws attention to limiting conditions, the things and their relations are functionally identical, despite appearances. Animals do *not* stand in for the indolent (and insolent) poor; the poor are badly fed animals. "The wisest legislator will never be able to devise a more equitable, a more effectual, or in any respect a more suitable punishment, than hunger is for a disobedient servant. Hunger will tame the fiercest animals, it will teach decency and civility, obedience and subjection, to the most brutish, the most obstinate, and the most perverse."[111] By implication, the island's newly arrived predators are no different from the privileged orders in English society: they too play their part in nature's balance. Whatever Townsend's intentions, the story that he told all too readily suggests that human beings, all of them and not just the poor, are animals.[112] This is no analogy from nature—this *is* our nature.

When Malthus shocked readers in 1798 with *An Essay on the Principle of Population,* dispensing with analogy no doubt compounded the shock. To see

---

109. Ibid., VIII, 37.
110. Ibid., 38.
111. Ibid., IV, 27.
112. Cf. Polanyi, *Great Transformation:* "Hobbes had argued the need for a despot because men were *like* beasts; Townsend insisted that they were *actually* beasts and that, precisely for that reason, only a minimum of government was required" (114, original emphasis).

how we, as animals, are subject to the same laws of nature that other animals are, we can take "any spot on earth, this island, for instance"—the island in question the one on which Malthus and seven million other people lived and not an imagined island whose only inhabitants are feral animals. If we accept that survival of the human species depends on the ability to procreate and the availability of food, and that population, if unchecked, will increase much more rapidly than the means of subsistence, then we must ask what conditions or events might limit population before food ran out. Emigration is one answer, but not if we "take the whole earth, instead of one spot, and suppose that the restraints to population were universally removed."[113] At the limit, the world, as nature, constitutes a closed set of relations.

By Malthus's calculation, if there were no check on the natural increase in people and the supply of food, "population would be to the means of subsistence as 512 to 10," and this in just 225 years. Just 75 years later, the ratio would be 4,096 to 13.[114] Comparing ratios over a period of years takes the form of an analogy (A is to B as C is to D) to subvert the constant relation, or proportion, that analogies presuppose in the construction of similarity. For Malthus nature—*our* nature—is a source of peril and disorder because the laws of nature do not have a proportionate relation, and they cannot together fulfill their potential. Townsend's "new kind of balance" is nothing but a euphemism, a metaphor fetched from the past, masking the extent and variety of human misery that our animal natures make inevitable.

As a fixed set of relations, Malthus's conception of the natural world resembles Hobbes's state of nature. Each is a world of limits. Within such a world, competing tendencies produce outcomes that no one would attribute to a nature whose laws constitute an order, or see as the work of an omniscient intelligence. The difference between this view and Locke's, for example, is epistemic. Neither Hobbes nor Malthus represented nature as an "ordered table," to use Foucault's words. Yet Hobbes's state of nature and Malthus's natural world also differ from each other epistemically.

While Hobbes had his players on a stage, today we put them in a game, and we call the state of nature a prisoner's dilemma with many players.[115] We see the prisoner's dilemma everywhere (the name suggests a series of similitudes extensible to the limits of our collective imagination), to the point that we venture to make inferences about rational choice as a human universal—just

113. Thomas R. Malthus, *An Essay on the Principle of Population* (1798; Amherst, N.Y., 1998), chap. 2, at 21, 25.
114. Ibid., 25–26.
115. Gregory S. Kavka, *Hobbesian Moral and Political Theory* (Princeton, N.J., 1986), chap. 3.

as Hobbes did. By contrast, Malthus started with a natural world full of living things, including human beings, ascribed to them a number of necessary attributes, and proceeded to consider aggregate behavior in diverse circumstances. This is nature stripped of its analogical power, rejected as a template for order and reason, and forced to yield its secrets, one by one, to positivist science.

If the way Malthus thought about nature exemplifies an epistemic shift, he had predecessors. Hume's demonstration that memory gives the "notion of causation" its force, and not nature as such, undermines any claim about nature's immanent order. Independently, the great French naturalist Comte de Buffon made a similar argument in the discussion of method that begins his monumental and immensely influential *Histoire naturelle* (1749–88).[116] Buffon's entire project was to put aside systems of classification in favor of assembling as many closely observed details of the natural world as he could (Buffon published thirty-six volumes of the *Histoire naturelle* before his death in 1788), so that "we can see how particular effects depend on more general effects, where we can compare Nature with herself in her great operations."[117] These sober recommendations on methods appropriate to a new natural history nevertheless hint at the reigning view of nature, in which humanity is providentially equipped "to further the plans and intentions of nature. In this teleological conception, nature is virtually personified."[118] Even as Buffon dispensed with the ordered tables of his time, he ordered the earth's history into seven epochs, the last of which features humanity actively taming a wild and hostile nature, not always with the greatest success.[119] This is, of course, conjectural history on the grandest scale.

Buffon's view of nature shows him straddling successive epochs in the epistemic history of modernity. In this he had good company—Smith, for example.[120] Another example is Thomas Jefferson, who deployed Buffon's

116. "A series of like facts or, if you wish, a frequent repetition . . . of the same events, make up the essence of physical truth: what one calls physical truth is thus no more than a probability, but a probability so great that it equals a certainty" (*Premier discours*, Vol. 1, *Histoire naturelle, générale et particulère*, Vol. 1 [1749], quoted in Jacques Roger, *Buffon: A Life in Natural History*, trans. Sarah Lucille Bonnefoi [Ithaca, N.Y., 1997], 90).
117. Ibid., again quoting Buffon's *Premier discours*. Also see generally chap. 6.
118. Clarence J. Glacken, *Traces on the Rhodian Shore: Nature and Culture in Western Thought from Ancient Times to the End of the Eighteenth Century* (Berkeley and Los Angeles, 1967), 664.
119. Buffon, *Histoire naturelle de l'homme*, 3, *Histoire naturelle* (1754); *Les époques de la nature*, 5 supp., *Histoire naturelle* (1774). See Glacken, *Traces on the Rhodian Shore*, 655, 663–81; Roger, *Buffon*, chaps. 11, 23.
120. For a thorough assessment, see Charles L. Griswold Jr., *Adam Smith and the Virtues of Enlightenment* (Cambridge, U.K., 1999), chap. 8.

methods in assembling his *Notes on the State of Virginia* (1785). He regarded Buffon "the best informed of any Naturalist who has ever written," but he took him severely to task for comparing the size of animals, including human beings, in the New and Old Worlds and concluding on the basis of flimsy evidence that animals are smaller, human beings less vigorous, and nature more oppressive in the latter.[121] Yet Jefferson is justly famous for declaring his faith in a universal natural order that confers on humanity the faculties that make us moral persons.[122] To say that we are fated to live in nature *as* animals but that we have rights and duties *as if* by nature's design suggests a measure of epistemic dissonance that persists to this day. With Malthusian readings of Hobbes and Locke disguising the dissonance, positivist science and liberal theory almost seem to belong together.

---

121. Thomas Jefferson, *Notes on the State of Virginia*, ed. William Peden (New York, 1954), Query 6, at 55. Also see Antonello Gerbi, *The Dispute of the New World: The History of a Polemic, 1750–1900,* rev. and enlarged ed., trans. Jeremy Moyle (Pittsburgh, 1973), 3–34, 252–75, and James W. Ceaser, *Reconstructing America: The Symbol of America in Modern Thought* (New Haven, Conn., 1997), 29–37.
122. On Jefferson's conflicting views of nature, see Charles A. Miller, *Jefferson and Nature: An Interpretation* (Baltimore, Md., 1988), chaps. 2–3.

5
Nation
Making

Early modern thinkers often prefaced their inquiries into the human condition with the claim that we are naturally sociable. By implication, we *need* each
other to flourish—so said Aristotle and Stoic philosophers such as Cicero.
Whether we should commit ourselves to the common good or rely on ourselves, doing what we do best takes care of most needs collectively but unevenly; extraordinary need calls for specific assistance. There is no general
duty to come to the aid of others because need resists generalization. Instead, we should be responsive to others' needs. This is, as Adam Smith understood, a virtue and not a rule.

Aristotle and the Stoics nevertheless offered a rule—a rule so informal
that it is never described as such—to help us know when to help others. Our
assistance should not disrupt the natural order of the household writ large:
everyone occupies a fixed place in this order, everyone knows everyone's
place, and with each place come the appropriate privileges and duties. Considerations of status and honor shape everyone's response to anyone's needs.
Always sensitive to these considerations, the church had made a duty of
charity.

Among early modern writers, Samuel Pufendorf had perhaps the bleak-
est view of the human condition. "It is quite clear that man is an animal extremely desirous of his own preservation, in himself exposed to want, unable
to exist without the help of his fellow-creatures, fitted in a remarkable way to
contribute to the common good, and yet at all times malicious, petulant, and
easily irritated, as well as quick and powerful to do injury."[1] Our circum-

---

1. Samuel Pufendorf, *De jure naturae et gentium libri octo,* trans. C. H. Oldfather and
W. A. Oldfather (Oxford, 1934), II, iii, § 15, 207–8.

stances are so dire that we must assist each other simply to survive. Among these circumstances, none is more compelling than that of our birth. We are completely vulnerable and utterly dependent: "scarcely any other animal is attended from birth with such weakness [*imbecillitas*]."[2]

We enter the world helpless and never fully outgrow our dependence on others, beginning with our families. Pufendorf insisted that nature supplies paternal authority (*patria potesta*) in the degree necessary to secure parental support.[3] Organized around paternal power, the household is the primary vehicle for meeting our needs, and the family writ large is the primary analogy for all other social arrangements. Yet the household thus conceived is not simply a repetition of a figure, a sign with interchangeable signifiers, that makes an appearance wherever we look. In short, the Renaissance fascination with similitudes fails to explain the analogy's force.

Instead, the household takes form in nature, and the analogy's force is due to the fact that it represents the natural order of things. In this early modern way of thinking (in Michel Foucault's terminology, the classical *episteme*), paternal authority has its place in the family and society because both are natural in form and function, and they therefore belong together in a class of things subject to systematic comparison. In Pufendorf's assessment of our natural condition, we never outgrow our need for help. As a result, we rely on rationalized and generalized paternal authority to meet our needs. Watchful guardians of the common good must care for us as parents care for their children.

Throughout the eighteenth century, German teachers and writers developed a science of administration—*Cameral-Wissenschaft*—for the promotion of public order and well-being. As Keith Tribe has pointed out, "concepts such as wealth, liberty, need, and happiness" were "linked in a chain of meaning which is founded on the economy as a constitutive moment." Linking them is the imperative to regulate human conduct. Yet "this process of regulation cannot be conceived in terms of state intervention in the economy, for state and economy have no independent existence—or put another way, they are the same thing."[4]

---

2. Samuel Pufendorf, *On the Duty of Man and Citizen* (1673), trans. Michael Silverstone (Cambridge, U.K., 1991), I, iii, § 3, 33. Also see II, i, § 4, 115–16.

3. Ibid., II, iii, §§ 1–2, 124.

4. Keith Tribe, *Strategies of Economic Order: German Economic Discourse, 1750–1950* (Cambridge, U.K., 1995), 8–31, at 12. Also see ibid., 19–118, and Liah Greenfeld, *The Spirit of Capitalism: Nationalism and Economic Growth* (Cambridge, Mass., 2001), 162–84.

Whether household, agrarian estate, or kingdom provides the social context, rationalized paternal authority permits a comprehensive response to every conceivable need and eliminates threats to the statuses and privileges ordering society. This is the classical *episteme* in defense of the old regime. With the advent of the modern *episteme* (again, Foucault's terminology), paternal authority assumed a new form and a different function. It did so in response to a changing sense of what the nation is, itself a complex response to the vicissitudes of the old regime in an age of revolutions. As before, paternal authority gave the social body its head. Yet the nation-body was different; it transformed the economy from "a constitutive moment" to a living, growing thing. That nineteenth-century nation making had more to do with human needs than natural rights changed Smith's kind of history into national histories. That nineteenth-century nation makers took for granted nation-bodies with heads possessing cognitive powers, including volition, took them beyond early modern thinking.

"Qu'est ce que c'est une nation?"

Enlightenment writers had been using the term *nation* informally and reflexively for several decades when abbé Emmanuel Joseph Sieyès, one of the great architects of republican France, asked his portentous question, "Qu'est ce que c'est une nation?" in 1789.[5] David Hume, for example, said in 1748 that "a nation is nothing but a collection of individuals" nevertheless distinguishable by "a peculiar set of manners" that are "habitual" to them. Because "the human mind is of a very imitative nature," social intercourse tends to make us alike, "as it were, by contagion."[6] With Hume, Montesquieu assumed that a nation has a character discernible in its distinctive manners, but, far more

---

5. Emmanuel Joseph Sieyès, *What Is the Third Estate?* trans. M. Blondel (New York, 1964), 58. "In the 18th century, 'nation' became a word of fashion" (Guido Zernatto, "Nations: History of a Word," *Review of Politics* 6 [1944]: 351–66). Cf. Jacques Godechot, "The New Concept of the Nation and its Diffusion in Europe," in Otto Dann and John Dinwiddy, eds., *Nationalism in the Age of the French Revolution* (London, 1988): "In 1789, the word *nation* became the favourite word of the revolutionary generation" (14). On the Revolution and French national identity, see Hans Kohn, *Prelude to Nation-States: The French and German Experience, 1789–1815* (Princeton, N.J., 1967), pt. 1; Liah Greenfeld, *Nationalism: Five Roads to Modernity* (Cambridge, Mass., 1992), chap. 2; and Mlada Bukovansky, *Legitimacy and Power Politics: The American and French Revolutions in International Political Culture* (Princeton, N.J., 2002), chap. 5.
6. David Hume, "Of National Characters," *Essays Moral, Political and Literary*, ed. Eugene F. Miller (Indianapolis, Ind., 1985), 198, 202.

than Hume, he thought that climate and topography determined manners. In effect, nations are indistinguishable from the countries—"cold countries," "fertile countries"—that shape their characters.[7] Montesquieu also invested these manners with moral significance. "The various characters of the nations are mixtures of virtues and vices, of good and bad qualities."[8] Such is the spirit of nations. They are moral persons, even if circumstances condemn them to morally reprehensible histories.

For Hume and Montesquieu, a nation is a collection of people who are, for all their differences, distinguishable as a people. What distinguishes them is the experience of living together and becoming like-minded. Montesquieu held that the particular features of place helped make the people living there a nation, and that national character shapes the political life of the country, while Hume held that being "united into one political body" was the crucial determinant of nationhood.[9] Despite these different emphases, the Enlightenment conception of a nation seems conspicuously modern in comparison with traditional understandings of the term *natio* still current in the eighteenth century: any people who live together (for example, university students) because they happen to come from the same place.[10]

Yet the Enlightenment conception of nation lacked one element that we now treat as central: it failed to consider whether people think themselves a people. This is precisely what Sieyès had hoped to evoke when he asked his famous question, thus mobilizing an emerging sense of national identity. Sieyès' answer to this question did not require the language of consciousness, which is unavoidable in contemporary discussions of the question. Ever since René Descartes' meditation on thinking and being, European writers separated subjective experience and the objects of the world: I think and therefore am conscious of myself; I think about myself, and I see an individual being who is also a social animal. With most of his contemporaries, Sieyès located himself on the objective side of the Cartesian divide.

Because he was not concerned with individual consciousness, Sieyès did not need to postulate a group consciousness. Since he paid little attention to manners, and his prose is noticeably free of references to the nation's *esprit*,

---

7. Montesquieu, *The Spirit of the Laws,* trans. Anne M. Cohler et al. (Cambridge, U.K., 1989), bk. 14, chap. 2, 232, bk. 18, chap. 2, 286.
8. Ibid., bk. 19, chap. 10, 313.
9. Ibid., chap. 14, 315–16; Hume, "Of National Characters," *Essays,* 202.
10. On the shifting sense of the term from its Roman and medieval uses to its modern meaning, see Zernatto, "Nations"; Greenfeld, *Nationalism,* 4–12; and E. J. Hobsbawm, *Nations and Nationalism since 1780: Programme, Myth, Reality,* 2nd ed. (Cambridge, U.K., 1992), 14–24.

we cannot infer an unconscious presumption of group consciousness (not that we should make any such inference about Montesquieu and Voltaire just because they do make conspicuous use of this term). Sieyès did, nevertheless, grant intentions to nations, emphasizing their wants and needs: "the people wants to become *something*, and in fact, the least thing possible." To use a Cartesian formula, collective entities are "thinking things." "Gone is the day," wrote Sieyès, "when the three orders were moved by the single thought of defending themselves against ministerial despotism and were ready to unite against their common enemy. Today, however, the nation cannot turn circumstances to advantage or take the slightest step towards social order without the third estate deriving some side-benefits thereby."[11]

The "least thing" that a nation can possibly be is a "body of associates." As John Locke's analysis of personal identity suggests, a body, not Cartesian self-awareness, is the first requirement of moral personality. Only bodies can have continuous identities, powers and rights, needs and wants. A collective body thus is something more than "a collection of individuals," to quote Hume, something other than a shapeless, undifferentiated mass or unencumbered spirit, ever changing in shape and direction. "It is impossible to create a body for any purpose," Sieyès explained, "without giving it the organisation, procedures and laws appropriate for it to fulfil its intended functions. This is called the *constitution* of this body." Even if nobody actually creates such a body and it arises spontaneously, as the unintended consequence of many bodies using their faculties and responding to their wants and needs, it will spontaneously develop a constitution in order to fulfill its unintended functions.[12]

Sieyès adopted the standard Enlightenment model of historical development. First "a fairly considerable number of isolated individuals . . . wish to unite; by this fact alone, they already constitute a nation." Responding to "public needs," they work together, and by doing so form "a common will." In due course, "they put a few of their number in charge," and, finally, they "delegate" responsibility to some "body of representatives" who act on behalf of the whole body.[13] In other words, a nation is, or soon becomes, a political

---

11. Sieyès, *What Is the Third Estate?* 67, 140, emphasis in translation. "*Res cogitans*"—thinking thing—is Descartes' famous formula for the meditating self.
12. Ibid., 58, 123, emphasis in translation. The Aristotelian resonances in this way of thinking are unmistakable. For a discussion of Aristotle's impact on early modern thinkers, see Nicholas Onuf, "Institutions, Intentions, and International Relations," *Review of International Studies* 28 (2002): 211–28. On the properties of institutions that arise spontaneously, see Peter Onuf and Nicholas Onuf, *Federal Union, Modern World: The Law of Nations in an Age of Revolutions, 1776–1814* (Madison, Wisc., 1993), pt. 1.
13. Sieyès, *What Is the Third Estate?* 121–22.

body. Sieyès thus echoed Hume, who argued that a collection of individuals becomes distinguishable as a nation when it takes form as a political body.

Political bodies have heads—individuals with heads and bodies, intentions and powers—whose office it is to act on behalf of other members. Even if the head is a body of officers, they too must act on behalf of a single head. This is Thomas Hobbes's conception of agency as representation, his great contribution to the theory of moral personality. Sieyès differed from Hobbes, however, on the issue of priority and thus necessity. For Hobbes the formation of the body politic presupposes the existence of a "Naturall Person" who becomes its head.[14] For Sieyès "the nation is prior to everything," including its political institutions. The head represents the body only insofar as the body, consisting itself of many heads, suffers the head to do so.[15] Representation is a *function* for which any number of institutional arrangements may prove to be suitable.

In this respect, the British constitution was hardly an adequate model. "Look at the national representation! See how imperfect it is in every respect, as the English themselves admit!"[16] Sieyès saw little value in the British example, nor did he need Hobbes and Locke to appreciate the properties of bodies politic. France had a long history of identifying the body of the king with the body politic. As Antoine de Baecque has remarked, "no 'History of France' is complete without a chapter on the body or bodies of the king thought of as metaphors."[17] During the seventeenth century, the king became more than the head he had always been; all of France was absorbed into his metaphorical person.[18] A century later, the potency of the king and the perpetuation of the royal line were subjects of intense public interest. The popular belief that King Louis XVI was impotent may have subverted the traditional identification of the king's body and the body politic, thus preparing the way for his execution in 1793.[19]

The issue for Sieyès was not the king's body. That Louis XVI lost his head could not mean that France had no head, or that the nation had expired with the king. Yet it was certainly possible to reach such a conclusion in 1789. "What

---

14. Thomas Hobbes, *Leviathan,* ed. Richard Tuck (Cambridge, U.K., 1991), I, xvi, 111.
15. Sieyès, *What Is the Third Estate?* 124.
16. Ibid., 113. Although Sieyès was aware of contemporaneous constitutional developments in the United States (see 192 n. z), he seems not to have considered them relevant to the situation of the French nation, perhaps because British North America had limited experience with the old regime of privileged orders.
17. Antoine de Baecque, *The Body Politic: Corporeal Metaphor in Revolutionary France, 1770–1800,* trans. Charlotte Mandell (Stanford, Calif., 1997), 76.
18. Ibid., 89–90. It should be noted, however, that, at least in de Baecque's judgment, Hobbes's writings significantly contributed to this process.
19. See ibid., chap. 1.

is the foundation of monarchical government?" asked one pamphleteer.[20] "It is neither a headless body, as in Poland, nor a bodiless head, as with the Turks; it is this: in France, the king is the head of the state; the armed forces are the hands; the magistrates . . . are the mouth, eyes, and ears; they are the organs of the brain, which is the king. The king is also the heart, the stomach; and the magistrates are the vitals. Nobles are the trunk that surrounds them; the people are the arms, the thighs, the legs, and the feet." Each part of the body performs a specific function or, in the case of "the monarch-brain-heart-stomach," "functions." Obviously, the body dies if there is no king, while the people are interchangeably available for their many secondary functions.

The political implications of this sort of functional anatomy are clear. The French nation cannot survive without its head and heart, and it cannot function as a healthy being unless its parts are properly arranged. Relations among France's three estates, and between the estates and the crown, must not change. Sieyès sought to refute this conclusion, which draws on an old anatomical tradition, in order to make it metaphorically plausible for the third estate to head the French nation. As de Baecque has masterfully shown, Sieyès and his compatriots turned to recent advances in clinical medicine—thereby anticipating a distinctively *modern* way of thinking about life—to make the case for a fundamental rearrangement of political institutions.

> This body of clinical medicine is a political weapon . . . : in it, the principle
> of life is neither localized nor organized into a hierarchy . . . , while the blood
> and nerves reconstruct one single, unique body, the indivisible "I," . . . . This
> nonhierarchical connection between each member, first principle of life, "con-
> stituent energy of the 'great citizen body'" even before the just paramountcy
> of the monarchical *caput*, and especially before the effective localization of
> privileges, thus meets its most precise correspondence in the circulation of
> the blood.[21]

The purpose of the Revolution, as Sieyès saw it, was to divest the nobility and the clergy of their ancient privileges because neither of these bodies contributed to the health and well-being of the whole body. Sieyès insisted that "the so-called usefulness of a privileged order to the public service is a fallacy." Is not the third estate the one body "containing within itself everything needful to be a complete nation? It is like a strong and robust man with one arm still in chains. If the privileged order were removed, the nation would

---

20. Bénigne Victor Aimé Noillac, *The Strongest of Pamphlets*, quoted ibid., 86–87.
21. Ibid., 86–96, at 93.

not be something less but something more."[22] Hobbes had imagined stripping away statuses in order to investigate the human condition; Sieyès
stripped statuses from useless bodies to benefit the nation as a whole. If the
king lost his life, if the magistrates lost their offices, if the nobility lost everything, then a rejuvenated body politic would regenerate its necessary parts,
starting with a new, more representative institution at its head.[23]

"Was ist das Volk?"

French revolutionaries, like their Enlightenment predecessors, could talk
the way they did about the French nation because France was already a political body and had been one for a very long time. Other European countries with a distinguishable people and stable political arrangements were
nations too: this was a distinguishing feature of European civilization. There
was, however, a crucial exception to this general point of view. There might
be a place called Germany, and a German people, but there was no such political body. Following a century of religious turmoil, the Thirty Years' War
left Germany with dozens of political bodies, each with its own head, for
which the Holy Roman Empire provided a nominal head of heads, disconnected from any body. As Pufendorf famously observed, the empire was a
monstrosity, defective by its very nature.[24]

The Revolution in France and the wars that followed made educated
Germans conscious of the *nation* as idea and ideal—and, in their own case,
a quandary. The French had destroyed the empire in 1806, and with it the
fiction that Germany could be considered a *nation* in the fullest sense of the
term. Johann Gottlieb Fichte's epochal *Addresses to the German Nation* (delivered in 1807) offered an implicit solution to the conceptual problem of a
once-German nation with many princely heads: a would-be German nation
of German nations. A hundred years later, Friedrich Meinecke popularized
Fichte's solution in *Weltbürgertum und Nationalstaat* (1907), his magisterial
history of the rise of German national identity after the Enlightenment. "Despite all the obvious reservations that can be made, we can still divide nations
into cultural nations and political nations, nations that are based primarily on

---

22. Sieyès, *What Is the Third Estate?* 56–57.
23. On the concept of regeneration in Revolutionary discourse, see de Baecque, *Body
Politic,* chap. 3.
24. On Pufendorf, see Onuf and Onuf, *Federal Union, Modern World,* 65–68. On the political backdrop and its relation to the conceptual issues then under debate, see Constantin Fasolt, *The Limits of History* (Chicago, 2004), chaps. 2–4.

some jointly experienced cultural heritage and nations that are primarily based on the unifying force of a common political history and constitution."[25]

Cultural nations come first. When they acquire a "firm territorial base," stable institutional arrangements will eventually produce political nations such as England and France. In these cases, "it is difficult to distinguish cultural and political nations from each other" and pointless even to try. Political experience brings cultural nations to life. "We can distinguish an early period in which nations have a more plantlike, impersonal existence and growth and a later period in which the conscious will of the nation awakens. In this later period, if only through the agency of its leaders, the nation becomes aware of itself as a great personality, as a great historical unit, and it now lays claim to self-determination, the mark and privilege of the mature personality." Political nations have bodies; they are persons; they make their way in the world. Cultural nations either remain vegetables or, thanks to their political embodiment, become moral persons possessed of a "conscious will."[26]

In Fichte's time, the cultural nation of Germany still possessed a "vegetative character"; it lacked "the inner impulse to become a political nation and to create a national state that would circumscribe it."[27] Nor did it possess a third estate that could be given a head and launched into action. In France, at least according to Sieyès, the third estate was a body that included farmers, merchants, and "all sorts of occupations, from the most distinguished liberal and scientific professions to the lowest of menial tasks."[28] But German society developed quite differently over the centuries, making a revolution in the French manner inconceivable. Most occupations had acquired corporate identities that were secured by an elaborate set of status markers. "The entire disjointed and amazingly ornate world of the *ancien régime*, the entire system of the regional, local and social institutions worked against nationalization from above. The patrimonial powers and the corporations divided and absorbed the public spirit to a great extent. The idea of the whole was visible only in innumerable refractions."[29]

25. Friedrich Meinecke, *Cosmopolitanism and the National State*, trans. Robert B. Kimber (Princeton, N.J., 1970), 10, footnoted omitted. Whether Meinecke's history can be thought of as liberal in any meaningful sense is debatable. See Louis L. Snyder, *German Nationalism: The Tragedy of a People*, 2nd ed. (Port Washington, N.Y., 1969), chap. 11. In charting the liberation of German national identity from the constraints of Enlightenment cosmopolitanism, it nevertheless follows a conjectural model of progressive development.
26. Meinecke, *Cosmopolitanism and the National State*, 10, 11, 12, footnote omitted.
27. Ibid., 14.
28. Sieyès, *What Is the Third Estate?* 53–54.
29. Meinecke, *Cosmopolitanism and the National State*, 14.

The king's plan to convene the Estates General in 1789 gave the priest Sieyès his vocation as "doctor of the body politic."[30] Prussia's humiliation on the battlefield in 1805 gave Fichte, *Bildungsbürger* and onetime cosmopolitan, his vocation as cultivator of the German spirit.[31] To bring the cultural nation of Germany out of its vegetative state, Fichte sought to make German people proud of themselves or, more accurately, of their German character. Fichte had no doubt that Germany had a national character, however undeveloped. Distinguishing the German people even from other Teutonic peoples is an "honest diligence and earnestness in all things"; as a people with a "living language," it "is really and truly in earnest about all mental culture [*Geistesbildung*]"; all the people are "capable of education."[32]

Fichte's *Addresses* are largely concerned with *Bildung*—education in the general sense of the development of character—and its relation to the development of the people as a whole. Thus, "a people in the higher meaning of the word" consists of "the totality of men continuing to live in society with each other and continually creating themselves naturally and spiritually of themselves, a totality that arises together out of the . . . law of divine development [*Entwicklung des Göttlichen*]." This law determines "the national character of a people [*Nationalcharakter eines Volks*]."[33] Just as humanity has a common character diversely expressed in individual human beings, so it is with nations. "Only when each people, left to itself, develops and forms itself in accordance with its own peculiar quality, and only when in every people each individual develops himself in accordance with that common quality, as well as in accordance with his own peculiar quality—then, and only then, does the manifestation of divinity appear in its true mirror as it ought to be."[34] Left to themselves, nations will develop as they must, and their peoples will fulfill their human potential.

Fichte reminded his auditors in 1807 (they were few) that several years earlier he had proposed closing Prussia to the world, thereby insuring that its people would be left to themselves and their "peculiar mode of life." In these circumstances, "a high degree of national honour and a sharply distinguished

---

30. This is de Baecque's turn of phrase, chapter title, *Body Politic*, 76.
31. On "*Bildungsbürgertum:* The Dangerous Class," section title, see Greenfeld, *Nationalism,* 293–302.
32. Johann Gottlieb Fichte, Fourth Address, *Addresses to the German Nation*, trans. R. F. Jones and G. H. Turnbull (New York, 1968), 60–61; idem, *Reden an die Deutsche Nation* (Hamburg, 1955), 74.
33. Fichte, Eighth Address, *Addresses*, 115, and Fichte, *Reden,* 129.
34. Fichte, Thirteenth Address, *Addresses*, 197–98.

national character are bound to arise very quickly."[35] Closed borders and reliance on domestic goods would make the cultivator's work easier. The people would no longer wish to imitate the artificial manners of Europe's self-styled civilized nations, borrow from an alien legal heritage, or receive in trade "the booty of other worlds."[36]

Without surgically separating Germany from the world—an act as revolutionary as any Sieyès proposed—Fichte's political program to enable the German nation to fulfill its divine destiny consisted of "the new national education," which he made the subject of five of his fourteen *Addresses*. Fichte argued that the state should take the lead in instituting a universal scheme of public education, but he saw little chance that any of the existing German states would rise to the challenge. It remained for "well-disposed private persons" to shoulder the burden.[37] Given the highly differentiated, corporate character of German society, Fichte's proposal was nothing more than a dream, and a deeply liberal dream at that.

In Fichte's Germany, the romantic reaction against Enlightenment rationalism had already given rise to a conservative reaction against liberal sentiments. No German writer articulated the new conservatism more clearly than Adam Müller, whose most substantial work, *Die Elemente der Staatskunst*, appeared in 1809.[38] Müller's solution to the problem of nation making was to enhance the position of the state. To do this he had to ignore the German problem—the problem of many actual German states—and to imagine a virtual identity between state and nation. *"The state is the totality of human affairs, their union into a living whole."*[39] Yet this "living whole" was nothing other than the cultural nation, which, as Müller eloquently

---

35. Ibid., 196–97. Johann Gottlieb Fichte, *The Closed Commercial State* (1800), trans. H. S. Reiss and P. Brown, in Reiss, ed., *The Political Thought of the German Romantics, 1793–1815* (New York, 1955), 86–102, at 102.

36. Fichte, Thirteenth Address, *Addresses,* 196.

37. Ibid., Eleventh Address, 170.

38. Perhaps surprisingly, there is no English translation of this book. For an excerpt, however, see Reiss, *Political Thought of the German Romantics,* 143–71. On the German romantics and their political thought, see ibid., 1–11; Meinecke, *Cosmopolitanism and the National State,* 49–70; Kohn, *Prelude to Nation-States,* 168–86; and Greenfeld, *Nationalism,* 322–52. On Müller, see Meinecke, *Cosmopolitanism and the National State,* 95–117, and, Kohn, *Prelude to Nation-States,* 187–93. On romanticism and conservatism with particular reference to Müller, see Karl Mannheim's classic study, *Conservatism: A Contribution to the Sociology of Knowledge,* trans. David Kettler and Volker Meja (London, 1986), 111–52. Also of interest is Carl Schmitt's *Political Romanticism,* trans. Guy Oakes (2nd ed., 1925; Cambridge, Mass., 1986), where the German romantics, exemplified by Friedrich Schlegel and Müller, are pilloried for their political vacuity.

39. Adam Müller, *Die Elemente der Staatskunst,* in Reiss, ed., *Political Thought of the German Romantics,* 157, emphasis in translation.

explained, had no need of being awakened from the vegetative trance that Fichte had found it in.

In reply to the question, *"was ist das Volk?"* they [Sieyès and his compatriots] answered, "the collection of ephemeral creatures with heads, two hands, and two feet which happened to be standing, sitting or lying side by side, displaying all the external signs of life, at the present miserable moment upon the stretch of earth called France," *instead of answering,* "a people is the sublime community of a long succession of bygone generations, together with generations yet to come, all of whom are bound together in a great, intimate association for life and unto death, in which each generation—and within each generation, every single human individual—stands surety for the association as a whole and in turn is given surety by the association for its own existence in its wholeness. And this beautiful and immortal community presents itself to the eyes and to the senses by means of a common language, common customs and laws, thousands of beneficent institutions, many long-flourishing families [*i.e.,* noble families] singled out to tie and even chain the ages together, and, finally, the one immortal family placed at the centre of the state, the reigning family and—to come even closer to the very heart of things—the present head of this family and the bearer of its estate."[40]

At the time affiliated with the Weimar court, Müller could hardly have believed that Saxe-Weimar was a "living whole." Lecturing in Dresden, he was no more likely to have believed Saxony was such a whole, or that the ruler of either state was the "head" at the "very heart of things." Prussia and its king might be construed this way, but then the totality in question could not be the German nation that Fichte had addressed. At least it could not be the German nation without a program of political unification under Prussian auspices, a project that neither Müller—a Catholic convert who ended up in Vienna—nor his princely patron and aristocratic audience would have found appealing. If Müller was conveniently vague about the mechanics of nation making, he and Fichte supplied necessary and complementary components to its realization. Müller emphasized the need for political leadership in an inclusive state, while Fichte promoted a national system of education that would teach Germans their history, customs, and institutions in their own "living language." Such a language "unites within its domain the whole mass of men who speak it into one single and common understanding, which is the

40. Adam Müller, *Die Elemente der Staatskunst,* ed. Jacob Baxa (Jena, 1922), 145, quoted in Mannheim, *Conservatism,* 98, emphasis in translation.

true point of meaning and mingling for the world of the senses and the world of the spirits."[41]

When millions of Germans became individually conscious of all they have in common, they will constitute a body. When this body has an appropriate head, it will function *as if* a living body—an animal's body and not just a vegetative mass. Such a body need not be "conscious" as a whole; it only needed an organ consciously capable of acting on behalf of the whole and of directing the action of the body's many parts. Yet German writers went further than this. The combination of Immanuel Kant's philosophical legacy and the romantic yearning for the ineffable blurred the Cartesian line between subjective consciousness and objective circumstances: a body of human beings acting *as if* conscious of itself as a whole *is* a self-conscious being; it *has* consciousness. No term makes this clearer than *Geist,* the term Fichte used in the passage just quoted to signal his attack on the Cartesian separation of objective and subjective worlds.

Indicatively, G. W. F. Hegel published in 1807 a philosophical treatise called *The Phenomenology of Spirit* (or *Mind: Phänomenologie des Geistes*), devoted, as one commentator has said, to "the experience of consciousness," not its "embodiment."[42] In Hegel's last major work, *The Philosophy of Right,* nations are, or function as, embodied individuals because they are independent states.[43] Nevertheless, subjective experience dominates the concluding paragraphs of *The Philosophy of Right,* which address the relation of the "spirits of nations" to "universal spirit" and thus the prospective development of the world as a whole.[44] "The history of spirit is its own *deed;* for spirit is only what it does, and its deed is to make itself—in this case as spirit—the object of its own consciousness, and to comprehend itself in its interpretation of itself to itself." While nations "have their objective actuality and self-consciousness as *existent* individuals," all such individuals "are at the same time the unconscious instruments and organs" of a generalized and thus disembodied spirit, which "in and for itself prepares and works its way towards the transition to its next and higher stage."[45]

---

41. Fichte, Fourth Address, *Addresses,* 59.
42. John Russon, *The Self and Its Body in Hegel's* Phenomenology of Spirit (Toronto, 1997), 3.
43. G. W. F. Hegel, *Elements of the Philosophy of Right,* trans. H. B. Nisbet (Cambridge, U.K., 1991), III, III, A, § 322, 359.
44. Ibid., B, § 340, 371, C, §§ 341–60, 372–80.
45. Ibid., §§ 343, 340, 344, 371–73, emphasis in translation. On the state as an "actuality" possessing a "particular *self-consciousness,*" see ibid., III, § 258, 275, emphasis in translation.

Hegel's transcendent cosmopolitanism may not have captured the German imagination, but, as this formulation suggests, the idea that nations are somehow conscious beings was becoming a commonplace, and not just among German speakers. When the French theologian Ernest Renan repeated the question, "What is a nation?" in an influential Sorbonne lecture in 1882, his answer might seem rhetorically romantic: "A nation is a soul, a spiritual principle." He said this to emphasize what a nation is not. "Man is the slave neither of his race, nor his language, nor his religion, or of the windings of his rivers and mountain ranges. That moral consciousness which we call a nation is created by a great assemblage of men."[46]

Moral consciousness ("*conscience morale*") is the subjective state that a body of conscious persons must possess to be a moral person. When, in *The Division of Labor in Society* (1893), Émile Durkheim wanted to characterize the "totality of beliefs and sentiments common to average citizens of the same society," he adopted the "well-worn expression, collective or common conscience [or consciousness: *conscience collectif*]."[47] This was not just a well-worn expression but a highly ambiguous one, as Durkheim noted in limiting his use of it to "social likenesses." If Durkheim expressly refrained from identifying collective consciousness with "the total psychic life of society," his readers were unlikely to be as fastidious, especially when faced with the methodological difficulties of establishing a totality of beliefs or identifying an average citizen. Even less would Renan's auditors construe moral consciousness narrowly as the aggregate of a people's beliefs, especially after hearing that the nation *is* "a spiritual principle."

Nevertheless, Renan was no slave to his romantic rhetorical inclinations. In favor of "modest empirical solutions," he offered an explanation for national solidarity: "A nation, like the individual, is the fruit of a long past spent in toil, sacrifice, and devotion."[48] The past is not an objective state of affairs but an ensemble of memories, cumulatively sorted, repeated, and invested with significance. Lockean personal identity depends on the body's continuous existence; Humean personal identity depends on memory. When people

---

46. Ernest Renan, "What Is a Nation?" in Omar Dahbour and Micheline R. Ishay, eds., *The Nationalism Reader* (Amherst, N.Y., 1999), 153, 154.
47. Émile Durkheim, *The Division of Labor in Society,* trans. George Simpson (New York, 1964), 79–80. In French, *conscience* can mean *conscience* or *consciousness* as those terms are ordinarily understood in English. "*Conscience* [*Gewissen*] expresses the absolute entitlement of subjective self-consciousness to know *in itself* and *from itself* what right and duty are, and to recognize only what it thus knows as the good" (Hegel, *Elements of the Philosophy of Right,* II, II, § 137, Remarks, 164, emphasis in translation).
48. Renan, "What Is a Nation?" 155, 153.

share their memories with each other, they alter what they think they remember, and the memories are shared: they no longer belong to anyone in particular, even if they blend with private memories to constitute particular identities.

People construe their shared memories as history. "The modern nation," according to Renan, "is the historic consequence of a series of facts converging towards the same point." As he emphasized, history involves forgetting as well as remembering. "To forget and—I will venture to say—to get one's history wrong, are essential factors in the making of a nation; and thus the advance of historical studies is often a danger to nationality."[49] Renan's conclusion that historians threaten a nation by reminding its people of what they have forgotten is problematic. In fact, historians such as Meinecke have significantly contributed to nation making in the nineteenth century by authoritatively selecting and interpreting events to comport with the claims of national identity.

In any event, the nation is, as Renan claimed, an unfolding product of history and, as such, "a daily plebiscite."[50] Or, as we say today, the nation is a social construction, always subject to change by virtue of what people choose to remember. From Sieyès to Renan, from Müller to Meinecke, the idea of the nation deepened and colored; it came alive. The move from anatomy to history, from the nation as a living thing to the nation as lived history maps a world becoming modern. If revolution and war brought the world of nations to the brink of modernity, then history—the modern history of nations, one by one but never as one, at peace and in war—maps the arc of an age.

Self-Determination

In a passage quoted earlier, Meinecke averred that "the nation becomes aware of itself as a great personality" and, in doing so, it "lays claim to self-determination, the mark and privilege of the mature personality." German thinkers were preoccupied with the concept of self-determination [*Selbstbestimmung*] ever since Kant sought to base moral action in the autonomous will. Only rational beings possess wills because they alone are free and able

---

49. Ibid., 145–46, 145. Also on memory and forgetting, with particular reference to Renan, see Benedict Anderson, *Imagined Communities: Reflections on the Origin and Spread of Nationalism,* rev. ed. (London, 1992), chap. 11.
50. Renan, "What Is a Nation?" 154.

to set ends for themselves.[51] Linking will and self-consciousness, Hegel held that "anyone can discover in himself an ability to abstract from anything whatsoever, and likewise to determine himself, to posit any content in himself by his own agency."[52] Hegel imputed self-consciousness to the nation but failed to specify how it might exercise its agency in any practical sense. Meinecke was specific but off-handed: "if only through the agency of its leaders, the nation becomes aware of itself."

To this day, writers speak of *will*. Ernest Gellner did so in a chapter of his influential *Nations and Nationalism,* unsurprisingly entitled "What Is a Nation?" In his judgment, "effective and cohesive nations . . . do in effect will themselves to be such, and their life may indeed constitute a kind of continuous, informal, ever-reaffirming plebiscite."[53] Yet nations do not actually "will themselves" to be anything at all, and daily life constitutes a "plebiscite" only in the vaguest possible sense. Gellner resorted to this kind of language because he wanted to establish nationalism as an autonomous force: "It is nationalism which engenders nations, and not the other way round."[54]

Like so many other recent writers, Gellner attributed conscious agency to nationalism, but with even less warrant than its conventional attribution to the nation. If nationalism "is not what it seems to itself," if indeed, it is a "self-deception," we are left wondering what it might be.[55] Gellner's answer subverts the premise that nationalism is an expression of collective consciousness: "nationalism is, essentially, the general imposition of a high culture on society, where previously low cultures had taken up the lives of the majority, and in some cases of the totality, of the population." Imposition takes the form of "a school-mediated, academy-supervised idiom, codified for the requirements of reasonably precise bureaucratic and technological communication." This process depends on particular agents—educators, journalists, civil servants, "print-capitalists"—most of whom embrace modernity

---

51. Immanuel Kant, *Groundwork of the Metaphysics of Morals,* trans. Mary Gregor (Cambridge, U.K., 1998), Sections II–III: "Rational nature is distinguished from the rest of nature by this, that it sets itself an end" (44).

52. Hegel, *Elements of the Philosophy of Right,* intro., § 4, Remarks, 37. See generally Ernst Tugendhat, *Self-Consciousness and Self-Determination,* trans. Paul Stern (Cambridge, Mass., 1986).

53. Ernest Gellner, *Nations and Nationalism* (Ithaca, N.Y., 1983), 53.

54. Ibid., 55.

55. Ibid., 56–57. Elsewhere Gellner scorned the "group mind" theory in the course of defending the explanatory relevance of social factors not reducible to the properties and dispositions of individual human beings (Ernest Gellner, "Explanations in History" [1956], in John O'Neill, ed., *Modes of Individualism and Collectivism* [London, 1973], 248–63, at 251).

and its trappings, although many are not nationalists in any self-conscious sense.[56]

Linguistic standardization is undoubtedly implicated in, and perhaps indispensable to, making people conscious of belonging to a nation. They may come to believe that the nation has a will or life of its own; indeed, they are quite likely to believe this. To the extent that such beliefs are widely shared, it is no doubt convenient to speak of nationalism and plausible to say that modern cultural elites have made nationalism a force to be reckoned with, whether they had this end in mind. Yet there is more to national self-determination than making people conscious of belonging to a nation. Somebody—some body of agents consciously acting on behalf of the nation—must convince the rest of the world that the nation, not nationalism, is the force to be reckoned with.

Contemporary practice has firmly established the principle that peoples, or nations, should be free to choose their destinies. Writers typically trace the concept back to the revolutions in British North America and France, and this genealogy explains the decided tendency both to construe self-determination as a natural right and to find its proper expression in the votes of a majority of the inhabitants in a particular territory.[57] In the case of the barely united states of British North America, self-appointed agents took up arms on behalf of a people for whom identity and will were far more the result of the struggle and its aftermath than its cause. The peace treaty with Britain transferred territory, and the adoption of the Constitution retroactively confirmed the corporate identity of the people residing therein. In France's case, overwhelming military success enabled people conscious of being French to join their compatriots through the transfer of territory to France. Plebiscites expedited the process by establishing the majority will within regions subject to annexation, although votes against unification did not always deter French expansionism.

---

56. Gellner, *Nations and Nationalism,* 57, and Anderson, *Imagined Communities,* chap. 3, for "print-capitalists." Anderson emphasized "largely unselfconscious processes" in the development of "print-languages." "But as with so much else in the history of nationalism, once 'there,' they could become formal models to be imitated, and, where expedient, consciously exploited" (45). We should note that the obliteration of "low culture" involves considerably more violence and dislocation than Gellner's description suggests.

57. The literature on this subject is predictably enormous. Alfred Cobban's classic study, *The Nation-State and National Self-Determination,* rev. ed. (New York, 1970), remains useful. For good general treatments, also see U. O. Umozurike, *Self-Determination in International Law* (Hamden, Conn., 1972), and Antonio Cassesse, *Self-Determination of Peoples: A Legal Reappraisal* (Cambridge, U.K., 1995). Reference specifically to national self-determination dates only from the late nineteenth century.

In both the United States and France, readily identifiable agents effected the process of self-determination. They did so with a determination otherwise absent in the people and with resources not generally available to cultural elites. Yet neither the self-declared United States nor revolutionary France constituted the model case of national self-determination. In such a case, the nation lies within and substantially fills the bounded territory of a state, and the state, as an apparatus of rule, provides the nation with direction. The coincidence of state and nation permits an organic whole to function as if it were a conscious being fully able to care for its own needs.

The model case of self-determination assumes that Gellner's modernizing elites dominate the state apparatus. France before the Revolution offers an example (as Meinecke suggested). Whether Spain does depends on judgments about the degree to which people were conscious of being Spanish after 1492 and the relation of national consciousness to the activities of modernizing elites, if indeed there were any. The Dutch republic at its commercial zenith is perhaps a more ambiguous example than one might think.[58] Britain offers the best example, well before and even after its American colonies revolted.[59]

A British people conscious of its nationhood—a modern nation—could only approximate the model case of self-determination because Britain was also a gens, authenticated as such by the jus gentium, familiar to nineteenth-century Europeans as international law, *droit des gens* or *Völkerrecht*. After the Napoleonic settlement, there were few states that could be more or less identified with modern nations, and quite a number of states in which nations, at least in any modern sense of a nationally conscious people, simply did not exist. Modern nations relate to each other as states, and the agents of states decide whether nations constitute states and therefore qualify for regular relations with other nations as states. Such a nation is *not* to be confused with the *natio,* although most contemporary commentaries fail to remark on the difference.

Formed as states, nations resemble one another in decisive respects. This is because they are standardized according to a general jurisprudential

---

58. "There was no national consciousness in the Dutch Republic, the identity of the Dutch Republic was not national and the Republic was not a nation," so Liah Greenfeld has argued, against the prevailing view, in reference to the Dutch "Golden Age" of the seventeenth century (*Spirit of Capitalism*, 96, see generally chap. 2).

59. Linda Colley, *Britons: Forging the Nation, 1707–1837* (New Haven, Conn., 1992); Greenfeld, *Nationalism,* chap. 1; Greenfeld, *Spirit of Capitalism,* chap. 1; and Kenneth Robert Olwig, *Landscape, Nature, and the Body Politic: From Britain's Renaissance to America's New World* (Madison, Wisc., 2002), xviii–xxx, chap. 3.

template. Formed by cultural elites, nations are different by design. This is because the process of standardizing them internally sets them apart from other nations. Meinecke's distinction between political and cultural nations helps capture the difference.[60] We must bear in mind, however, that political nations are not simply willed into existence as an act of self-determination. Other political nations, recognizing each other as states, must recognize claimant political nations as states like themselves.

On philosophical grounds, Hegel held that recognition (*Anerkennung*) is a requirement of individual selfhood.[61] In the world of states, recognition emerged as a conscious practice by which to identify members of international society as a legal order. Under the law of nations, national self-determination could never refer to the process through which people come to be conscious of belonging to the *natio*. Instead, it must refer to the process by which a well-formed gens achieves recognition as a functioning state. Once recognized, the state is in a position to expedite the process by which people identify the gens, as one nation among many, with the *natio*, the one nation to which they have an exclusive attachment.

When nation and state coincide, we may plausibly speak of the *right* of national self-determination. The right attaches to the state, the agents of which are conscious of belonging to the nation. By helping other people to become conscious of belonging to the cultural nation, they exercise this right on behalf of the people as a political nation. The agents of other states have a corresponding duty not to interfere in this process.

All too obviously, nation and state rarely coincide so neatly. Agents of a state may claim to represent a nation some part of which lies within the territorial limits of another state, and the latter's agents will respond that such actions violate their state's rights. Or agents may claim to represent a nation contained within a multinational empire and not rightfully represented by the imperial apparatus of rule. Both situations lend themselves to the medical

---

60. Also see Cobban, *Nation State and National Self-Determination*, 108–14. The difference between gens and *natio* parallels the distinction between *Einzelheit,* "mere oneness" (one among many of the same kind) and *Einzigheit,* "uniqueness" (the only one of its kind)—the latter reflecting the "aesthetic and sociohistorical idiom of German Romanticism" (Rogers Brubaker, *Citizenship and Nationhood in France and Germany* [Cambridge, Mass., 1992], 9, drawing on Georg Simmel). Cf. Foucault's conjecture that classical thinking fixates on the *kind*, modern thinking on the *one*.

61. In *The Phenomenology of Spirit,* Hegel argued that conscious beings must recognize others as self-conscious in order to be fully conscious of themselves as selves. The absence of mutual recognition in the relation of master and slave prevents the master from achieving full self-consciousness (See Robert R. Williams, *Hegel's Ethics of Recognition* [Berkeley and Los Angeles, 1997]).

imagery so characteristic of nation making. In the first situation, the "doctors of the body politic" perform surgery on nation-bodies, perhaps by precipitating a war leading to the transfer of territory and the relocation of large numbers of people. Alternatively, the doctors may get together and deal with the problem by agreeing to form a single state or to redefine the territorial limits of both states, perhaps guided by plebiscites designed to elicit the will of the majority of the affected people. Where discontented minority populations afflict newly configured states, doctors have an implicit mandate to purge nation-bodies of foreign elements through policies such as linguistic standardization and forced emigration.

Given vested interests and murky circumstances, agreements involving transfer of territory are difficult to achieve. Fomenting irredentist agitation and civil war are often tempting alternatives, and pretexts for forcible intervention and occupation are always available. Where one state has greater capacities than its neighbors, including the ability to mobilize national sentiments, the messy and extended process of realigning states and nations is likely to be expedited, particularly when affected states go to war. Revolutionary France provides the first instance of territorial consolidation in the name of national unification, while the creation of modern Germany and Italy exemplifies a process in which statecraft benefited from the inseparable glorification of war and nation. Peace treaties and international recognition complete the surgery, but the process of making nation-states functional wholes only ends when wounds heal.

Metaphorically speaking, the second situation is more obstetric than surgical. Agents claiming to represent a nation—a political nation awaiting birth and the chance to grow up as a cultural nation—may be said to function as midwives. With their assistance, the new nation exercises its bodily right of self-determination and enters the modern world of nation-states. State doctors will repudiate these claims and take other measures as they see necessary to protect the functional integrity of the imperial body. The latter will succeed unless the new nation is equipped to survive the rigors of birth and the world into which it is born.

If the new nation is to survive, self-appointed national agents must be able to mobilize national sentiments and material resources. Simultaneously, they must attack and discredit the imperial body politic, and they must organize the functional elements of a body politic for the new nation. A declaration of independence marks the moment at which the new nation is said to act for itself, but it is not yet the moment of birth. At some point, national agents will have organized sufficiently to campaign for outside support, including support from the agents of other states, ranging from public professions of sympathy and solidarity to clandestine material support.

Although not inevitable, civil war is exceedingly likely. Substantial military operations may prompt agents on both sides to recognize a state of war subject to the international law of war. Agents of other states will respond to such a war with particular care, because substantial material support is an obvious violation of international law and a prelude to active involvement in the war. If state agents cannot prevail in a drawn-out war and national agents are able to exercise the normal functions of state in the regions they control, then the former may accept the loss of territory and acknowledge that the new nation is indeed a nation-state. Or agents of other states will begin to see that the advantages of recognizing the new nation as a state outweigh the disadvantages of offending an imperial state in distress, and the latter has little choice but to accept the consequences. Either way the process ends in the birth of a new nation-state.

The revolt of the Dutch against Spain and that of the colonists in North America against Britain offer examples of the process in which multinational empires gave birth to new nation-states. Whether the Dutch republic or the United States were cultural nations before they were political nations and then nation-states is beside the point. The American South offers an example of national self-determination that proceeded very quickly both in cultural and political terms. As the Civil War gained in ferocity, Britain considered recognizing the Confederacy, only to realize that such an act would constitute intervention against the Union.[62] However much the wartime blockade did cost British manufacturing interests, a hostile Union could have cost Britain far more. Denied recognition and attendant material support, the Confederacy failed the final test of nationhood.

More or less at the same time, the formation of cultural nations within the Austro-Hungarian Empire launched the process of imperial dissolution. Yet the relatively slow development of political nations retarded their birth until World War I, after which the principle of national self-determination helped states' agents redraw the map of Europe. The principle found impressive reinforcement in the United Nations Charter and the subsequent development of international law. Rapid decolonization after World War II produced nation-states where, in some instances, neither cultural nor political nations existed in any meaningful sense; many of the beneficiaries of decolonization were hardly in a position to determine much of anything for themselves. In recent decades, states' agents have resisted the claim that self-determination

---

62. Nor was Britain alone: France and Russia also considered recognition, but all maneuvering ended with the British decision against intervention in any form (See Howard Jones, *Union in Peril: The Crisis over British Intervention in the Civil War* [Chapel Hill, N.C., 1992], chap. 9).

is a right of nations, as opposed to a principle of international law. By implication, such a right is natural, nations are primordial, and no state can prevent any nation from fulfilling its destiny, whatever the consequences for the state in question. By contrast, the principle of self-determination, as a matter of statecraft, presumes that every nation must be made to order before it can occupy its place in the modern world of nation-states.

In the end, self-determination hinges on the willingness of agents acting on behalf of states—the doctors of the bodies politic—to issue a birth certificate. Unless there are unusual circumstances, such as world war or massive decolonization, the doctors need to be persuaded that any new state is well formed and healthy. This in turn depends on meeting formal requirements designed to show that the would-be state can indeed function as a state. A less formal requirement is no less important. Given the model of one nation, one state, the nation to which the new state corresponds must be credible as a nation that can flourish in a world of nation-states.

Self-Reliance

As we have seen, nineteenth-century commentaries emphasized the cultural and political properties of the nation, in keeping with the two ways that we normally speak of self-determination. It was also possible to emphasize the economic properties of a nation in order to make credible claims on its behalf. Here the point is not self-determination but self-reliance. Not to be confused with the Aristotelian goal of a self-sufficient *polis* (or Fichte's call for a closed state), self-reliance is a practical virtue and always a matter of degree. Those persons, individual or collective, possessing this virtue are enterprising enough to care for their own needs. Only they can hope to avoid dependence on others and benefit fully from the division of labor.

British settlers in North America dealt with isolation and harsh conditions by becoming self-reliant in practice. In keeping with their circumstances, they denied that others might be their betters, they were quick to assert their rights, and they emphasized future possibilities over past failures and personal limitations. A risky war of independence ratified a collective disposition to go it alone more or less together. The West always beckoned. Americans identified themselves as such by affirming their like-minded attachment to individualism, which, in turn, gave liberal ideas a pragmatic relevance altogether missing in Europe.

In a European context, Jean-Jacques Rousseau had prescribed rural simplicity as an antidote to the mannered excesses of a commercial civilization predicated on a division of labor. For Smith nostalgia for a lost age of innocence reversed an equation that he thought was a given. From Smith's historical perspective, it was clear that if individuals intent on self-improvement were left to their own devices, they could count on collective benefits. In Rousseau's conjectural history, the collective consequences of an unimpeded division of labor undermined individual self-reliance; "slavery and misery" were the inevitable result.[63] If some Europeans romanticized a rustic past, Thomas Jefferson and his followers extolled a rusticated republic far removed from the status preoccupations, mercantilist policies, and chronic conflict of Europe's royal houses.[64]

Both versions of self-reliance came to be associated with what had been lost, not gained. Ralph Waldo Emerson's famous essay "Self-Reliance" (1841) starts as an inspirational anthem and ends as an indictment of civilization. "The civilized man has built a coach, but has lost the use of his feet." Emerson indicted the civilization whose history Smith had extolled: "reliance on Property, including the reliance on governments which protect it, is the want of self-reliance." As if Rousseau had come back to life in the New World, Emerson chastised all those who "measure their esteem of each other by what each has, and not by what each is."[65] Of course, he was talking about his property-owning compatriots.

By contrast, Alexander Hamilton had argued that the economic development of the United States hinged on policies and improvements enabling people to take advantage of the division of labor, associate productively, exchange what they produced, and improve their lives.[66] In turn, the nation would be able to assure its independence and increase the general level of prosperity in a world where some nations—Britain most of all—benefited

---

63. Jean-Jacques Rousseau, *Discourse on the Origin and Foundations of Inequality among Men,* in Victor Gourevitch, ed., *Rousseau: The Discourses and Other Early Political Writings,* trans. Gourevitch (Cambridge, U.K., 1997), pt. 2, 166.

64. On self-reliance as a "strategy for development," see J. Ann Tickner, *Self-Reliance versus Power Politics: The American and Indian Experiences in Nation-Building* (New York, 1987), chap. 1; on self-reliance as Rousseau's and Jefferson's strategic alternative to development, see chaps. 2, 4. On debates over political economy in the United States during its formative period, see Cathy D. Matson and Peter S. Onuf, *A Union of Interests: Political and Economic Thought in Revolutionary America* (Lawrence, Kans., 1990) and John E. Crowley, *The Privileges of Independence: Neomercantilism and the American Revolution* (Baltimore, Md., 1993).

65. Ralph Waldo Emerson, "Self-Reliance," in *The Collected Works of Ralph Waldo Emerson,* Vol. 2 (Cambridge, Mass., 1979), 48–49. On the relation of the self-reliant individual to society in Emerson's work, see George Kateb, *Emerson and Self-Reliance* (Thousand Oaks, Calif., 1995), chaps. 5–6.

66. Jacob E. Cooke, ed., *The Reports of Alexander Hamilton* (New York, 1964). Also see Tickner, *Self-Reliance versus Power Politics,* chap. 5, and Crowley, *Privileges of Independence,* chap. 7.

from the vulnerabilities of other nations. A self-reliant nation nurtured the self-reliant individuals on whom the nation could rely. The policies and improvements needed to set this virtuous spiral in motion included a national banking system for rational debt management, the protection of manufacturing for a balanced internal division of labor and better prospects in the world division of labor, and investment in transportation for the better circulation of goods and thus the development of the home market. Borrowing a phrase from Hamilton, Henry Clay gave the *American System* its most coherent expression in 1820, and he and others pressed it for many years.[67]

The American System was predicated on the existence of a nationwide customs union. The states of the union could not exact levies on goods crossing their respective borders. Nor could they do so with respect to foreign goods. Only the federal government could set tariff rates and, as a primary source of revenue, collect duties. Smith's critique of the mercantile system was aimed, at least in the first instance, against barriers to exchange within nations by eliminating corporate privileges and immunities. When representatives of the several states constituted the United States as a customs union, they achieved this aim of Smith's. Yet by giving the federal government the power to set tariff rates, they guaranteed the new nation a significant source of internal stress even as they equipped it with an indispensable instrument of foreign policy in a world still dominated by imperial ambitions and mercantilist practices.

Had the United States not been set up as a customs union, it is difficult to imagine it surviving very long in a world of nation-states. Nevertheless, the new nation's federal arrangements left open the extent to which the government could take additional measures to strengthen the national economy. Diverging conceptions of self-reliance associated with Jefferson and Hamilton precipitated party alignments and factional politics, played out over mat-`ters such as debts, tariffs, and public works. The last of these matters raised anew the problem of corporate privilege. The Supreme Court definitively affirmed that private corporations had a place in the new nation (1819) and that they could function as monopolies in providing public services (1837).[68] Incorporated business firms played an important role in promoting the rapid

---

67. George Dangerfield, *The Awakening of American Nationalism, 1815–1828* (New York, 1965), chap. 7; Maurice G. Baxter, *Henry Clay and the American System* (Lexington, Ky., 1995), chaps. 5–7; and James E. Lewis Jr., *The American Union and the Problem of Neighborhood: The United States and the Collapse of the Spanish Empire* (Chapel Hill, N.C., 1998), chaps. 4, 5.

68. *Trustees of Dartmouth College v. Woodward; The Proprietors of the Charles River Bridge v. The Proprietors of the Warren Bridge. United States Supreme Court Reports,* 4 Wheaton (1819), 518–714, 11 Peters (1837), 420–649.

growth of manufacturing and improvements in transportation, as did the nation-building projects of the federal government, a rapidly growing work-force, open land for settlement, and even a managed degree of foreign competition.

These developments were unevenly distributed across the country. Later in this book, we explore the way in which tariff policies reflected and then reinforced sectional differences already defined by reference to economic relations with the rest of the world. Both Northern beneficiaries of protec-tion and Southern beneficiaries of free trade began to see their sections as economic nations. With slavery the wedge between them, they even began to see their sections as cultural nations. For both, control over westward ex-pansion became the key to self-reliance for their respective nations.

Friedrich List was one of the foremost advocates of national self-reliance or what today is called "economic nationalism."[69] Born in a free city of the Holy Roman Empire, sometime civil servant, journalist, political activist, and prisoner, List sought refuge in the United States from 1825 to 1830, where he raised funds for a railway to his coal mine, became a citizen, and, as an editor of a German-language newspaper, emerged as "a powerful champion of the 'American System.'"[70] On his return to Europe, he urged the French to consider the advantages of a national railway system and worked tirelessly for the creation of a customs union and a railway system to bring the German states into a single, national-scale market. In 1841, List published *Das na-tionale System der politischen Œconomie,* for which he drew extensively on earlier work published in the United States and on his practical experience in the development of a national economy.

List situated the national system of political economy, or, more simply, na-tional economy, between private economy on the one hand and "cosmopo-litical" economy on the other. The former refers to what individual human beings do for themselves and their families, while the latter refers to "the whole human race."[71] Binding them together is the national economy, to which both are inextricably connected. Yet Smith and his followers, whom

---

69. See, for example, Eric Helleiner, "Economic Nationalism as a Challenge to Economic Liberalism? Lessons from the 19th Century," *International Studies Quarterly* 46 (2002): 307–29, at 308–14.

70. W. O. Henderson, *Friedrich List: Economist and Visionary, 1789–1846* (London, 1983), 70. For other assessments of List and his ideas, see Snyder, *German Nationalism,* chap. 4; Tickner, *Self-Reliance versus Power Politics,* chap. 3; Roman Szporluk, *Communism and Nationalism: Karl Marx versus Friedrich List* (New York, 1988), chaps. 7–9; and Green-feld, *Spirit of Capitalism,* 199–214.

71. Friedrich List, *The National System of Political Economy,* trans. Sampson S. Lloyd (Lon-don, 1928), 97–100, 132–33.

List called "the popular school," disregarded this central fact. Instead, they believed that the pursuit of individual self-interest connects the private and cosmopolitical economies directly: "in order to attain to the highest degree of national prosperity, we have simply to follow the maxim of letting things alone (laisser faire et laisser aller)."[72] Following this maxim also produces the highest degree of prosperity for the whole human race. If leaving people to pursue their own interests is best for everyone, then national prosperity is just one aggregate index of many that are possible, there is no need for the apparatus of state, and talk of nations is not just vacuous but misleading.

Smith took for granted the nation as an institutional framework. The term he used to frame his discussion of the home market is *society;* at worst, he can be accused of hazy thinking about markets, nations, and societies in relation to each other. Thomas Cooper, a free trade economist from cotton-exporting South Carolina, provided a better target for List, if only because he took the school's position "to extremes." According to List, Cooper "denies even the existence of nationality; he calls the nation 'a grammatical invention,' . . . a nonentity, which has no actual existence save in the heads of politicians."[73] By taking such a position, Cooper had in effect made the methodological claim (as we would say today) that the whole of humanity is nothing more than the sum of the individuals composing it. Just such a claim underlies laissez faire as a maxim, or empirical generalization, about the effects of maximizing behavior for *any* aggregate of individuals.

List was committed to quite a different empirical generalization. Human beings have always organized themselves to provide for their needs. These entities, to which List gave the generic label *nation,* cannot be reduced to individuals and their dispositions.

> Between each individual and entire humanity . . . stands THE NATION, with its special language and literature, with its peculiar origin and history, with its special manners and customs, laws and institutions, with the claims of all these for existence, independence, perfection, and continuance for the future, and with its separate territory; a society which, united by a thousand ties of mind and of interests, combines itself into one independent whole, which recognises the law of right for and within itself, and in its united character is still opposed to other societies of a similar kind in their national liberty, and consequently can only under the existing conditions of the world maintain self-existence and independence by its own power and resources.[74]

---

72. Ibid., 133, citing *Wealth of Nations,* IV, ii, where Smith invoked the "invisible hand."
73. Ibid., 133, 99.
74. Ibid., 141.

In time, nations acquire singular identities, just as individual human beings do, and they must then deal with each other, as nation-states, in what can only be styled a liberal society.

List made no claims about a group mind or spirit, and his characterization of the nation bears only a superficial resemblance to Müller's.[75] Nor did he need to make such a claim to demonstrate that the nation is (as Durkheim would later say) a *social fact*. Even before addressing the implicit question, What is a nation? he emphasized what nations do, which is to provide for human needs not otherwise met and, in the process, shelter the *"mental capital of the present human race."* If the "present state of the nations is the result of the accumulation of all discoveries, inventions, improvements, perfections, and exertions of all generations which have lived before us," then nations do what individuals fail to do for themselves: "mere individuals do not concern themselves for the prosperity of future generations—they deem it foolish (as Mr Cooper really demonstrates to us) to make certain and present sacrifices in order to endeavour to obtain a benefit which is as yet uncertain and lying in the vast field of the future."[76] Organized to meet needs over time, nations link the needs of future generations to the experiences of past generations, and they are better able to do so as members of the nation, and especially its organized element, draw on these experiences to develop the nation's functional capacities.

List considered the full and balanced development of a nation to be its "normal state."

A nation in its normal state possesses one common language and literature, a territory endowed with manifold natural resources, extensive, and with convenient frontiers and a numerous population. Agriculture, manufactures, commerce, and navigation must be all developed in it proportionately; arts and sciences, educational establishments, and universal cultivation must stand in it on an equal footing with material production. Its constitution, laws, and institutions must afford to those who belong to it a high degree of security and liberty, and must promote religion, morality, and prosperity; in a word, must have the well-being of its citizens as their object.[77]

Nevertheless, "an infinite difference exists in the condition and circumstances of the various nations: we observe among them giants and dwarfs,

---

75. For scholarly opinion on the degree to which List drew inspiration from Müller, see Szporluk, *Communism and Nationalism,* 99–101.
76. List, *National System of Political Economy,* 113, emphasis in translation, 140.
77. Ibid., 142.

well-formed bodies and cripples, civilised, half-civilised, and barbarous nations."[78] Not all of these differences are fixed by circumstances. Organized
as states, nations can adopt policies helping them to develop well-formed
bodies. List drew on a long metaphorical heritage—less German than
French—to make the case for balanced development and self-reliance.

> *A nation which only carries on agriculture, is an individual who in his mat-*
> *erial production lacks one arm.* Commerce is merely the medium of exchange
> between the agricultural and the manufacturing power, and between their
> separate branches. A nation which exchanges agricultural products for foreign
> manufactured goods is an individual with one arm, which is supported by a
> foreign arm. This support may be useful to it, but not so useful as if it possessed
> two arms itself, and this because its activity is dependent on the caprice of the
> foreigner.[79]

List's metaphors make nations seem like living beings, with bodies, limbs,
heads, powers unimpeachably their own. If they lack human consciousness,
they embody features that make them at least potentially capable of a degree
of self-reliance beyond that which we, as needy individuals, can hope to
achieve. List's running critique of Smith and "the popular school"—for example, that "his doctrine at once sinks deeper and deeper into materialism,
particularism, and individualism"—makes him sound like a conservative romantic; before List, Müller had used a crude caricature of Smith for target
practice.[80] Nevertheless, List had personal experience with the benefits (and
perils) of individual initiative for private economy, and he favored self-
reliance—within limits.

> As individual liberty is in general a good thing so long only as it does not run
> counter to the interests of society, so is it reasonable to hold that private
> industry can only lay claim to unrestricted action so long as the latter consists
> with the well-being of the nation. But whenever the enterprise and activity of
> individuals does not suffice for this purpose, . . . there ought it for the sake of
> its own interests to submit to legal restrictions.[81]

---

78. Ibid., 141.
79. Ibid., 130, emphasis in translation.
80. Ibid., 111. On Müller and the conservative romantic reaction against *Smithianismus*, see
    Greenfeld, *Spirit of Capitalism*, 196–99.
81. List, *National System of Political Economy*, 139.

Some of these restrictions follow from the ineluctable fact of human need. "In North America millers are bound under a penalty to pack into each cask not less than 198 lbs. of good flour, and for all market goods market inspectors are appointed, although in no other country is individual liberty more highly prized. Everywhere does the State consider it to be its duty to guard the public against danger and loss."[82] The nation as state also imposes restrictions and otherwise intervenes in private economy to protect the nation and its individual members from the self-interested conduct of other nation-states and their members. List's position here is standard political realism: "so long as other nations subordinate the interests of the human race as a whole to their national interests, it is folly to speak of free competition among the individuals of various nations."[83]

Had Smith given as much thought as List had to the nation and its relation to the world, he would not necessarily have rejected List's conclusion. "The arguments of the school in favour of free competition are thus only applicable to the exchange between those who belong to one and the same nation. Every great nation, therefore, must endeavour to form an aggregate within itself, which will enter into commercial intercourse with other similar aggregates so far only as that intercourse is suitable to the interests of its own special community."[84] From this general conclusion, List derived specific policy recommendations already familiar to him in the form of the American System, starting with tariffs to protect and promote manufacturing.

As a Briton, Smith had no incentive to think through the relation between cosmopolitical and national economy, because Britain had the world's most advanced economy. Having developed first, Britons could sell manufactured goods and buy agricultural goods on advantageous terms; if free trade benefits the world, it benefits Britain most of all. "The popular school betrays an utter misconception of the nature of national economical conditions if it believes that such nations"—here List was referring to the United States— "can promote and further their civilisation, their prosperity, and especially their social progress, equally well by the exchange of agricultural products for manufactured goods, as by establishing a manufacturing power of their own." Yet List did not support a comprehensive system of protection, for self-sufficiency was not the point. "Neither is it at all necessary that all branches of industry should be protected in the same degree. Only the most important branches require special protection, for the working of which

82. Ibid., 134–35.
83. Ibid., 139.
84. Ibid.

much outlay of capital in building and management, much machinery, and therefore much technical knowledge, skill, and experience, and many workmen are required."[85]

List's cogent defense of protectionism depends on a view of national history as proceeding through a familiar series of four stages in economic and social development: hunting and gathering, herding, agriculture, and commerce. As we have seen, Smith was a principal in developing this sort of conjectural history. List extended and adapted the scheme to include manufacturing in the last stage.[86] In cosmopolitical fashion, Smith and his contemporaries had a decided tendency to offer their conjectures in universal terms, to generalize about the development of a European civilization, and thus to minimize national differences. List could write in an Enlightenment idiom: "The more industry and agriculture flourish, the less can the human mind be held in chains, and the more are we compelled to give way to the spirit of toleration, and to put real morality and religious influence in the place of compulsion of conscience."[87] Yet even here, List's frame of reference is the quest for civilization within nations.

Appropriately protected, those nations "favoured by nature"—"*the countries of the temperate zone*"—would achieve full and balanced development and thus self-reliance. On that distant day, and only then, would free trade favor all nations (even those destined to remain agricultural nations forever), and only then would civilization take on cosmopolitan proportions. "*The popular school has assumed as being actually in existence a state of things which has yet to come into existence.* It assumes the existence of a universal

85. Ibid., 144–51, at 145. Conversely, some British advocates of free trade had serious misgivings about exporting machinery and capital (Bernard Semmel, *The Rise of Free Trade Imperialism: Classical Political Economy, the Empire of Free Trade, and Imperialism, 1750–1850* [Cambridge, U.K., 1970], chap. 8).

86. "As respects their economy, nations have to pass through the following stages of development: original barbarism, pastoral condition, agricultural condition, agricultural-manufacturing condition, and agricultural-manufacturing-commercial condition" (List, *National System of Political Economy*, 143). Also see List, *National System of Political Economy*, 184–88, and Bert F. Hoselitz, "Theories of Stages of Economic Growth," in Hoselitz et al., *Theories of Economic Growth* (Glencoe, Ill., 1960), 193–238, at 198–204. Hoselitz wrongly held that "there is little distinction between the last two stages" (199). The last stage differs from the one preceding it because the nation no longer needs to restrict foreign commerce to develop; the last stage, and that stage alone, affords the well-formed nation the luxury of balanced development of agriculture, commerce, and manufacturing. On List's reckoning, only Britain had reached the last stage, but France was close; Germany and the United States were to be found in the preceding stage, while Spain, Portugal, and the Kingdom of Naples remained in the agricultural stage (List, *National System of Political Economy*, 93).

87. Ibid., 168.

union and a state of perpetual peace, and deduces therefrom the great benefits of free trade. In this manner it confounds effects with causes."[88]

For List nation making comes first, and world making follows in train. By this logic, the American South should have sought self-determination, but only if such a nation made economic sense—something that List might well have doubted, given its marginal place in the temperate zone. By the same logic, the North should have pursued its own destiny, or resisted the South with all its might, depending on a judicious assessment of economic consequences. The logic of nation making turns conjectural history outside in. As an Enlightenment cosmopolitan and moral historian, Smith could hardly have recognized it. In List's time, liberal historians began to write national histories, and to do so self-consciously. Most of them still do, although they are perhaps less conscious of doing so. Not many years after List's death in 1846, the logic of nation making brought civil war and great carnage to the liberal world.

---

88. Ibid., 131, 102, emphasis in translation.

PART II

Markets, Nations, and War

The Civil War looms large in the national imagination. It is a defining moment for Americans, yet its outcome and impact remain ambiguous. The union survived, perhaps with "a new birth of freedom"—perhaps not even with that, given the subsequent history of race and civil rights in the United States. Because the carnage seems so excessive, if not pointless, questions of causation have proven endlessly controversial.

Were the great sacrifices of the Civil War the price Americans had to pay in order to destroy slavery and reaffirm their fundamental commitment to freedom? Did Civil War constitutional amendments ending slavery and extending civil rights to freedmen finally complete the American founding? Or was emancipation the unintended by-product of a war fought for other, less exalted reasons? Did the war come, as revisionists suggested, because a "blundering generation" squandered the founders' precious legacy of union, thus plunging the nation into a bloodbath? Or, as apologists for the Confederacy claim, was the war the result of an assault on fundamental principles of states' rights and minimal government that demolished an alternative, more truly American way of life? All of these questions take the national narrative as a given. Northern victory and the restoration of the union sustained that narrative, whether or not the promise of American nationhood was fulfilled.

A curious result of all these efforts to make sense of the Civil War—to explain its "coming" in light of its outcome—has been to discount and dismiss the ideas and intentions of its protagonists. Surely good Americans could not have foreseen such a horrific outcome. The tragic mode so often deployed in depictions of the Civil War gives the senseless slaughter a kind of dignity and gravity. Abraham Lincoln recognized "the hand of God in this terrible visitation." Because of "our own faults and crimes as a nation and as individuals," a country that was "once, by the blessing of God, united, prosperous and happy, is now afflicted with faction and civil war."[1]

We think that Lincoln knew better. Southerners and Northerners knew exactly what they were doing, as much as any historical actors *can* know what they are doing. The best approach to understanding their thinking is to situate them in the modern world we have described—the world as contemporaries conceived it—*not* in the American national narrative.

On the brink of war, Southerners and Northerners had come to see themselves as members of two distinct and hostile nations. The secession crisis and the war that followed gave definition and substance to those two nations, enabling powerful governments to mobilize resources and sacrifice lives on an unprecedented scale. We emphasize the crucial, co-constitutive link between modern war and modern nationhood; in doing so, we reject the romantic mythology of sectionalism, that North and South were embryonic proto-nations that discovered their essential, irreconcilable differences through a series of crises that progressively revealed the union's tenuous character. What precocious nationalists claimed for their would-be "nations" and the actual perceptions and behaviors of their putative peoples were radically divergent. Southern "nationalists"—like nationalists everywhere—sought to give their project a legitimating pedigree by inventing a distinctive sectional history and thus imagining a distinctive communal identity. If Northern protectors of the union rejected these Southern pretensions, insisting that union and nation were coterminous, their obsession with the "slave power"—the vast conspiracy of slaveholding oligarchs to exercise mastery over nominally "free" as well as slave states—pointed in the same direction: the persistence of the "peculiar institution" south of the Mason-Dixon Line gave rise to distinctive forms of rule and distinctive conceptions of what it meant to be civilized.

A widely shared and meaningful sense of national identity, of belonging to a particular "people," is both the *product* and the *predicate* of conceptual developments that take substantial, institutional form in the "real" world of politics and war. Our task is to explain how some Americans could come to think of other Americans as "foreigners," and therefore potential enemies, without tracing the outcome back to some supposedly original difference or divergence—Virginians' purchase of a few slaves in 1619?—that made the war "inevitable." The focus on sectional exceptionalism and its more or less distant origins makes sections seem "natural" and the union artificial: without

---

1. Lincoln, Proclamation of a National Fast Day, Aug. 12, 1861 in Roy Basler, ed., *The Collected Works of Abraham Lincoln,* 9 vols. (New Brunswick, N.J., 1953–55), 4:482.

a genuine national history, the heterogenous plurality of peoples who called themselves "American" could only share the most minimal sense of common identity. But this is nonsense. Revolutionary Americans were inspired by patriotic commitments to their common, continental cause, and subsequent generations were equally fervent in espousing their new nation's providential role in world history—including the generation that plunged into war, as Lincoln's wartime eloquence makes clear. There was no patriotism deficit in 1861. Quite the contrary, a surfeit of patriotic feeling (or what the revisionists called "an excess of democracy") that was generated by deepening sectional conflict—and frustrated by the compromises and the corrupt party politics that kept the union together—helped bring on the Civil War.[2]

Yet there was nothing "inevitable" about this conflict. If anything, the sectional crisis reinforced loyalty to the union, in the South as well as the North, although agreement on what "union" meant and entailed was increasingly elusive. As William W. Freehling has so forcefully argued, there were "many Souths" and the likelihood they would ever coalesce into a single, unified South—if, in fact, they ever did—was highly problematic and contingent.[3] During the protracted secession crisis, the future boundaries of the Confederate nation were subject to various determinants: investment (financial, legal, and social) in racial slavery, border state commercial and cultural connections with the "Cotton Kingdom" of the Deep South and free states to the north, and calculations of the future balance of political and military power. Under these confusing circumstances—in the "fog" of prewar mobilization—Southern nationhood was the project of revolutionary agitators, not a political or social fact. Southern nationalists had to overcome tremendous obstacles, within and beyond the South, in order to fulfill their aspirations. Most crucially, they had to exploit and redirect powerful patriotic commitments to the existing union.

Students of Civil War causation may be asking the wrong question when they look for more or less remote origins or seek to identify a precise moment when violent conflict became inevitable. We might ask instead, why did the union survive as long as it did? Given powerful centrifugal tendencies in the federal system toward the formation of regional alliances and the coincidence of leading sectors of the economy with particular sections—not to mention chronic conflict over slavery and its westward expansion—the survival of the

---

2. The phrase is from the title of David Donald's *An Excess of Democracy* (Oxford, 1960).

3. William W. Freehling, *The Road to Disunion: Secessionists at Bay, 1776–1854* (New York, 1990); idem, *The South against the South: How Anti-Confederate Southerners Shaped the Course of the Civil War* (New York, 2001).

union seemed as "miraculous" as the founding fathers' success in establishing one in the first place.

The founders hoped that an increasingly harmonious and interdependent union of interests would secure the success of their experiment. A developing continental economy would mitigate and transcend conflicts of interest among disconnected colonies in the British imperial trading system; ultimately, nation and market would converge. To a remarkable extent, the founders' prophecy was fulfilled. Through the antebellum decades, a dynamic national economy fostered the rapid expansion of population, capital, and credit across the continent, strengthening intersectional ties and blurring sectional distinctions. But even as markets brought Americans together, those markets drove them apart. The new nation continued to depend on access to foreign markets for its agricultural exports, and the extent to which it could—or should—achieve genuine economic "independence" in a self-sufficient continental economy remained controversial.

Debates over foreign commercial policy framed the question of the new nation's relation to the world in stark terms: should Americans exploit their advantages in Atlantic markets or should they sacrifice immediate profits in order to develop their home market? Of course, support for free trade or protection reflected the conflicting interests of advocates. But Americans also recognized that debates over the tariff and other controversial issues in political economy raised fundamental questions about the character of the new nation and its relation to the larger world. Protectionists sought to deal with other nations—particularly with Britain—from a position of strength by developing the new nation's internal resources; they were convinced that prosperity and power were inextricably linked in an anarchic, war-torn world. Free traders embraced a more benign view of the prospects for world peace and prosperity, insisting that a liberal trading regime benefited all participants, and particularly a new nation with such extraordinary natural advantages. Independence and union were means to the end of freer and fuller participation in an expanding world market; the need for a protective, activist national state would diminish as obstacles to free trade were progressively eliminated.

Antebellum Americans understood that the union was a sacred legacy, that its preservation alone could guarantee the success of their world-redemptive experiment in republican government. The great desideratum was to preserve peace among the states while providing for their collective security in a dangerous world. Debates over foreign commercial policy exposed immanent contradictions in the patriotic consensus, pivoting on disagreement about the source of threats, external or internal, to vital interests and about the federal government's role in promoting national economic development. These debates necessarily gave rise to conflicting conceptions of union and nation. Devotion to the union was constantly tested by conflicts of interest that, with the spread of antislavery and proslavery sentiment, were increasingly framed in moral terms. The problematic relation between the federal state and nationalist sentiment became increasingly conspicuous as protectionists sought to forge closer links between union and nation and between the nation and a more potent federal state. In response, many Americans—especially in the South but also in the Democratic North—proclaimed their patriotic loyalty to a limited, consensual union and weak federal government.

That national political parties during the period of the "second party system" could build effective, long-lasting intersectional alliances despite pervasive conflicts of interest and ideology was an impressive achievement. Partisan political success ultimately proved demoralizing, however, because coalition building depended on avoiding and suppressing controversial issues, most notably over slavery, because partisans so relentlessly and effectively challenged their opponents' good faith, and because the ordinary business of lawmaking and political patronage was, from the moralist's perspective, inevitably corrupt. When the national political parties no longer effectively tapped or expressed popular national patriotism, they imploded. Only then were their sectionalist successors in a position to foment disunionist sentiment or take advantage of waning national loyalties.

Our goal is to understand nationalist thinking in Civil War America while avoiding the teleology of the conventional national historical narrative or of its sectionalist variants. Why should we think that the American experiment in nation building was providentially destined to succeed? Why shouldn't two nations, North and South, have emerged in the place of one, and isn't it at least possible that these two nations would have given fuller expression to nationalist sentiments and achieved greater legitimacy and efficacy than the antebellum federal union—or its postbellum successor?

We are interested in how nationalist thinking could flourish in the United States even as the old union collapsed and alternative nationalisms and conflicting nation-states emerged in its place. Our contention is that these developments were not only historically contingent but that they could only have taken place at a specific moment in the rise of a liberal world of national markets and international exchange, of an international society of bellicose yet civilized nations. Americans could think themselves *out of the union*—and did so repeatedly from the beginning of the new nation's history. During the debates over the ratification of the federal Constitution they rehearsed the dangerously anarchic consequences of disunion, imagining a regression to the chronic state of war that plagued the Old World, and consciousness of these grave risks constituted the unionist creed of subsequent generations. It was something altogether different, however, for Americans to think themselves *into separate nations.* Indeed, Northerners' resistance to secession was a measure of their continuing devotion to the founders' union. Yet if the preservation of the union depended finally on coercion not consent, on a willingness to deploy the instrumentalities of federal state authority against fellow Americans, then clearly the meaning of the union was transformed: its identity with the nation was complete. By seceding, Southerners arrived at a similar result. If their nation was radically severed from the old union, it was inextricably linked to a new union and to a new federal state that, in the crucible of war, would exercise extraordinary power.

Nationalist sentiment in the new Confederate nation did not emerge spontaneously from the Southern soil—or from a slaveholders' conspiracy to promote their "peculiar institution" at the expense of the free people of the Northern states or of their own nonslaveholding neighbors. Instead, loyalty to the new Southern nation drew deeply on American nationalist sentiments that had flourished throughout the antebellum decades, even as successive sectional crises threatened to rupture the union. The most divisive controversies, over the expansion of slavery into new Western territories and states, testified to the pervasiveness of the image of the United States as a great nation with a "manifest destiny." Few Americans doubted that their nation was destined to achieve unprecedented prosperity and power, that it would inspire and promote (if not impose) the spread of freedom (or slavery) in the hemisphere and, ultimately, across the world. That the United States must expand was a moral certainty; that slavery and freedom, slave states and free states, could coexist peacefully in an expanding union was a moral impossibility.

The assertion that "a house divided against itself," half slave and half free, could not stand violated a taboo long cherished by temporizing, union-loving Americans. The taboo implicitly acknowledged the assertion's irresistible logic, for Northerners and Southerners alike agreed that every great nation had a distinctive genius and destiny, that the United States was destined to be wholly free, with slavery "in the course of an ultimate extinction," or wholly dedicated to the institution's perpetuation.[4] Of course, slavery and freedom had coexisted in the founding fathers' union, and the federal Constitution had been artfully (or shamefully) constructed to make a "more perfect union"

---

4. Lincoln, Fourth Debate with Douglas, Charleston, Sept. 18, 1858, in Basler, ed., *Collected Works of Abraham Lincoln* 3:181.

of slave states and free. But the development of more concrete, less abstract conceptions of the "people," embodied and incorporated in the "nation," made such a union seem increasingly anomalous and compromised its moral integrity. Even Southerners, ostensible champions of the founders' union, belligerently insisted on strong national guarantees for their "peculiar institution," not only in their own states but throughout the national territory. They would, as Abraham Lincoln warned, promote the "nationality," even the "universality" of slavery: if freedom survived in a union dominated by the "slave power," it would be the local exception, not the general rule.[5]

Secessionists ultimately abandoned the union and, by constructing a new Confederacy, mobilized and redirected nationalist sentiments in the South. Invoking the fathers' resistance to British tyranny in the imperial crisis and emphasizing the primal rights of their states to withdraw from an illegitimate union, Confederates insisted that they were the patriotic heirs and true custodians of American Revolutionary values. As they identified union and nation and sought to suppress the rebellion, Lincoln and fellow Northern defenders of the union also claimed to be Constitutional conservatives. Yet, ironically, the two nations that confronted each other on Civil War battlefields resembled each other much more than the single, increasingly disunited nation that had so recently commanded their loyalties and affections. Divergent nationalisms drew on a common stock of patriotic sentiments that remained powerful until the outbreak of war. Until confronted with the necessity of choosing one side or the other, most Americans continued to think and act as Americans, and most undoubtedly would have agreed that unpatriotic, irresponsible, irrational "extremists"—whether abolitionists or fire-eaters, or both—had brought on a tragically unnecessary conflict. These patriotic Americans were nonetheless primed for wartime mobilization and ready to embrace new loyalties and identities, with remarkable alacrity, as the crisis unfolded.

The conventional view is that Northerners and Southerners had come to a fateful crossroads by the eve of the Civil War, that they had developed radically different, irreconcilable conceptions of what "America" was and should be. This was doubtless the case for the vanguard elites who led the rush toward war. But we argue that commonalties and shared values are equally important. The universal belief that the United States was a great nation with a progressive, providential role in world history helped prepare the way toward war. In the American exceptionalist narrative, this conflict is a tragedy, with slavery the fatal flaw. But the outbreak of war between great

5. Lincoln, Address at Cooper Institute, New York City, Feb. 27, 1860, ibid., 3:549.

and expansive nations is a much more predictable outcome in the modern history of the "civilized" West.

Indeed, the *similarity* of nations helps explain their rivalries and wars, as they compete for territory, geopolitical advantage, and scarce resources. Great nations are by definition expansive: this was something certainly that Americans knew about themselves in the antebellum decades and that was all too clear to foreign observers. No longer contained by the "peace pact" of the collapsing union, the rivalries that had long characterized federal politics provided ample pretext for escalating, ultimately violent conflict.[6] By the time of the war, American political elites had long since learned to think of their sectional rivals as "foreigners" and "enemies." The differences they cultivated combined with their commonalties to produce an explosive, cataclysmic outcome.

Successive generations warned themselves of "the evils of dismemberment," even as they prepared to jettison the founders' union. Ritually invoking the fathers' wisdom, the sons and grandsons agreed that the breakup of the union and the "separate governments, or confederacies" that emerged in its wake "would of course have rivalries and jealousies and wars." The new nation would then "exhibit the picture of Europe to the world," the Virginian Thomas Roderick Dew lamented in 1836, "with governments perhaps less balanced and more sanguinary in their wars."[7] The Old World was a sorry model for the New, as Dew explained in his earlier *Lectures on the Restrictive System* (1829): "all Europe is in consternation," as its hostile and divided nations "exhaust their resources and wealth on the field of battle, and in constant and never-ending exertion for the maintenance of the balance of power." Certainly Southerners, outraged as they might be by high, protective tariffs, should look carefully before leaping off such an awful precipice. But if they did so, Dew concluded, it would not be their fault; quite to the contrary, the "fatal and ungenerous policy" of Northern and Western protectionists was responsible; "the sin will, and ought to be, laid at their doors." By projecting evil intentions on to sectional enemies, Dew—and growing

---

6. On the concept of union, see Paul C. Nagel, *This Sacred Trust: American Nationality, 1798–1898* (New York, 1971); Peter S. Onuf, *Jefferson's Empire: The Language of American Nationhood* (Charlottesville, Va., 2000); and Rogan Kersh, *Dreams of a More Perfect Union* (Ithaca, N.Y., 2001). The best systematic treatment of the problem of union and disunion is David C. Hendrickson, *Peace Pact: The Lost World of the American Founding* (Lawrence, Kans., 2003).

7. Thomas Roderick Dew, *An Address on the Influence of the Federative Republican System of Government upon Literature and the Development of Character* (Richmond, 1836), 21.

numbers of his countrymen in the South and the North—embraced the prospect of disunion, war, and the "universal impoverishment and degradation" that would follow, with a self-righteous anticipation approaching eagerness. In other words, they began to think—and imagine acting—as devoted patriots, preparing themselves for the ultimate sacrifice. But this national feeling was directed at fellow Americans, not against the "foreigners" who once had threatened American independence.[8]

Our goal in the second part of *Nations, Markets, and War* is to trace the development of the nationalist thinking in the antebellum federal republic that enabled Americans to think themselves out of the old union and into two separate and hostile nations. We do not pretend to offer a comprehensive account of the coming of the war or its putative causes. Instead, we will show how patriotic Americans could come to such radically different, ultimately irreconcilable conclusions about the character and destiny of their nation. Over the antebellum years, slavery certainly became, as Lincoln claimed, the "apple of discord" that threatened the union's survival. But divergent trajectories of nationalist thinking antedated deep intersectional divisions over the future of the "peculiar institution."[9]

Ongoing debates over national commercial policy illuminated fundamental disagreements over the new nation's proper place in the world. Cosmopolitan free traders saw the world as a great, competitive market for American exports and sought to eliminate mercantilist barriers to trade at home and abroad; their protectionist opponents argued that Americans would only reap the full benefits of foreign trade if they first protected and developed their home market, thus neutralizing the unequal advantages of more highly developed trading partners. Adam Smith, an exemplary Enlightenment figure and the subject of chapter 6, seemed to authorize both views. Smith's famous arguments against mercantilism in *The Wealth of Nations* inspired free traders, but the bulk of his influential book was devoted to promoting market freedom *within* Britain and thus to enhancing its leading position in the trading world. The tension between nation-as-market and world-as-market was not critical to Smith because Britain's advanced economy so obviously stood to benefit from the liberalization of world trade; furthermore, he suggested, as other nations progressed through the stages of

---

8. Thomas Roderick Dew, *Lectures on the Restrictive System Delivered to the Senior Political Class of William and Mary College* (Richmond, 1829), 185–86.
9. Lincoln, First Debate with Douglas, Ottawa, Aug. 21, 1858, in Basler, ed., *Collected Works of Abraham Lincoln* 3:18.

economic development (Smith was particularly impressed with the colonies' extraordinarily rapid progress), the distinction between national and world markets would disappear.

Americans loved Smith. Some questioned the applicability of his market maxims to American circumstances, however, particularly in times of diplomatic crisis and war when their commerce was vulnerable to assault and their access to foreign markets was disrupted. Vindicating national independence, protectionists insisted, depended on developing a robust home market capable of surviving wartime dislocations. The post–War of 1812 debate over a protective tariff and other, associated nation-building measures focused on these issues, as we show in chapter 8. Free traders and protectionists divided over the likelihood of future wars and therefore over the need for an energetic federal government that would promote manufacturing and a balanced, interdependent national economy. Discounting threats to national security, free traders questioned protectionist motives, charging that a corrupt alliance of protected interests sought to capture—and transform—the federal state. These suspicions expressed and exacerbated powerful libertarian, strict constructionist, and states' rights tendencies in American political culture, challenging the link between union and nation that protectionists sought to strengthen. Critics of nation-building initiatives were nonetheless "nationalists," convinced that their resistance to the consolidation of power was the epitome of Americanism.

The memory of the Revolution and persistent Anglophobia provided a deep well of national feeling for all Americans, regardless of their positions on foreign trade policy. Conflict with the former mother country could even turn philosophical free traders such as the Anglophobic Thomas Jefferson toward protection, although ideology and interest pointed the other way when commercial provocations subsided. No one had a more exalted sense of the new nation's providential, progressive role in world history than Jefferson, the subject of chapter 7. Because Jefferson's conception of national greatness was predicated on his exaggerated estimation of the dominant position of American staple exports in the Atlantic economy, he was less concerned about the development of the home market than about the unnatural resistance of European imperial powers to the ongoing expansion of the new nation's "empire for liberty."

Jeffersonians favored territorial expansion; market relations and republican institutions would inevitably fill the continental void. Disentangled from the European balance of power, the American nation could expand peacefully, its greatness manifest in the freedom and prosperity of its people. Conversely, however, when foreign enemies threatened, American power would be irresistible for, as Jefferson proclaimed in his first inaugural address, the

United States had "the strongest Government on earth."[10] In Jefferson's mind—and in the minds of later Jeffersonians and Jacksonians—the default "enemy," the greatest potential threat, was always Britain. Territorial controversies with the British in Canada, in the Oregon country, and in Texas kept Anglophobic fires burning, even for Southern cotton producers who argued for free trade with the British, their best customers. Rumors that British abolitionists hoped to negotiate an end to slavery in independent Texas gave a radical edge to Southern Anglophobia, as Britain yet again threatened to block the spread of "American" institutions.

Anglophobia spurred and rationalized territorial expansion. Southerners and Northerners shared the conviction that westward expansion was "natural," although controversy over the spread of slavery precipitated recurrent crises of the union, and this conviction made peaceful coexistence of separate nations doubtful. We trace the history of another strain of Anglophobia in chapter 9, the increasingly sectionalized protective nationalism of Whigs and Republicans that reaffirmed the connection between nation and union that Southerners had called into question. Protectionists concluded that the only way for the United States to escape from a degrading condition of neocolonial dependency on the former imperial metropolis was to develop a truly independent national economy. Henry Carey, the leading Whig economist, warned that British "free trade imperialism" would ultimately impoverish the United States, as it had already destroyed the economies of Ireland and India; Britain's relentless quest for world domination perpetuated slavery, stripped raw materials from the underdeveloped colonial periphery, and preempted the development of manufactures. Territorial expansion that simply strengthened British domination of world markets was pathological, not a mark of a robust and rising great young nation.

Nationalism in the northern remnant of the union drew on diverse sources. Northerners certainly were not immune to the territorial appeal; Republicanism, after all, grew out of the Free-Soilers' anti–slave power expansionism. But the protectionists' conception of internal, balanced development pointed toward an idea of the nation that had only been elaborated previously during wartime, or in war's shadow. The "protective" idea of nationhood presupposed conflict among nations; nations as corporate persons with interests that transcended the aggregate of their populations were, in some sense, *made* for war. The parallel development of Southern nationalism, discussed in chapter 10, exemplifies this powerful tendency in nationalist thought.

---

10. Jefferson, First Inaugural Address, Mar. 4, 1801, in Merrill D. Peterson, ed., *Thomas Jefferson Writings* (New York, 1984), 493.

The protectionist conception of the nation—grounded in national econo-mists' apotheosis of the home market and "realistically" postulating inevitable conflicts between and among nations—was embraced in the South as well as the North. As hostile neighbors, both nations necessarily embraced protec-tionist tenets.

Slavery proved crucial in the genesis of Southern nationalism. Southern-ers' sensitivity to potential threats to their "peculiar institution" had made them suspicious about the uses of federal power and thus predisposed to dis-tinguish the nation from the union. During the tariff controversies, the in-terests and ideology of staple-exporting free traders who challenged protec-tionist commercial policy reinforced antistatist tendencies in the South. Yet the prospect of the union's imminent collapse brought countervailing ten-dencies to the fore.

Cotton producers might imagine a regime of peaceful, reciprocally bene-ficial commercial and diplomatic relations between an independent South and its chief European trading partners, but they had no illusions about the inevitability of geopolitical and economic conflict with the rump Union in a disunited North America. Nor could they overlook pervasive opposition to slavery throughout the civilized world, a potent threat to the vital interests of the first new nation dedicated to the perpetuation of that "relic of bar-barism."[11] "King Cotton" could give rule to the trading world as long as man-ufacturers depended on the precious staple, but exaggerated moral scruples might trump interest, dictating a search for alternative sources or an alter-native (putatively "free") labor supply. Perhaps, some Southerners feared, Britain would spearhead a war against Southern slavery in order to eliminate competition with less efficient producers in its own far-flung imperial possessions.

The most radical antiunionists in the South, those who with Thomas Cooper, president of South Carolina College, first began to "calculate the value of our union," were the most precocious proto-nationalists: they rec-ognized both the need for region-wide mobilization (and therefore the in-sufficiency of state sovereignty) and the need to deal with the larger world from a position of strength.[12] They also recognized the need to justify their national project in moral terms, to convince themselves and the civilized

---

11. Slavery and polygamy were "twin relics of barbarism," according to the Republican Party platform in 1856 (Donald Bruce Johnson, comp., *National Party Platforms, 1840–1976* [Urbana, Ill., 1978], 27–28).

12. Speech of Thomas Cooper, July 27, 1827, in *Niles Weekly Register* (Baltimore) 33 (Sept. 8, 1827), rpt. in William W. Freehling, ed., *The Nullification Era: A Documentary Record* (New York, 1967), 25.

world generally, that slavery was no relic of barbarism but rather a benign, improving, civilized solution to the conflicts between capital and labor and between the races that threatened to retard and reverse the worldwide progress of civilization. Proslavery thought thus played a crucial role in the development of Southern nationalism. The presence of slaves made white Southerners a distinct "race," or people, with a unique purpose and destiny in world history, and the great wealth produced by slave-grown staples was the engine for prosperity in the civilized world. By declaring and vindicating their independence, the Confederate nation would point the way toward a better future, not only for the white race but for humanity as a whole. Southerners would discover their own better selves; they would show a better way to the pious hypocrites who questioned the morality of slavery.

The Civil War *was* about slavery, because slavery was critical to the sudden coalescence of a collective consciousness among white Southerners of their identity as a separate people. Yet that consciousness was equally indebted to ideas about nationhood that had emerged throughout the civilized world in the antebellum decades as well as to a common stock of ideology and sentiment that Southerners shared with their Northern enemies. Two modern nations made war against each other in North America from 1861 to 1865 because they were profoundly, irreconcilably alienated from each other. At the same time, the war showed how profoundly and irreconcilably these two nations—as modern nations, with the capacity and will to assert and vindicate their vital interests—resembled each other.

6
Adam Smith, Moral Historian

Adam Smith is recognized as one of the founders of modern economics. He was also, much less famously, a historian whose understanding of moral progress reached back to the great teachers of antiquity and looked forward to the fulfillment of human potential at history's end. Thus there are two Smiths: the *economist* whose image as a theorist was perfected through the history of the discipline he helped to found, and the *historian* whose moral concerns no longer define the practice of history. Drawing on the two Smiths, opposed perspectives shaped the great debates over political economy in the nineteenth century. These debates in turn helped to give the modern world some of its most distinctive features—ones that we broadly recognize today as *liberal*.

Key passages in *The Wealth of Nations,* published in 1776, reveal Smith as a moral historian. As a historian, Smith attached particular importance to the expansion of European commerce and power in the age of discovery. "The discovery of America, and that of a passage to the East Indies by the Cape of Good Hope, are the two greatest and most important events recorded in the history of mankind."[1] Smith understood these momentous events as marking the emergence of a world market. Only in the context of such a market can human beings fulfill their potential. That Britain had achieved a well-formed market made Britons better off materially and better able to develop their civic institutions and exercise their "natural liberty."[2] Britons and other Europeans also benefited enormously from the expansion of market relations to distant parts of the world. Yet Smith had profound misgivings about

---

1. Adam Smith, *An Inquiry into the Nature and Causes of the Wealth of Nations,* ed. R. H. Campbell and A. S. Skinner (Indianapolis, Ind., 1981), IV, vii.c, § 80, 626.
2. Ibid., IV, ix, § 51, 687.

the impact on native peoples. "The savage injustice of the Europeans rendered an event, which ought to have been beneficial to all, ruinous and destructive to several of those unfortunate countries."[3]

Smith's indictment is not of the natural propensity of all human beings to exchange the fruits of their labors to improve their circumstances, but, rather, it is of the irresistible temptation—and perhaps also natural propensity—to use superior force to exploit weak peoples. "The superiority of force happened to be so great on the side of the Europeans, that they were enabled to commit with impunity every sort of injustice in those remote countries."[4] The plunder of native peoples is, for Smith, the antithesis of free exchange in advanced commercial societies. In condemning these injustices, Smith revealed his moral indignation. By contrast, market behavior, which is neither selfish nor selfless, fulfills the moral destiny of humanity. As with his Enlightenment contemporaries, Smith held the conviction that history is a chronicle of moral improvement. That morally advanced Europeans should treat others with such "savage injustice" provoked his indignation and, at the same time, illuminated the complexity of historical development.

In principle, European expansion should have benefited the whole world, bringing together "the most distant parts of the world" and "enabling them to relieve one another's wants, to increase one another's enjoyments, and to encourage one another's industry." Here Smith recapitulated his faith in the efficacy of market relations, as developed in the famous opening pages of *The Wealth of Nations,* to promote human betterment. Yet if the "general tendency" of expanding markets "would seem to be beneficial," the historical record told a different story, for which Smith's analysis of market relations is hardly adequate. "To the natives . . . both of the East and West Indies, all the commercial benefits which can have resulted from those events have been sunk and lost in the dreadful misfortunes which they have occasioned." Smith's use of terms such as *seem* and *can* tell the large story: *seem* marks the discrepancy among theory and practice, promise, and result; *can* marks the utter contingency of human history. "These misfortunes . . . seem to have arisen rather from accident than from any thing in the nature of those events themselves."[5]

Smith emphasized the historically contingent character of European encounters with the larger world. These "discoveries" took place at "a particular time"—a time when European civilization enjoyed an immense technological advantage. In a contingent world, these injustices might be rectified;

---

3. Ibid., IV, i, § 32, 448.
4. Ibid., IV, vii.c, § 80, 626.
5. Ibid.

"the natives of those countries may grow stronger, or those of Europe may grow weaker, and inhabitants of all the different quarters of the world may arrive at that equality of courage and force which, by inspiring mutual fear, can alone overawe the injustice of independent nations into some sort of respect for the rights of one another."[6] The commercial prosperity of European nations depended on a balance of power and a degree of normative restraint among them. Commercial prosperity for the whole world calls for a balance of power for all nations.

"Just Indignation"

Smith developed a powerful moral theory long before he wrote *The Wealth of Nations* and continued to refine it to the end of his life. The first edition of *The Theory of Moral Sentiments* appeared in 1759, and a sixth edition—the last Smith was to revise himself—in 1790. We have no reason to suppose that Smith put his moral concerns aside when he wrote *The Wealth of Nations*, or limited them to occasional outbursts of indignation. To see his indignation as an integral feature of his historical imagination, and thus his history of modern opulence as a moral history, we need to examine Smith's moral theory.[7]

When Smith expressed his indignation over the "savage injustice" of Europeans in *The Wealth of Nations*, he was articulating a broader conception of history that informs the entire treatise and that gives his famous indictment of mercantilist statecraft its peculiar moral resonance. Indeed, history for Smith was a moral chronicle, even—or, rather, especially—when understood in terms of a people's progress through the ages. The moral dimensions of Smith's historical imagination are systematically elaborated in *The Theory of Moral Sentiments*, but they are never far below the surface of *The Wealth of Nations*.

---

6. Ibid.
7. The literature on Smith is vast. We draw on Richard Teichgraeber III, *"Free Trade" and Moral Philosophy: Rethinking the Sources of Adam Smith's Wealth of Nations* (Durham, N.C., 1986); Donald Winch, *Riches and Poverty: An Intellectual History of Political Economy in Britain, 1750–1834* (Cambridge, U.K., 1996); Charles L. Griswold Jr., *Adam Smith and the Virtues of Enlightenment* (Cambridge, U.K., 1999); Emma Rothschild, *Economic Sentiments: Adam Smith, Condorcet, and the Enlightenment* (Cambridge, Mass., 2001), without always being faithful to these important works. Also useful are various of the essays in Istvan Hont and Michael Ignatieff, eds., *Wealth and Virtue: The Shaping of Political Economy in the Scottish Enlightenment* (Cambridge, U.K., 1983); John Cunningham Wood, ed., *Adam Smith: Critical Assessments*, 3 vols. (London, 1983); and Peter Jones and Andrew S. Skinner, eds., *Adam Smith Reviewed* (Edinburgh, 1992).

The advanced commercial societies of western Europe generated unprecedented wealth and power; they also created the conditions of moral improvement. Yet as a moral historian, Smith could not be complacent, for unforseen contingencies could subvert these progressive conditions. The wheel of fortune could turn against modern European imperial powers, as it had against the great empires of antiquity; so too, powerful and privileged classes within these advanced societies could seek their selfish advantage at the expense of their countrymen, thus retarding or even reversing the natural course of historical progress. Smith's indignation was most conspicuously aroused when Europeans yielded to the temptation of their superior power to exploit the natives of the Indies. But his critique of mercantilism also expressed a pervasive and profound moral animus. The object of his indignation in both cases was the misguided policies of ruling elites who failed to take the long—the historical and therefore moral—view of their own and their peoples' best interests.[8]

Smith's moral historical perspective in *The Wealth of Nations* is obscured by the plethora of empirical detail that illustrates and demonstrates the supposedly transhistorical axioms of classical economics. His prolix, inductive method may have enabled Smith to discover the instrumental propensities of humanity and the optimizing properties of markets, but contemporary readers are disinclined to retrace his clumsy steps. Yet to ignore Smith's accumulation of details is to mistake his fundamental purpose: to shape state policy in the face of complexity and contingency with a view toward the progressive improvement of nations particularly and of humanity generally *within history*.[9] His axioms are empirical generalizations, glosses on economic

8. As T. W. Hutchison has written, "nothing is more passionately and constantly condemned throughout *The Wealth of Nations* than this monopolistic drive, both generally and in its particular manifestation in colonial policies" ("Adam Smith and *The Wealth of Nations*," *Journal of Law and Economics* 19 [1976]: 507–28, rpt. in Wood, ed., *Smith: Critical Assessments* 2:172–92, at 184). For a good recent discussion of conceptions of history and progress in the Scottish Enlightenment, see Joyce E. Chaplin, *An Anxious Pursuit: Agricultural Innovation and Modernity in the Lower South* (Chapel Hill, N.C., 1993), 26–37. On Smith's "Historical Theory," see Andrew S. Skinner, *A System of Social Science: Papers Relating to Adam Smith*, 2nd ed. (Oxford, 1996), 76–105. On Smith's patron Lord Kames, as a moral historian, see Ari Helo, "Thomas Jefferson's Republicanism and the Problem of Slavery" (Ph.D. diss., Tampere University, Finland, 1999) and Ari Helo and Peter Onuf, "Jefferson, Morality, and the Problem of Slavery," *William and Mary Quarterly* 60 (2003): 583–613.
9. In a postmodern interpretation quite at odds with ours, Michael Shapiro has called *The Wealth of Nations* an "untroubled story"—one "barren of detail"—"in which people smoothly sort themselves into places within the division of labor" (*Reading "Adam Smith": Desire, History, and Value*, new ed. [Lanham, Md., 2002], 54–59, at 57).

behavior characteristic of advanced commercial societies. Perhaps they are immanently universal, as these societies advance *through* history and empirical conditions ever more closely approximate universal laws of nature. Yet Smith was less overtly teleological than Immanuel Kant and G. W. F. Hegel: peace is hardly inevitable; history has no foreseeable end.

Smith's moral concerns shaped his understanding of human nature, which in turn shaped his conjectures about the large patterns in human history. Conjectural history is an apt description, not just of Smith's labors of a lifetime but for the labors of his fellows in the Scottish Enlightenment, and perhaps for those of Enlightenment writers elsewhere. The remarkable achievement of these writers was to comprehend the history of nations within a universal, secular, and comparative framework. Such a framework presupposes a fixed standard—understood temporally as stages of historical development—against which to assess the contingent circumstances of particular nations.

Smith's Enlightenment sensibilities took him beyond history to the potential fulfillment of human nature's immanent tendencies. Yet the statesman could only act within and on specific historical circumstances. Smith's *Wealth of Nations* provided an exhaustive and timely review of these circumstances for the statesmen of his own day; his *Theory of Moral Sentiments* showed how the "impartial spectator"—virtuous subject, moral historian, or statesman—could reconcile the particular and the universal, individual experience and collective norms. His point of departure, and fundamental premise, was to distinguish self—the individual capable of making moral judgments—from selfishness: we are, he insisted, self-regarding social animals.

The first sentence of *The Theory of Moral Sentiments* warns readers not to make an unduly simple judgment about selfishness or any other human disposition. "How selfish soever man may be supposed, there are evidently some principles in his nature, which interest him in the fortune of others, and render their happiness necessary to him, though he derives nothing from it except the pleasure of seeing it."[10] In *The Wealth of Nations*, Smith used the term *selfish* just three times to describe people who are either frivolous or, at the other extreme, "averse to all social pleasure and enjoyment."[11] The distinctive property of being selfish is to feel "anxious about small matters for their own sake."[12] Human beings are capable of feeling much else, and of acting on those feelings. We are neither fearful nor greedy by nature; we are not selfish in the sense of being ruthlessly self-centered,

10. Adam Smith, *The Theory of Moral Sentiments,* ed. D. D. Raphael and A. L. Macfie (Indianapolis, Ind., 1981), I, I, i, § 1, 9.
11. Smith, *Wealth of Nations,* II, iii, § 42, 349; IV, ix, § 13, 668; V, iii, § 1, 907, at 668.
12. Smith, *Theory of Moral Sentiments,* III, vi, § 6, 173.

even if we are afraid or envious or, for that matter, anxious or indignant when circumstances warrant such feelings.

Smith started with feelings—*our* feelings. "As we have no immediate experience of what other men feel, we can form no idea of the manner in which they are affected, but by conceiving what we ourselves should feel in the like situation." The specifically human "faculty" enabling us to feel what others feel by putting ourselves in their places is "imagination," and this faculty is "the source of our fellow-feeling," not just "for the misery of others" but for "their happiness" as well. Finding no single term for the entire range of feelings, or "passions," that we experience on others' behalf, Smith appropriated the term *sympathy,* but only after explicitly ridding it of exclusively positive connotations.[13]

Smith knew that the joy and grief that others experience "inspire us with some degree of the like emotions," if only fleetingly. For our sympathies to acquire the depth and durability that leads to the possibility of moral action, we need to know what may have caused someone else to experience such strong feelings. "Sympathy, therefore, does not arise so much from the view of the passion, as from that of the situation which excites it."[14] Fear of dying illustrates the point.

> We sympathize even with the dead, and overlooking what is of real importance in their situation, that awful futurity which awaits them, we are chiefly affected by those circumstances which strike our senses, but can have no influence upon their happiness. It is miserable, we think, to be deprived of the light of the sun; to be shut out from life and conversation; to be laid in the cold grave, a prey to corruption and the reptiles of the earth; to be no more thought of in this world, but to be obliterated, in a little time, from the affections, and almost from the memory, of their dearest friends and relations. . . . And from thence arises one of the most important principles in human nature, the dread of death, the great poison to the happiness, but the great restraint upon the injustice of mankind, which, while it afflicts and mortifies the individual, guards and protects the society.[15]

The expressive power of this passage, which ends the first chapter of *The Theory of Moral Sentiments,* is remarkable. Even more remarkable is the way it links the perceptual, cognitive, and affective powers of human beings to the conditions under which we can expect to live together, in mutual toleration,

---

13. Ibid., I, i, i, §§ 2–5, 9–10.
14. Ibid., §§ 8, 10, 11–12.
15. Ibid., § 13, 12–13.

with generally beneficial consequences. Our powers of sympathy, manifest as feelings or *sentiments*, make us self-regarding social animals. Exercising these powers, we protect ourselves from our own worst tendencies, "the injustice of mankind." We guard and protect society, but not by intention or design.

Smith's starting point is the individual *self*, but not "self-love"—whatever his readers might later claim. Indeed, he took the trouble to dissociate himself from those for whom self-love was the point of departure.[16] Thanks to our capacity for fellow feeling, Smith asserted, we see what situations bring joy, sorrow, gratitude, anxiety, or indignation to others, and we take action to alter these situations, as best we can, to makes us feel good about ourselves and our lives. The unintended consequences are, on balance, beneficial. For Smith this is an empirical generalization, to which he attached a great deal of moral significance. Nevertheless, our sentiments have normative properties even before they yield collectively beneficial consequences.[17]

In Smith's account, again expressed with extraordinary eloquence, no one experiences fellow feeling without additionally passing judgment on the feelings that others express for themselves.

> The man who resents the injuries that have been done to me, and observes that I resent them precisely as he does, necessarily approves of my resentment. The man whose sympathy keeps time to my grief, cannot but admit the reasonableness of my sorrow. He who admires the same poem, or the same picture, and admires them exactly as I do, must surely allow the justness of my admiration. He who laughs at the same joke, and laughs along with me, cannot well deny the propriety of my laughter.[18]

Those who feel the same way about some situation will have a favorable view of each other. Conversely, those who judge a situation differently will be less favorably disposed toward each other.

> If my animosity goes beyond what the indignation of my friend can correspond to; if my grief exceeds what his most tender compassion can go along

---

16. Ibid., I, I, ii, § 1, 13–14; much later in the book, he named Thomas Hobbes, Samuel Pufendorf, and Bernard Mandeville as theorists whose systems start with self-love. "Sympathy," he maintained in this context, "cannot, in any sense, be regarded as a selfish principle" (VII, III, i, 315–17, at § 4, 317).
17. Ibid., IV, i, § 10, 184; Smith, *Wealth of Nations*, IV, ii, § 9, 456. Smith's famous "invisible hand" is foreshadowed here. He made only passing reference to the "invisible hand" in *Theory of Moral Sentiments* and, again, perhaps ironically but to canonical effect, in *Wealth of Nations*. See Rothschild, *Economic Sentiments*, chap. 5, for a subtle discussion of Smith's sense and use of this famous metaphor.
18. Smith, *Theory of Moral Sentiments*, I, iii, § 1, 16.

with; if my admiration is either too high or too low to tally with his own; if I laugh loud and heartily when he only smiles, or, on the contrary, only smile when he laughs loud and heartily; in all these cases, as soon as he comes from considering the object, to observe how I am affected by it, according as there is more or less disproportion between his sentiments and mine, I must incur a greater or less degree of his disapprobation: and upon all occasions his own sentiments are the standards and measures by which he judges of mine.[19]

Whatever feelings we have for others and their situations are always accompanied by another feeling that we cannot suppress, a positive or negative response, which we sense as approval or disapproval. When we speak of these feelings, we use the language of judgment, invoking terms such as *justness* and *propriety*. We think that others are right or wrong depending on how we think they feel about some situation and, by extension, on how they act on their feelings. Our sentiments are the standard by which we judge the sentiments of others.

Where do these standards come from? On first reading, Smith seems to be saying that we always disapprove of everyone who feels differently about something, and that we therefore judge that everyone else is wrong. Yet this conclusion does not fit the way we see Smith constructing his moral theory. If we take into account how we feel about the feelings others have for us, we will seek to avoid expressing feelings we know will meet with their disapproval. "Nature, when she formed man for society, endowed him with an original desire to please, and an original aversion to offend his brethren. She taught him to feel pleasure in their favourable, and pain in their unfavourable regard."[20]

Smith did not stop here. "But this desire of the approbation, and this aversion to the disapprobation of his brethren, would not alone have rendered him fit for that society for which he was made. Nature, accordingly, has endowed him, not only with a desire of being approved of, but with a desire of being what ought to be approved of; or of being what he himself approves of in other men."[21] We judge our feelings on the basis of standards shared by others. If we can persuade others to feel differently about something, then they have adopted our standard. If we doubt that everyone will see things as we do, we will be disposed to change our feelings to meet everyone else's

---

19. Ibid., 16–17.
20. Ibid., III, ii, § 6, 116.
21. Ibid., § 7, 117.

standard. Either way, the standard is social and it is normative. It tells us what others expect from us, and therefore it tells us what we ought to do.

If we desire the approval of others and recognize that we can gain that approval by meeting approved standards, we are not going to be admired by others for that reason alone. "When the sentiments of our companion" surprise us with "their uncommon and unexpected acuteness and comprehensiveness," then "he appears to deserve a very high degree of admiration and applause. For approbation heightened by wonder and surprise, constitutes the sentiment which is properly called admiration, and of which applause is the natural expression." Smith proceeded to illustrate the point by reference to "talents," such as "the acute and delicate discernment of the man of taste" exemplified in conduct, and not to sentiments as such.[22]

Admiration arises from conduct so greatly exceeding approved standards as to make them seem more or less irrelevant; it is excellence we admire. "Emulation, the anxious desire that we ourselves should excel, is originally founded in our admiration of the excellence of others. Neither can we be satisfied with being merely admired for what other people are admired. We must at least believe ourselves to be admirable for what they are admirable. But, in order to attain this satisfaction, we must become the impartial spectators of our own character and conduct." While anxious desire is the engine that drives us, the engine's governor is the cool detachment that we achieve by standing apart from ourselves in constant judgment. As if standing in lonely watch, Smith's impartial spectator is surely the best-remembered feature of his moral philosophy. Nevertheless, its importance follows from our unending need for "love and admiration," sentiments that we and others cannot form simply by recourse to available standards.[23]

Hatred and contempt are Smith's direct counterparts to love and admiration: "As the love and admiration which we naturally conceive for some characters, dispose us to wish to become ourselves the proper objects of such agreeable sentiments; so the hatred and contempt which we as naturally conceive for others, dispose us, perhaps still more strongly, to dread the very thought of resembling them in any respect."[24] If contempt is to disapproval as admiration is to approval, then indignation involves something more. Smith made this clear when he observed that the "insolence and brutality of anger," of fury unchecked, is "the most detestable" sort of conduct. "But we admire that noble and generous resentment which governs its pursuit of the

---

22. Ibid., I, ɪ, iv, § 3, 19–20.
23. Ibid., III, ii, § 3, 114.
24. Ibid., § 9, 117.

greatest injuries, not by the rage which they are apt to excite in the breast of the sufferer, but by the indignation which they naturally call forth in that of the impartial spectator."[25] Any of us observing a great injury to someone else should feel indignant. Since each of us has an impartial spectator within ourselves, we can feel rage, hatred, and contempt for any injury done to us, and we can be outraged at the same time. By implication, we should act on our indignation, which others, as impartial spectators, are also likely to feel, and not on the hatred or contempt that we feel for those who have injured us or anyone else whose injuries have aroused our sympathetic identification.

Smith used the pairings "hatred and indignation" and "contempt and indignation" a number of times in *The Theory of Moral Sentiments*.[26] At least as often, he spoke of "just indignation." Here is a typical instance: "There can be no proper motive for hurting our neighbour, there can be no incitement to do evil to another, which mankind will go along with, except just indignation for evil which that other has done to us."[27] Neither hatred nor contempt suffices as a motive. There must be an injury so great as to be an evil in the eyes of every spectator. In this event, we are justified in taking action, in the first instance by expressing our indignation. When we see great injury against others, we should, in good conscience, do the same.

"Just indignation" is a central motif in Smith's moral theory. He assumed that we all have occasion to "vent our indignation" over the character and conduct of other people, both on our own behalf and on behalf of others.[28] He believed that none of us have any great difficulty in knowing when our indignation is warranted; the impartial spectator is neither passive nor dilatory. Indeed, he thought it entirely appropriate to invoke the "indignation of mankind," as if impartial spectators have access to natural, universal standards by which to judge what they see. We can hardly be surprised, then, to

---

25. Ibid., I, I, v, § 4, 24. It might seem that indignation corresponds to applause, which Smith saw as following from admiration. He implied as much in speaking of "applause or indignation" (VII, III, i, § 3, 317). There is an important way in which these terms do not correspond, however: *applause* is presumably spontaneous and frequently partisan, while *indignation* is the result of contempt that "the great inmate of the breast" (this is Smith's memorable description of the impartial spectator; III, iii, § 1, 134) has inspected and certified as objectively warranted.

26. See, for example, ibid., II, II, ii, § 2, 83 and III, ii, § 9, 118, for hatred and indignation; III, iii, §§ 5–6, 138 and III, iii, § 24, for "contempt and indignation"; VII, II, ii, § 12, 298, for "hatred, contempt, or indignation." In *Wealth of Nations*, an indignant Smith used the phrase "malignant and contemptuous indignation" to describe the sentiments of feudal lords toward free and increasingly prosperous peasants (V, ii.g, § 6, 854).

27. Smith, *Theory of Moral Sentiments*, II, II, i, § 1, 82.

28. Ibid., VII, II, iv, § 10, 311; compare this with "the sympathetic indignation which naturally boils up in the breast of the spectator" (II, i, v, § 6, 76).

find Smith venting his indignation over "savage injustice," or indeed for injustice, including "the injustice of mankind," to be a recurring concern for Smith in all of his work.[29]

Natural Ethics

The idea of just indignation links the subjective experience of moral sentiments with the objective condition of injury and injustice. Indeed, "the violation of justice is injury: it does real and positive hurt to some particular persons, from motives which are naturally disapproved of."[30] Objective conditions imply that widely held standards, or general rules, are available for the reliable assessment of such conditions. If great injury warrants an indignant response, then we need to know when a particular injury is great enough for this response and not some other, or none at all.

Smith's concern with justice—and with the "savage" injustices so conspicuous in European encounters with the natives of the Indies—might lead us to expect that his *Theory of Moral Sentiments* would offer a systematic account of "natural jurisprudence," or of the rules of justice that ought to govern our behavior.[31] Smith anticipated such an expectation, promising at the conclusion of the first edition that a future work would review "the general principles of law and government, and of the different revolutions they have undergone in the different ages and periods of society, not only in what concerns justice, but in what concerns police, revenue, and arms, and whatever else is the object of law."[32] But Smith had a different agenda in *The Theory of Moral Sentiments*, which is better understood as an inquiry into what we might call *natural ethics*—an inquiry into the natural foundations of ethics,

---

29. See Ibid., II, III, ii, § 2, 105 and III, iii, § 6, 138, for the "indignation of mankind"; VII, II, iv, § 10, 311, for "the ignorance and injustice of mankind."
30. Ibid., II, II, i, § 5, 79.
31. By "natural jurisprudence," Smith meant the natural foundations of jurisprudence. "Jurisprudence is the theory of the rules by which civil governments ought to be directed." So began Smith's lectures on jurisprudence at the University of Glasgow, 1762–63, according to the notes of one of his students (Adam Smith, *Lectures on Jurisprudence*, ed. R. L. Meek et al. [Oxford, 1978], Report of 1762–63, i, 1, 5).
32. Smith, *Theory of Moral Sentiments*, VII, iv, § 37, 342. The promise remains in the sixth edition, along with the quite appropriate claim that he "partly executed this promise" in *The Wealth of Nations*, "at least as so far concern police, revenue, and arms," and a wry disclaimer about the likelihood of living long enough to undertake the project (Advertisement, 6th ed., 3). See *Wealth of Nations*, V, 689–947, for Smith's extensive discussion of the legal institutions associated with "police, revenue, and arms."

accompanied by an extensive, but not exhaustive account of the "practical Rules" that moral discourse brings to attention.[33]

Smith's theory of natural ethics makes virtue, not rules, its chief concern, thus following the lead of the ancients and their "systems of moral philosophy."[34] Stoic thought is supposed to have had a great influence on Smith, and Aristotle's thinking about virtue (*aretē*, excellence) may have been particularly influential.[35] But when Smith identified justice as "the last and greatest of the four cardinal virtues," the context is Plato's system. In that brief discussion, Smith said nothing of the other three cardinal virtues, no doubt because, in Plato's account, justice "comprehends in it the perfection of every sort of virtue."[36] At other points in *The Theory of Moral Sentiments,* Smith considered the remaining cardinal virtues, but never in a unified exposition.[37] He may have expected his readers to be familiar with Cicero's cogent, and exceptionally influential, discussion of the four cardinal virtues in *De officiis.*

In Cicero's formulation, the four cardinal virtues—wisdom, a sense of justice, greatness of spirit, and a sense of decorum or seemliness—define "everything that is honourable."[38] Smith also linked virtue to honor and, by

---

33. Smith, *Theory of Moral Sentiments,* VII, iv, 327, and see §§ 36–37, 340–41. By folding natural jurisprudence into natural ethics, thereby contextualizing Smith's sense of what justice entails, we part company with Knud Haakonssen, *The Science of a Legislator: The Natural Jurisprudence of David Hume and Adam Smith* (Cambridge, U.K., 1981), 54–62, 147–51, and Winch, *Riches and Poverty,* chap. 4, both of whom have emphasized the "centrality of justice" in interpreting Smith's thinking as a whole (Winch, 97).

34. Smith, *Theory of Moral Sentiments,* VII, "Of Systems of Moral Philosophy," II, i, §§ 1–47, 266–93.

35. See, for example, D. D. Raphael and A. L. Macfie, intro., ibid., 5–10, where Smith's ambivalence about Stoicism is barely noticed (9). Cf. Gloria Vivenza, *Adam Smith and the Classics: The Classical Heritage in Adam Smith's Thought,* trans. Clive Cheesman and Nicola Gelder (Oxford, 2001), 212: "Perhaps he [Smith] meditated on Stoicism so deeply in order to discover why this philosophy, which left no room for sentiment, and could not serve as a guide for human behavior, attracted him so much." Also see Vivienne Brown's careful treatment in *Adam Smith's Discourse: Canonicity, Commerce and Conscience* (London, 1994), chaps. 3–5. On Smith's "closeness to Aristotle," see Samuel Fleischacker, *A Third Concept of Liberty: Judgment and Freedom in Kant and Adam Smith* (Princeton, N.J., 1999), chap. 6, and, on the way Smith "turned Aristotle to non-teleological and egalitarian uses," see chap. 7, at 120.

36. Smith, *Theory of Moral Sentiments,* VII, II, i, § 10, 270.

37. Scholars have only recently granted their attention to Smith's recourse to the cardinal virtues. For an assessment, see Vivenza, *Adam Smith and the Classics.*

38. "Everything that is honourable arises from one of four parts: it is involved either with the perception of truth and with ingenuity; or with preserving fellowship among men or with assigning to each his own, and with faithfulness to agreements one has made; or with the greatness of spirit of a lofty and unconquered spirit; or with order and limit in everything that is said and done (modesty and restraint are included here)" (Cicero, *On Duties,* trans. Margaret Atkins [Cambridge, U.K., 1991], I, § 15, 7).

linking honor and approval, connected virtue to the fellow feeling on which he based his ethical theory. Smith and Cicero ranked the cardinal virtues in a different order. For Cicero the first and "foremost of all the virtues is the wisdom that the Greeks call *sophia.*" It takes wisdom to recognize that human sociability "is something of the greatest importance" and that "the duty that is based on sociability is also of the greatest importance."[39]

Justice is "the most wide-reaching" of the remaining cardinal virtues in Cicero's catalogue, because it concerns "the reasoning by which the fellowship of men with one another, and the communal life, are held together."[40] For Smith, however, a sense of justice is not just the second but the most important of the cardinal virtues. In his account, justice is natural: our sense of justice derives from knowing "the governing principles of human nature" and their purpose, our collective well-being. "The happiness of mankind . . . seems to have been the original purpose intended by the Author of nature"; "we . . . may therefore be said, in some sense, to co-operate with the Deity, and to advance as far as in our power the plan of Providence."[41]

The priority of justice for Smith reflects his historical awareness. Cicero was an ahistorical thinker: recognizing each other's "human sociability," people pursue justice in order to sustain and perfect their "communal life." Smith reversed the order. A "sense of justice" is natural to humanity, a universally inclusive category transcending specific communities; justice enables the whole of humanity to achieve happiness, its ultimate purpose. Justice thus defines the trajectory of history, its point of departure and its final destination. Because we have the power to understand nature's plan, our sense of justice makes our duties toward others so eminently clear that we can formulate them as general rules with "the greatest exactness." This is hardly the case with the other virtues. Any effort to formulate precise rules for their application smacked of "the most absurd and ridiculous pedantry."[42]

A transhistorical sense of justice was foundational to Smith's understanding of humanity as a whole. Because the requirements of justice could be

---

39. Ibid., § 153, 59. Here Cicero followed the Greeks in distinguishing *sophia* from *phronesis* (in Latin, *sapentia* and *prudentia*); earlier in the text (§ 15, 7), he conjoined them as first of the cardinal virtues. In general, his term of choice is *sapentia*. Atkins translated *prudentia*—"the knowledge of things that one should pursue and avoid"—as "good sense" (§ 153, 59), although "prudence" seems entirely appropriate. See, for example, Cicero, *De officiis*, trans. Walter Miller (London, 1961), § 15, 17, with Latin text on facing page. Note, however, that Smith used the term *prudence* in quite a different sense: see elsewhere in this essay.

40. Cicero, *On Duties*, trans. Atkins, § 20, 9.

41. Smith, *Theory of Moral Sentiments*, III, v, §§ 6–7, 165–66.

42. Ibid., vi, §§ 9–10, 174–75.

formulated as general rules, it could provide none of the circumstantial detail that could illuminate humanity's slow and erratic moral progress through history. By contrast, the various, often conflicting definitions of the other virtues—wisdom, greatness of spirit, and decorum—embraced by peoples of other times and places enabled the historically minded observer to discern broader patterns of change over time. The historian could trace the developing relationship between justice and the other historically contingent cardinal virtues and so follow the bright line of moral development into the present age.

Smith embraced the conceptual framework of the "ancient moralists" *because* he was a moral historian. And because history is a chronicle of moral progress, its immanent tendencies were most apparent in the advanced commercial society of modern Britain. In any society, as Cicero wrote, the cardinal virtues are "bound together and interwoven," and this was as true for modern Britain as for ancient Rome.[43] The difference between these ethical regimes was that modern Britain was much closer to fulfilling nature's design: a sense of justice became increasingly manifest in relation to the *other* cardinal virtues that determined the character of the people.

Smith devoted little attention to justice because its implications for our common existence and collective well-being seemed so obvious. Because we can formulate the rules of justice precisely, a single example sufficed:

> If I owe a man ten pounds, justice requires that I should precisely pay him ten pounds, either at the time agreed upon, or when he demands it. What I ought to perform, how much I ought to perform, when and where I ought to perform it, the whole nature and circumstances of the action prescribed, are all of them precisely fixt and determined. Though it may be awkward and pedantic, therefore, to affect too strict an adherence to the common rules of prudence or generosity, there is no pedantry in sticking fast by the rules of justice.[44]

Smith's justice is fairness. Where our sense of fairness is skewed by self-deception, our shared knowledge of the rules is usually a sufficient corrective. When people nonetheless disagree on the relevance of the rules to their disagreements, the institutions of justice come into play.

Smith did not elaborate or interrogate the premises of his natural jurisprudence in *The Theory of Moral Sentiments*. Previous writers in the jurisprudential tradition sought to reconcile conflicting communal and individ-

---

43. Cicero, *On Duties*, I, § 15, 7.
44. Smith, *Theory of Moral Sentiments*, III, vi, §§ 9–10, 174–75.

ual property claims and explain the origins of private property. Cicero had held that "no property is private by nature" but that, by justice, "each man should hold on to whatever has fallen to him."[45] By contrast, Smith had almost nothing to say about property. What he did say focused on the indignation that people exhibit at the violation of their supposed property rights, and not from inspection of the general rules of natural justice constituting property rights *as* rights.[46] In other words, Smith was more interested in the fact of property—and as we shall see, its relation to rank, respect, and prosperity—than in its ultimate origins or legitimacy.

The ancients' four cardinal virtues are inextricably bound together in *The Theory of Moral Sentiments*. Precisely because of this interdependence, justice per se merited so little attention. Far from disappearing in Smith's text, it is omnipresent, pervading the more elaborate discussions of other virtues. His treatment of greatness of spirit, the third cardinal virtue in Cicero's catalogue, set the stage for his assault on mercantilist statecraft and its manifest injustices in *The Wealth of Nations*. Tempting as it might be to see this virtue as courage or valor in the face of danger, neither Cicero nor Smith paid much attention to war and warriors. Cicero instead insisted, and Smith agreed, that "public life," and the conduct of "public business," was the proper arena for the display of great spirit.[47]

While Smith, unlike Cicero, remained at the margins of public life, his great treatises—animated by his own "sense of justice"—subjected public men and their policies to rigorous analysis on moral grounds.[48] Modern

---

45. Cicero, *On Duties*, I, § 21, 9.
46. "The most sacred laws of justice, therefore, those whose violation seems to call loudest for vengeance and punishment, are the laws which guard the life and person of our neighbour; the next are those which guard his property and possessions; and last of all come those which guard what are called his personal rights, or what is due to him from the promises of others" (Smith, *Theory of Moral Sentiments*, II, II, ii, § 2, 84). Even in *The Wealth of Nations,* Smith had surprisingly little to say about property. There too he seems to have taken for granted the justice of private property, even when it is "valuable and extensive," and thus in need of the protection of civil government (V, 1.b, § 2, 710).
47. Cicero, *On Duties*, I, §§ 72–73, 29. "Most men consider that military affairs are of greater significance than civic; I must deflate that opinion" (§ 74, 29).
48. In private matters both attached a great deal of importance to liberality or magnanimity, which for Cicero is perhaps a branch of justice but for Smith is clearly separate from justice—the reciprocities of generosity and gratitude are not subject to precise rules. Cicero said that justice and liberality are "connected," and that "nothing is liberal if it is not also just." Ibid., I, §§ 20, 43, 9, 19. Smith introduced his discussion of magnanimity by reference to conduct in situations of "great distress," and he offered some examples of "heroic magnanimity," which, even in "common life," reveal what Cicero called greatness of spirit. *Theory of Moral Sentiments,* I, III, i, §§ 13–14, 47–48; on generosity and gratitude, see III, vi, § 9, 174.

statesmen failed to display "greatness of spirit" not because they lacked courage in the conventional sense or because they fell short in their private obligations, but, rather, it was because they did not rise to the moral standard of the public they ostensibly served. According to Smith, "the common character of the people" differed at different stages of historical development: some nations are characterized by "liberality, frankness, and good fellowship," others by "narrowness, meanness, and a selfish disposition." The virtues of statesmen could only be assessed in relation to a people's virtues, or "common character," at a particular historical moment. If people individually and collectively were "liberal and generous," the plans and systems statesmen crafted for the public benefit must meet the same high standard. For Smith, "Mr. Colbert, the famous minister of Lewis XIV," was the antithesis of the enlightened, great-spirited modern statesman: "instead of allowing every man to pursue his own interest his own way, upon the liberal plan of equality, liberty and justice, he bestowed upon certain branches of industry extraordinary privileges, while he laid others under as extraordinary restraints." Jean-Baptiste Colbert was a man of probity, industry, and experience, but he lacked greatness of spirit when he instituted the unfair and shortsighted measures of the "mercantile system."[49]

The last of the cardinal virtues, seemliness, or in Cicero's Latin, *decorum,* was the most subjective and culturally relative, and thus furthest removed from Smith's conception of justice. Cicero defined *decorum* as "a sense of shame and what one might call the ordered beauty of a life, a calming of the agitations of the spirit, and due measure in all things."[50] This virtue could hardly be reduced to precise rules applicable at all times and places. Yet Smith lavished extraordinary attention on what he called "prudence," a close approximation to Cicero's *decorum.* The traits that Smith associated with prudence were, as many commentators have noted, precisely the ones he personally admired and therefore cultivated in himself. "The prudent man is always sincere," he wrote in a well-known, almost autobiographical passage from part 6 in his last edition of *The Theory of Moral Sentiments,* "and feels horror at the very thought of exposing himself to the disgrace which attends upon the detection of falsehood. . . . Both in his conduct and conversation, he is an exact observer of decency, and respects with an almost religious scrupulosity, all the established decorums and ceremonials of society."[51]

---

49. Smith, *Wealth of Nations,* IV, ix, § 13, 668, § 3, 663–64; "liberal and generous system," § 24, 671.
50. Cicero, *On Duties,* I, § 93, 37. See generally §§ 93–159, 37–62.
51. Smith, *Theory of Moral Sentiments,* VI, i, §§ 8–10, 214.

Smith's discussion of what we would identify as the fourth cardinal virtue reads like a synopsis of the "Protestant ethic," a culturally specific and normative idealization of conduct that Max Weber would later make famous.[52] If seemliness is a virtue for anyone in any society, its specific features vary according to a society's particular features and the positions particular individuals occupy in it. The same is true for wisdom and greatness of spirit. Justice, on the contrary, does *not* depend on the particulars of station, and this is why Smith could say that the general rules of justice can be formulated with "the greatest exactness." Like cases are always to be treated alike; in matters of justice, we are all supposed to be equals. For the other three virtues, we are equals only in the limited sense that some number of us hold the same or similar rank in society.

The connection among Smith, Britons of his station, and the future happiness of humanity is historical. The character of the people in an advanced commercial society moves progressively toward the synthesis of the ancients' four cardinal virtues at the highest stage of development, with justice assuming its properly primary place. The ancient moralists celebrated ordered ranks as an end in itself for all communities: their virtues promoted an ethos of honor. Summarizing the particulars of station and arranging them in a binding order, ranks are marked by signs recognizable to everyone. Moreover, the relations between ranks are subject to rules that are conspicuously supported and assiduously followed.

As a moral historian, Smith read different lessons in the succession of ethical regimes, or particular rank orderings, that constituted human history. Smith's version of the "Protestant ethic" is thus both culturally specific and contingent—as the historian was well equipped to see—and immanently universal, anticipating nature's design for humanity generally. To use the language of our time, the rising "middle class" for which Smith supposedly spoke was thus a class-to-end-all-classes, the vanguard of an emergent moral order in which a universal sense of justice transcended the class distinctions created and supported by the ancients' virtues.

Smith's subjects of middling station were emphatically products of history, people like himself whose position in society afforded them the luxury of living in seemly modesty and frugality. His parochial conception of prudence is most conspicuous in his preoccupation with frugality at a time when relatively few people, even in the most advanced societies, had very much control over their daily expenses. "In the steadiness of his industry and frugality,

52. Max Weber, *The Protestant Ethic and the Spirit of Capitalism,* trans. Talcott Parsons (New York, 1930).

in his steadily sacrificing the ease and enjoyment of the present moment for the probable expectation of the still greater ease and enjoyment of a more distant but more lasting period of time," Smith wrote, "the prudent man is always both supported and rewarded by the entire approbation of the impartial spectator, and of the representative of the impartial spectator, the man within the breast."[53] Although "the man within the breast" and the "prudent man" are potentially at odds, as they would have been throughout history, Smith saw them in the process of becoming one.

If the historical self-consciousness Smith cultivated emphasizes the great distance between the ancients and the moderns, it also focused attention on the radical imperfections of his time. What today we think of as middle-class virtues were far from universal, as Smith well knew, and middle-class people in any case would only act according to the canons of prudence under particular and contingent political conditions. This is why modern policy, particularly in the realm of political economy where questions of justice were most salient, absorbed so much of Smith's attention. But even if justice shaped the development of modern statecraft—and this was by no means certain—Smith did not imagine that it would obliterate the other ancient virtues. To the contrary, the more precise definition of the public realm and its clear distinction from the private would enable those virtues to flourish. Far from rejecting the ancients' teachings, Smith grounded his moral psychology in virtue ethics. He did not deduce his moral theory from market behavior, as a simple gloss on the class interests of "possessive individualists." Instead, Smith's psychology—his reading of the ancient moralists— preceded and shaped his understanding of market relations and their effects on the ethos of modern commercial societies.

For self-regarding social animals, Smith taught, the desire for the approval, admiration, and applause of others implies a natural propensity to seek to better ourselves. "It is because mankind are disposed to sympathize more entirely with our joy than with our sorrow, that we make parade of our riches, and conceal our poverty. . . . Nay, it is chiefly from this regard to the sentiments of mankind, that we pursue riches and avoid poverty. For to what purpose is all the toil and bustle of this world?"[54] We imagine those who have had the greatest success in the pursuit of riches to be the happiest among us, the ones to admire and emulate. We feel the same way about those who have power over us.

> Upon this disposition of mankind, to go along with all the passions of the rich
> and the powerful, is founded the distinction of ranks, and the order of

---

53. Smith, *Theory of Moral Sentiments*, VI, I, § 11, 215.
54. Ibid., I, III, ii, § 1, 50.

society. . . . We are eager to assist them in completing a system of happiness that approaches so near to perfection; and we desire to serve them for their own sake, without any other recompense but the vanity or the honour of obliging them. Neither is our deference to their inclinations founded chiefly, or altogether, upon a regard to the utility of such submission, and to the order of society, which is best supported by it.[55]

Smith's theory of sentiments and his system of natural ethics thus explain the stratified nature of every society, offering a powerful tool for thinking morally and acting responsibly in a world of statuses, where questions of honor and respect always intrude and our duties are no less compelling because they are situationally delimited.

Modern commercial societies would remain rank ordered, even as the middle-class's sense of justice gained ever-wider currency through the extension of market relations. Indeed, as justice enjoined respect for private property, it would secure the unequal wealth distribution that sustains rank. Smith's moral perspective thus resolved the apparent tension between the equality enjoined by the universal principle of justice and the inequalities that constituted any particular, necessarily rank-ordered society.[56] Yet just as Smith completed his masterful reconstruction of virtue ethics, two new and opposed systems of ethics, Kantian and Benthamite, came to the fore, both emphasizing autonomy and equality as universal values and discounting the ephemera of rank and reputation. These famously "liberal" theorists reversed Smith's historical approach, treating equality not as the end but rather as the premise and point of departure for moral theory. While history and morality constituted a single domain for Smith, they diverged progressively in his successors' dismantling of virtue ethics.

It would be a mistake to conclude, however, that Smith's moral theory was anachronistic, or irrelevant to the liberal world that emerged from—or was ratified by—his economic theory. To the contrary, Smith's closely connected conceptions of *nation* and *market*, elaborated in *The Wealth of Nations* from premises set forth in *The Theory of Moral Sentiments*, constitute the

55. Ibid., § 3, 52.
56. Smith resolved this tension more successfully—at least in theory—than his famed predecessor in the lineage of liberalism, John Locke, who argued in the same breath for the natural equality of all humanity and respect for the social inequalities reflecting the contingencies of age, merit, and birth (John Locke, *The Second Treatise of Government*, vi, § 54, in idem, *Two Treatises of Government,* ed. Peter Laslett [Cambridge, U.K., 1988], 304). Also see John Marshall, *John Locke: Resistance, Religion and Responsibility* (Cambridge, U.K., 1994), chap. 7. Locke was, of course, well acquainted with Cicero's treatment of the cardinal virtues in *De officiis.*

conceptual framework for liberal modernity. The idea of nation, however integral it may be to our understanding of the *international* system that defines the modern world, is anomalous and anachronistic in the ahistorical, deductive tradition of modern liberal theorizing. For Smith, by contrast, the emerging regime of *market* relations in advanced commercial societies progressively converged with, and was bounded by, the *nation* through history. Far from dissolving or obliterating all prior social relations, the perfection of the market would enable ranks and interests *within* national society to achieve a "natural" balance and interdependence.

The end of mercantilist interference in the market and its attendant injustices to property owners would strengthen and stabilize advanced commercial societies *and* the natural ordering of ranks that constitute societies in general. Justice requires equal treatment of property owners within the context of the market. The unequal treatment resulting from the government's interference jeopardized harmonious social relations and retarded the market's extension and perfection. Mercantilist governments exceeded their proper role as the dispenser of justice narrowly defined and guarantor of the national interest. Just as they committed injustices against their own subjects, so too did their efforts to beggar one another and project their power through conquest or unequal alliance violate nature's design for the wealth and welfare of all nations. These violations of justice were endemic in the policies of modern nations, but they were most conspicuous in the depredations of advanced commercial societies against nations at an earlier and lower stage of development.

Improvement

Smith addressed a fundamentally historical problem in *The Wealth of Nations:* How and why had Britain ascended so rapidly from barbarism to its present flourishing condition as an advanced commercial society? His answer seems straightforward: The extension and perfection of market relations were the engine of Britain's remarkable progress. But Smith's historical perspective on the role of "the sovereign" (what today we would call the sovereign state) in this development was fundamentally ambiguous. Indeed, Smith was disinclined to give Britain's rulers much credit for the nation's progress. If anything, the mercantilist tendencies of modern statecraft had retarded the nation's development. The challenge for a more enlightened generation of statesmen was to follow the lead of myriad enterprising individuals who pursued their own interests *within* the market and thus promoted the wealth of the entire community. Yet even as Smith showed that the chief threats to a modern market regime came from the state, he recognized that the market could not have emerged in the first place—and would not be perfected in the future—without an effective "civil government" that guaranteed collective security, dispensed justice, and raised taxes.[57]

Smith's fundamental insight, which he announced at the beginning of *The Wealth of Nations,* is that the division of labor—the functional specialization of "productive powers"—is the engine of human progress. The increasing division of labor promotes exchange, which in turn promotes the division of labor. "As it is the power of exchanging that gives occasion to the division of labour," he wrote in book 1, chapter 3, "so the extent of this division must always be limited by the extent of that power, or, in other words, by the extent of the market."[58] By producing greater wealth, the division of labor facilitates the balanced development of ranks and fosters the virtues that Smith elaborated in *The Theory of Moral Sentiments.* Without the division of labor, the result of a natural propensity to exchange what we produce for our own benefit, societies cannot advance and civilization is impossible.[59]

Our wish to improve our circumstances, to better ourselves, is related to our quest for approval. Thus implicated in our moral sentiments, improvement is never simply an objective condition. Ill-gotten and unjust gains are to be condemned, not applauded, just as foolish, mean-spirited, selfish, or extravagant conduct is the proper subject of our indignation. Nevertheless, Smith recognized that differences in wealth, power, rank, and reputation deny some of us any chance of betterment and reward others for their vices. Nor did Smith shirk from the moral implications of this enduring state of affairs: "the care of the universal happiness of all rational and sensible beings, is the business of God and not of man. To man is allotted a much humbler department, one more suited to the weakness of his powers and the narrowness of his comprehension; the care of his own happiness, of that of his family, his friends, his country."[60] In these circumstances, betterment, whether material or moral, is uncertain, uneven, and yet cumulatively discernible in human history.

---

57. See generally Smith, *Wealth of Nations,* V, i, 689–816.
58. Ibid., I, i, § 1, 13; iii, § i, 31. Also see chapter 1, above, on human powers and chapter 2 on the "extent of the market."
59. The thrust of Smith's argument is apparent in the title of *The Wealth of Nations:* "Of the Causes of Improvement in the Productive Powers of Labour, and of the Order according to which its Produce is naturally distributed among the different Ranks of the People" (I).
60. *Theory of Moral Sentiments,* VI, II, iii, § 6, 237. While this assessment may seem to be at odds with Smith's claim, quoted earlier, that we are duty bound to advance "the happiness of mankind . . . as far as in our power," it should be recalled that the context for this claim is justice—the only virtue where duties follow from general and exact rules known to us all.

The market mediates between individual psychology—the will and ability to improve one's situation—and the collective welfare. Individuals may be thwarted in their quest for improvement, but society as a whole will benefit from their efforts. We are morally obliged to care for ourselves, our family, our friends (and others of our rank), and our country. Caring is a social activity, involving, as Cicero put it, "degrees of fellowship" to which there are corresponding degrees of obligation.[61] In caring for ourselves, we also take care of others and others of us. When we improve our circumstances, the good effects will be felt by those closest to us, making all of us happier. Well-being and good feeling will generally correspond. There is, however, no necessary relation among using one's faculties to achieve a goal, achieving that goal, and benefiting oneself or anyone else in the process. As an empirical generalization, Smith believed that good intentions and useful activities produce concentric circles of benefit, and that overlapping circles of benefits lead to the general improvement of society.

The Wealth of Nations proceeds from the premise of man's natural propensity to improve his condition and the resulting progress of a division of labor that had promoted the wealth and welfare of expanding associations of people throughout history. Smith's propositions about human beings and their propensities and powers are based on the moral historian's empirical observations: they are not deductions from the behavior of "economic man," a notional figure in an ahistorical, abstract world constituting the domain of modern economics.[62] The progression of Smith's argument from the notional individual to ever-larger worlds of human experience, from empirical generalizations about self-improvement to universal history, illuminates the moral dimension of his project.

Smith situated his economic and social history of Britain in the progress of European civilization. Yet with "the discovery of America," European civilization could only be conceived in the context of a still larger world. It is the

---

61. Cicero held that "the first fellowship exists in marriage itself, and the next with one's children." Yet, "of all the fellowships none is more serious, and none dearer, than that of each of us with the republic" (Cicero, *On Duties*, I, §§ 53–57, 22–24). Smith no doubt would have said the same for country in the event that its existence were threatened.

62. *Theory of Moral Sentiments* offers a number of such propositions about human propensities. Smith resisted the tendency to reduce the number of such propensities by relating them to each other systematically. This he called "a propensity, which is natural to all men, but which philosophers in particular are apt to cultivate with a peculiar fondness, as the great means of displaying their ingenuity, the propensity to account for all appearances from as few principles as possible" (VII, II, ii, § 14, 299). His contrary predilection leaves him open to the charge that at least some of his empirical generalizations contradict each other.

fundamental incompatibility of the evident moral progress of Europe and the savagery of Europeans in their encounters with native peoples that provoked Smith's strongest language. The mercantile system—the subject of book 4 of *The Wealth of Nations*—provides the more general context for Smith's indignation over the way Europeans conducted themselves in the New World. Indeed, the mercantile system, of which the colonial exploitation was an integral part, was a more general source of Smith's indignation.[63] In his view, there was no justification for systems of privileges and preferences benefiting some artisans, merchants, and their public patrons at the expense of the nation as a whole. Justice calls for them to be eliminated. "All systems either of preference or of restraint, therefore, being thus completely taken away, the obvious and simple system of natural liberty establishes itself of its own accord. Every man, as long as he does not violate the laws of justice, is left perfectly free to pursue his own interest his own way, and to bring both his industry and capital into competition with those of any other man, or order of men."[64]

Smith's indignation about the ways mercantilist policies impeded social and economic progress in Britain at a particular moment in national history was expressed in bold, unequivocal generalizations that seemed universally applicable and therefore axiomatic. To the extent that Britain, the most advanced commercial society, could be seen as a model for the future, generalizations drawn from British market behavior could be seen as immanent axioms. But Britain had hardly reached its fullest development, and the mercantilist system—the source of Smith's indignation—was dangerously behind the times, all too oblivious to market realities. If it was imperative that Britain withdraw from its pervasive and intrusive interference in the market, it was by no means clear that other nations at different stages of historical development should follow the same course.

Smith conjectured that societies proceed through a sequence of four historical ages predicated on the way they provide for their material needs— from hunting and gathering to pastoral, agricultural, and commercial regimes. This developmental map enabled him to compare different nations at any given time according to a universal standard. Far from implying

63. In eulogizing Smith, Dugald Stewart observed that his views of the mercantile system "are expressed in a tone of indignation which he seldom assumes in his political writings" ("Account of the Life and Writings of Adam Smith, L.L.D.," read by Dugald Stewart, Jan. 21, and Mar. 18, 1793, to the Royal Society of Edinburgh; rpt. in Adam Smith, *Essays on Philosophical Subjects*, ed. W. P. D. Wightman and J. C. Bryce [Oxford, 1980], 269–351, at 316).

64. Smith, *Wealth of Nations*, IV, ix, § 51, 687.

synchronous development, universal history focused attention on the temporally distinct trajectory of particular national histories. The emphasis on development through time stood in apparent counterpoint to the emphasis, exemplified by David Hume and Montesquieu, on the variable relation of manners to material conditions across space.

The differences between historical and environmental orientations should not be exaggerated. Both sought to account for the cultural differences that Europeans encountered in the age of discovery, and both reinforced the growing conviction that European civilization was superior to all others. Hume, Montesquieu, and Smith shared an interest in the material circumstances that gave rise to an international division of labor. By emphasizing the progress of civilization, all of these writers superimposed a universal history of humanity on a world whose natural history is heterogeneous beyond all human reckoning.

History conceptualized in progressive stages constitutes the common sense of the Scottish Enlightenment, and perhaps to a lesser degree, of the Enlightenment as a whole. By synthesizing spatial and historical perspectives, this way of thinking provided the template for *The Wealth of Nations.* As individuals' natural propensities gave rise to social tendencies and the progress of development accelerated, the immanently universal character of human history became increasingly manifest. At some future time, when national markets merged seamlessly into a single world market, the nation might wither away.

Yet this was at best a distant prospect. The present-day circumstances of different nations—and therefore the policy imperatives that governments faced—still differed radically. The role of any particular government was contingent on its nation's stage of development relative to other nations. The *market* and its prospective extent thus proved to be a protean, ambiguous concept, conflating a description of commerce as an actual state of affairs with the visionary prospect of a liberal world of free exchange. The market was both *national,* or at least prospectively so, when all barriers to free exchange were dismantled within a particular country, and *global,* as foreign trade flourished and mercantilist regimes were dismantled.

Some nations stood at a higher stage of development than others and would therefore gain more from the rapid extension of the world market. This was the case, Smith well knew, in the history of the European conquest of the New World. "By opening a new and inexhaustible market to all the commodities of Europe," he wrote, "the discovery of America . . . gave occasion to new divisions of labour and improvements of art, which in the narrow circle of the ancient commerce, could never have taken place for want of a market to take off the greater part of their produce." In theory, this "new sett of exchanges . . . should naturally have proved as advantageous to the new, as it certainly did to the old continent."[65] Unfortunately, the Europeans' military preponderance—a function of their more highly developed economies—made irresistible the conquest of less civilized peoples and the expropriation of their wealth.

By tracing advanced commercial societies through stages of development that reflected the progressive perfection of market society, Smith and his fellow conjecturalists could also explain differences among nations across space. Smith's "natural liberty" made the most sense in exchange among societies at the same stage of development, although the history of British commercial relations with France and other European nations suggested that trade would always be subject to the kinds of political interference Smith grudgingly endorsed. Nations at different stages of development were much more likely to resort to force, both because more advanced societies could not resist exploiting their preponderant power and because the survival of weaker, less developed nations depended on forceful resistance to encroachments on their rights.

Smith urged policy makers in societies at an advanced stage of development to keep the domains of economics and politics as distinct as possible, promoting the wealth of nations through reciprocally beneficial market exchanges. But weak societies on the periphery of the expanding European market had to move in the opposite direction, building up effective warmaking states even if European nations might begin to dismantle theirs. The goal was for "the inhabitants of all the different quarters of the world . . . [to] arrive at that equality of courage and force which, by inspiring mutual fear, can alone overawe the injustice of independent nations into some sort of respect for the rights of one another." Smith recognized that the beneficial effects of a global market depended on the prior achievement of a rough political equality, or balance of power, among the nations of every "quarter" of the world. This did not mean that less developed nations should avoid contact with the world, for the extension of market relations promoted the economic development—the movement through history—that alone could equalize power. Indeed, "nothing seems more likely to establish this equality of force than that mutual communication of knowledge and of all sorts of improvements which an extensive commerce from all countries to all countries naturally, or rather necessarily, carries along with it." The antimercantilist Smith thus advocated something very much like mercantilism as he urged less

---

65. Ibid., IV, i, § 32, 448.

developed nations to manage foreign trade relations in ways that would promote national power and enable them to redress European "injustices."[66]

Home Market

The Wealth of Nations is best known for its powerful attack on mercantilism
and its endorsement of market freedom. These were not necessarily the
same thing in Smith's time, although his legatees customarily conflate them.
Subsequent generations of free traders routinely invoked his authority as
they sought to dismantle international trade barriers. But Smith was less interested in promoting foreign trade than in illuminating the pernicious implications of mercantilistic regulation in the domestic economy. Mercantilists were certainly misguided when they interfered with free foreign trade,
but their biggest mistake was to take foreign trade too seriously, to imagine
that a favorable international balance of trade was crucial to a nation's prosperity. Smith instead insisted that the fullest possible extension of the market *within* the nation was the first great desideratum, for the wealth of a nation depended on the full development of its own productive resources.
Smith's preference for the home market was a function of his conjectural history, according to which the development of separate societies would ultimately lead to a unified world market.

Smith's most forceful denunciation of mercantilism and its injustices
came in the concluding passages of *The Wealth of Nations,* in his famous
commentary on the contemporaneous American crisis. His major concern
here was with perfecting and extending Britain's national market—and with
equalizing tax burdens throughout the empire—and not with instituting an
international regime of free trade. The best outcome of the crisis would be
a full incorporation of the colonies in the British home market; next best
would be the most cordial, freest possible trade relations with an independent United States. In other words, nation came first, and world followed, a
sequence that tracked Smith's historical understanding of the stages of societal development.[67]

Smith's preference for the home market not only called into question the
relative importance of foreign trade but also the value of free trade under

66. Ibid., IV, vii.c, § 80, 626–27.
67. Winch, *Riches and Poverty,* 156–65; Skinner, *System of Social Science,* 209–30; Eliga
H. Gould, *The Persistence of Empire: British Political Culture in the Age of the American Revolution* (Chapel Hill, N.C., 2000), 140–45.

particular historical circumstances. The "inland or home trade," he wrote in book 4, was "the most important of all, the trade in which an equal capital affords the greatest revenue, and creates the greatest employment to the people of the country," but it was one that mercantilists considered "as subsidiary only to foreign trade."[68] Smith also celebrated the superior virtue and patriotism of the "small proprietor," "of all improvers the most industrious, the most intelligent, and the most successful."[69] Smith's bias in favor of the home market—often construed as an agrarian bias—is apparent in his juxtaposition of the farmer to the merchant who, "it has been said very properly, is not necessarily the citizen of any particular country." Capital was safer at home; it also generated more wealth as it circulated in the home market. In time of war, a nation with a well-developed home market would be better able to vindicate its independence against external threats.[70]

For Smith the main impediments to national economic development were legally sanctioned monopolies. Corporate interests employed them to exploit their countrymen; mercantilist regulations projected them into the arena of foreign trade. Increasing the ambit of "natural liberty" at home and abroad was obviously the key to national prosperity. Given Britain's dominant position in the commercial world, Smith had no reason to fear that freer foreign trade would wreak significant damage on any major sector of the domestic economy. Dissolving barriers between national and world markets would serve Britain's interests.[71]

This was not necessarily the case in the new United States. In a country of continental dimensions, the extension of the home market could support a sufficiently elaborate division of labor to promote a rapid pace of economic

---

68. Smith, *Wealth of Nations*, IV, i, § 10, 435.
69. Ibid., III, iv, § 19, 423. See Nicholas Phillipson, "Adam Smith as Civic Moralist," in Hont and Ignatieff, eds., *Wealth and Virtue*, 179–202, at 192, for a discussion of this passage. Smith's "new voluntarist language of provincial morality" pivoted on "neighbourhood" and "regionality" (Ibid., 192–202).
70. On the civic dimensions of Smith's agrarian bias, see John Dwyer, "Virtue and Improvement: The Civic World of Adam Smith," in Jones and Skinner, eds., *Adam Smith Reviewed*, 190–216.
71. Bernard Semmel, *The Rise of Free Trade Imperialism: Classical Political Economy, the Empire of Free Trade, and Imperialism, 1750–1850* (Cambridge, U.K., 1970). As George Fitzhugh astutely noted in 1854, Smith's "country . . . was an over-match for the rest of the world. International free trade would benefit his country as much as social free trade would benefit his friends. This was his world, and had it been the only world his philosophy would have been true. But there was another and much larger world, whose misfortunes, under his system, were to make the fortunes of his friends and his country" (*Sociology for the South: or, The Failure of Free Society* [1854; New York, 1965], 12).

development.[72] But extension could proceed too rapidly, particularly when an underdeveloped economy was drawn into the orbit of a more advanced commercial economy. Market expansion thus had to be combined with a sufficient concentration of population and productive resources in order to foster optimal development. Smith did not worry about the concentration of capital at "home," because it seemed to him a natural phenomenon: "home is in this manner the center, if I may say so, round which the capitals of the inhabitants of every country are continually circulating."[73] Centrifugal tendencies were more pronounced at the periphery, however, and the concentration of productive resources therefore much more problematic. Would weaker, less developed economies ever develop a home market, given the tendency of capital to return to its "home" in the most advanced commercial societies?

The unequal distribution of wealth and power within and among nations represented the operation of the division of labor across time and space. Smith dismissed the physiocrats' contention that agriculture was the source of all value. A growing population gave rise to manufactures, increasing productivity and concentrating wealth in towns: "the inhabitants of a town, though they frequently possess no lands of their own, yet draw to themselves by their industry such a quantity of the rude produce of the lands of other people as supplies them, not only with the materials of their work, but with the fund of their subsistence." The same pattern had taken place in Europe, and it was now taking place in the world as a whole: "what a town always is with regard to the country in its neighbourhood, one independent state or country may frequently be with regard to other independent states or countries."[74]

In the fullness of time, inequalities among nations would diminish as they converged at the highest stage of development. Inveterately suspicious of the motives and measures of politicians, Smith warned that improvement should not be forced and that a "landed nation" would only squander its capital stock if it sought "to raise up artificers, manufacturers and merchants . . . prematurely, and before it was perfectly ripe for them."[75] This, of course, was a favorite passage of free traders who opposed protectionist efforts to foster

---

72. "In an immense country, with every variety of soil, and climate, and geological structures," one part of the country "could produce what another part cannot," and all would enjoy "the vast advantage of having a market nearer and surer" ("The Infancy of American Manufactures: A Brief Chapter of Our National History," *American Whig Review* 1 [Jan. 1845]: 49–58, at 55).

73. Smith, *Wealth of Nations*, IV, ii, § 6, 455.

74. Ibid., ix, § 37, 667.

75. Ibid., § 26, 672.

"infant industries."[76] Historically, Smith wrote, government-sponsored monopolies had given "traders and artificers in the town an advantage over the
landlords, farmers, and labourers in the country," breaking "down that natural equality which would otherwise take place in the commerce which is carried on between them."[77] As he acknowledged, "natural equality" did not
mean an equal distribution of wealth. And notwithstanding the tendency of
townspeople to combine and conspire against agriculturalists in the countryside, Smith recognized that towns promoted economic development and the
progress of civilization. Indeed, Smith's conception of the nation hinged on
the domestication of mercantile capital: "no part of it can be said to belong to
any particular country, till it has been spread as it were over the face of that
country, either in buildings, or in the lasting improvement of lands."[78]

Smith couched his historical account of Britain's rise as a market society in
terms of the obstacles that impeded its optimal development. If bad policies
were the problem, then better policies could indeed solve the problem. At
least by comparison with his indignant critique of bad policies, he was noticeably reticent in proposing good policies, no doubt because he was so sensitive to the historical complexity of Britain's development. His self-appointed
legatees interpreted this reticence as a matter of principle, yielding a preference for *no* policies: the unobstructed pursuit of individual interests would
have collective consequences all the more beneficial for being unintended.

Smith's account of the home market was too empirical, too grounded in
Britain's particular situation, to be fully satisfactory to succeeding generations
of classical economists. They took on themselves the task of discovering and
elaborating Smith's "theory" of market society.[79] In doing so, they would conceptualize the homogeneous space where the modern laws of economics play
out. What for Smith had been a particular, historically situated *home* market
now took on the character of *the* market. To make sense out of Smith, to en-
list him as the founder of their discipline, classical, free trade economists thus
had to suppress the historical dimension of *The Wealth of Nations*. Their
polemical opponents, the "national" or "historical" economists who advocated regulation of foreign trade and protection of manufactures, moved in

76. Douglas A. Irwin, *Against the Tide: An Intellectual History of Free Trade* (Princeton,
   N.J., 1996).
77. Smith, *Wealth of Nations*, I, x, § 19, 142.
78. Ibid., III, iv, § 24, 426.
79. "One of the criticisms of Smith, in the period of reconstruction of political economy in
   the 1790s and 1800s, was indeed that he was too little concerned with the simple principles of the thing, or too much concerned with all the details of economic life" (Rothschild, *Economic Sentiments*, 237).

the opposite direction, foregrounding contingent historical conditions that justified limits on market freedom and deferring the free trade millennium until a far distant future.[80]

The historical logic of *The Wealth of Nations* was most conspicuous in book 5, "Of the Revenue of the Sovereign or Commonwealth." When Smith addressed the American crisis, his attention shifted to the problematic boundaries of Britain's national market. Were the colonies part of the "nation," and would they participate fully in its market regime? Would the Americans pay their fair share of the costs of civil government? In an enlightened nation where monopoly privileges had been abolished, the costs of defending the nation's sovereignty would be borne equally by all taxpayers.

The nation thus defined the boundaries of the internal, home market, and it was only within that bounded domain that a regime of free trade was possible. The "freedom of interior commerce," Smith explained, was "the effect of the uniformity of the system of taxation" and "perhaps one of the principal causes of the prosperity of Great Britain."[81] Freedom was linked with taxation because Britain and other European nations operated within a diplomatic system that pivoted on a balance of political and military power. Britain's power depended on incorporating distant provinces into both the state and a growing internal market. "The extension of the custom-house laws of Great Britain to Ireland and the plantations, provided it was accompanied, as in justice it ought to be, with an extension of the freedom of trade," would be in the highest degree advantageous to both." Free trade "between all the different parts of the British empire" and a system of uniform taxation would create "an immense internal market for every part of the produce of all its different provinces."[82]

Britain's comparative advantage in Europe was a function of the superior development of its home market. By contrast, the British overseas empire was riddled with mercantilistic regulations that impeded market freedom and economic development. Mercantilists were dazzled by the apparent

---

80. Edward Mead Earle, "Adam Smith, Alexander Hamilton, Friedrich List: The Economic Foundations of Military Power," in Edward Mead Earle, ed., *Makers of Modern Strategy: Military Thought from Machiavelli to Hitler* (Princeton, N.J., 1943), 117–54; Istvan Hont, "Free Trade and the Economic Limits to National Markets: Neo-Machiavellian Political Economy Reconsidered," in John Dunn, ed., *The Economic Limits to Modern Politics* (Cambridge, U.K., 1990), 41–120; Bernard Semmel, *The Liberal Ideal and the Demons of Empire: Theories of Imperialism from Adam Smith to Lenin* (Baltimore, Md., 1993); Keith Tribe, *Strategies of Economic Order: German Economic Discourse* (Cambridge, U.K., 1995).

81. Smith, *Wealth of Nations*, V, ii.k, § 69, 900.

82. Ibid., iii, § 72, 935.

advantages of monopolizing the colony trade, failing to recognize the distorting effects of its artificially high profits on "that natural balance which
would otherwise have taken place among all the different branches of British
industry."[83] Privileged interests both at home and in the colonies flourished
at the expense of the nation as a whole.

Colonial taxpayers, spared most of the costs of imperial administration,
were among the immediate beneficiaries of this corrupt mercantilist regime.
Nevertheless, the denial of their market freedom—that is, of full integration
in the British national market—would stunt their future prospects. Given
the colonies' "present state of improvement," imperial regulations of colonial
trade may "have not hitherto been very hurtful." This would no longer be
true, however, as the colonies moved rapidly to a higher stage of development. It would then become apparent that it was "a manifest violation of the
most sacred rights of mankind," Smith concluded, "to prohibit a great people . . . from making all that they can of every part of their own produce, or
from employing their stock and industry in the way that they judge most advantageous to themselves."[84]

Smith's most highly charged and judgmental language rhetorically
marked the boundaries of the nation-as-market. At some glorious distant
day, market and world might coincide—a prospect that Smith's students
dwelled on much more than Smith did—but in the present state of historical development, the nation played a critical, progressive role in expanding
the ambit of market freedom. The British nation stood at an epochal con-
juncture in the imperial crisis leading up to the American Revolution. It
could either extend its boundaries westward, to Ireland and the "plantations," by incorporating subject peoples fully into the national market. Or it
could renounce its jurisdiction (in the colonies, at least) and acknowledge
American independence.

Incorporation would subject these peoples to a uniform system of taxation, and thus remove the "badges of slavery" that mercantilist regulations
had "imposed upon them."[85] Independence for the American colonies
would allow Britain to negotiate a treaty of commerce with them that "would
effectually secure . . . a free trade, more advantageous to the great body of
the people, though less so to the merchants, than the monopoly which she at
present enjoys."[86] Incorporation was the better choice, because free trade
would then not be hostage to political negotiations in a context of persisting

---

83. Ibid., IV, vii.c, § 43, 604.
84. Ibid., vii.b, § 44, 582.
85. Ibid.
86. Ibid., § 66, 617.

international rivalries. If incorporation was no longer possible, however, an early peace on favorable terms was clearly preferable to war.

Unfortunately, from Smith's point of view, British policy makers remained enthralled by the vision of "a great empire on the west side of the Atlantic," an empire that "has hitherto existed in imagination only."[87] Of course, these politicians, blinded by their own prejudices, would consider Smith the "visionary enthusiast" and reject any conciliatory project that jeopardized the monopoly of the colony trade. For their part, American patriots who were notoriously averse to all forms of taxation would hardly welcome the "heavier taxes" that incorporation in Smith's expanded nation promised.[88] The selfishness of British interests that benefited from the colonial monopoly combined with the equally selfish interests of colonists who had enjoyed tax exemptions under the mercantilist regime to make impossible any reciprocally advantageous outcome of the imperial crisis.

As a result, all parties would suffer from the devastation of an unnecessary war, the reverse image of the economist's vision of free trade, peace, and prosperity. From this historical perspective, Smith's condemnation of British policy in the American crisis sets forth a general principle of fundamental significance. Smith had no illusions about influencing present policy, but instead he sought to show how the nation protected and fostered the market. Previous discussions of mercantilist economics and of the development of the home market fleshed out Smith's historical understanding of this relationship, providing the appropriate context for his more familiar and influential formulations about markets, the division of labor, and the natural propensities of economic man.

---

87. Ibid., V, iii, § 92, 947.
88. Ibid., § 90, 945.

7
National
Destinies

In his inaugural address of March 4, 1801, Thomas Jefferson offered an inspirational vision of the United States as a great nation redeemed from the antirepublican heresies of his Federalist predecessors. Theirs was "the strongest Government on earth," the new president told his fellow Americans. "Unite[d] with one heart and one mind," they would spread liberty and enlightenment across a "chosen country, with room enough for our descendants to the thousandth and thousandth generation." His election was a "revolution," he later claimed, reversing powerful centrifugal tendencies that had nearly torn the union apart during the party struggles of the 1790s. The monarchical regimes of the Old World were in a constant state of war with each other and with their own peoples. But because governors and governed were one under the new republican dispensation, prosperous and peace-loving American citizens would make any sacrifice to defend their liberties and the nation's independence against any threat.[1] The power of a free people was irresistible, Jefferson exulted in a letter to his friend Joseph Priestley; it was something "new under the sun." Indeed, "this whole chapter in the history of man is new. The great extent of our Republic is new. Its sparse habitation is new. The mighty wave of public opinion which has rolled over it is new."[2]

---

1. Thomas Jefferson (hereafter TJ), First Inaugural Address, Mar. 4, 1801, in Merrill D. Peterson, ed., *Thomas Jefferson Writings* (New York, 1984), 493–94. TJ coined the phrase "revolution of 1800" in a letter to Spencer Roane, Sept. 6, 1819, ibid., 1425. See the essays collected in James P. Horn, Jan Ellen Lewis, and Peter S. Onuf, *The Revolution of 1800: Democracy, Race, and the New Republic* (Charlottesville, Va., 2002).
2. TJ to Joseph Priestley, Mar. 21, 1801, in Peterson, *Thomas Jefferson Writings*, 1086.

For the Anglophobic Jefferson, a despotic and corrupt British Empire was the new nation's antitype and foil, the most compelling image of the awful fate it had escaped in 1776. Yet the differences between empire and nation— between monarchical past and republican future—were clearer in rhetoric than in reality. As Adam Smith recognized, commercial exchange in a dynamic transatlantic market economy tended to make Britons and their Anglo-American cousins a single people. The challenge for enlightened statesmen, Smith thought, was to realign politics and economics, thus synchronizing nation and market. In his draft of the Declaration of Independence, Jefferson expressed similar sentiments, with a similar sense of futility. "We might have been a free and a great people together," but because King George failed to heed his American subjects' pleas, we must "forget our former love" for our former fellow British subjects "and hold them as we hold the rest of mankind, enemies in war, in peace friends."[3] For both Smith and Jefferson, the boundaries of the nation—whether conceived in terms of market relations or of affective, quasi-familial ties—were contingent and arbitrary, the result of failed British statesmanship.

In retrospect, geography might seem to dictate separation between the British metropolis and its distant American provinces. Yet Jefferson was not daunted by "the great extent of our Republic," nor did Smith foresee limits to the spread of market relations and a reciprocally beneficial division of labor. Revolutionary cosmopolitans abjured the British connection (although it soon became clear that there was no viable alternative to continuing trade relations), but they did not turn away from the larger world. To the contrary, they hoped that independence would facilitate fuller integration into the Atlantic trading system and into a progressively more enlightened state system. Nationalism and cosmopolitanism were inextricably linked for Jefferson and his fellow Revolutionaries. By forming their own nation—itself a compound of different European nations, with little common history—Americans would break down mercantilist barriers among nations in the trading world. National self-determination, republican government based on consent not coercion, and a liberal free trade regime would inaugurate a new chapter in the "history of man."

Smith and Jefferson both rejected the corrupt, mercantilist politics of the old regime and shared an expansive vision of national greatness in the modern world. Neither objected to the imperial dimensions of their respective nations. Smith imagined a happy resolution to the American crisis in which enlightened statesmen incorporated Britons in Ireland and the plantations

---

3. TJ's draft of the Declaration, July 4, 1776, ibid., 23.

into a greater Britain, thus aligning nation with market; Jefferson's new American nation would expand westward in *anticipation* of developing market relations. With republican government preceding and facilitating settlement, the new republican empire would escape the political and economic conflicts that had destroyed the British Empire and still wracked the Old World. The contingencies of the imperial crisis thus gave rise to distinctive geopolitical perspectives. Jefferson departed from Smith and the Scots in his belief that regime change could hasten and direct the progress of historical development. Jefferson's faith in the efficacy of politics resembled that of British politicians who cherished an imaginary "project of an empire . . . on the west side of the Atlantic" and thus resisted the American independence movement. Jefferson may have abjured the British connection, but he too embraced an imperial vision of the new nation's destiny, "amus[ing]"—or inspiring—the American "people with the imagination that they possessed a great empire" to the west.[4]

The Chosen Country

Jefferson's identification of a particular people and its "chosen country" evoked later, more familiar romantic ideas of national identity.[5] The revolutionary republican principles of citizen equality, government by consent, and popular sovereignty he so eloquently articulated demolished the props of old regime despotism, imaginatively creating the political space the new nation would fill. But Jefferson's Enlightenment vision was not the perfect prototype of conceptions of nationhood that developed in America and Europe over the next century. Jefferson's ideas about the role of the new nation in the progress of civilization in the world as a whole pointed toward the end of history. When he looked forward—and westward—the republican millennium seemed close at hand: self-determining, self-perfecting, self-transcending nations would merge into an all-encompassing world society.

---

4. Adam Smith, *An Inquiry into the Nature and Causes of the Wealth of Nations,* ed. R. H. Campbell and A. S. Skinner (Indianapolis, Ind., 1981), V, iii, § 92, 946. For a fuller elaboration of this theme, see Peter S. Onuf, *Jefferson's Empire: The Language of American Nationhood* (Charlottesville, Va., 2000).
5. The best study of the revolutionary origins of American nationalism is David Waldstreicher, *In the Midst of Perpetual Fetes: The Making of American Nationalism, 1776–1820* (Chapel Hill, N.C., 1997). For the rising tide of nationalist fervor in the post–War of 1812 "Era of Good Feelings," see Wilbur Zelinsky, *Nation into State: The Shifting Symbolic Foundations of American Nationalism* (Chapel Hill, N.C., 1988).

The union of American republics, living together in perpetual peace, prefigured the union of all societies.

Nevertheless, when Jefferson looked back—eastward across the Atlantic—the prospects for world peace seemed still distant. At some point in the future, he wrote his old friend John Adams in 1823, all the nations of Europe "will attain representative government," first by curbing, finally by abolishing monarchical power: "to attain all this however rivers of blood must yet flow, and years of desolation pass over." Jefferson's distant historical horizon was here measured by the quantity of blood yet to be shed on a continent still reeling from the carnage of the Napoleonic Wars. Only at the end of their own bloody history would Europeans begin to enjoy the peace and prosperity the Americans now enjoyed.[6]

The American Revolution was the pivotal moment in world history, providing an inspirational model for republican revolutions in Europe. European revolutionaries still faced enormous obstacles, however, both in destroying their own old regimes and in resisting the coalition of counterrevolutionary powers that sought to restore the old status quo. Jefferson's stubborn attachment to the French Revolution as it descended into the Terror reflected his consciousness of these obstacles. Every new nation in the Old World would be baptized in "rivers of blood," and the flow would be infinitely harder to stanch than it had been in the new United States. As Jefferson had written in 1787, before the French Revolution began, "the tree of liberty must be refreshed from time to time with the blood of patriots and tyrants."[7] The birth of the nation—the planting and nurturing of the "tree of liberty"—was the decisive and defining moment in history. For Jefferson, revolutionary nation making telescoped Whig history—the centuries-long struggle of liberty against power—into a single, brilliantly illuminating moment of truth. Yet even as Jefferson and his countrymen celebrated the world historical significance of their revolution, their precocious achievement underscored *differences* among nations. The peoples of the Old World would have to experience much more "history"—and much more bloodshed—before they could fulfill their national destinies.

---

6. TJ to John Adams, Sept. 4, 1823, in Lester Cappon, ed., *The Adams-Jefferson Letters: The Complete Correspondence between Thomas Jefferson and Abigail and John Adams*, 2 vols. (Chapel Hill, N.C., 1959), 2:596. The "rivers of blood" trope was a favorite of TJ's. See, particularly, the famous letter to Benjamin Austin, Jan. 9, 1816, in Andrew A. Lipscomb and Albert Ellery Bergh, eds., *The Writings of Thomas Jefferson* (Washington, 1903–4), 14:387–93.

7. TJ to William Smith, Nov. 13, 1787, in Julian Boyd et al., eds., *The Papers of Thomas Jefferson* (Princeton, N.J., 1950–), 12:356. This was TJ's famous justification of Shays's Rebellion, an agrarian uprising in Massachusetts.

Every nation found itself in distinctive circumstances. In historical terms, the nations of the world could be arrayed along a continuum of political progress, according to their ability to assert and maintain independence and self-government. The stage of political progress was in turn related to economic development and geopolitical circumstances. But these particularities tended to disappear in Jefferson's vision of a new American nation at the edge of the European world and heading toward the end of history: time and space converged in his vision of the West as the American future. The first new nation was also, providentially, the *only* civilized nation in the American hemisphere. Because it did not have to contend with powerful neighbors, its boundless potential could extend to its farthest, natural limits. Under these uniquely propitious circumstances, the revolutionary promise of the national idea for humanity as a whole, and not just for this particular people, would be most fully realized. Disentangled from the bloody affairs of Europe, the United States would offer not only a model of nation making but also a model order for the world of nations: the federal union, a republic of republics. In the absence of hostile neighbors, the immanent tendency of the nation thus was to transcend itself, to become the world.

Jefferson's thinking about the national idea was most fully developed after his retirement from the presidency, in an exchange with the French ideologist Antoine Louis Claude Destutt de Tracy about Destutt's *Commentary and Review of Montesquieu's Spirit of the Laws.*[8] Jefferson was so enthusiastic about the *Review* that he translated one major portion of the text and arranged for its full translation and publication by William Duane, the prominent Jeffersonian Republican editor, in 1811. Jefferson and Destutt agreed on the fundamental point, that the American and French revolutionary idea of the nation would transform the world. Recognizing the radically different circumstances of their respective nations, Jefferson acknowledged—but discounted—his disagreements with Destutt, most notably on the role of an

8. Antoine Louis Claude Destutt de Tracy, *A Commentary and Review of Montesquieu's Spirit of the Laws. Prepared for the Press From the Original Manuscript, in the Hands of the Publisher* (Philadelphia, Pa., 1811; rpt. New York, 1969). TJ's response is elaborated in TJ to A. L. C. Destutt de Tracy, Jan. 26, 1811, in Peterson, ed., *Thomas Jefferson Writings*, 1241–47. On the relationship between TJ and Destutt, we are indebted to the brilliant essay by Joyce Appleby, "What Is Still American in the Political Philosophy of Thomas Jefferson?" *William and Mary Quarterly* 39 (1982): 287–309, rpt. in her *Republicanism and Liberalism in the Historical Imagination* (Cambridge, Mass., 1992), 291–319. See also Emmet Kennedy, *A Philosophe in the Age of Revolution: Destutt de Tracy and the Origins of "Ideology"* (Philadelphia, Pa., 1978), 167–83, 208–13, and Dumas Malone, *The Sage of Monticello*, vol. 6 of *Jefferson and His Time* (Boston, 1981), 208–12.

energetic, centralized state administration. The new American nation was already secure in the full enjoyment of the liberties that embattled France was still struggling to vindicate against powerful enemies. As a result, Destutt's geopolitical analysis focused on the nation in history and *in* the world. Given the fortunate situation of the United States, Jefferson could instead imagine the nation *as* the world, beyond history.

The distinction between Destutt's short-term realism and his long-term idealism might have seemed insignificant to Jefferson in 1811, for he could still tell himself then, as he told Adams in 1823, that the passage of time—and the shedding of blood—eventually would bring the old European nations up to the new nation's standard. Jefferson certainly understood that the new nation's struggles were not yet over. European states still exercised enormous power and influence in the hemisphere, and the United States preserved at best a tenuous neutrality in their ongoing conflicts. Indeed, Jefferson's successor James Madison would soon lead the nation into yet another war with Britain, a second war for national independence. In such moments of crisis, Jefferson proved himself a political realist of the most conventional sort: power must be met with power. The oscillation between his republican optimism—looking to the end, and beyond history—and this geopolitical realism—responding to geopolitical imperatives within history—was characteristic of his entire career.

Jefferson's ambivalence set the parameters for a broader American debate about the new nation's place in the world after the War of 1812. National Republicans seized on Jefferson's famous acknowledgment, in a letter to Benjamin Austin in 1816, that the United States could only enjoy true independence in a dangerous world if it developed its own productive—and military—capacities by fostering manufactures. In response, free traders harked back—as did Jefferson in later years—to the famous passage in the *Notes on the State of Virginia* in which he urged his fellow Americans to "let our work-shops remain in Europe" as long as possible.[9] Jefferson's Revolutionary optimism was based on the comforting idea that New World and Old were separated by a great ocean, but always coexisted, more or less uncomfortably, with his faith in America's advantageous position in the Atlantic

---

9. TJ to Benjamin Austin, Jan. 9, 1816, in Lipscomb and Bergh, eds., *Writings of Thomas Jefferson;* TJ, *Notes on the State of Virginia,* ed. William Peden (Chapel Hill, N.C., 1954), Query 19, "Manufactures," 165. For an interpretation of TJ's foreign policy focusing on these contradictory positions, see Walter LaFeber, "Jefferson and an American Foreign Policy," in Peter S. Onuf, ed., *Jeffersonian Legacies* (Charlottesville, Va., 1993), 370–91.

trading system. Politically, the ocean was a great natural boundary; economically, it linked Americans to an increasingly elaborate and interdependent system of market relations. Could Americans trade freely with Europeans without compromising their independence? This simple question, which Jefferson at different times answered affirmatively and negatively, divided Americans along sectoral and sectional lines in the antebellum years and ultimately eroded the foundations of their union.

Jefferson, Destutt, and Montesquieu

Jefferson told Destutt that his *Review* was "the most precious gift the present age has received," and he hoped that it would become "the political rudiment of the young, and manual of our older citizens."[10] Montesquieu, Destutt and Jefferson agreed, did not anticipate the new order of things in the world that the American and French revolutions created. Modern nations would fulfill their destinies as "representative democracies" or republics, expanding to their natural limits—or to the limits that a competitive international system permitted. The nation grew as market relations were extended and a progressively elaborate division of labor promoted its prosperity and power. Bigger was better: Montesquieu had been wrong to think otherwise.

Jefferson had long been troubled by Montesquieu's "paradoxes" and "heresies"; as early as 1795 he had predicted that Montesquieu's "doctrine, that small States alone are fitted to be republics" would "be exploded by experience."[11] Jefferson was most troubled by the great philosophe's apparent relativism. Montesquieu's typology of regimes showed how each—the classic triad of republic, aristocracy, and monarchy—could be best sustained by its corresponding "spirit" or ethos—virtue, honor, and fear—and was best suited to countries of differing extent, from small to large. This meant that republicanism was only one form of government among many, that it was

---

10. TJ to A. L. C. Destutt de Tracy, Jan. 26, 1811, in Peterson, ed., *Thomas Jefferson Writings*, 1242, 1243.

11. TJ to Thomas Mann Randolph, May 30, 1790, in Lipscomb and Bergh, eds., *Writings of Thomas Jefferson* 8:31; TJ to François D'Ivernois, Feb. 6, 1795, in Peterson, ed., *Thomas Jefferson Writings*, 1024. For a similar prediction, see Joel Barlow, *To His Fellow Citizens of the United States*, Letter II (Philadelphia, Pa., 1799): "Not many years will pass" before it would universally be accepted that "the republican principle is not only proper and safe for the government of any people; but, that its propriety and safety are in proportion to the magnitude of the society and the extent of the territory" (4–5).

only preferable under specific conditions—conditions that did not and could not exist in the great nations of the modern world.[12]

Destutt earned Jefferson's applause because he cut through Montesquieu's categories, collapsing all regimes into two fundamental "classes": "one of these I denominate *national*, in which social rights are common to all; the other *special*, establishing or recognizing particular or unequal rights." A properly "national" regime is founded on "the principle, that all rights and power originate in, reside in, and belong to, the entire body of the people or nation; and that none exists, but what is derived from, and exercised for the nation."[13] "Special" is synonymous with "imperfect" or "defective," as when a monarch exercised rule over the people solely for his own benefit. More complicated regimes such as Britain's, where "different powers or sovereignties exercised in the same society" enter into "formal or tacit stipulations, which cannot be changed without the mutual consent of all the contracting parties," give the appearance of being "national," but they were in fact "special."[14] Such a regime could be described as an institutionalized state of war, in which the people—in Britain, the commons—are simply one of many powers. "This balancing is not securing peace," Destutt concluded, "it is declaring war": the "pretension to a power independent of the people at large, and capable of contending against the people, is the cause of that constant warfare which is every where seen between the rich and the poor."[15]

Destutt's analysis was appealing to Jefferson because its hostility to British-style mixed and balanced government resonated with Jefferson's Anglophobic bias. More significantly, Destutt's conception of the "nation" obliterated the distinctions within society—and the economy—that Jefferson identified with the old regime. According to Destutt, republican revolutions spurred the movement from "special" to "national" regimes that marks the progress of civilization. The moderns' great discovery of representation makes it possible to eschew crude proxies for both "the people" and the privileged classes embodied in the branches of government in a mixed regime. Representation enables a "special" regime to become "national." Under its aegis, a "simple democracy"—an ephemeral form of government characteristic of "hordes of savages" in "the infancy of a state"—could escape the inevitable cycle of

---

12. This was hardly a fair reading of the *Spirit of the Laws.* Far from being an advocate of ancient virtue, Montesquieu celebrated the mixed regime that sustained the rule of law in Britain, the quintessential modern commercial republic. Montesquieu, *Spirit of the Laws,* trans. Anne M. Cohler et al. (Cambridge, U.K., 1989) bk. 11, chap. 6, "On the constitution of England," 156–66.
13. Destutt de Tracy, *Review of Montesquieu,* 12–13, original emphasis.
14. Ibid., 13–14.
15. Ibid., 117–18.

classical politics, in which democracy degenerating into "anarchy . . . brings on aristocracy or tyranny." Representative democracy "is democracy rendered practicable for a long time and over a great extent of territory."[16]

"Simple democracy," Destutt concluded, "is the true state of nature; representative democracy is that of nature, in a perfect state."[17] Montesquieu's small republic is a "simple democracy" suitable for savages and irrelevant to the modern world. The heroic "virtue" of the ancients—their "gloomy enthusiasm" for "voluntary privations" and "self-denials"—reflects the savage impulses that primitive communities had to suppress, or at least contain, in order to survive. By "exciting men to hardihood and devotedness," classical virtue "renders them at the same time malignant, austere, ferocious, sanguinary, and above all unhappy."[18] Like Destutt, Jefferson embraced a conception of virtue more suitable for an enlightened and improving modern age, in accord—not at war—with the progressive fulfillment of man's true nature.[19] Man as such, not man as adapted to the peculiar requirements of a "special" regime that distorted his nature, was the ultimate product of representative democracy, the end point of the progress of civilization.

Jefferson and his fellow Revolutionaries proclaimed their "attachment to the general rights of mankind," insisting that their republican experiment initiated a new epoch in world history.[20] They were, like Destutt, "nationalists" who cherished the principle of popular self-rule, but they were also cosmopolitans. If republicanism enabled the peoples of the world to govern themselves and claim the "*separate* & equal station to which the laws of nature and of nature's God entitle them," it also brought them together, progressively merging them into universal society. In the fullness of time, Montesquieu's taxonomy of regime types and distinctive national characters would thus be rendered obsolete.[21]

In time, the classical republican "citizen," with his parochial attachments and blind prejudices, would also be superseded by the modern "man," with his "love of order, of industry, of justice, and reason."[22] The "principle of

16. Ibid., 18–19.
17. Ibid., 19.
18. Ibid., 24, 20, 24.
19. Jean M. Yarbrough, *American Virtues: Thomas Jefferson on the Character of a Free People* (Lawrence, Kans., 1998).
20. TJ, Response to the Citizens of Albemarle, Feb. 12, 1790, in Peterson, ed., *Thomas Jefferson Writings*, 491.
21. TJ, Declaration of Independence, July 4, 1776, ibid., 19, original emphasis.
22. Destutt de Tracy, *Review of Montesquieu*, 33. On the theme of moral progress, see Ari Helo and Peter Onuf, "Jefferson, Morality, and the Problem of Slavery," *William and Mary Quarterly* 60 (2003): 583–614.

preservation" in a representative democracy, Destutt wrote, was "love of country, and equality of rights"—his "national" principle—"and, if you will, the love of peace and justice." This was just the sort of patriotism Jefferson extolled in his first inaugural. The Americans' republican government was "the only one where every man, at the call of the law, would fly to the standard of the law, and would meet invasions of the public order as his own personal concern"; because it put all citizens on an equal plane and so transcended the internal conflicts and resistance—the so-called balance—of even the best constituted governments of the old regime, it would be able to mobilize unprecedented power and so prove itself "the strongest Government on earth."[23]

Taking issue with the ancients, Destutt insisted that commerce was not antithetical to virtue, but it was instead "not only the foundation and basis of society" but in "effect the fabric itself; for society is nothing more than a continual exchange of mutual succours, which occasion the concurrence of the powers of all for the more effectual gratification of the wants of each."[24] Following Smith's lead, Destutt emphasized the importance of the home market, rejecting the traditional mercantilist obsession with foreign commerce as a barely sublimated form of political conflict among the great trading powers, in which, in Smith's words, the "interest" of nations supposedly "consisted in beggaring all their neighbours."[25] Reversing priorities, the classical economists invoked reciprocally beneficial exchange in the home market—liberated from the distorting influence of corporate privilege and mercantilist regulation—as the template for a free trade regime for the world as a whole. Foreign trade was useful when "it enlarges the *extent of the market* for the productions of every part of the country," thus serving as a supplement to, but not substitute for, the home market.[26]

The economists suggested a sequence, from the perfection of the home market to the expansion of foreign trade, in order to widen the sphere of reciprocally beneficial exchange and promote the continuing division of labor as the engine of economic progress, mirroring Destutt's conception of the progress of civilization within the nation and radiating out from the nation to the world. The conflation of these processes was not surprising, for the

---

23. TJ, First Inaugural Address, in Peterson, ed., *Thomas Jefferson Writings*, 493.
24. Destutt de Tracy, *Review of Montesquieu*, 205–6. On Enlightenment thinking about commerce, see Albert O. Hirschman, *The Passions and the Interests: Political Arguments for Capitalism before Its Triumph* (Princeton, N.J., 1977).
25. Smith, *Wealth of Nations*, IV, iii.c, § 9, 493. Destutt criticized Montesquieu for considering foreign trade as "the means of making a profit on strangers," or "of fleecing foreign nations of a few dollars" (Destutt de Tracy, *Review of Montesquieu*, 214, 219).
26. Destutt de Tracy, *Review of Montesquieu*, 219, original emphasis.

"nation" and the classical economists' "market" emerged simultaneously and were, to some significant degree, reciprocally constitutive. Yet the role of the modern state in creating and extending these homologous domains remained obscure and controversial to the Revolutionary generation. Jefferson and Destutt were both reform-minded "liberals" who tended to advocate a minimalist, laissez-faire state: the Revolutionaries' struggle for national self-determination and the economists' crusade for market freedom were both predicated on dismantling the old regime state. Yet neither hesitated to endorse the use of state power to meet both internal and external threats. They defined those threats differently, however, and it was these divergent perspectives that led Jefferson to question some of Destutt's conclusions on the proper size and constitution of the large and expanding democratic republic.

Jefferson's criticisms of Destutt focused on two related points. He first questioned Destutt's "preference of a plural over a singular executive" in a "great nation," and then proceeded to challenge Destutt's argument for a unified regime, *"un et indivisible,"* and against federalism. Destutt's advocacy of a plural executive followed from his commitment to the principle of representation, reinforced by his distaste for monarchy. Like lawmaking, "the execution of the laws" should not be "confided to a single person": "it may on the contrary be said, that the affairs of a great nation, directed in general by a legislative body, requires in its execution to be conducted in an uniform manner, and according to the same system." Division of the executive would keep a nation from degenerating into a "special," despotic regime under the rule of a single man.[27]

Jefferson disagreed, arguing instead that the broad distribution of authority within a great nation was critical to the preservation of its liberties. Thus, while Destutt would unify the regime and divide executive power, Jefferson argued for dividing the regime and unifying it in its federal head. "The true barriers of our liberty in this country are our State governments," Jefferson wrote, "and the wisest conservative power ever contrived by man, is that of which our Revolution and present government found us possessed." The fatal error of the French revolutionaries was to demolish provincial authorities. By preserving the integrity and independence of the separate colony-states, the Americans had preserved their liberties, showing that republican government could survive and prosper over an extended—and expanding—domain: "seventeen distinct States, amalgamated into one as to their foreign concerns, but single and independent

---

27. TJ to Destutt de Tracy, Jan. 26, 1811, in Peterson, ed., *Thomas Jefferson Writings*, 1243, 1246; Destutt de Tracy, *Review of Montesquieu*, 127.

as to their internal administration, regularly organized with legislature and governor resting on the choice of the people, and enlightened by a free press, can never be so fascinated by the arts of one man, as to submit voluntarily to his usurpation."[28]

The obvious explanation for the different attitudes toward federalism was that the geopolitical circumstances of the sister republics were so radically different. The "confederative system" might answer well for Americans, Destutt acknowledged, "because they have no powerful neighbors." But if "France had adopted this form, it is doubtful whether it could have resisted all Europe, as it did by remaining one and indivisible."[29] For Destutt, federal arrangements constituted "mere essays or experiments" as statesmen groped toward "true ideas of a representative system." Unlike the American states, newly reformed as perfect republics, French provinces were bastions of entrenched privilege and impediments to the free flow of goods, people, and ideas that would make a great nation prosper. In this respect, he had no doubt, the French Revolution had been an unequivocal success. Notwithstanding the "calamities" it suffered at the hands of its enemies, France's "population and agriculture have augmented considerably, "enabling the nation to supply "immense funds from taxes" and expend "vast sums in public works." It "can accomplish all this without borrowing; such is her power on the continent of Europe, that nothing can resist it; and were it not for the British navy, France might subdue the universe."[30]

Jefferson and Destutt expressed their shared conviction in the fundamental transformation of world history in remarkably similar assertions of national greatness: Jefferson claimed that the United States had "the strongest Government on earth," while Destutt boasted that France was powerful enough to "subdue the universe"—or would be, if Britain did not still rule the waves. Both Jefferson and Destutt glimpsed new sources of power in the Revolutionary upheavals that had destroyed the old regime. By overcoming internal conflicts and unleashing the productive powers of their enterprising peoples, these postrevolutionary states had become "great nations." As the Old World gave way to the New, Destutt proclaimed, "special" regimes predicated on "unequal rights" became "national." The Revolutionary conception of nationhood, founded on the principles of equality and consent set forth in Jefferson's Declaration of Independence, was based on the great truth "that all rights and power originate in, reside in, and belong to, the entire body of

28. TJ to Destutt de Tracy, Jan. 26, 1811, in Peterson, ed., *Thomas Jefferson Writings*, 1245–46.
29. Destutt de Tracy, *Review of Montesquieu*, 82–83.
30. Ibid., 64.

the people or nation."[31] The power of these new national regimes was both greater than that which the states of the old regime could possibly mobilize and qualitatively different, for it would ultimately promote the prosperity and happiness of humanity generally as well as of particular peoples.

Jefferson and Destutt agreed about the direction of world history, through the formation of true nations, toward a cosmopolitan end. By emphasizing the mobilization of popular power, the development of the national economy, and the spread of market relations and enlightened reform across the continent, Destutt could discount the importance of regime change and chronic constitutional crisis in France. As long as it continued to respect the fundamental principle of popular sovereignty, the government would continue to be "national." The nation could even choose, as France apparently did, to "intrust all its power, or only the executive power to one man, either for life, or in hereditary succession."[32]

Emphasizing the "nation" enabled Destutt to keep the revolutionary faith in trying times, to overlook or explain away the French government's many deviations from the republican principles his American friend so conspicuously cherished. For his part, Jefferson was remarkably tolerant—critics would say, willfully obtuse—about developments in France. Bloody excesses notwithstanding, the important thing about the French Revolution was that it vindicated the principle of national self-determination, both for France and for the nations it "liberated." As Jefferson famously wrote his young protégé the diplomat William Short in 1793, he would be willing to see "half the earth devastated" as long as "there was an Adam & an Eve left *in every country*, & left free."[33] The constitutional arrangements that would sustain that freedom were certainly important to Jefferson, an obsessive constitutionalist, but the nation—the existence of a truly independent people capable of giving itself a constitution—necessarily came first. Jefferson's commitment to the national idea helps explain both his enthusiasm for Destutt's *Review* and his hostility to Montesquieu's "heresies." Jefferson and Destutt agreed on the fundamental premise of national self-determination; they also agreed that the measure of a nation's greatness was the freedom that the people generally enjoyed in pursuing their individual interests and thus in promoting the wealth and welfare of the community as a whole. Jefferson's language evoked primitive

31. Ibid., 12.
32. Ibid., 13.
33. TJ to William Short, Jan. 3, 1793, in Boyd et al., eds., *Papers of Thomas Jefferson* 25:14–17, emphasis added. For further discussion see Onuf, *Jefferson's Empire*, 170–73. TJ's most virulent critic on this issue is Conor Cruise O'Brien, *The Long Affair: Thomas Jefferson and the French Revolution* (Chicago, 1996).

beginnings—each nation had its own Adam and Eve—but pointed to a glorious future: the modern world would be a world of nations, progressively coming together through the spread of commerce and civilization.

The different circumstances of postrevolutionary France and the United States showed that a new day may have dawned, as both Jefferson and Destutt so fervently believed. Yet the sun did not shine equally on all quarters of the globe. Montesquieu taught that nations differ in their vulnerability. If, as Jefferson and Destutt realized, the modernizing economies of France and the United States made these two nations powerful, their geopolitical situations made them strikingly different.

Jefferson imagined that the peace-loving American republics would never launch wars of conquest, but that they would be prepared to rebuff the assaults of the great European powers, including (ironically) Napoleon's France. France faced more immediate dangers from hostile neighbors and therefore could not afford to assume the Americans' more passive, defensive posture. Perhaps, Jefferson could have added, the political ignorance and inexperience of the French people presented an even greater obstacle to the establishment of a durable republican regime. These differences would disappear in the fullness of time, however, and Jefferson and Destutt could both look forward with confidence—whatever their immediate circumstances—to the better day coming.

Nation and World

Jefferson and Destutt could minimize their differences on constitutional questions because of their confidence in the future. But the idea of the "nation" they both embraced proved protean and problematic. All nations were not created equal: they stood at different stages of economic, social, and political development and therefore at a greater or lesser distance from fulfilling their historical destinies; their situation in an anarchic world of hostile states required them to participate effectively in the traditional, old regime balance of power; their interests in expanding the domain of market freedom and thus realizing their productive potential depended both on leveling obstructions to exchange in the home market and on opening trade opportunities—and risking new entanglements—abroad. All of these challenges raised questions of boundaries: What, in short, was the relation between the nation and the world?

Jefferson and Destutt both worked within this broad geopolitical framework. Because the nation was "natural"—"representative democracy" was true to "nature, in a perfect state," Destutt wrote—it should expand to its "natural boundaries." Because a nation could be any size, it should seek "the best possible boundaries, and when obtained should never pass them." The "best possible boundaries" were the most extensive ones that could be obtained in competition with neighboring states, and they were only "naturally" limited by the extent of reciprocally beneficial market relations.[34] The United States was blessed by an immense continental domain and the absence of other powers who could inhibit its continuing expansion. According to Jefferson's interpretation, "nature" decreed that the Mississippi watershed, including the vast region purchased from France in 1803, should form the heart of one great nation; looking south and north, he envisioned extending the new nation's natural limits at the expense of neighboring imperial powers. Once Cuba was annexed, he told his successor Madison, "I would immediately erect a column on the southernmost limit of Cuba, and inscribe on it a *ne plus ultra* as to us in that direction. We should then have only to include the north in our Confederacy, which would be of course in the first war, and we should have such an empire for liberty as she has never surveyed since the creation."[35]

In Destutt's sense, the United States was the only true "nation" on the continent and therefore free to expand to its limits. France's European neighborhood was, in stark contrast, fraught with danger. In a remarkable passage, Destutt imagined the nations of the world as "islands," secure in their natural borders. "Of all natural limits," he wrote, the sea is "the best":

the advantages of an island for happiness and liberty are very great. This is so true, that if we suppose the surface of the globe divided into islands of a proper extent and distance from each other, it would be covered by rich and industrious nations, who would not stand in need of any land armies, consequently ruled by moderate governments only. Having the most convenient communication among themselves, and scarcely any ability to hurt each other without affecting their reciprocal relations, their differences would soon cease by means of their mutual dependence and wants. If, on the contrary, we

34. Destutt de Tracy, *Review of Montesquieu,* 19, 91.
35. TJ to James Madison, Apr. 27, 1809, in Lipscomb and Bergh, eds., *Writings of Thomas Jefferson* 12:274–77. On Jefferson's geopolitics, see Robert W. Tucker and David C. Hendrickson, *Empire of Liberty: The Statecraft of Thomas Jefferson* (New York, 1990); James E. Lewis Jr., *The American Union and the Problem of Neighborhood: The United States and the Collapse of the Spanish Empire, 1783–1829* (Chapel Hill, N.C., 1998); and Peter J. Kastor, *The Nation's Crucible: The Louisiana Purchase and the Creation of America* (New Haven, Conn., 2004). On "natural rights" claims to territory, see Albert K. Weinberg, *Manifest Destiny: A Study in Nationalist Expansionism in American History* (Baltimore, Md., 1935).

suppose the earth without sea, nations would then be without commerce, always in arms, in constant fear of neighboring nations, ignorant of others, and living under military governments: the sea is one obstacle to all kind of evil, and a means of numerous advantages.[36]

Destutt conceived of the "nation" as an "island" with the sea, its natural boundary, keeping it at a safe distance from other nations. Kept apart, nations would engage in peaceful commercial relations rather than in the never-ending contest to secure extensive limits. This was another way of saying that nations were *otherwise* boundless, that their natural tendency to expand in order to promote prosperity through a progressively elaborate division of labor would lead to constant warfare, not peace. Destutt thus proceeded from the "realistic" premise of the balance-of-power theorists, that "Nations, as they respect each other, stand in precisely the same relations as savages."[37] International trade mitigated chronic conflict, however, teaching nations to cultivate reciprocally beneficial relations. Ultimately, when "civilized nations . . . reached that point at which society is organized and somewhat more perfect, by the establishment of social duties and rights"—that is, when "special" regimes became truly "national"—they would move toward a "third state of civilization" by establishing "among themselves, a common tribunal, and a power sufficient to enforce its decisions, such as takes place in the interior of a confederation, among the members of the confederacy."[38] The nation that fulfilled its "national" destiny in a society of true nations would thus ultimately transcend nationality.

The American federal republic was a working model of the new, improved world Destutt imagined in his world of island nations. The Jeffersonian Joel Barlow thus urged Europeans to follow the American lead by "republicanizing" their nations along the lines Destutt suggested, and then "federalizing" them into a more perfect union.[39] But until the happy moment when the Old World caught up with the New, the United States would have to function as a "power"—in the conventional sense—in the European state system. Jefferson's federalism reflected his posture as a "half-way pacifist," in, but not

---

36. Destutt de Tracy, *Review of Montesquieu*, 80.
37. Ibid., 86.
38. Ibid., 88.
39. Barlow, *To His Fellow Citizens*, Letter II, n. 8. For further discussion, see Peter Onuf and Nicholas Onuf, *Federal Union, Modern World: The Law of Nations in an Age of Revolutions, 1776–1814* (Madison, Wisc., 1993), 135–44. For a superb discussion of Barlow, see Philipp Ziesche, "American Expatriates in European Networks of Revolution and Counter-Revolution" (Ph.D. diss., Yale University, 2006), chap. 2.

of, the world of power politics.[40] Similarly, his patriotic rhetoric promised peace but also evoked the image of irresistible popular power, the Revolutionary "Spirit of 1776," that had enabled the Americans to defeat Britain on the battlefield.[41]

Jefferson's posture was always defensive, never—he liked to think—belligerent. Jeffersonians routinely juxtaposed their "pacific system" to the perpetual state of war, the *"bellum omnium in omnia* of Europe."[42] Assuming the "natural" distinction between the two worlds, Jefferson could only conclude that "the whole system of Europe towards America" was "an atrocious and insulting tyranny." The balance of power kept European "lions and tigers" at each other's throats and thus worked to the Americans' advantage, but a passive posture could not guarantee peace.[43] "When our strength will permit us to give the law of our hemisphere," Jefferson concluded, "the meridian of the mid-Atlantic should be the line of demarkation between war and peace, on this side of which no act of hostility should be committed."[44]

Jefferson apparently dissented from Destutt's emphasis on maritime boundaries—and connections—when he celebrated the American union as a regime of good neighbors *sharing* territorial boundaries in perpetual peace. But the boundaries of the American states were not the international frontiers that Destutt had in mind. Having delegated the powers of war and peace to the federal government, the states effectively disarmed themselves. Comity among the states, the security of property rights, and a dynamic, mobile population that moved freely from state to state muted "national" distinctions and mitigated conflicts of interest. The realistic Alexander Hamilton, writing as "Publius" during the ratification controversy, might have been right that republics were no more peaceful than other forms of government and that, in the absence of a strong union, an anarchic state of nature would emerge among the American states. It was "an axiom in politics," he wrote in *The Federalist* no. 6, "that vicinity, or nearness of situation, constitutes nations natural enemies."

---

40. The phrase comes from Reginald C. Stuart, *The Half-way Pacifist: Thomas Jefferson's View of War* (Toronto, 1978). For a much more critical account of TJ's foreign policy, see Tucker and Hendrickson, *Empire of Liberty.*
41. On the centrality of the "Spirit of 1776" in TJ's conception of nationhood, see Onuf, *Jefferson's Empire,* 98–102, passim.
42. Kent Co., Del., Democratic-Republicans to TJ, Jan. 13, 1807, Jefferson Papers (Library of Congress).
43. TJ to Clement Caine, Sept. 16, 1811, in Lipscomb and Bergh, eds., *Writings of Thomas Jefferson* 13:90.
44. TJ to Dr. John Crawford, Jan. 2, 1812, ibid., 13:119. For similar sentiments on a "meridian of partition" between the "two hemispheres," see TJ to William Short, Aug. 4, 1820, ibid., 15:263. On the importance of "lines of distinction" in Jefferson's thought, see Onuf, *Jefferson's Empire,* 113–17.

The ratification of the Constitution changed all that, Jefferson believed, inaugurating a regime of peace among the states, what Hamilton described as "the happy empire of perfect wisdom and perfect virtue" that had been such a "remote" prospect under the Articles of Confederation.[45] Under the Constitution, provisions for collective security were linked to prohibitions on state interference with the free movement of people and goods, thus fostering the development of regional and national markets.

Federalists and Republicans alike agreed that the Constitution solved the problem of the extended republic, but their interpretations of that solution differed radically. Hamiltonian High Federalists were centralizers, sharing Destutt's impatience with a broad federal distribution of authority that impeded national development. Jefferson and his allies reasoned in the opposite direction, arguing that a limited delegation of power to the federal government facilitated the development of more perfect republican regimes in the states by guaranteeing peace and collective security. While Federalists thus tended to conflate the "nation" with the government of the union, Republicans identified the "nation" with the people, distinguishing it from either state or federal governments. As a model world order, the union showed what conventional, war-prone nations could become—perfect republics, or Destutt's "national" regimes—at a higher level of civilization. In the progressive scheme that Jefferson and Destutt embraced, national self-determination was a crucial step toward the "happy empire" Hamilton mocked, when the rights and true interests of people were generally recognized and secured. The American nation in Jefferson's inspirational language was a nation-to-end-nations, a local microcosm of humanity, a preview of the new world in the making, moving toward the end of history.

Destutt shared Jefferson's enthusiasm for the new nation's bright prospects. But the fate of the national idea in Europe, where nations struggled to promote their peoples'—or rulers'—interests in competition with "formidable neighbors" and without the "immense regions of fertile and uncultivated lands" that beckoned enterprising Americans, was bound to follow a much different course.[46] Destutt's island-nation fantasy—his acknowledgment of Britain's fortuitous position in the European balance of power, as well as of its historical maritime and commercial advantages—reflected the primacy of geopolitical considerations in his thinking. The first challenge for the modern nation was to secure its existence against powerful enemies—in

---

45. Jacob E. Cooke, ed., *The Federalist* (Middletown, Conn., 1961), no. 6 (Hamilton), 35. See the brilliant discussion of this passage in Gerald Stourzh, *Alexander Hamilton and Republican Government* (Stanford, Calif., 1970), 145–65.
46. Destutt de Tracy, *Review of Montesquieu*, 82, 181.

effect, to make itself into an island—and *then* to make enemies into friends through enlightened, reciprocally beneficial trade relations. The United States, like Britain, was blessed by its "insular" situation and a great ocean boundary that simultaneously served as the medium for the commercial connections that promoted world peace and prosperity.[47] Until European nations achieved the same level of political development that the new nation had already achieved, thanks to its fortunate circumstances, the link between nation and state would remain powerful. Without strong central governments, Old World nations could neither perfect their regimes at home—by eliminating barriers to free exchange and economic development (which, in France's case, were so closely tied to provincial and corporate privileges)— nor protect themselves against external threats.

As a political economist, Destutt recognized that expanding commerce was crucial to national development. Building on the work of Smith and Jean-Baptiste Say, Destutt argued that merchants contributed as much to the national wealth and welfare as agriculturalists or manufacturers. Like "all other industrious persons," and in contrast to "conquerors and courtiers" who take "the goods of others by force or deceit," merchants "seek only for reward in their talents, by means of free agreements entered into with good faith and guaranteed by the laws." Merchants not only made productive activity possible but the trade relations they fostered were "the source of all . . . moral sentiments; and the first and most powerful cause of the improvement of their mutual sensibility and reciprocal benevolence." The progress of civilization was a function of expanding commerce: "it commences by uniting all the men of the same tribe; it afterwards unites those societies with each other, and finishes by connecting all parts of the universe."[48] By contrast, agriculture, the dominant activity at a primitive stage of social development, exploited the unskilled and ignorant class of laborers, "the last in rank in society, because almost destitute of intellectual knowledge."[49]

Destutt attempted to demystify agriculture by arguing that the land was nothing more than a "machine."[50] Beguiled by the "false idea of a sort of

---

47. Felix Gilbert, *To the Farewell Address: Ideas of Early American Foreign Policy* (Princeton, N.J., 1961).
48. Destutt de Tracy, *Review of Montesquieu*, 232.
49. Ibid., 186.
50. "Mr. Say likewise pronounces, without hesitation, book I, chap. 5, *that a tract of land is only a machine;* yet influenced by [Smith's] authority . . . he permits himself to be dazzled by the illusions he has so completely destroyed" and "persists in considering a tract of land, as a possession of a particular nature, its productive service as something else than a utility to be derived from a tool; and its rent as different from the interest given for a capital lent" (Ibid., 189., original emphasis).

magical virtue attributed to the earth," the economists continued to hold forth on "the dignity and utility of agriculture" and thus to imagine, in Jefferson's words, that "those who labour in the earth are the chosen people of God . . . whose breasts he has made his peculiar deposit for substantial and genuine virtue." Destutt dismissed such views as atavistic survivals of the old regime. Agrarians confused love of country with a timeless—and mindless—attachment to the land, leading them to embrace the absurd premise of the old "feodal system," that "an inanimate tract of land" has "rights." They thus arrived at the profoundly mistaken "notion that there are no true citizens in a state but the proprietors of land, and that they alone constitute society."[51]

Such citizens might indeed be "virtuous" in the classical sense, stupidly sacrificing their interests—and themselves—for a meaningless abstraction. But these were not the enlightened, cosmopolitan citizens who would promote the nation's wealth and welfare and therefore the progress of human civilization generally. For Destutt, in fact, it was patriotism of the old sort— the feudal attachment to particular tracts of land and the corollary belief that the conquest of new land (and the people attached to it) was the key to national power—that had kept the old regime in a nearly constant state of war and led him to imagine a world of island nations. Destutt's contempt for agriculture thus followed from his conception of the progressive role of the postrevolutionary nation in world history.

Jefferson gave no indication of being troubled by his French friend's derogatory comments about farmers and agriculture. The important thing for Jefferson both in this case and on the related issue of federalism was that he and Destutt were in fundamental accord on the progress of civilization. Jefferson's enterprising and enlightened farmer could not, in any case, be confused with Destutt's ignorant peasant. "In the United States of America," Destutt wrote, "the people are intelligent and their faculties untrammelled by absurd institutions or establishments."[52] They were certainly not tied to the land, which they exploited in just the instrumental way—for its productive potential (or to strip its resource endowment)—that Destutt prescribed. The situation of societies on either side of the Atlantic mirrored that of their citizens (or subjects). European nations were constrained by finite resources and conflicting claims, and this was why Destutt imagined each nation as an island with "natural boundaries" and access to the markets of the world.

The differing geopolitical circumstances of New World and Old explain the different pathways to the glorious future that both Jefferson and Destutt

---

51. Ibid., 186. The TJ quote is from Query 19, "Manufactures," in Peden, ed., *Notes on the State of Virginia*, 164–65.
52. Destutt de Tracy, *Review of Montesquieu*, 247.

imagined. In optimistic moments, Jefferson exulted that the republican millennium had already arrived. Providing for collective security, guaranteeing peace among the state-republics, and liberating enterprising Americans to pursue their own happiness, the federal union anticipated the future state of the world. "Who can limit the extent to which the federative principle may operate effectively?" Jefferson asked in his second inaugural address.[53] The boundlessness of the nation's expansive energies—and of the market that tied Americans together—was matched by the boundlessness of a continent with land enough for countless future generations.

Yet Jefferson's bright vision was shadowed by extraordinary contingencies that threatened to retard or reverse the new nation's natural progress. Without a clearly defined boundary, the New World could never be fully disentangled from the Old. Europe continued to be present in America, in its colonial possessions, in commercial connections with American interests, in political links with the "monocrats" and "aristocrats" who constituted Jefferson's disloyal opposition. At moments of crisis, European powers threatened to become "formidable neighbors" who would limit the growth of the union, or even destroy it. At such moments, Jefferson's New World converged with Destutt's Old and history's horizon receded. Perhaps the United States would then, like France, have to take on the form of the revolutionary nation-state before it could move on to the last stage of political development.

National Republicanism

Many bloody chapters in European history remained to be written, as the final phases of the Napoleonic Wars made clear. Despite its determination to remain neutral—to maintain its disentangled distance from the Old World—the United States had been sucked into the vortex of European violence. Repeated embarrassments on land and sea revealed the weaknesses of the federal state under Madison's leadership. The War of 1812 was hardly a testimonial to the irresistible power of popular patriotism that Jefferson imagined. Its identification with the Revolution as a second "War for Independence" may have kindled patriotic fervor in some, although certainly not all, parts of the country. The chief significance of this identification was instead to define war aims in such limited terms that the Americans simply could not lose, notwithstanding their best—or worst—efforts: the

---

53. TJ, Second Inaugural Address, Mar. 4, 1805, in Peterson, ed., *Thomas Jefferson Writings,* 519.

British had no intention of reversing the Revolution's outcome and recolonizing America. When peace was finally negotiated, on surprisingly favorable terms, the people may have exulted that they had once again vindicated their independence, but chastened Republicans knew better: the next war might lead to another, less fortunate outcome.[54]

Jefferson recognized that the new nation remained vulnerable. The emphasis in his postwar commentary was on the "depravity" of the great European powers, Britain and France, and the final, devastating collapse of the Old World balance of power. He was characteristically reticent about the failures of his countrymen to live up to his exalted standard, although he did single out perfidious New Englanders—traditional scapegoats who were little better than foreigners—for bitter condemnation and possible sanction.[55] Yet if the people were—with this conspicuous exception—blameless, Jefferson nonetheless agreed with the emerging cohort of reform-minded National Republicans that the United States must be better prepared for the next war: the federal government must take the lead in strengthening the union. Jefferson articulated this new position—an acknowledged change of heart—in his remarkable letter of 1816 to Austin, a proponent of domestic manufactures and a protective tariff.[56]

Jefferson's endorsement of manufactures commanded the most attention, at the time and in subsequent decades. Recanting his famous opposition to domestic "work-shops" in *Notes on Virginia,* he now insisted "that to be independent for the comforts of life we must fabricate them ourselves." His conclusion, that "we must now place the manufacturer by the side of the agriculturist," became a protectionist mantra, one of the most frequently quoted sayings of the Sage of Monticello.[57] But most of the Austin letter focused on the extraordinary circumstances that explained this deviation

---

54. The best treatment of the war is J. C. A. Stagg, *Mr. Madison's War: Politics, Diplomacy, and Warfare in the Early American Republic, 1783–1830* (Princeton, N.J., 1983). On the identification of the War of 1812 with the Revolution, see Roger H. Brown, *The Republic in Peril: 1812* (New York, 1964). For suggestive comments on popular responses to the American "victory," we are indebted to Drew R. McCoy, *The Last of the Founders: James Madison and the Republican Legacy* (New York, 1989), 9–12.
55. Onuf, *Jefferson's Empire,* 121–29.
56. TJ to Benjamin Austin, Jan. 9, 1816, in Lipscomb and Bergh, eds., *Writings of Thomas Jefferson.*
57. Ibid., 14:391. For the text of Benjamin Austin's letter to TJ, Dec. 9, 1815, seeking clarification of his position on "domestic" and "foreign work-shops," see *Niles Weekly Register* (Baltimore), supplement to vol. 18 (1832–33): 37–38. See the discussion in Malone, *Sage of Monticello,* 137–50, which properly emphasizes TJ's limited, circumstantial commitment to protection: he "spoke as a relativist, not a doctrinaire" in the Austin letter (147).

from his lifelong commitment to free trade principles. For the time being, geopolitics trumped economics: the new nation may have survived, but fulfillment of the national idea in Europe had suffered a serious, although certainly temporary, setback. International free trade could only flourish with permanent peace, and nations could only live at peace when they determined their own destinies.

Jefferson held Napoleon *personally* responsible for the "rivers of blood" that had deluged Europe. Bonaparte's "atrocious egotism," his "parricide treason" against the French nation in betraying his sacred trust "as a republican magistrate, to the subversion of that republic and erection of a military despotism for himself and his family," had "checked the salutary progress" of the great principle of national self-determination that Jefferson and Destutt had embraced.[58] By condemning Napoleon, Jefferson could thus exonerate the French nation. The violence that engulfed Europe began with the "conspiracy of kings" against France's republican revolution, climaxing in the late 1790s in one of the most disgraceful epochs in "the history of man," as England—the only remaining counterrevolutionary power—and France "descended from" their high rank as "civilized nations" to the anarchy of savages, "setting at defiance all those moral laws established by the Author of nature between nation and nation, as between man and man" and covering "earth and sea with robberies and piracies, merely because strong enough to do it with temporal impunity."[59] The antinational coalition had thus diverted France from fulfilling its national destiny into a war for its survival, thus setting the stage for Napoleon's "parricide treason."

Jefferson predicted further bloodshed in Europe, but the responsibility would not be France's, despite Napoleon's derelictions and continuing divisions among the French. "There is still an awful void between the present and what is to be the last chapter" of French history, he told Austin. Echoing Destutt's paean to the great nation's destiny, Jefferson looked forward to the day when France would throw off the shackles of an unequal, humiliating peace. "That nation is too high-minded, has too much innate force, intelligence and elasticity, to remain under its present compression," Jefferson

---

58. TJ to Benjamin Austin, Jan. 9, 1816, in Lipscomb and Bergh, eds., *Writings of Thomas Jefferson* 14:388–89. For an extended attack on Napoleon as a "moral monster," with "millions of human lives" on his hands, see TJ to John Adams, Feb. 25, 1823, in Cappon, ed., *Adams-Jefferson Letters* 2:589.
59. TJ to Benjamin Austin, Jan. 9, 1816, in Lipscomb and Bergh, eds., *Writings of Thomas Jefferson* 14:390–91. "The Cannibals of Europe are going to eating one another again," TJ told John Adams in a mocking characterization of the European state system, or "henyard" (TJ to John Adams, June 1, 1822, in Cappon, ed., *Adams-Jefferson Letters* 2:578).

insisted: "Samson will arise in his strength, as of old, and as of old will burst asunder the withes and the cords, and the webs of the Philistines." Presumably France had been "compressed" within unnatural boundaries, and the inevitable reaction, with all its accompanying "scenes of havoc and horror," would finally culminate "in a representative government, in a government in which the will of the people will be an effective ingredient." The vindication of France's national rights would in turn inspire the other nations of Europe to throw off their shackles: "this important element has taken root in the European mind, and will have its growth." "What a germ have we planted," Jefferson concluded, "and how faithfully should we cherish the parent tree at home!" This, of course, was the "tree of liberty," emblem of self-determining nationality.[60]

The true nation should and must ultimately expand to its "natural boundaries."[61] Just as Jefferson's United States was the only civilized nation in the New World, Jefferson's France, the first great European nation to plant its own liberty tree, was the only true nation in the Old World. The difference was that France was surrounded by hostile powers who would seek to restrain that nation in order to suppress the national aspirations of their own peoples. The emergence of the "Holy Alliance," the coalition of legitimists dedicated to preserving the unregenerate status quo on the continent, seemed to fulfill Jefferson's dark prophecy and guarantee that the "last chapter" of European history would be a very long and bloody one indeed.[62] In effect, the idealistic Jefferson came around to a realist's assessment of the European state system's anarchic tendencies because of his commitment to the principle of national self-determination and its ultimate fulfillment in representative government. Jefferson was convinced that the "holy allies"

---

60. TJ to Benjamin Austin, Jan. 9, 1816, in Lipscomb and Bergh, eds., *Writings of Thomas Jefferson* 14:388–89.

61. According to the German national economist Friedrich List, "a well-shaped territory is one of the first requisites of a nation; that the desire of meeting this requisite is legitimate; and that it may sometimes be the legitimate cause of war" (Friedrich List, *National System of Political Economy*, trans. G. A. Matile, including the notes to the French translation by Henri Richelot, with a preliminary essay and notes by Stephen Colwell [1841; Philadelphia, Pa., 1856; rpt. New York, 1974]).

62. "A first attempt to recover the right of self-government may fail; so may a 2d. a 3d. etc., but as a younger, and more instructed race comes on, the sentiment becomes more and more intuitive, and a 4th. a 5th. or some subsequent one of the ever renewed attempts will ultimately succeed. In France the 1st. effort was defeated by Robespierre, the 2d. by Bonaparte, the 3d. by Louis XVIII. and his holy allies; another is yet to come, and all Europe, Russia excepted, has caught the spirit, and all will attain representative government, more or less perfect" (TJ to John Adams, Sept. 4, 1823, in Cappon, ed., *Adams-Jefferson Letters* 2:596).

could never keep the peace and that the people would recoil from their suppression with redoubled force. Given the history of unending conflict over the course of the previous generation, it seemed unlikely to Jefferson that the United States could keep out of harm's way. Americans therefore should be ready to fight; they should also resist Britain's commercial domination. Anyone "who is now against domestic manufacture," he told Austin, "must be for reducing us either to dependence on that foreign nation, or to be clothed in skins, and to live like wild beasts in dens and caverns"; he must be determined "to keep us in eternal vassalage to a foreign and unfriendly people."[63]

Jefferson's conception of nationhood looked toward the republican millennium of peace and prosperity at the end of history. Paradoxically, it also justified dire predictions of continuing bloodshed during the protracted "last chapter" of European history. The defeat of Napoleon would bring war, not peace; the old regime, gaining a new lease on life because of the self-proclaimed emperor's great betrayal of the republican principle, was constitutionally incapable of regenerating itself. The forward progress of history and the ultimate redemption of the nations of Europe thus would exact an extraordinary toll in blood. But Jefferson was prepared to pay the price—or, rather, he was prepared to see millions of hapless Europeans die—in order to vindicate the national idea. In the meantime, Americans should jealously protect their own independence, throwing off their commercial vassalage to Britain.

National Republicanism grew out of the Madison administration's embarrassments in conducting the War of 1812 and the expectation that more fighting would inevitably follow. Convinced of the inevitability of war in an anarchic world, Jefferson tentatively embraced the new gospel of preparedness and protection. His letter to Austin endorsed the National Republicans' key premise, that the United States could only achieve genuine independence by breaking free of British commercial domination. Jefferson's vision of an enduring, "natural" boundary that would protect the New World from the "havoc and horror" of the Old underscored the need for a balanced, self-sufficient continental economy: "we must now place the *manufacturers* by the side of the agriculturist." Fostering the home market was "the true *American System*," a meeting of Louisiana protectionists insisted in 1832. Jefferson's words thus epitomized the revolutionary principles "which have been supported from the formation of the confederacy, and the adoption of

---

63. TJ to Benjamin Austin, Jan. 9, 1816, in Lipscomb and Bergh, eds., *Writings of Thomas Jefferson* 14:392–93.

the federal constitution, by Washington, Adams, Jefferson, and all our presidents, to the present administration."[64]

Jefferson's conception of the nation, reinforced by a powerful Anglophobia that survived the Napoleonic Wars, drew him toward protectionism.[65] As a union of free republics, the United States might banish national rivalries in the New World, thus providing a model for war-torn Europe when the last chapter of its bloody history was finally written. But as long as the affairs of the two worlds remained entangled, Jefferson's United States, like Destutt's France, must prepare for war in order to vindicate its national rights and secure its natural boundaries. The new nation must expand, extending the "empire for liberty" across the continent; it must also move forward in time, extricating itself from European entanglements—the politics of the past—in order to fulfill its destiny at the next, highest stage in the progress of civilization. One day, at the end of history, the nation would be the world. In the meantime, protectionists promised, development of the home market would "render us a world within ourselves, deriving, from a friendly intercourse with foreign nations, all the advantages which we now do, but exempt from the continual shocks which our industry has heretofore sustained from a too close connection with that of Europe."[66]

Protectionists made the most of Jefferson's turn toward geopolitical realism and his brief flirtation with a more energetic, neo-Hamiltonian nation-state. The centralizing tendencies of National Republicanism ran against the grain of the Jeffersonians' hallowed "Principles of 1798," Henry Clay's protests notwithstanding, while protectionism challenged the party's ideological commitment to free trade.[67] War and the immediate threat of more

---

64. Tariff Meeting, Opelousas, La., Apr. 28, 1832, *Niles Weekly Register* (Baltimore) (June 16, 1832): 284, original emphasis. For other references to the Austin letter, see "Debate in Congress on the Bill to amend the several Acts for imposing Duties on Imports," *North American Review* (July 1824): 253, and "Memorial of the New-York Convention, To the Congress of the United States. Presented Mar. 26, 1832, and referred to the Committee on Manufactures," bound with [Alexander Everett], *Address of the Friends of Domestic Industry, Assembled in Convention, at New York, October 26, 1831, To the People of the United States* (Baltimore, Nov. 10, 1831), 129–74, at 148; List, *National System of Political Economy*, 174.

65. On protectionism in this era, see Lawrence A. Peskin, *Manufacturing Revolution: The Intellectual Origins of Early American Industry* (Baltimore, Md., 2003).

66. [Everett], *Address of the Friends of Domestic Industry*, 167.

67. Our discussion of National Republicanism is indebted to Lewis, *American Union and the Problem of Neighborhood*. For Clay's fealty to Jeffersonian principles, see his Speech on Internal Improvements, Jan. 14, 1824, in James F. Hopkins, ed., *The Papers of Henry Clay*, vol. 3 (Lexington, Ky., 1963): "I am happy, in the outset, to state my hearty concurrence with the gentleman from Virginia, in the old, 1798, republican principles, (now become federal, also,) by which the constitution is to be interpreted" (581).

war provided ample justification for this radical reorientation of policy as Jefferson's visionary, protean conception of the nation suddenly took on a more familiar political form, centered on the federal state. These crisis conditions proved ephemeral, however, and heightened postwar anxieties ironically prepared the way for an increasingly pervasive sense of security. The normalization of Anglo-American relations, the failure of the French "Samson" to burst its chains, the onset of a period of political stability in Europe and the apparent quiescence of would-be republican revolutionaries—all gave the lie to Jefferson's overheated imagination.

Jefferson continued to wax eloquent on the inevitable European holocaust, despite these developments—and nondevelopments. Yet he was increasingly detached and complacent about European politics: when "rivers of blood" inundated the Old World, Americans would be spared—although, of course, their humanitarian sensibilities might be assaulted. Meanwhile, domestic threats loomed increasingly large in Jefferson's mind. The measures that an energized federal state would have to take to prepare to meet foreign threats could be deployed by an unscrupulous administration against American liberties, states' rights, and vital sectional interests. Jefferson characteristically responded to this ambiguity about the source of threat—from hostile foreign powers or from domestic "consolidationists"—by calling for strict construction of—or amendments to—the federal Constitution.[68] In doing so, he simultaneously reaffirmed his faith in the nation, acting in its constitutional capacity to resolve and preempt conflicts, and promoted a diffusion of authority to the states and a pervasive distrust of federal authority that finally severed the nation from the state—and justified the claims of the states as "separate nations."

Thomas Jefferson was the great theorist of American nationhood. His exchange with Destutt de Tracy demonstrates their fundamental agreement on the role of nation building in the progress of civilization. They disagreed on the proper constitution of a great self-governing nation: ever alert to France's precarious position in the European state system, Destutt was a centralizer; Jefferson, imagining that the United States had escaped from Europe and the past, advocated a radically decentralized federal union of republics. But this disagreement proceeded from different geopolitical circumstances, not from principle. During moments of crisis, when the United States was sucked into the vortex of war—and back into history—the convergence between Jefferson's and Destutt's thinking was complete.

---

68. The literature on TJ's constitutionalism is voluminous, but on this point, see particularly John Lauritz Larson, "Jefferson's Union and the Problem of Internal Improvements," in Onuf, ed., *Jeffersonian Legacies*, 340–69.

In the escalating, increasingly sectionalized struggles over American foreign trade policy, protectionists and free traders alike could invoke Jefferson's
authority. Each side emphasized one dimension of Jefferson's conception of
the new nation's destiny—and its role in the world, now and in the future—
while suppressing the other. Protectionists seized on Jefferson's recognition,
during a period of world war and instability, that the United States would
have to act energetically to secure its independence. With Jefferson, they emphasized the need for market expansion, integration and balance at home in
order to secure American interests abroad. And they cultivated a Jeffersonian strain of Anglophobia that enabled them to sustain a sense of a continuing external threat even in peacetime. Yet protectionists did not share Jefferson's Enlightenment cosmopolitanism and historicism: the nation was not the
self-transcending means toward an all-embracing world society, but, rather,
it was an end in itself, the means of surviving in a perpetually dangerous, anarchic world, or even—as skeptical critics charged—the means for promoting particular, selfish interests under the guise of the "general welfare."

If protectionists slighted the future, free traders ignored the past. Following the lead of the new school of "classical" economists, they proclaimed that
the glorious future—a world of nations tied together through free trade—
had already arrived. They thus embraced Jefferson's cosmopolitan vision of
nations dissolving into a world society, organized around an increasingly
elaborate and reciprocally enriching division of labor. As nations dissolved,
enterprising individuals, the true authors of the wealth of nations, stepped to
the fore, secure in their rights and pursuing their happiness as Jefferson had
enjoined. With Jefferson and Smith, free traders assaulted the benighted,
mercantilist policies of Old World imperial states: protectionists threatened
to resuscitate the discredited old regime. Yet there was a curious elision in
the free traders' worldview. Somehow, they suggested, the regime change
that Jefferson and Destutt had so vigorously championed, their notion that
the nations of the world could only fulfill their destinies through revolutionary change, was no longer necessary. The liberalization of national societies
might follow the liberalization of international trade and politics—but, then
again, it might not. The great desideratum—the immanent reality—was
instead international free trade. For free traders, unlike Jefferson, the world
was fine, almost perfect, just the way it already was. All that remained for enlightened statesmen was to eliminate lingering impediments to free exchange in the world market. Jefferson's historicism and his conception of the
nation in, and progressing beyond, history thus faded from their view. The
nation's destiny was to simply disappear.

8
War and Peace
in the New World

The debates over American commercial policy following the War of 1812 revolved around the prospects for future wars. Optimistic revolutionaries conceived of their federal union of free republics as a peace plan for the New World that would insulate them from the perpetual conflicts that characterized the history of the European balance of power. But they also recognized that Europe remained a powerful, destabilizing presence in America and that transatlantic trade relations remained vital to the new nation's prosperity and power. The visionary ideal of a complete separation between New World and Old stood in stark counterpoint to the reality of continuing entanglement.

The final spasm of the Napoleonic Wars, the Americans' War of 1812, showed how easily the United States could be drawn into European conflicts. When the devastation finally came to a halt with the Treaty of Ghent in 1815, a broad coalition of Jeffersonian Republicans rallied behind policy initiatives—a new national bank, internal improvements, and a protective tariff—that would prepare the new nation to better meet future threats to its vital interests and very survival. When the next war failed to materialize, however, the coalition began to fall apart: "National" Republicans remained convinced that the new nation's independence was still at risk, if not from conventional attack then from the more insidious and ultimately more devastating threat of British commercial domination. Meanwhile, "Old" Republicans, reflexively suspicious of all concentrated power, gained new recruits from skeptical merchants and staple producers who advocated free trade and discounted the threat of war.[1]

---

1. For a superb analysis of the founders' intentions, see David C. Hendrickson, *Peace Pact: The Lost World of the American Founding* (Lawrence, Kans., 2003). See also Peter Onuf and Nicholas Onuf, *Federal Union, Modern World: The Law of Nations in an Age of*

American Revolutionaries understood that peace in the New World depended on peace in—and with—the Old. After all, the 1783 Peace of Paris terminating the wider European war that the American colonial rebellion had initiated constituted the true beginning of American national history.[2] In subsequent decades, American statesmen avoided European entanglements as much as possible, hoping to persuade the belligerent powers to adhere to the canons of neutrality, a controversial principle not yet fully incorporated in the modern law of nations, at the very time when the European balance and the legal regime it had supported was collapsing.[3] From the "quasi war" with France in the 1790s to commercial warfare during the Jefferson and Madison administrations and finally to a second war for independence in 1812, the new nation's destiny thus remained subject to the vagaries of European diplomacy and war. Recent history gave little reason to hope that the Treaty of Ghent would inaugurate a lasting peace, particularly in view of the failure of negotiators to resolve the full range of maritime and commercial issues that had led to war in the first place.[4]

Yet if the history of chronic warfare underscored the need for military preparedness and economic self-sufficiency, the logic of foreign trade relations pulled in the other direction, toward greater involvement in the world trading system in order to promote American prosperity and greater reliance on international commercial interdependence to mitigate the threat of war. The tendencies toward withdrawal from and further integration into the Atlantic trading system could only be reconciled as long as protection was seen as temporary: tariff barriers would promote national security by developing national resources while forcing recalcitrant trading partners to offer commercial concessions. The memory of recent war and the expectation of future war sustained the balance between diverse interests and conflicting policy prescriptions in the Republican alliance. Improving prospects for

Revolutions, 1776–1814 (Madison, Wisc., 1993). For harsh assessments of the "failure" of Jeffersonian commercial diplomacy, see Bradford Perkins, *The Creation of a Republican Empire, 1776–1865*, vol. 1, *The Cambridge History of American Foreign Relations* (New York, 1993), 111, and Doron S. Ben-Atar, *The Origins of Jeffersonian Commercial Diplomacy* (New York, 1993). Our analysis of Republican divisions in the postwar period is indebted to James E. Lewis Jr., *The American Union and the Problem of Neighborhood: The United States and the Collapse of the Spanish Empire, 1783–1829* (Chapel Hill, N.C., 1998). See also Lewis, *John Quincy Adams: Policymaker for the Union* (Wilmington, Del., 2001).

2. David Armitage, "The Declaration of Independence and International Law," *William and Mary Quarterly* 59 (2002): 39–64.

3. Onuf and Onuf, *Federal Union, Modern World.*

4. For a review of the new nation's international history, see Peter S. Onuf and Leonard J. Sadosky, *Jeffersonian America* (Oxford, 2002), chap. 4.

peace and stability in the postwar years fractured the party, however, as protectionist-minded nationalists sought to promote home manufactures while free traders insisted that permanent peacetime trade barriers were counterproductive, provocations *to* war rather than preparations *for* war.[5]

Republican divisions pivoted on differing assessments of the likelihood that the nations of the world would turn away from the "barbarous" policies of the past, promote an expanding regime of free trade, and eschew recourse to war. In their increasingly bitter controversies, Jeffersonians divided between exponents and opponents of vigorous state action, between nationalists and cosmopolitans. These divisions were further, more profoundly complicated by the politics of federalism: as Americans argued about the new nation's proper relation to the world at large, they were forced to reconsider the character of their federal union. Southern advocates of free trade and states' rights took the lead in challenging the authority of the federal government, exalting the sovereignty of the state governments and therefore in distinguishing the nation from the union. In doing so, they prepared the way for the union's collapse and the emergence of two "civilized nations" in the place of one.

The clash between National Republican protectionists and Old Republican free traders reflected Thomas Jefferson's ambivalence about the likelihood of future European wars and their implications for the United States. The threat of war made Jefferson into a political realist who relied on the exercise of conventional state power to secure and promote vital national interests; peace brought the liberal exponent of minimal government to the fore.[6] Jefferson's most fundamental ideological commitments convinced him that the European—and therefore American—peace would be ephemeral. Napoleon's perversion of the French Revolution and the frustration of France's national destiny in his career of imperial conquest had given old regime legitimists a new, unnatural lease on life. Europe's revolutionary transformation remained a historical necessity for Jefferson: to believe otherwise would be to call into question the world historical significance of the American Revolution. The idea that the "holy alliance"—a peace plan for the reactionary status quo—could sustain political stability on the continent

---

5. The best study of commercial policy, partisan political competition, and sectionalism is Brian Schoen, "The Fragile Fabric of Union: The Cotton South, Federal Politics, and the Atlantic World, 1783–1861" (Ph.D. diss., University of Virginia, 2004). On the nexus between commercial agriculture and foreign policy, see Drew R. McCoy, *The Elusive Republic: Political Economy in Jeffersonian America* (Chapel Hill, N.C., 1980).

6. Robert W. Tucker and David C. Hendrickson, *Empire of Liberty: The Statecraft of Thomas Jefferson* (New York, 1990); Reginald C. Stuart, *The Half-way Pacifist: Thomas Jefferson's View of War* (Toronto, 1978); Lawrence S. Kaplan, *Jefferson and France: An Essay on Politics and Political Ideas* (New Haven, Conn., 1967).

was inconceivable to Jefferson. If "rivers of blood" had already inundated Europe during the French revolutionary wars, much more would surely flow before the last chapter of European history was finally written. Only then, with the advent of the republican millennium in the Old World, would the New World be safe.

Given his conviction that European warfare must inevitably resume, it is not surprising that Jefferson would renounce his well-known opposition to the development of American domestic manufactures and align himself with the National Republicans' post–War of 1812 campaign for commercial independence. What is surprising is that Jefferson's commitment to this position, and that of so many Southern Jeffersonians, proved so tenuous.[7] One explanation is the discrepancy between his exaggerated expectations of future warfare and the relatively stable and peaceful conditions that actually emerged in post-Napoleonic Europe. In the meantime, the postponement of revolutionary violence simply underscored the historical distance between reactionary Old World and republican New. Peace in the Atlantic trading system (ironically under Britain's aegis) gradually led Jefferson to believe that America's republican experiment was no longer threatened by Old World entanglements, even when the European wars finally resumed. The new geopolitical dispensation gave the United States the kind of natural boundaries that a great nation required—and that would give it the overwhelming prosperity and power to resist future encroachments and incursions from abroad.[8] At the same time that the new nation's relative power grew, European nations wasted their resources in sustaining coercive regimes; when the blood did finally start to flow, these powers would grow progressively weaker until finally redeemed and revivified by republican revolutions.

---

7. The most convincing explanation of this shift, focusing on Southerners' sense of disinterested sacrifice on behalf of the union—and particularly on behalf of Northern commercial and manufacturing interests—is Brian Schoen, "Calculating the Price of Union, Republican Economic Nationalism and the Origins of Southern Sectionalism, 1790–1828," *Journal of the Early Republic* 23 (2003): 173–206.

8. Even the Anglophobic Jefferson recognized that American security was predicated on an emerging community of interests between Britain and America (Eliga H. Gould, "The Making of an Atlantic State System: Britain and the United States, 1795–1825," in Julie Flavell and Stephen Conway, eds., *Britain and America Go to War: The Impact of War and Warfare in Anglo-America, 1754–1814* [Gainesville, Fla., 2004], 241–65). Britain was the "one nation" that "could disturb us" in "our endeavor . . . to make our hemisphere that of freedom," Jefferson wrote James Monroe, Oct. 24, 1823, but "she now offers to lead, aid, and accompany us" in resisting Spain's efforts to reestablish its American empire. "Great Britain is the nation which can do us the most harm of any one, or all on earth; and with her on our side we need not fear the whole world" (Merrill Peterson, ed., *Thomas Jefferson Writings* [New York, 1984], 1481–82).

Smith's Legacies

Jefferson's growing sense that the new nation's existence did not depend on the vagaries of the European balance of power confirmed his faith in American exceptionalism. In the absence of external threats, his attention shifted from the character of the European state system as a whole to the separate development of its member states. Jefferson and Antoine Louis Claude Destutt de Tracy thus focused on the *internal* sources of power and prosperity while de-emphasizing conventional military and diplomatic capabilities. The less the nation was in fact challenged by foreign powers, the easier it was to distinguish a nation's "real" wealth and power from its occasional, extraordinary manifestation on the battlefield, when it could be brought to bear through the mobilization of a willing, patriotic people. The underlying, economic premise of this modern, postrevolutionary conception of the nation was developed most influentially by Adam Smith in his *Wealth of Nations*.

Smith's polemic against mercantilism resonated with Americans who sought to liberate themselves from the corruption, coercion, and corporate privileges of the British imperial state. Just as Smith's program would liberate the British economy from the incubus of a wealth-destroying regulatory regime, the Revolutionaries' new nation would tap new sources of prosperity and power by promoting enterprise and development. Smith anticipated modern conceptions of the nation by emphasizing the formal equality of market participants and delegitimating the parasitic and unproductive political sociology of the old regime. Smith's equation of market society and nation was particularly appealing to republican revolutionaries wary about potential abuses of political power. Antimercantilism thus pointed, paradoxically, both to the expansion of national power through economic development and to a distinction between the domains of politics and economics that nation-states breached at their peril.

Jefferson's ambivalence about the relation between nation and state reflected Smith's distinction between a nation's true wealth and power and conventional military capabilities. Of course, a nation at war would have to be powerful enough in the conventional sense to secure its vital interests, but its long-term prospects depended on the full development of its resources. A world of nations dedicated to promoting their peoples' wealth and welfare would be a world without war, a world in which conventional, war-making, mercantilist states withered away. The same historical logic, the movement from promoting the wealth of particular nations to promoting the wealth of all nations, was implicit in Smith's great book and explicit in the works of his cosmopolitan successors in the classical school.

Free trade principles were broadly appealing in an export-driven colonial economy long before the publication of Smith's *Wealth of Nations* in 1776; Revolutionary patriots who mobilized against British imperial trade regulations were naturally predisposed to endorse his arguments against mercantilism.[9] Americans were flattered to read in Smith that "the most sacred rights of mankind" were at stake in the Americans' struggle against mercantilism.[10] Dismantling the colonial monopoly would vindicate American rights, but it would also benefit the entire trading world, including Britain. Smith thus provided a rationale for American independence and affirmed the revolution's world historical significance. Not surprisingly, Smith's stock rose steadily in the United States throughout the antebellum years. "No person yet has carefully perused" *The Wealth of Nations,* Smith's American disciple Thomas Cooper wrote a half century after its publication—and the declaration of American independence—"without becoming a convert to his leading doctrines."[11]

In theory, every extension of the market fostered a more elaborate and productive division of labor. The free traders' Smith thus celebrated the benefits of foreign trade: "a more extensive market" provided a vent for domestic surpluses and promoted the development of a nation's "productive powers."[12] Furthermore, the mercantilists' policy of "beggaring all their neighbours" was obviously misguided: "a nation that would enrich itself by foreign trade is certainly most likely to do so when its neighbours are all rich, industrious, and commercial nations."[13] The division of labor "is highly beneficial to mankind throughout the civilized world," according to John Taylor of Caroline, an early American advocate of Smith's political economy: it was nature's design to "diffuse and equalize her blessings" across the globe.[14] The political econo-

---

9. On early American free traders, see Cathy D. Matson and Peter S. Onuf, *A Union of Interests: Political and Economic Thought in Revolutionary America* (Lawrence, Kans., 1990). On the reception of Smith, see Joseph Dorfman, *The Economic Mind in American Civilization,* vol. 2 (New York, 1961). See also Paul Conkin, *Prophets of Prosperity: America's First Political Economists* (Bloomington, Ind., 1980) and Allen Kaufman, *Capitalism, Slavery, and Republican Values: Antebellum Political Economists, 1819–1848* (Austin, Tex., 1982). See more generally Douglas A. Irwin, *Against the Tide: An Intellectual History of Free Trade* (Princeton, N.J., 1996).
10. Adam Smith, *An Inquiry into the Nature and Causes of the Wealth of Nations,* ed. R. H. Campbell and A. S. Skinner (Indianapolis, Ind., 1981), IV, vii.b, § 43–44, 582.
11. Thomas Cooper, *Lectures on the Elements of Political Economy,* 2nd ed. (1830; New York, 1971), 34.
12. Smith, *Wealth of Nations,* IV, I, § 31, 447.
13. Ibid., IV, iii.c, §§ 9, 11, 493, 495.
14. John Taylor, *Tyranny Unmasked,* ed. F. Thornton Miller (1822; Indianapolis, Ind., 1992), 24.

mist Thomas Roderick Dew agreed. "An active and free commerce will enable each section and each latitude to produce the commodity which naturally befits it," Dew wrote, but "when the system of restriction and encouragement begins, these fair prospects are clouded; labour and capital are no longer left to take that profitable course which interest and a more humane and liberal national policy would point to" as best adapted to different climates.[15] Governments were ill advised to interfere with market exchanges that increased the wealth of all nations by forcing the premature development of "infant" manufactures.

Yet if free trade ideas remained attractive for most Americans—at least in theory—the bitter experience of chronic warfare and perennial concern about the threat of British commercial domination fostered countervailing protective tendencies in American economic thought and practice. At first, protectionists found themselves at a rhetorical and ideological disadvantage in countering the free traders' reading of Smith. They could emphasize Smith's qualifications on free trade—to protect industry crucial to national security, to equalize tax burdens on imports, to retaliate against foreign trade regulations, or to prevent dumping of "cheaper foreign goods"—agreeing with him that "defence . . . is of much more importance than opulence."[16] But these were all limited exceptions, contingent on what Smith insisted were unusual conditions: an actual state of war or an international commercial dispute that pointed toward war.

The protectionists' campaign for an activist federal state gained more leverage from Smith when they focused instead on the primacy of the American home market and compared its situation to that of Britain. *The Wealth of Nations* provided a broad historical narrative that illuminated inequalities among nations at different stages of development and emphasized the role of the state in securing vital national rights and interests. Read in the light of the *differences* among nations, *The Wealth of Nations* provided powerful arguments for tariff protection and the balanced development of interdependent interests in the domestic economy. Protectionists discovered that Smith had anticipated their own interest in the development of the home market.[17]

---

15. Thomas Roderick Dew, *Lectures on the Restrictive System Delivered to the Senior Political Class of William and Mary College* (Richmond, 1829), 22–23.
16. Smith, *Wealth of Nations*, IV, ii, §§ 40, 30, 469, 464–65.
17. See "American System," *North American Review* 32 (1831): "The home trade is admitted by all, including Adam Smith, the great authority of the opponents of the protecting policy, to be a steadier, safer, and, on the whole, more eligible branch of business than the foreign; and the increase of it evidently indicates a favorable change in the general state of industry" (145).

In the 1850s the great Whig economist Henry C. Carey offered the full-est reading of Smith in this new key, distinguishing the master from David Ricardo, Thomas Malthus, and the other "English politico-economical writ-ers, who, while claiming to belong to [his] . . . school . . . , repudiate all his doctrines, praising what he denounced, and everywhere denouncing what he advised—to wit, the careful cultivation of the home market."[18]

American protectionists recovered the historical dimension of Smith's *Wealth of Nations,* distinguishing the circumstances of a specific nation at a particular stage of development from the long-term tendency of national markets to merge into an inclusive international market. From a British per-spective, Smith's ambiguity about markets was easily overlooked: if the par-ticular circumstances of Britain's "home market" were not yet universal, they would become so as other nations reached the same stage of development and free trade drew them increasingly into a single global market. But the dis-tinction between "nation" and "world" was much more conspicuous from the underdeveloped periphery, in a "young," developing country far removed from the European markets on which it relied. Distance in space underscored the temporal gap: the United States would have to move rapidly through the stages of its own historical development before it could secure an equal position in the trading world. Was it more likely to do so simply by throwing open its markets, as free trade absolutists insisted?[19] Or would a regime of

18. Henry C. Carey, *The Prospect: Agricultural, Manufacturing, Commercial, and Finan-cial. At the Opening of the Year 1851* (Philadelphia, Pa., 1851), 6. Carey claimed that his conversion from free trade to protectionism resulted from his analysis of the beneficent effects of the 1842 tariff and was confirmed by a "reperusal of *The Wealth of Nations,*" where he found that Smith's "essential object . . . had been to teach the people of Great Britain, that the system, against which it has been the object of protection among our-selves to guard, was not less manifestly destructive of themselves than it was violative 'of the most sacred rights of mankind'" (Ibid., 5). See Conkin, *Prophets of Prosperity,* for discussions of protectionist economics (171–99) and Carey (267–301). On Carey, see George Winston Smith, *Henry C. Carey and American Sectional Conflict* (Albuquerque, N.M., 1951). There is no broad study of the intellectual history of protective economics equivalent to Douglas A. Irwin's study of free trade, cited elsewhere in this essay. But see Roman Szporluk, *Communism and Nationalism: Karl Marx versus Friedrich List* (New York, 1988) and Keith Tribe, *Strategies of Economic Order: German Economic Dis-course* (Cambridge, U.K., 1995).

19. "Universal association and absolute free trade, may possibly be realized centuries hence," Friedrich List acknowledged, but Smith and the theorists regard "them as real-izable now. Overlooking the necessities of the present and the idea of nationality, they lose sight of the nation, and consequently of the education of a nation with a view to its independence" (Friedrich List, *National System of Political Economy* [1856 ed.; New York, 1974], trans. G. A. Matile, including the notes to the French translation by Henri Richelot, with a preliminary essay and notes by Stephen Colwell, 64).

"neomercantilist" trade regulations force trading partners to offer equitable terms, thus compensating through political means for the new nation's unequal state of development?[20]

As we have seen, *The Wealth of Nations* is a rich text, profoundly informed by Smith's historical sensibility. Even Smith's apparently ahistorical passages could be read in terms of his conjectural approach to history: his axioms are empirical generalizations, glosses on economic behavior characteristic of advanced commercial societies. Yet because Smith believed that his generalizations prefigured the "laws" that would govern relations under perfect market conditions, his self-appointed heirs felt amply justified in dispensing with his empirical approach and suppressing his moral historical vision. American free traders enthusiastically embraced this antihistorical reading of Smith, conflating his polemic against mercantilism with the revolutionary struggle against British imperial despotism: only the most rigorously limited state— and only the most self-effacing "statesman"—could avoid the onus of old regime, mercantilist corruption.[21] In dialectical fashion, however, doctrinaire free traders invited protectionists to distinguish the "real free-trade school" of "Dr. Smith" from "the system of the modern British school" and its American expositors and to recover the historical dimension of Smith's text, thus giving the conjectural history of developmental stages a new lease on life in nineteenth century debates on political economy.[22] "Real" free trade would only be achieved through the mobilization of productive resources and perfection of markets *within* nations and *through* history.

The great American debate about free trade and protection justified radically different readings of Smith's *Wealth of Nations*. The very title of Smith's masterpiece was subject to different interpretations. Did Smith mean "nations" *collectively*, and was the commercial freedom he prescribed therefore now applicable to the world as a whole? "English politico-economical writers" and their American avatars had no doubt that this was the case. "By increasing

20. John E. Crowley, *The Privileges of Independence: Neomercantilism and the American Revolution* (Baltimore, Md., 1993). For an excellent recent discussion of Smith's reception in the United States, emphasizing his broad influence on the founders and the relative insignificance of the free trade principles that would dominate interpretations of *The Wealth of Nations* in subsequent generations, see Samuel Fleischacker, "Adam Smith's Reception among the American Founders, 1776–1790," *William and Mary Quarterly*, 3rd Ser., 59 (2002): 897–924.

21. For testimonials to Smith as the founder of the "science of political economy," see Dew, *Lectures on the Restrictive System*, 195, and Cooper, *Lectures on Political Economy*, 34. Also see "The Prospect before us . . . ," *North American Review* 13 (1823): 191.

22. "What Constitutes Real Freedom of Trade?" *American Whig Review*, New Ser., 6 (1850): 353.

the general mass of productions," Ricardo wrote, free trade "diffuses general benefit, and binds together, by one common tie of interest and intercourse, the universal society of nations throughout the civilized world."[23] Because this "universal society" already existed, the dismantling of trade barriers *anywhere* would benefit participants *everywhere*. Significantly, however, the classical economists' optimism about global free trade was balanced by their increasingly "dismal" assessment of the implications of population growth, capital accumulation, and rent for the domestic economy. Protectionists reversed these tendencies, offering a more optimistic account of the progressive development of the home market, even while questioning the wisdom of liberalizing global trade relations. They insisted that Smith's primary concern was with "nation," not "nations," that his prescriptions for the perfection of the *British* national market had to be adapted to the specific circumstances of the other nations, including the United States. Ricardo's "universal society" would only emerge when all the nations of the world had achieved the same stage of market freedom and economic development, at the end of history.

Protection and Free Trade, War and Peace

National Republicanism grew out of the Madison administration's embarrassments in conducting the War of 1812 and the expectation that other wars would inevitably follow. Without an efficient or energetic central government, without even a bank to manage the national revenue (the charter of the First Bank of the United States had expired on the eve of the war), the United States had barely survived its second war for independence. The rapid emergence of domestic manufactures during the interruption of foreign trade from the onset of the embargo in 1807 to the end of the war in 1815—the most encouraging development in the national economy—was the inadvertent consequence of the *failure* of Jeffersonian commercial diplomacy. At war's end, National Republicans hoped to protect this emerging manufacturing sector from the anticipated flood of cheap British imports, recognizing the strategic importance of a balanced, interdependent, and independent national economy in future international conflicts. War cut off revenue from import duties when it was most desperately needed; so, too, a nation that depended on foreign trade for vital war materiel, even for textiles to clothe its soldiers, could not claim to be truly independent.

---

23. David Ricardo, *On the Principles of Political Economy and Taxation* (London, 1821), chap. 7, § 11, Library of Economics and Liberty, Apr. 15, 2005 http://econlib.org/library/Ricardo/ricP2a.html.

Tariff protection was the centerpiece of a broader, neo-Hamiltonian program of nation building that included chartering the second Bank of the United States in 1816 and federal funding for internal improvements, thwarted by President James Madison's stunning veto of the Bonus Bill in 1817 on constitutional grounds.[24] Madison believed that the proposed expansion of federal powers was critical for national security, but it could only be authorized by a constitutional amendment. Seizing on Madison's scruples, Old Republican opponents of nationalist initiatives were increasingly successful in downplaying the national security concerns that had originally framed the debate. The real issue, they insisted, was not the new nation's place in a hazardous, war-prone world, but, rather, it was the perpetuation of a federal union which "presumes a perfect equality and community of interests among all the parties concerned."[25] Would policies ostensibly designed to secure collective interests against external threats instead subjugate one part of the country to the tyranny of another, provoking Thomas Cooper and his fellow Southerners "to calculate the value of our union; and to enquire of what use to us is this most unequal alliance?"[26]

The success of tariff proponents in sustaining a moderately protective tariff in 1820 and progressively higher rates in 1824 and 1828 (the infamous "tariff of abominations") generated a powerful backlash among staple export producers and transatlantic traders. As the threat of renewed war apparently receded, free traders became convinced that the tariff constituted a tax on the most productive sectors of the economy, diverting capital from agriculture to manufactures that would not survive, much less compete effectively, without protection. Free traders were able to sustain an intersectional coalition during the tariff debates that mirrored the alliance of protected interests—including Louisiana sugar producers—and that gave Henry Clay and his fellow tariff proponents congressional majorities. But the tendency of

---

24. John Lauritz Larson, "Jefferson's Union and the Problem of Internal Improvements," in Peter S. Onuf, ed., *Jeffersonian Legacies* (Charlottesville, Va., 1993), 340–69; idem, *Internal Improvement: National Public Works and the Promise of Popular Government in the United States, 1783–1862* (Chapel Hill, N.C., 2001); Bray Hammond, *Banks and Politics in America: From the Revolution to the Civil War* (Princeton, N.J., 1957). On the development of protectionist thought, see Lawrence A. Peskin, *Manufacturing Revolution: The Intellectual Origins of Early American Industry* (Baltimore, Md., 2003).

25. "Cotton Manufacture," Nov. 27, 1833, in Condy Raguet, ed., *The Examiner, and Journal of Political Economy; Devoted to the Advancement of the Cause of State Rights and Free Trade,* 2 vols. (Philadelphia, Pa., 1834–35), 1:135.

26. Speech of Thomas Cooper, July 27, 1827, in *Niles Weekly Register* (Baltimore) 33 (Sept. 8, 1827), rpt. in William W. Freehling, ed., *The Nullification Era: A Documentary Record* (New York, 1967), 25.

tariff politics in the period leading up to the controversy over nullification in the early 1830s was increasingly sectional, as John Taylor of Caroline and other precocious Old Republican critics had recognized from the outset.[27]

Daniel Webster's famous Senate debate with Robert Hayne over the character of the union reflected a critical sectional realignment. Webster's great speech against protection in 1824 had made him the darling of free traders across the country, but he now followed the lead of influential constituents who abandoned free trade and embraced protection as their capital shifted from commerce to manufacturing. Meanwhile, producers of cotton—the new nation's most lucrative export—saw profits plummet as overproduction drove down prices in world markets. In South Carolina and other older, less fertile regions of the cotton South, planters were hard pressed to compensate for declining prices by expanding production. As a result, Carolinians proved particularly receptive to arguments that the tariff was an inequitable, even unconstitutional form of taxation, and they ultimately threatened to bolt from the union, asserting their right to nullify federal legislation that encroached on their state's sovereignty. The nullifiers backed down in the face of President Andrew Jackson's vigorous vindication of federal authority. But free traders now gained the upper hand, and protectionists were thrown on the defensive.[28]

The Tariff Compromise of 1833 secured manufacturers against immediate drastic rate reductions. Clay, its author, insisted that the progressive reduction of tariff rates over the next nine years to a revenue level that would offer only incidental protection did not jettison the protective principle. At worst, he insisted, manufacturers were given plenty of time to prepare for

---

27. For a succinct account of the history of the tariff, see Jonathan J. Pincus, "Tariff Policies," in Jack P. Greene, ed., *Encyclopedia of American Political History*, 3 vols. (New York, 1984), 3:1259–70. For a fuller history of antebellum tariff battles, see Maurice Baxter, *Henry Clay and the American System* (Lexington, Ky., 1996), 16–33, passim; Merrill D. Peterson, *The Great Triumvirate: Webster, Clay, and Calhoun* (New York, 1987), 68–84, 146–64; and J. J. Pincus, *Pressure Groups and Politics in Antebellum Tariffs* (New York, 1977).

28. Webster's speeches are reprinted in Charles M. Wiltse, ed., *The Papers of Daniel Webster: Speeches and Formal Writings*, vol. 1 (Hanover, N.H., 1974): on the tariff, Apr. 1–2, 1824, 113–60, and second reply to Robert Y. Hayne, Jan. 26–27, 1830, 285–348. See also Peterson, *Great Triumvirate*, 171–79. For the best study of the nullification controversy, see William W. Freehling, *Prelude to Civil War: The Nullification Controversy in South Carolina, 1816–1836* (New York, 1965). See also Freehling's insightful discussion of the "eccentricity" of Carolina politics in his *The Road to Disunion: Secessionists at Bay, 1776–1854* (New York, 1990), 213–86. South Carolina at this period was by no means typical of the South. On the South Carolina economy, see Peter A. Coclanis, *The Shadow of a Dream: Economic Life and Death in the South Carolina Low Country, 1670–1920* (New York, 1989).

the new regime, and it was always possible that protectionists could mount a new campaign for a higher tariff under more congenial circumstances in the future.[29] But Mathew Carey and Hezekiah Niles, the most ardent and influential proponents of tariff protection, were not persuaded: the "price of the union" would not be paid by cotton planters, the self-styled victims of high tariffs, but rather by the free labor of the northeast and free farmers of the West.[30] Protection enjoyed a revival in 1842, as briefly ascendant Whigs enacted the last protective tariff in the antebellum years. But the Democrats' Walker Tariff of 1846 marked the definitive triumph of free trade and demise of the protective principle in the antebellum period.

The history of tariff politics is usually, and appropriately, cast in terms of conflicting interests, with deepening polarization over slavery—the paramount interest of the Southern states—roiling just beneath the surface. Yet the definition of these interests was predicated on assumptions about the future of American foreign trade relations—and the likelihood that they would be interrupted by war. If cotton producers were convinced that dismantling tariff barriers would promote world peace and prosperity, they also feared that protection would lead to commercial warfare—countervailing tariffs, embargoes, and other sanctions, perhaps war itself—as other trading states sought to secure their own vital interests. Alternatively, Britain and France, the leading customers of Southern cotton, might develop new sources of supply, with devastating results for both regional and national economies.[31]

For their part, protectionists would prepare for war in order to secure true national independence and a more durable peace. And as the threat of an early resumption of war receded, protectionists persuaded themselves that this "peace" was merely nominal, a disguise for a British commercial empire that had already blighted Ireland and India and ultimately threatened the

---

29. Freehling emphasizes Clay's success in sustaining protection in *Road to Disunion,* 385–86. On Calhoun's complicated role in tariff negotiations, see John Niven, *John C. Calhoun and the Price of Union: A Biography* (Baton Rouge, La., 1988), 179–99. See also Peter B. Knupfer, *The Union as It Is: Constitutional Unionism and Sectional Compromise, 1787–1861* (Chapel Hill, N.C., 1991), 102–18.

30. On protectionists' responses to the Tariff Compromise of 1833, see Kenneth Wyer Rowe, *Mathew Carey: A Study in American Economic Development* (Baltimore, Md., 1933) and Philip R. Schmidt, *Hezekiah Niles and American Economic Nationalism: A Political Biography* (New York, 1982). Carey conceded defeat in a letter to Duff Green, the editor of the *Daily Telegraph,* on Mar. 29, 1833: "I have withdrawn from the arena in consequence of the utter destitution of co-operation throughout the whole of last year, on the part of those vitally interested, and the hopelessness of any in future" (rpt. in *Niles Weekly Register* [Baltimore] 44 [Apr. 13, 1833]: 104).

31. The best treatment of this theme is in Schoen, "Fragile Fabric of Union."

United States as well.[32] Free traders and protectionists undoubtedly sought to promote their interests. They clearly recognized that control of the federal government, and therefore of national commercial policy, was the great desideratum. But they also developed dialectically opposed, ultimately irreconcilable understandings of the way the world had worked in the past and would work in the future. Fundamental principles were implicated in these opposing worldviews.

The great debate between protectionists and free traders pitted "history"—the American experience over the previous four decades of chronic conflict—against "theory," the economists' gloss on the longer history and future prospects of an inherently rational, progressively peaceful international division of labor. Dispute thus moved from an apparently straightforward empirical question—what had been the frequency of war in U.S. history, or in the modern history of the European state system—to more fundamental questions about the character of international relations. New York manufacturers thus assured Congress in 1832 that another war was inevitable: "Should the international relations of the great powers of the Christian world be on no worse a footing for the next two centuries than they have been for the two last—and it would surely be rash, whatever we may wish and hope, to reason and act on the hypothesis that the next following age will be better than the best in the history of our race—we must still calculate, as your memorialists have already remarked, that on an average, every alternate year will be one of war."[33] In 1828 the protectionist political economist Willard Phillips calculated that the United States had been involved in wars or victimized "by the wars of other nations" for eighteen of the first fifty years of national history. "Admit that the prospect in future is more favourable, and assume that we shall either be at war, or that our foreign trade will be exposed to interruption and embarrassment from foreign wars, one year out of five."[34]

Free traders were not impressed with such calculations. Protectionists assumed, with Thomas Hobbes, "that the natural state of man is WAR." But American history belied the Hobbesian dogma, as a free trade writer noted in 1834, "for we have been at war only four of five years out of the fifty-one

32. Bernard Semmel, *The Rise of Free Trade Imperialism: Classical Political Economy, the Empire of Free Trade, and Imperialism, 1750–1850* (Cambridge, U.K., 1970).
33. "Memorial of the New-York Convention, To the Congress of the United States. Presented Mar. 26, 1832, and referred to the Committee on Manufactures," bound with [Alexander Everett], *Address of the Friends of Domestic Industry, Assembled in Convention, at New York, October 26, 1831, To the People of the United States* (Baltimore, Nov. 10, 1831), 129–74, at 149.
34. Willard Phillips, *A Manual of Political Economy* (Boston, 1828), 188.

that have elapsed since the treaty of peace which established our independence." Protectionists perversely insisted that "we ought to foster manufactures, by high protecting duties in peace, to have them cheap and plentiful in war. In other words, that in order to diminish possible difficulties for five years, we should endure a most oppressive and unequal taxation for fifty!"[35] In any case, protectionists would have to acknowledge that the frequency of wars was likely to decrease, for, as Thomas Cooper wrote in 1830, it was the common sense of the age that "War is seldom the interest of any nation, and is likely to be less so in future than formerly."[36] The premise of the protectionists' crude historicism, projecting past patterns into the future, was fundamentally "unphilosophical and inconclusive," Dew concluded: peace, not war, was the "most natural state of nations," whatever "the past history of Europe, during its most barbarous and unsettled state."[37]

Free traders waxed eloquent about the beneficent effects of commerce for the "whole human family": free trade, Cooper asserted, makes "one family of all the nations on earth."[38] The economist Henry Vethake insisted that the progressive implementation of free trade principles contributed "to the peace of the world, and to the general progress of human civilisation," giving the lie to the mercantilist notion that one nation's gain was necessarily another's loss.[39] In the free traders' broad conception of progress, the stages of historical development were both simplified and universalized: "free trade" was "the offspring of a grand movement, the first fruits of a rich harvest, the precursor of a mighty, world-embracing revolution."[40] In "the present enlightened and civilized age," statesmen rejected "barbarous and unenlightened" injunctions of mercantilist statecraft, now recognizing that the growing prosperity and power of nations depended on peaceful, reciprocally beneficial relations, not on conflict and conquest.[41]

The free trade "revolution" was nothing less than the "dawn of a new day," promising "peace on earth, and good will toward men."[42] The difference between old and new, "barbarous" and "enlightened," was as clear as night and day. The new dispensation would secure the true wealth and welfare of all nations, exposing the fundamental mercantilist fallacy of "considering a nation in a corporative capacity, entirely distinct from the individuals who compose

35. "M.," "Suiting Facts to Theory," in Raguet, ed., *The Examiner,* Feb. 5, 1834, 1:216.
36. Cooper, *Lectures on Political Economy,* 62.
37. Dew, *Lectures on the Restrictive System,* 128, 128 n.
38. Cooper, *Lectures on Political Economy,* 195.
39. Henry Vethake, *The Principles of Political Economy* (Philadelphia, Pa., 1838), 284.
40. "Free Trade," *Democratic Review* 9 (1841): 329.
41. Dew, *Lectures on the Restrictive System,* 190.
42. Cooper, *Lectures on Political Economy,* iv.

it."[43] "National prejudices would be corrected," and "the relations of distant people would be made so close and vital, that it would be next to impossible to foment a war."[44] There would be no more wars in a free-trading world because there would no longer be *nations,* at least according to the conventional definition of the term. "We do not believe that free trade could at once make the world what it should be," the editors of the *Democratic Review* acknowledged in 1841, "but it would give it the opportunity to become so, and put it on the way. It would bind diverse interests into a solemn league of good-will."[45] Democrats envisioned "the moral amelioration of society"—a *single,* world society—as nation-states disappeared and diverse "interests" were reconciled and bound together in an all-embracing "covenant."

The polarization of positions on the prospects for war and peace generated by the tariff battles also led protectionists away from history and toward the kinds of broad generalization, or "theory," they claimed to disdain. "Nations are to them conflicting powers," a hostile critic charged, "set to jostle and tear each other in a rough contest for supremacy."[46] Protectionists did not hesitate to characterize the world in just such terms. "The globe is divided into different communities," Clay told Congress in his great speech on the tariff in 1824, "each seeking to appropriate to itself all the advantages it can, without reference to the prosperity of others." "Whether this is right or not," Clay would leave to the liberal moralists, but "it has always been, and ever will be, the case."[47] The protectionist economist Daniel Raymond insisted that nation and world necessarily constituted radically distinct moral domains. "Every nation," he wrote, must "consult its own interests exclusively, without any regard to the interests of other nations," and regardless of misguided "doctrines of universal philanthropy": "the old adage, 'charity begins at home,'" was the fundamental principle of good statesmanship.[48]

Wars were inevitable under the anarchic conditions of international society, and nations should always be ready to fight. "The romance of the Free-Trade doctrine," the Whig economist Calvin Colton wrote in 1848, was "the assumption that all nations are one family, and that therefore a system of perfect Free Trade would be best for their aggregate interests." This was far

43. Dew, *Lectures on the Restrictive System,* 11; Cooper, *Lectures on Political Economy:* "a nation or a community consists essentially of the individuals who compose it" (16).
44. Dew, *Lectures on the Restrictive System,* 146; "The Home League," *Democratic Review* 9 (1841): 552.
45. "Free Trade," *Democratic Review,* 341.
46. "Home League," ibid., 553.
47. Clay, Speech on Tariff, Mar. 30–31, 1824, in James F. Hopkins, ed., *The Papers of Henry Clay,* vol. 3 (Lexington, Ky., 1963), 712.
48. Daniel Raymond, *Thoughts on Political Economy* (Baltimore, Md., 1820), 320.

from the case. Quite to the contrary, Colton insisted, the premature dismantling of protective barriers would constitute a form of unilateral disarmament, making "the young and weak nations slaves to the old and strong" and ultimately giving "one nation, probably Great Britain, an ascendency over all the rest."[49] This was the "peace" of total capitulation and defeat, a new, more insidious and subversive form of the "universal monarchy" that the despots of old sought to establish by force of arms.

At the peak of the tariff controversy in 1831, Alexander Everett elaborated the key premises of the protectionists' quarrel with free trade cosmopolitanism. The free trade position was predicated on idealized and unrealistic conceptions both of human nature and of the unity of mankind. The "imaginary condition of individual independence . . . absurdly called the state of nature" never existed, Everett charged, except "in the dreams of poets and philosophers."[50] If men were not naturally independent, then the "philanthropists'" corollary, that there was a universal society of all mankind, was equally fallacious. The distribution of "mankind into different communities" or nations, Everett insisted, was natural, even providential. Mankind would have descended into a Hobbesian state of nature if men had not been "separated originally by confusion of tongues, and prevented from all rushing together into the most favored latitudes, by local attachments and foreign antipathies, which are the germs of national preservation, by means of national emulation."[51]

Friedrich List, the founding father of "national economics" (recall chapter 5 in this essay), blasted Cooper and the free traders for failing to grasp the reality of the nation. Cooper argued that the idea of the nation as a "moral entity" was sheer mystification, a merely "grammatical being . . . clothed in attributes that have no real existence except in the imagination of those who metamorphose a word into a thing."[52] "But the American nation," List responded, was no abstraction: "it has all the qualities of a *rational being* and real existence. It has body and real possessions; it has intelligence, and expresses its resolutions to the members by laws, and speaks with its enemy—not the language of individuals, but at the mouth of cannon."[53]

49. Calvin Colton, *Public Economy of the United States* (New York, 1848), 62.
50. "Memorial of the New-York Convention, To the Congress of the United States. Presented Mar. 26, 1832, and referred to the Committee on Manufactures," bound with [Everett], *Address of the Friends of Domestic Industry*, 129–74, at 165.
51. [Everett], *Address of the Friends of Domestic Industry*, 21–22.
52. Cooper, *Lectures on Political Economy*, 28.
53. Friedrich List, *Outlines of American Political Economy in a Series of Letters to Charles J. Ingersoll, Esq.* (1827), rpt. in Margaret Esther Hirst, *Life of Friedrich List and Selections from his Writings* (New York, 1965), 216–17.

As free traders deconstructed the nation, protectionists put it back together again, insisting first that individuals and nations were utterly dissimilar but then imputing to nations a transcendent, organic unity—or "corporative capacity"—analogous to that of the individual. The simple difference was that "real" individuals depended on society for their existence—"property," the foundation of individual rights claims in modern times, was "itself . . . the creation of society"—while the independence and individuality of nations was, in a crucial sense, more "natural" and less "imaginary" (or conventional) than that of individual human beings.

Cosmopolitan free traders imaginatively banished the nation, only to have the repressed return with a vengeance in protectionist rhetoric. The full-blown, romantic conception of the nation grew out of this transvaluation of values, in the imaginative embodiment of particular national societies *as if they were individuals* in opposition to the economists' "enlightened" vision of the universal society of humanity. List's idea of the nation thus filled in the space "between the individual and the whole human race" that Cooper and the "cosmopolitical" economists sought to empty.[54] Proceeding from Smith's focus on the home market, national economists emphasized the interdependence of sectors of the economy, classes, and regions. Smith did not need to distinguish the *British* home market from that of other nations: clearing away the rubbish of mercantilism clearly would promote "natural liberty" at home and promote the emergence of an international free trade that inevitably would benefit Britain. Protectionist economists had to work out the implications of Smith's teachings for less happily situated nations, subject to the commercial domination of better developed metropolitan economies, namely Britain.

In making the case for the nation as more than a legal entity, one gens among many, national economists invested the "home market" with layers of meaning, suggesting that the nation was an organic whole, a *natio,* uniquely

---

54. "Between the individual and the whole human race there is the nation with its special language and literature, with its own origin and history, with its manners and habits, its laws and its institutions; with its claims to existence, its independence, its progress, its duration, and with its distinct territory; an association having not only an entirely separate existence, but having an intelligence and interest peculiarly its own, a whole existing for itself, acknowledging within itself the authority of the law, but claiming and enjoying full exemption from the control of similar associations, and consequently in the actual state of the world, able to maintain its independence only by its own strength and proper resources. As an individual acquires chiefly by the aid of the nation and in the bosom of the nation, intellectual culture, productive power, security, and well-being, human civilization can only be conceived as possible by means of the civilization and development of nations" (List, *National System of Political Economy,* 263).

defined by a common historical experience and sharing common interests mediated through attachments to the land. This was not Smith's "nation," but its genealogy could be traced to his conception of the home market in *The Wealth of Nations* and the efforts of history-minded readers to adapt its teachings to their own circumstances. The "corporate spirit" Smith sought to extirpate in Britain emerged with growing force over the course of the next century, notwithstanding the ascendancy of classical economics throughout the liberal world. As weaker nations sought to overcome inequalities in world political and commercial systems, they discovered the countervailing moral historical dimension of Smith's teachings; as nationalists leveled distinctions and created the homogenous space *within* the nation that enabled market relations to flourish, they also revived and rehabilitated the "corporate spirit" in the world of nations.

Crises of the Federal Union

The American debates over commercial policy focused on the place of the new nation in the trading world, pivoting on divergent interpretations of the meaning of the American Revolution and on the proper relationship between the British metropolis and its former colonies. These debates were further complicated by the peculiar constitution of the United States as an "extended" or "compound" federal republic embracing a diverse and not always harmonious array of primary interests. Under the federal Constitution, authority was divided between a single government for the union as a whole and an expanding number of quasi-sovereign states; sectional blocs of states, seeking advantage within the federal arena, constituted an incipient third level of authority that became manifest during recurrent crises of union. Inevitably, these debates took on a constitutional cast.

In the antebellum era, "nationalists" followed Smithian precepts in seeking to preserve and perfect a continent-wide free trade zone. The "freedom of interior commerce" had been the key to Britain's economic power, Smith explained, "every great country being necessarily the best and most extensive market for the greater part of the productions of its own industry."[55] But the efforts of the Marshall Court to fulfill Smith's mandate, to make a nation by perfecting its market—most notably through broad constructions of the Constitution's commerce clause—raised the specter of a powerful central government that would obliterate states' rights and destroy the federal

---

55. Smith, *Wealth of Nations*, V, ii.k, § 69, 900.

union.[56] Doctrinaire free traders thus tended to be strict constructionists, challenging the "elastic" clauses of the Constitution that nationalists invoked in their campaign to expand the powers of the federal state.[57]

In the view of John Marshall and like-minded Smithian nationalists, the perfection of the market in America entailed the *expansion* of the federal state's powers at the expense of other, putatively subordinate jurisdictions, not its progressive withering away. A powerful central government would, in turn, be able to promote the national interest—which, in circular fashion, only could be said to exist if there was a home market in the first place—by exercising effective power in the Atlantic trading system. An assertive, neomercantilist commercial diplomacy thus could promote the international political conditions under which a free trade regime would *ultimately* flourish, just as the development of the home market would promote market freedom domestically.

By contrast, critics feared the enlargement of the federal state, its interference with free trade, and the inevitably corrupting consequences. They borrowed liberally from Smith's strictures against mercantilism and insisted on the universal applicability of the axioms of market behavior they drew from the opening chapters of *The Wealth of Nations*. In other words, they ignored the moral historical dimension of Smith's treatise. If they thought about the home market at all, it was as the spontaneous product of a free trade regime that already existed, an American preview of the future state of a free-trading world. Overlooking history, they discounted the importance of nation- and market-making politics.

The "freedom of interior commerce" was not a compelling concern for staple-producing agriculturalists, or for merchants who shipped their products to foreign markets in exchange for manufactured goods. They were instead much more impressed by Smith's strictures against the mercantilist

---

56. R. Kent Newmyer, *John Marshall and the Heroic Age of the Supreme Court* (Baton Rouge, La., 2001), 210–66; idem, *Supreme Court Justice Joseph Story: Statesman of the Old Republic* (Chapel Hill, N.C., 1985), 115–54, 305–43; G. Edward White, *The Marshall Court and Cultural Change, 1815–1835*, abr. ed. (New York, 1991), 595–673.

57. The "general welfare" theme was a central pivot of Calhoun's constitutionalism: "For Congress . . . to undertake to pronounce what does, or what does not belong to the general welfare—without regard to the extent of the delegated powers—is to usurp the highest authority—one belonging exclusively to the people of the several States in their sovereign capacity" (John C. Calhoun, *Discourse on the Constitution and Government of the United States*, in Ross M. Lence, ed., *Union and Liberty: The Political Philosophy of John C. Calhoun* [Indianapolis, Ind., 1992], 246–47). For a sustained effort to link constitutional and political economic issues, see Condy Raguet, *The Principles of Free Trade, Illustrated in a Series of Short and Familiar Essays; Originally published in the Banner of the Constitution* (Philadelphia, Pa., 1835).

regulations that clogged and stunted foreign trade. Free exchange in a global context was their great goal, and they fervently embraced the Smith who sought to open "the whole world for a market to the produce of every sort of labour."[58] From their global perspective, efforts of "nationalists" to promote balanced and integrated development in the home market were fundamentally misguided.

The conduct of foreign commercial policy thus proved increasingly controversial to American free traders, even though this was one area where the federal government apparently had a clear constitutional mandate. If the market that mattered was transatlantic in scope, efforts to promote the home market at the expense of a direct free trade with foreign trading partners were fundamentally misguided. The great achievement of Southern statesmen, culminating in John C. Calhoun's theory of the "concurrent majority," was to translate sectional grievances about the unequal impact of tariff policy into constitutional language, thus calling into question the value of the union—and eventually its survival. In doing so, Southern disunionists enacted another Smithian script, looking beyond a factitious American "nation" toward full integration in a dynamic, expansive, interdependent global market.[59]

For Smithian cosmopolitans, an overly energetic federal government was the problem, not the solution. The machinations of bankers, internal improvement advocates, and protection-minded manufacturers showed that the federal government, not the states, was most vulnerable to capture by corrupt alliances of partial interests. Politicians could not be trusted. Smith had no illusions about the wisdom of "that insidious and crafty animal, vulgarly called a statesman or politician, whose councils are directed by the momentary fluctuations of affairs."[60] "Statesmen" would continue to blunder into war, as they did in the American imperial crisis, fomenting commercial rivalries and national prejudices, heedless of their real costs.[61] In antebellum

---

58. Smith, *Wealth of Nations*, I, iii, § 3–4, 33–34.
59. Jesse T. Carpenter, *The South as a Conscious Minority, 1789–1861: A Study in Political Thought*, with a new intro. by John McCardell (1930; Columbia, S.C., 1990), 77–126.
60. Smith, *Wealth of Nations*, IV, ii, § 39, 468. On Smith and statesmanship, see Peter McNamara, *Political Economy and Statesmanship: Smith, Hamilton, and the Foundation of the Commercial Republic* (DeKalb, Ill., 1998), 18–22.
61. Only "the most visionary enthusiast" would "propose that Great Britain should voluntarily give up all authority over her colonies," however advantageous independence and a "new treaty of commerce" might be. Indeed, it was "as absurd as to expect that an Oceana or Utopia should ever be established" as "to expect . . . that the freedom of trade should ever be entirely restored in Great Britain" (Smith, *Wealth of Nations*, IV, vii.c, § 66, 616–17, IV, ii, § 43, 471).

America, Smith's caricature of the "statesman" seemed to come to life in the career of Clay and his notorious "American System." [62] Professions of patriotism barely disguised the interested motives of a corrupt phalanx determined to impose a pseudorepublican version of mercantilism on a credulous people. Cynical free traders were convinced that Clay and company were all too prone to whip up "national prejudices" as a pretext for promoting partial, corporate interests; so too, the protectionists' professed solicitude for workers in particular industries (or, rather, for manufacturers' capital) should be discounted. Free markets would redeploy labor and capital most efficiently—as long as the politicians left them alone.

Concerns about congressional corruption raised more profound questions about majority rule and minority rights.[63] Majority rule, as the framers of the Constitution so acutely understood, was not a sufficient safeguard against abuses of government and the true interests of the people as a whole. It was axiomatic, Cooper acknowledged, that *every political community or nation, ought to be considered as instituted for the good and the benefit of the* MANY *who compose it, and not of the FEW who govern it.*" The peculiar vulnerability of republics was that interests that sought to use state power to their particular advantage could form a coalition, or what Madison called "majority faction"—as protectionists did in 1824 and, most notoriously, in 1828— that could gain control of Congress and enable the corrupted "MANY" to exploit, impoverish, and subjugate *"the FEW."* [64] The Southerners' solicitude for minority rights (meaning the right to exploit slave labor) may not commend itself to modern democrats, but it underscored a fundamental tension between republican majoritarianism and the liberal determination to secure property rights and market exchanges from state interference. The need to keep these domains inviolate inspired Revolutionary patriots to break with the British Empire; a later generation of states' rights advocates, reinforced by the teachings of Smith and the economists, elaborated the distinction in a more rigorous, doctrinaire fashion as they sought to sustain the liberal-republican synthesis.[65]

---

62. Peterson, *Great Triumvirate,* 68–84; Baxter, *Clay and the American System.*
63. James H. Read's forthcoming study of Calhoun's political and constitutional thought offers a fresh perspective on the crucial theoretical issues. See also Lacy K. Ford Jr., "Inventing the Concurrent Majority: Madison, Calhoun, and the Problem of Majoritarianism in American Political Thought," *Journal of Southern History* 60 (1994): 19–58.
64. Cooper, *Lectures on Political Economy,* 33, original emphasis.
65. Our understanding of Southern liberalism is indebted to Jan Ellen Lewis, "The Problem of Slavery in Southern Discourse," in David Thomas Konig, ed., *Devising Liberty: Preserving and Creating Freedom in the New American Republic* (Stanford, Calif., 1995), 265–97.

The identification of the union, as a state system, with the international system was a logical response to the protectionists' emphasis on the inevitability of war and therefore on the persistence of a state of war in the larger world. Strict constructionists of the Old Republican school were predisposed toward such an identification in any case. As Calhoun later explained in his *Discourse on the Constitution and Government of the United States* (1851), the federal Constitution was "a treaty—under the form of a constitutional compact—of the highest and most sacred character" that governed "the exterior relations of the States among themselves."[66] The presumption was that, in the absence of such a "treaty," the disunited states would seek to promote their conflicting interests by making "war" on one another, just as independent sovereignties presumably did—or so protectionists claimed—in the Atlantic world.

At first blush, free trade advocates and jealous defenders of states' rights might seem to offer radically divergent accounts of the natural tendency of political communities toward war and peace. But the point of securing states' rights was to prevent legislation that would bear unequally on different parts of the union and thus interfere with free trade both within and beyond the union—and, of course, to protect the "domestic" institution of slavery from outside interference. The most immediate and insidious threat to a liberal trading system came from within, free traders insisted, because manufacturers and other beneficiaries of federal largesse sought to rig national commercial policy in ways that would perpetuate and promote their privileged interests. "The Cause of State Rights and Free Trade" was thus a single cause, as the Philadelphia economist Condy Raguet insisted.[67] Mirroring the identification of part (manufacturers) and whole (the nation) in protectionist rhetoric, Raguet argued that the sovereign states—the union's constituent parts—played a critical defensive role in preempting the concentration of power in the federal government that jeopardized the peace and prosperity of the whole union.

The Old Republicans' defense of a strictly construed federal Constitution had the paradoxical effect of calling into question the union it was supposed to perfect and perpetuate. Their crucial move was to relocate the source of

66. Calhoun, *Discourse on the Constitution and Government of the United States,* in Lence, ed., *Union and Liberty,* 147.

67. Raguet did so in the title of his journal, *The Examiner, and Journal of Political Economy; Devoted to the Advancement of the Cause of State Rights and Free Trade,* cited elsewhere in this chapter. On Raguet and his circle, see H. Arthur Scott Trask, "The Constitutional Republicans of Philadelphia, 1818–1848: Hard Money, Free Trade, and State Rights" (Ph.D. diss., University of South Carolina, 1998).

threat. A benign view of a progressively enlightened, stable, and peaceful world order organized around reciprocally beneficial market relations thus was juxtaposed to a federal political arena in which the "weaker party" was dominated "by the stronger."[68] Of course, "strength" and "weakness" in the union did not reflect the real wealth—and potential power—of its separate members, but rather the domination of an adventitious and artificial "majority." In effect, the Constitution made strong states weak by disarming them, and the predictable result was a kind of "war" through the scheme of unequal, redistributive taxation that the tariff authorized.

In the absence of a genuine foreign threat, the union was therefore worse than useless, as the South Carolina governor George McDuffie explained in his 1835 inaugural address: "The rights and liberties of the minority States . . . are in much greater jeopardy from the majority States, acting through the federal government, under an assumed and practical omnipotence, than they possibly could be, if there existed no compact of Union, and each were separate and independent." Turning Jefferson's distinction between bloody Europe and peaceful America on its head, McDuffie now claimed to "conscientiously believe that the smallest state on the continent of Europe, amidst the gigantic struggles of warring monarchies, holds its rights and liberties by much surer guaranties, under the laws of nations, than South Carolina now holds her rights and liberties, under the federal constitution, subject to a construction which absolutely inverts its operation, rendering it a chain to the oppressed, and a cobweb to the oppressor."[69]

McDuffie's horrific vision of constitutional "warfare" relocated the anarchic state of nature from the world at large, where consensual relations premised on reciprocal interest now "governed," to the operations of the federal system. McDuffie thus emphasized the distinction between corrupt politics and enlightened economics that Smith and the political economists endorsed. In doing so, however, he imagined that the world had *already* arrived at a postpolitical state of perfect and perpetual peace—and without

---

68. "Adjournment of Congress," Mar. 9, 1831, in Raguet, ed., *The Examiner* 1:276.
69. M'DUFFIE'S Inaugural Address, Jan. 7, 1835, in Raguet, ed., *The Examiner* 2:185–86. According to Calhoun, "no two distinct *nations* ever entertained more opposite views of policy than these two *sections* do" (The Fort Hill Address [July, 26, 1831], rpt. in Lence, ed., *Union and Liberty*, 386, emphasis added). Calhoun elaborated on this theme in his *Discourse on the Constitution and Government of the United States* [1851]: "Never was there an issue between independent States that involved greater calamity to the conquered, than is involved in that between the States which compose the two sections of this Union. The condition of the weaker, should it sink from a state of independence and equality to one of dependence and subjection, would be more calamitous than ever before befell a civilized people" (in Lence, ed., *Union and Liberty*, 267).

the benefit of revolutionary republican regime change that Jefferson had insisted must come first. In effect, the free trading world had arrived at the end
of history, while the final chapter was yet to be written in the United States.
As Calhoun insisted in the 1828, the Southern states continued to be in
shackles, "serfs of the system."[70] Free traders did not banish the specter of
war: they simply displaced it.

Under the ostensible forms of majority rule, the federal government provided an arena for an insidious form of "warfare" that would subvert liberty
and property, the foundations of republican self-government. In this deeply
skeptical view, the peace and prosperity Americans supposedly enjoyed
within their federal union was only nominal, depending finally on the capacity of its members to enforce "that equality of protection to which all the citizens of the Union are justly entitled."[71] From the free traders' perspective,
"oppressive and unequal taxation" that promoted the development of one
sector of the economy—or section of the union—at the expense of others
was the moral equivalent of war. The protectionists' claim that the promotion of manufactures served the national interest, their identification of the
part with the whole, was thus called into question: a high tariff was inherently redistributive, taking from one sector—or one section—and giving to
another. This is, of course, what nations at war sought to achieve with respect
to each other, although much less efficiently and without the legitimacy that
the presumed "consent" of the victims through representation in Congress
conferred on the transaction.[72]

Skeptical critics depicted protectionist advocates of preparedness as war-
mongers who magnified the threat of future conflict in order to justify encroachments on states' rights and individual liberties. A strong federal state
conjured up images of the kind of despotic imperial authority the American
Revolutionaries thought they had destroyed.[73] Protectionists proceeded on
the premise that foreign trade was inherently unequal and conflictual, that

---

70. Calhoun, Exposition and Protest [Dec. 19, 1828], in Lence, ed., *Union and Liberty,* 320.
71. "The American Tariff," *Edinburgh Review* (Dec. 1828), quoted in [Alexander Everett],
    *British Opinions on the Protecting System, Being A Reply to Strictures on that System
    which have Appeared in Several Recent British Publications* (Boston, 1830), rpt. in
    Alexander Everett, *Journal of the Proceedings of the Friends of Domestic Industry; and
    British Opinions on the Protecting System* (New York, 1974), 15.
72. The classic and most influential statement of this argument may be found in John
    Taylor, *Tyranny Unmasked:* The protective "system pretended to be levelled against for-
    eigners, has only hit ourselves"; "this new war is to be carried on by foreign and native
    capitalists" at the expense of the great agricultural majority (at 48, 179).
73. This theme is elaborated in Peter S. Onuf, "Federalism, Republicanism, and the Origins
    of American Sectionalism," in Edward L. Ayers et al., *All over the Map: Rethinking
    American Regions* (Baltimore, Md., 1996), 11–37.

one nation's gain was always at the other's expense. Free traders pointed out this was the same fundamentally fallacious premise that had led mercantilists astray. Obsessed with bullion flows and the balance of trade, old regime policy makers kept up a constant state of war in order to beggar their rivals and achieve economic autarky—or what protectionists now called independence. Cooper complained that the mercantilist beast that Smith and his followers had slain was, incredibly, now resurrected in the protectionists' "*manufacturing system;* a system equally absurd and selfish, and equally jealous lest our neighbours should profit as well as ourselves."[74]

Protectionism, Cooper explained, was the second coming of mercantilism, "a system of monopoly, exclusive privilege, restriction, and prohibition; a system, which professes to make its gain, by depressing as far as possible the efforts of every other nation who using its natural advantages, seeks to make a profit by commerce and manufacture as well as ourselves." Such systems were unnatural: they distorted foreign trade—which, like exchanges in the home market, should be reciprocally beneficial—by subordinating it to the interests of belligerent states seeking to dominate one another. "Manufactures and commerce," when "protected" and promoted by neomercantilist governments, "are the great and perpetual sources in modern days of national quarrels. They are war-breeders. Three fourths at least of the wars in Europe for these one hundred and fifty years, have originated from the jealousies of trade, from the stupidity, and the selfishness of merchants and manufacture[r]s."[75]

Preparing for war, as the protectionists urged, was thus tantamount to making, or "breeding," war. And it was just such preparations that most jeopardized republicanism. The Revolutionary generation conceptualized the threat in terms of "standing armies," the "consolidation" of political authority, and high levels of taxation and indebtedness. The economists of Cooper's later career offered a more sophisticated analysis: the confusion and therefore "corruption" of the distinct domains of politics and economics, the illegitimate interference of governments in the private business of citizens, inevitably subverted the foundations of republican government. This monopolizing, despotic impulse had provoked American patriots to rise up in revolt; during the nullification crisis it justified resistance to the tariff in South Carolina.

While free traders turned protectionist rhetoric about the threat of war inside out, protectionists challenged the free traders' fundamental premises.

---

74. Cooper, *Lectures on Political Economy,* 10, original emphasis.
75. Ibid., 10, 131–32.

The progressive liberalization of international trade relations would, they insisted, reduce the United States and all the other nations of the world to a condition of servile dependence on Britain. Under these unnatural conditions, nations ultimately, inevitably would struggle to assert their independence, bursting the chains of commercial domination, inundating the world in "rivers of blood." "The experience of all mankind forbids us to hope for an exemption" from future wars, the protectionist Mathew Carey warned in 1819. Free trade on necessarily unequal terms would retard the development of national resources, rendering the nation weak and vulnerable. Under the specious pretense of liberality and reciprocity, Henry Brougham and his fellow British free traders wanted to strangle America's "rising manufactures . . . in the cradle." Free trade was nothing less than war by other, more insidious means. If we mean to be "really" and not merely "nominally independent," Carey concluded, we must recognize that "the cause of the manufacturers . . . is the cause of the nation."[76]

Protectionists argued that free trade constituted an insidious form of warfare that subverted national independence: "after having expended the best blood of the nation, and millions of treasure to shake off the yoke of colonization," Carey wrote, "we have voluntarily adopted the colonial policy of England, and placed ourselves with respect to her, and in truth to most of the world, in the situation of colonies." "Who can contemplate the result [of free trade] without horror? . . . The wealth of the country would be swept away, to enrich foreign, and probably hostile nations, which might," he ominously predicted, "at no distant period, make use of the riches and strength thus f[or]tuitously placed in their hands, to enslave the people who had destroyed themselves by following such baneful counsels."[77] Free trade, Clay concluded, leaves us "essentially British, in every thing but the form of our government."[78] We will not "possess a real national existence," a writer in the *North American Review* explained, we cannot claim to be "a self-subsisting substantive community" until "we shall have succeeded in relieving ourselves from the sort of colonial relation in which we have hitherto stood to the mechanical and intellectual workshops of Europe—when we shall have acquired an economical and moral, as well as a political independence."[79]

76. [Mathew Carey], *Addresses of the Philadelphia Society for the Promotion of National Industry* (New York, 1974), rpt. 5th ed. (1820), 74, 152, iv.
77. Ibid., 189, 18.
78. Clay, Speech on Tariff, Mar. 30–31, 1824, in Hopkins, ed., *Papers of Henry Clay* 3:722–23.
79. "American System," *North American Review* 32 (1831): 129.

Protectionists saw opportunities for commercial exploitation in the national differences that, for free trade economists, gave rise to a providentially benign international division of labor. "As a municipal principle," Everett acknowledged, "there is no question of the great advantages of Free Trade," but "as between foreign nations, there is no free trade—there never was—there never can be—It would contravene the arrangements of Providence."[80] The possibility of "a *perfect reciprocity*" in foreign trade, Niles explained, "must remain Utopian, until it shall please the Great Creator of all things to give the same soil and climate, wants and wishes, governments and customs, to all the human race."[81] Thus, as free traders calculated the value of the union, protectionists insisted that union was the necessary precondition of a genuinely free trade. As List pithily summarized the protectionist position: "political union always precedes commercial union." "In the actual state of the world," he added, "free trade would bring forth, instead of a community of nations, the universal subjection of nations to the supremacy of the greater powers in manufactures, commerce, and navigation."[82]

Two Nations

The worldviews of protectionists and free traders mirrored each other. Protectionists looked abroad—and particularly toward Britain—and saw a world of nations in perpetual conflict. They challenged the rosy projections of liberal cosmopolitans who imagined that the dismantling of trade barriers—indeed, the dismantling of nations—would inaugurate a regime of world peace and prosperity. "Peace," they insisted, was deceptive: it was best understood either as an interval in an unending succession of wars—the plausible premise of Mathew Carey and the first generation of protectionists—or as a cover for more insidious assaults on the independence of young, undeveloped, commercially dependent nations such as the United States. There could be no real, lasting peace among unequal states at different stages of development. By contrast, the federal union secured free trade, prosperity, and peace among the American state-republics, regardless of discrepancies of size, population, and wealth.

---

80. [Everett], *Address of the Friends of Domestic Industry*, 21.
81. [Hezekiah Niles et al., Central Committee, Convention of the Friends of Domestic Industry], *Memorial to the Senate of the United States* (Baltimore, July 4, 1832), rpt. in Everett, *Journal of the Proceedings of the Friends of Domestic Industry*, 180, original emphasis.
82. List, *National System of Political Economy*, 200.

Free traders inverted protectionist logic at every point. Optimistic about the prospects for peace in an increasingly interdependent, peaceful, and prosperous trading world, free traders saw the federal union as a zone of danger, an arena for warlike assaults on the vital interests and fundamental rights of embattled minority interests. Safety depended on a rigorous, "constitutional" distinction between the realms of economics and politics, putting "freedom of commerce . . . beyond the reach of any combined or corrupted majority in a central or consolidated Congress."[83] Free traders' logic subverted their faith in the efficacy of republican government to secure liberty and property and of the union to guarantee states' rights. Without the kinds of constitutional protections Calhoun's concurrent majority offered, Southerners would be better off seceding from the union altogether.

Yet free traders could not escape profound anxieties about the threat of war, however much they imagined the trading world a peaceful place. Their skeptical assessment of protectionists' motives underscored the likelihood of conflict in the event of disunion: if their fellow Americans constructively made war on them *within* the union, what would restrain them from more overt, violent assaults in the absence of union? Strict constructionist free traders had no reason to question the wisdom of the founders in constructing a union that would guarantee peace among potentially hostile states, for hostility and suspicion among Americans had never been more conspicuous. If, when they looked abroad, free traders could imagine that enlightened nation-states would coexist in peace, progressively withering away, they had no illusions about the future of American politics. The idea that states were "sovereign"—with a legitimate claim to the rights of fully independent states in an international society—and the displacement of the idea of the nation from the whole American people to the "separate nationalities" of the particular states and finally to two hostile sections constituted an implicit acknowledgment of the founders' wisdom. Americans experienced the imaginative demolition of the union in the tariff debates and in recurrent controversies over slavery and its westward expansion as a kind of virtual war—and as a rehearsal for the actual bloodbath that would finally fulfill the founders' most awful imaginings.

Conflicts over commercial policy reflected—and, to a significant extent, precipitated—the deepening crisis of the American union. The founders' primary goal had been to preempt the possibility of war, whether with foreign powers or among the American states. Ironically, their successful efforts to demonstrate the endemic threats to peace and security, to depict the

83. "Cotton Manufacture," Nov. 27, 1833, in Raguet, ed., *The Examiner* 1:139.

inexorable tendency of disunited states to slide into anarchy, paved the way toward subsequent confusion and conflict. The need to meet *external* challenges to American independence by establishing a more energetic federal regime was broadly appealing to most Americans, even moderate anti-Federalists—and future Jeffersonian Republican oppositionists—who feared the concentration of power in a potentially despotic central government.

Nevertheless, the Federalists' emphasis on the dangers of interstate—and intersectional—conflict, however effective it may have been in countering anti-Federalist concerns about "consolidation," underscored, even reinforced anxieties about *internal* threats to the American peace. In other words, the premise of the new federal peace plan was that war threatened in all quarters, whether from the counterrevolutionary great powers of Europe, or from conflicts among states or sections in the union. Under such dire circumstances, the survival—much less, the perfection—of the union was indeed something of a miracle. But it was a miracle that depended on a spirit of compromise and concession that proved increasingly difficult to sustain under the strain of sectional conflict.

The paradoxical effect of the post–War of 1812 campaign to bolster American independence and prepare for future wars was to call into question the legitimacy of the federal Constitution and the value of the union. Opponents of this campaign did not instantly forget the founders' warnings about the dangers of disunion and the likelihood of war among disunited states. However they might embrace the free traders' inspiring vision of an increasingly peaceful and prosperous *world* order, their resistance to nationalist initiatives revealed fundamental conflicts of interest—and belligerent tendencies—that only union could hold in check. Disunion meant war and, as the National Republicans had insisted, the threat of war required energetic national government. Critics of the American System thus accepted the founders' logic. They simply disagreed on the source of threat to the American peace.

Agreement on the founders' wisdom sustained powerful commitments to the union, despite deepening intersectional divisions. The deepest division was over the chief source of danger to liberty and union. Did it come from foreign powers in a dangerously anarchic European state system, or from the consolidation of power by a corrupt alliance of ambitious interests *within* the union? Unionist sentiments could not contain or suppress sectional tensions—particularly when, despite the disclaimers of its most fervent exponents, unionism took on an increasingly pronounced sectional inflection—and intersectional antipathies prepared the way for the emergence of two hostile nations in the place of one. Successive crises of the union did not banish the idea of the nation or lead Americans to imagine that they could transcend the threat of war. To the contrary, just as free traders displaced the threat of war from the larger world to the federal arena, the idea of the nation was displaced—first to the "separate nationalities" of sovereign states, prepared like nullifying South Carolina to mobilize its military force against Yankee consolidationists, and then to an emergent Southern nation.

The route toward Northern nationhood was apparently more direct, beginning with the defense of the union and a harmonious, interdependent balance of interests in the home market to a romantic conception of the American people as one great, inclusive family. "The home market," the protectionist Everett wrote in 1831, "is the palladium of home itself in all its most endearing and ennobling political and social relations; without which we have no common country, but should be reduced to the condition of dismembered and defenceless provinces."[84] But of course, this fervent nationalism was predicated on the denial of the deepening divisions among Americans, most notably over the future of slavery as a domestic institution, that had long since alienated Southerners. Northern nationalism was thus fixated on the preservation of the union, not on the acknowledged sense of sectional difference— and grievance—that inspired sectional nationalists in the South.

---

84. [Everett], *Address of the Friends of Domestic Industry*, 39.

9
The North and the Nation

The nullifiers' conception of states' rights "strikes at the heart of the union itself," John Quincy Adams told the House of Representatives in May 1832. The paradoxical result of this assault would be the emergence of separate peoples, "two great, transcendent, opposite, and irreconcileable interests, in deadly hostility to each other; each pervading the two great Atlantic sections of the country, each operating within its appropriate domain, with the irrepressible force of a law of nature." Adams was not alone in prophesying the inevitability of civil war should the union be sundered. But his vision of two "large masses of mankind" coalescing around "transcendent interests" was remarkably prescient. Southerners might subvert the idea that Americans collectively constituted a single nation, bound together by sacred ties of union, but they would not be able to suppress the "irrepressible force" of the national idea. The failure of one nation then would give rise to two separate nations, "situated in natural conflict with each other."[1]

The nullifiers, according to Adams, saw the union as nothing "but a partnership of corporate bodies without posterity, without soul, [and] without faith."[2] As the South Carolinian Thomas Cooper put it, the "nation" had "no

---

1. John Quincy Adams, for the Committee on Manufactures, May 24, 1832, *Niles Weekly Register* (Baltimore) 62 (June 2, 1832): 256. On the idea of union, see Paul C. Nagel, *This Sacred Trust: American Nationality, 1798–1898* (New York, 1971) and Peter B. Knupfer, *The Union as It Is: Constitutional Unionism and Sectional Compromise, 1787–1861* (Chapel Hill, N.C., 1991). The most illuminating studies of ideological developments in the North are Eric Foner, *Free Soil, Free Labor, Free Men* (New York, 1970) and Daniel Walker Howe, *The Political Culture of the American Whigs* (Chicago, 1979).
2. "Report of the minority of the committee on manufactures, prepared and submitted by Mr. Adams," Feb. 28, 1833, *Niles Weekly Register* (Baltimore) 64 (May 25, 1833): 211.

real existence except in the imagination of those who metamorphose a word into a thing."[3] Adams had no doubts about the reality of the nation or of its government, a "great organized engine of improvement, physical, moral, political."[4] "Protection was the right of the citizen," he told the House in 1833, "and the duty and obligation of the government." The federal government had done its duty by the South: the institution of slavery, "a certain interest which he need not more particularly designate," enjoyed "an especial protection peculiar to itself . . . under the constitution, and the *laws* of the United States." Southern domination of the federal government also translated into an aggressive (and expensive) policy of American Indian removal that cleared the way for the spread of plantation slavery and protected the vital interests of "the western and southern portions of this union."[5] "The most remarkable characteristic of the controversy" over the tariff, Adams concluded, "is, that it originated in the discontent of one great *protected* interest, with the *protection* extended by the existing laws to another. The controversy is sectional in its nature. It is the superabundantly, the excessively protected interest of the south, which revolts at the feeble and scanty protection of the laws enjoyed by the north, the centre, and the west."[6]

Adams anticipated the ironic trajectory of Southern nationalism. Southerners first demystified and finally destroyed the union, denying the reality of American nationhood as well as the great material benefits union afforded them. Unwilling to acknowledge the "protection" the union offered their vital interests, Southerners posed as victims of an overpowerful central government in order to extort still further benefits—territory for their plantations, protection for their slave "property"—while denying protection to Northern manufacturers and laborers against the depredations of British free trade imperialism. As the sectional crisis deepened, very few Southerners could agree with James Henry Hammond of South Carolina that the "slaveholders of the South" still ruled the nation—although growing numbers of

3. Thomas Cooper, *Lectures on the Elements of Political Economy*, 2nd ed. (1830; New York, 1971), 28.
4. "Report of the minority of the committee on manufactures, prepared and submitted by Mr. Adams," Feb. 28, 1833, *Niles Weekly Register* (Baltimore) 64 (May 25, 1833): 206.
5. Adams speech in House, Feb. 4, 1833, ibid., 63 (Feb. 23, 1833): 439, original emphasis.
6. "Report of the minority of the committee on manufactures, prepared and submitted by Mr. Adams," Feb. 28, 1833, ibid., 64 (May 25, 1833): 215, original emphasis. For an excellent analysis of Adams's unionism, see James E. Lewis Jr., *John Quincy Adams: Policymaker for the Union* (Wilmington, Del., 2001). On the role of the central government in serving Southern interests—and of the Southerners' tendency to deny that role—see Peter S. Onuf and Leonard J. Sadosky, *Jeffersonian America* (Oxford, 2002).

Northerners reached that uncomfortable conclusion.[7] Instead, they embraced a conception of "transcendent [sectional] interests" that pointed toward separate Southern nationhood, thus giving the mystical abstraction "nation" a "real existence" and transforming the "word" back into "thing." As Southerners began to contemplate the possibility of independence, they rediscovered and relocated the national idea: the repressed returned.[8]

Northerners moved in the opposite direction, positioning themselves as patriotic defenders of the nation against militant advocates of states' rights who threatened to destroy the union in order to promote sectional interests. Nationalism in the North followed various trajectories in the decades leading up to the Civil War. The common theme was identification with the union as a whole and the suppression of sectional particularism: the North was not the object of patriotic feeling. Northerners may have celebrated their region's economic, cultural, or moral superiority to other parts of the country, and the policies they promoted may have benefited them disproportionately. But Northerners disavowed sectionalist intent, and Southern skepticism simply lifted their nationalism to new rhetorical heights.

Protective Nationalism

As Adams made clear, this idea of the nation rationalized and romanticized a regime that benefited many Americans, *especially* Southern slaveholders. When Southerners finally and definitively rejected the union—fatally misled by mystifications of their own about their prospects for independent nationhood—Northerners reluctantly refocused their patriotic energies on

7. Hammond's speech in Congress, 1858, quoted in Leonard L. Richards, *The Slave Power: The Free North and Southern Domination, 1780–1860* (Baton Rouge, La., 2000), 1, 214. Richards's important new study is the clearest explication of this theme in the literature: it properly focuses on the extraordinary persistence of the dough-face phenomenon in Northern politics. Our understanding of how the national political parties functioned in relation to controversial economic issues—and how they ceased to function effectively when such issues were no longer on the table—is indebted to Michael F. Holt, *The Political Crisis of the 1850s* (New York, 1978). On Southern perceptions, the classic work is Jesse T. Carpenter, *The South as a Conscious Minority, 1789–1861: A Study in Political Thought,* with a new intro. by John McCardell (1930; Columbia, S.C., 1990). See also authoritative studies by William J. Cooper Jr., *The South and the Politics of Slavery, 1828–1856* (Baton Rouge, La., 1978) and Michael A. Morrison, *Slavery and the American West: The Eclipse of Manifest Destiny and the Coming of the Civil War* (Chapel Hill, N.C., 1997).
8. John McCardell, *The Idea of a Southern Nation: Southern Nationalists and Southern Nationalism, 1830–1860* (New York, 1979).

their own region. Thus, as Southerners moved from a sectional conscious-ness that subverted American nationhood to national pretensions of their own, nationalists in the North only acknowledged their distinctive sectional identity as they mobilized for a war to restore and rehabilitate the original union. A few abolitionists in the North concluded that Hammond's union, the union slaveholders dominated, was hopelessly bankrupt and should not be preserved, but the great majority of Northerners remained committed to—and ultimately went to war for—a conception of the union as a nation and of Americans as a single great people.

As long as the union survived, Northerners' continuing identification of union and nation gave Southerners the upper hand in recurrent struggles to determine the future direction of federal policy. Precociously conscious of a distinctive corporate identity, Southerners were quick to defend their own and their region's honor against any and all assaults, real and imagined; in con-trast, Northerners appeared insensible and pusillanimous because they de-nied and suppressed their sectional identity, continuing to imagine them-selves as part of an inclusive national community. Northern honor only came into play as sectional divisions deepened and popular sentiment finally could be unleashed against the nation's internal enemies.[9] In both parts of the country, persisting attachments to union mitigated sectional hostilities and slowed the progress toward war. But Southern unionism was colored by counsels of prudence and conservative appeals to vested interest, and ulti-mately it could not compete with the more sublime and transcendent de-mands of sectional honor. As long as sectional conflicts could be contained, Northern unionism apparently operated in the same way, cementing the so-called unholy alliance of the "lords of the lash" and "lords of the loom." Yet unionism in the North also expressed more profound patriotic impulses. Ap-peals to the harmony of interdependent interests in a progressively more per-fect home market served as the foundation for the construction of a broadly and deeply appealing conception of American nationhood. For patriotic Southern proto-nationalists, interest and honor seemed increasingly at odds; for Northern nationalists, by contrast, sectoral and sectional interests merged into a mystical, transcendent conception of union and nation, a corporate en-tity whose integrity and honor had to be redeemed on the field of battle.

The logic of sectional controversy guaranteed that nationalist feeling in the North would be overtly antisectionalist. Nullifiers' insistence that the union was contingent and provisional—that it could and should be dissolved

---

9. For an analysis of the apparent honor deficit in the North in the pre–Civil War decades, see Susan-Mary Grant, *North over South: Northern Nationalism and American National Identity in the Antebellum Era* (Lawrence, Kans., 2000) and Richards, *Slave Power.*

282 · Markets, Nations, and War

if the rights and vital interests of member states were threatened—led Daniel Webster and other Northern nationalists to insist that the union was "perpetual," sacred, and inviolable. In similar dialectical fashion, radical Southern challenges to the constitutionality and policy of protective tariffs valorized protectionism. Disunionist threats raised the specter of civil war, reviving postwar anxieties about the nation's vulnerability to external as well as internal threats—and enabling exponents of national economic development to shake off the stigma of pork barrel politics. Nullification also gave New Englanders, who had flirted with disunion before and during the War of 1812, a golden opportunity to refurbish their nationalist credentials. The nullifiers' apotheosis of state sovereignty—and patent solicitude for local interests—exonerated Northern defenders of the union from any lingering taint of separatism and self-interestedness. What was good for the North was good for the nation.

Advocates of a protective tariff linked promotion of manufactures, a disproportionately Northern interest, to the development of a balanced, interdependent national economy that would enable Americans to secure their independence in a dangerous world. Of course, not all Northerners were protectionists—commercial interests naturally gravitated toward free trade—and Southern hemp and sugar producers offered crucial support for high tariffs. But protection provided a broadly appealing framework for nationalist sentiment that transcended commercial policy. The protectionists' "nation" always reached toward the transcendent, promising future benefits for all sectors of the economy and sections of the country, even—and especially—for those sectors and sections called on to make present sacrifices. Protection also harked back to traditional conceptions of political obligation, the "protection covenant" that bound sovereign and subject; at the same time, it anticipated the broad reach of the modern welfare state in fulfilling its responsibilities to the great national "family." [10] In either case, the nation was conceived as a corporate entity, with a life that transcended the lives of its present citizens and a purpose that transcended their purposes. The nation existed both in history, in the chronicle of sacrifices by founders and patriots, and in the people's expectations of a glorious future.

American history was not shrouded in a distant, mythic past. The struggle for independence marked the new nation's birth, and preserving the Revolutionary fathers' legacy was the historical responsibility of succeeding

---

10. On the "protection covenant," see Peter S. Onuf, *Jefferson's Empire: The Language of American Nationhood* (Charlottesville, Va., 2000), 156–57; James Kettner, *The Development of American Citizenship, 1608–1870* (Chapel Hill, N.C., 1978), 165–73.

generations.[11] Of course, what this meant in practical terms was always controversial. Protection-minded Americans worried about continuing challenges to the nation's vital interests and independence from the former mother country. Britain's recognition of American nationhood remained begrudging and partial, they insisted, even after Americans once again vindicated their independence on the battlefield in the War of 1812. Protectionists thus tended to define *independence*—and therefore the *nation*—in much broader terms than their free trader antagonists, suggesting that true independence, embracing the full development of the nation's human and natural resources, would only be achieved through continuing struggle against formidable foes. Their concern with the insidious threats of British commercial domination thus situated the protectionist agenda in a legitimating narrative of national history (the Revolutionaries were the first protectionists) and pointed to a glorious end point, when the new nation could finally meet Britain and the other great powers on fully equal terms.[12]

The protectionists' conception of national development and international rivalry was elaborated in postwar tariff battles, but—like the idea of protection—remained compelling even when controversial policy issues were no longer on the table. Free trader critics were doubtless right when they charged that many protectionists were self-interested opportunists whose nationalist rhetoric should be radically discounted. (Protectionists did not hesitate to return the favor as they emphasized the selfish interests free trade served and questioned free traders' patriotism.) But nationalist rhetoric took on a life of its own and continued to shape conceptions of union and nation even when immediate interests were no longer being served. Protectionist Whig thought, particularly in the influential works of the economist Henry C. Carey, thus played a critical role in fostering national sentiment in the North in the years leading up to the Civil War even though prospects for tariff protection were so dim. Protectionists never lost sight of their broad policy goals (perhaps the ascendancy of the new Republican party would revive their fortunes), but they necessarily had to take a longer, more immediately disinterested view of the role of the state in promoting economic development.[13]

---

11. Michael Kammen, *A Season of Youth: The American Revolution and the Historical Imagination* (New York, 1978).
12. Bernard Semmel, *The Rise of Free Trade Imperialism: Classical Political Economy, the Empire of Free Trade, and Imperialism, 1750–1850* (Cambridge, U.K., 1970).
13. On Carey, see George Winston Smith, *Henry C. Carey and American Sectional Conflict* (Albuquerque, N.M., 1951) and Rodney J. Morrison, *Henry C. Carey and American Economic Development* (Philadelphia, Pa., 1986).

The protean character of protective nationalism in the North was apparent in the progressive elaboration—and sentimentalization—of the home market and the "homes" it supposedly sustained and nourished. There was no necessary connection in protectionist political economy between *home* and *home market*. But concern with British economic domination made Carey and his fellow protectionists increasingly conscious of the supposed conflict between extensive development within a global trading system and intensive, balanced, and interdependent development within a particular nation and, by logical extension, within regions and localities.[14] The regressive tendency in protectionist thought from world to neighborhood drew derisory commentary from free trade cosmopolitans, but it proved crucial in domesticating and familiarizing a highly abstract conception of the nation. Antiexpansionist protectionists wanted to preserve neighborhoods and households from the centrifugal, destructive effects of a too rapidly expanding agricultural frontier where the wasteful exploitation of fresh land simply reinforced industrial Britain's domination of world markets.[15]

The protectionist focus on balanced development in nation and neighborhood brought questions of social relations generally and labor relations particularly to the fore. As debates over commercial policy, constitutional interpretation, and the future of slavery became increasingly sectionalized and the second party system ceased to function effectively, Northern protectionists had to explain how all classes would benefit under a protective regime. Proslavery Southerners who invoked the authority of the new economics in debates over national commercial policy now emphasized the more "dismal" prospects of a free market society, racked by inevitable conflicts among capitalists, rentiers, and a rapidly expanding and increasingly underemployed laboring population. In response, protectionists groped toward a paternalist conception of free labor that mirrored proslavery paternalism, arguing that a

---

14. On antebellum political economy, see Paul Conkin, *Prophets of Prosperity: America's First Political Economists* (Bloomington, Ind., 1980). See also the valuable analyses, emphasizing Carey's influence, in James L. Huston, *The Panic of 1857 and the Coming of the Civil War* (Baton Rouge, La., 1987), 66–110, and Huston, *Securing the Fruits of Labor: The American Concept of Wealth Distribution, 1765–1900* (Baton Rouge, La., 1998), 152–83.

15. On Carey's conception of decentralized industrialization on a neighborhood scale under a protective regime, see Foner, *Free Soil, Free Labor, Free Men,* 36–38. The progress of rural industrialization in the Hudson Valley and other regions in the antebellum period made Carey's ideas seem plausible. See Martin Bruegel, *Farm, Shop, Landing: The Rise of a Market Society in the Hudson Valley, 1780–1860* (Durham, N.C., 2002).

protective tariff would secure capitalists and laborers alike from debilitating competition against pauperized foreign labor.[16]

Insisting that the British economists—particularly Thomas Malthus and David Ricardo—deduced their dismal axioms about the inexorable tendencies of population growth, rising rents, and surplus capital to spread human misery from a fundamental misreading of the progress of civilization, Carey and his colleagues offered a more compelling and theoretically coherent rejoinder to the proslavery assault on Northern institutions. Free laborers, they argued, would become progressively more productive and enjoy a rising share of the wealth they produced within the context of a protective national state that promoted a true "Harmony of Interests." The nation was the natural, necessary form of political and social organization that would enable people to fulfill their productive potential. By contrast, the single world market and worldwide division of labor that free traders envisioned would lead to Britain's progressive enrichment (although not to the enrichment of its working class) and to the deskilling, underdevelopment, and immiseration of all other nations.[17]

Perpetual Union, Perpetual Threat

When the framers of the federal Constitution established a "more perfect union," they were imagining a definitive solution to the classic dilemma of how to secure perpetual peace without obliterating the liberties of separate states.[18] The success of this federal republican experiment would enable a free people to flourish, to pursue happiness individually while developing their collective or national potential. Jeffersonian Republicans who saw themselves as guardians of the founders' legacy insisted that union and nation were distinct, in theory if not always in practice. The injunction to preserve the union and to pass it on as a sacred trust was timeless, for every generation stood poised on the brink of anarchy and war if it should fail, regardless of the progress of the American people to ever-higher levels of

16. Huston, *Panic of 1857*, 103–10; idem, *Securing the Fruits of Labor*, 248–51; Jonathan A. Glickstein, *American Exceptionalism, American Anxiety: Wages, Competition, and Degraded Labor in the Antebellum United States* (Charlottesville, Va., 2002), 183–210.
17. Henry C. Carey, *The Harmony of Interests: Agricultural, Manufacturing, and Commercial* (Philadelphia, Pa., 1851).
18. David C. Hendrickson, *Peace Pact: The Lost World of the American Founding* (Lawrence, Kans., 2003); Peter Onuf and Nicholas Onuf, *Federal Union, Modern World: The Law of Nations in an Age of Revolutions, 1776–1814* (Madison, Wisc., 1993).

civility, prosperity, and power. This was the political gospel for Americans of all persuasions in the antebellum decades, even—perhaps especially—for those who threatened to bolt the union and thus unleash the "dogs of war" if their most vital interests and fundamental rights were not secured.

The antebellum federal system encouraged brinkmanship, underscoring and exaggerating conflicts of interest along sectoral and sectional lines and therefore reinforcing the distinction between union and nation. But the opposite tendency, to conflate union and nation, was equally powerful, particularly when National Republicans and Whigs sought to mobilize the people and their productive capacities to meet dangerous foreign challenges. The convergence was complete in the domain of foreign affairs. The federal Constitution might secure perpetual peace among the state-republics, so enabling them to escape the sorry history of never-ending war and bloodshed that afflicted the peoples of Europe, but it could not guarantee them against conflict with foreign nations and empires. The government of the union therefore must be able to command the full resources of the nation in order to secure American independence and guarantee the success of the republican experiment.

Debate over land policy, the tariff, and other contentious issues exposed the fault lines of union, provoking Webster and other nationalists to define the union in progressively more exalted terms. In his famous Senate debate with Robert Y. Hayne of South Carolina, Webster focused on the future development of the nation's "vast internal resources." "Improvement" was necessarily a collective enterprise, depending on the agency of the federal government and requiring the "consolidation of our Union." The government of the union would always remain one of limited, delegated powers, for "the States are, unquestionably, sovereign" within their limited sphere of authority. But "in war and peace we are one," Webster insisted, and "in commerce, one" as well, "because the authority of the general government reaches to war and peace, and to the regulation of commerce."[19]

Of course, Webster's conflation of war, peace, and commerce was the controversial question in the tariff debates, and Hayne and his fellow free traders recognized Webster's formulation as the mark of his apostasy from their ranks. As the Marshall Court demonstrated in its commerce clause jurisprudence, "commerce" was a protean concept capable of indefinite

---

19. Webster's second reply to Hayne, Jan. 26–27, 1830, in Charles M. Wiltse, ed., *The Papers of Daniel Webster: Speeches and Formal Writings*, vol. 1 (Hanover, N.H., 1986), 308, 330, 304. For the context and significance of this famous exchange, see Maurice Baxter, *One and Inseparable: Daniel Webster and the Union* (Cambridge, Mass., 1984), 180–88.

extension.[20] Webster's apotheosis of the union, his juxtaposition of the Constitutional union to the mere "compact" created by the Articles of Confederation, and his vision of internal improvement and economic development provided a compelling narrative framework for national history.[21] Defenders of states' rights were quite right to be alarmed, for Webster's nation promised to transcend and subsume the states as true sovereignties. Webster's union was not merely a sacred legacy to be preserved but an end to be accomplished, the Constitution's "leading object." "By consolidating the Union," he "understood no more"—and no less—"than the strengthening of the Union, and perpetuating it." Perpetuity was secured by developing the nation's powers *through* and *in* history. The achievements of past generations warranted a glorious future. "We love to dwell on that union, and on the mutual happiness which it has so greatly contributed to acquire," and we do not "impose geographical limits to our patriotic feeling or regard."[22]

Webster provided a broadly appealing gloss on neo-Hamiltonian conceptions of union and nation that protectionists had elaborated in the tariff debates long before Webster disavowed his early advocacy of free trade. Webster also elaborated a version of national history that justified shifting positions on commercial regulation and exonerated New England from charges of disloyalty and disunionism culminating in the abortive Hartford Convention of 1814.[23] New Englanders certainly believed that Thomas Jefferson's embargo of 1807–9, the most comprehensive possible exercise of Congress's power to regulate commerce, was "unconstitutional," and they suffered grievously under its dispensation. At that time, John C. Calhoun and his fellow nationalists, original authors of "the 'accursed policy' of the tariff," demanded sacrifices from New Englanders that dwarfed the pretended hardships of the tariff. Unlike the nullifiers, New Englanders "did not take the law into our own hands, because we did not wish to bring about a revolution, nor to break up the Union." Webster defied Hayne to "find any thing in the history of Massachusetts, or New England, or in the proceedings of any legislative or other public body, disloyal to the Union, speaking slightingly of its

20. On Marshall's jurisprudence, see G. Edward White, *The Marshall Court and Cultural Change, 1815–1835,* abr. ed. (New York, 1991); Charles F. Hobson, *The Great Chief Justice: John Marshall and the Rule of Law* (Lawrence, Kans., 1996); and R. Kent Newmyer, *John Marshall and the Heroic Age of the Supreme Court* (Baton Rouge, La., 2001).
21. Webster's second reply to Hayne, in Wiltse, ed., *Papers of Daniel Webster* 1:332. Webster elaborated the constitutional argument in his most important antinullification speech, "The Constitution Not a Compact," Feb. 16, 1833, ibid., 571–619.
22. Webster's second reply to Hayne, ibid., 1:315, 304.
23. James M. Banner Jr., *To the Hartford Convention: The Federalists and the Origins of Party Politics in Massachusetts, 1789–1815* (New York, 1970).

value, proposing to break it up, or recommending non-intercourse with neighboring States, on account of difference of political opinion."[24]

Webster's paean to perpetual union gained him admirers throughout the union, even among disgruntled antinullificationists in South Carolina.[25] His defense of the union provided a capacious conceptual framework for imagining the American nation in time and space, through history and across the continent's vast expanses. But if Webster's union was capacious, it also remained protean and undeveloped. Negating the nullifiers offered a broad common ground for both preservation-minded unionists such as Andrew Jackson intent on securing the founders' precious legacy and development-minded nationalists such as Henry Clay with visions of the nation's future greatness.

At best, Webster's great speeches thus constituted only a prospectus for nationalism, subject to further elaboration—and contestation. The likelihood of war remained the crucial and controversial variable: concerns with national security, broadly defined, provided the major impetus to nationalist thinking and sentiment. For many Americans, however, the successive compromises that apparently secured the peace of the union combined with increasingly stable, peaceful, and prosperous conditions in the Atlantic trading system to mitigate historical anxieties about America's geopolitical vulnerability. The challenge for National Republicans and Whigs who continued to fear the dangerous implications of British commercial domination was to develop a more substantive conception of American nationhood.

During the tariff controversies of the post–War of 1812 period, protection-minded National Republicans insisted that British military and naval power continued to threaten American independence. At first they predicted another war with the former mother country. Increasingly, however, exponents of federally directed economic development argued that the new nation must respond to the more diffuse and insidious threat of British commercial domination to secure real independence. As they developed a broad conception of what American independence entailed, protectionists thus invoked a Hobbesian image of the state of war, a never-ending struggle for advantage—and survival—in an anarchic state of nature. "The experience of our own history," John Quincy Adams wrote in 1832, "has amply confirmed" the maxim that "preparation for war" was "the most effective security for the continuance of the blessings of peace."[26] The need for preparedness

---

24. Wiltse, ed., *Papers of Daniel Webster* 1:337, 319, 322.
25. Merrill D. Peterson, *The Great Triumvirate: Webster, Clay, and Calhoun* (New York, 1987), 172–80.
26. Adams, for the Committee on Manufactures, May 24, 1832, *Niles Weekly Register* (Baltimore) 62 (June 2, 1832): 253.

subverted the conventional distinction between war and peace, thus defining
the nation in terms of its capacity to resist the encroachments of other
powers—and to project its own power.

The protectionists' conception of the relations of nations as an anarchic
state of nature emerged in opposition to the cosmopolitan conception of a
liberal international society based on commerce and common practices.
Free traders believed that the dismantling of commercial regulations her-
alded the "dawn of the millen[n]ium" of peace, prosperity, and "universal
brotherhood."[27] In a lawless world, explained the Harvard economist Francis
Bowen, economic exchange would never supersede political conflict. "Independent communities" might not "always [be] at war with each other," but
they were "always rivals and competitors in the great market of the world,"
and their rivalries could always lead to war: "war is either a present evil to be
averted or alleviated, or it is a possible future event, the occurrence of which
is to be guarded against."[28]

Free traders imagined that international law would be self-enforcing under a regime of enlightened self-interest. But "the want of any superior tribunal to enforce its enactments" made "the law of nations . . . a very imperfect
code"—whose only real sanction, ironically, was the threat of war. The protectionists' critical point was that "nation" and "world" were distinct domains.
The free trader's great mistake was to repudiate "boundaries and nationality
in matters of foreign commerce" and to embrace "an absolute international
communism" on the premise "that the interest of each [nation] is identical
with that of each other, just as before, the interest of every individual in a community, as he himself calculates it, is identical with that of the community."[29]

Protectionists were geopolitical realists who defined the nation in terms of
its capacity to make war in order to protect its vital interests and preserve its
independence. Britain played a crucial role in the protectionists' understanding of national history as well as in their predictions of future perils. Americans' national identity was forged in these past struggles and would be perfected in fulfilling their destiny as a great power: they had been struggling "for
more than a century" to promote "industry, by the establishment and support
among us of new departments of productive labor," a Whig writer asserted in

27. "The Tariff of 1846," *American Whig Review* 12 (Sept. 1850): 309.
28. [Francis Bowen], Review of Willard Phillips, *Propositions concerning Protection*, *North
American Review* 72 (Jan. 1851): 420. Bowen incorporated the review of Phillips in *The
Principles of Political Economy Applied to the Condition, The Resources, and the Institutions of the American People* (Boston, 1856), 24–25.
29. [Bowen], Review of Phillips, *Propositions concerning Protection*, *North American Review* 72 (Jan. 1851): 421; Phillips, *Propositions concerning Protection*, 21.

1845.[30] Patriots "took up arms" in the Revolution, a later writer added, to overthrow a despotic imperial regime "which left untold wealth in England and nothing in America, all the plunder on one side, all the dependency and servility on the other."[31] In other words, although the Revolutionaries rose up against the constraints of British mercantilism and sought access to forbidden foreign markets—that is, free trade—they had always been "protectionists" in their determination to foster the infant nation's productive capacities.

The consistent object of British policy toward America was to stifle its economic development, "to confine our people, so far as possible, to the production of colonial staples."[32] Britain's halting, partial progress toward free trade, culminating in the repeal of the Corn Laws in 1846, served this fundamental purpose, for unprotected American manufactures could not survive an unequal competition against cheap British products. The doctrine of free trade held out the bait of universal peace and prosperity when, in fact, it "warred upon the manufacturing interest, in a way to almost paralyze it."[33] Under the old empire, mercantilist regulation of colonial commerce had promoted British wealth and power; now "free trade" achieved the same results, more insidiously and often with the unwitting cooperation of its victims. "Free trade is a license for depredation," the Whig polemicist Calvin Colton insisted in 1848, "because it is based on the principle of anarchy" and thus puts "the weaker party in the power of the stronger all the world over."[34] Under the pretext that unfettered commerce fostered a beneficent worldwide division of labor and community of interests, free traders suggested that national governments should retreat from interference in global markets— thus leaving the field clear for a new form of global imperium. The false promise of world peace disguised a radical new imbalance of power, creating

a power of wrong, which, for its comprehensiveness, energy, and for the remoteness of its influence, is unrivalled among all the known devices of injustice. On this system, a strong man—strong in his commercial position— living under one national jurisdiction, may crush hundreds and thousands of weak men, living under another jurisdiction; and the operation of the

---

30. "The Infancy of American Manufactures: A Brief Chapter of Our National History," *American Whig Review* 1 (Jan. 1845): 49.
31. "British Policy Here and There: 'Free Trade,'" ibid., 12 (Nov. 1850): 533.
32. "The Infancy of American Manufactures: A Brief Chapter of Our National History," ibid., 1 (Jan. 1845): 49.
33. [Nathaniel A. Ware], "A Southern Planter," *Notes on Political Economy, As Applicable to the United States* (New York, 1844), 13.
34. Calvin Colton, *Public Economy of the United States* (New York, 1848), 55.

principle is without limit over the face of the earth, till the rights of individuals, in countless groups, and those of whole nations, are devastated by it.[35]

As they vindicated their patriotic credentials and conjured up dire threats to American independence, Whigs expressed—and exploited—a powerful Anglophobic strain in American political culture. The British commercial system, according to Carey, "can be designated by no other term than that of 'satanic.'"[36] England, the *American Whig Review* explained, was "a bully and a beggar, an extortioner and a bankrupt—the exhauster of the world, now so utterly exhausted by her vices that she hangs for life upon the quiet or folly of her former enemies!"[37] "Free trade," charged Colton, was the mask and means of its bid for "universal dominion" and "world-wide despotism."[38]

It could hardly be claimed—yet—that Americans suffered seriously under British commercial hegemony, but the new nation's fate could be foreseen in the histories of Ireland and India: Ireland's incorporation in the United Kingdom—and free trade—was a "horrible tragedy," leading to the "nation's murder"; in India, Britain "killed the cotton manufacturer" and "beggared the people," "driving . . . women and children . . . to the labours of the field, and the men to the raising of sugar in the Mauritius."[39] Free trade meant deindustrialization and colonial (or neocolonial) dependency for staple export producers across the world, including the United States. Present prosperity disguised the unvarnished truth, that "'free trade' with England has made us tributary to her" and that, "with all our 'liberty,' WE ARE NOT INDEPENDENT."[40] "In all economical relations," British commentators happily agreed, "the United States will stand to England in the relation of colony to mother-country."[41] Echoing a favorite trope of the Revolutionaries, a

35. Ibid.
36. Henry C. Carey, *The Prospect: Agricultural, Manufacturing, Commercial, and Financial. At the Opening of the Year 1851* (Philadelphia, Pa., 1851), 51.
37. "British Policy Here and There: Who Feed England?" *American Whig Review* 12 (Dec. 1850): 656.
38. Colton, *Public Economy of the United States,* 63.
39. "British Policy Here and There: 'Free Trade,'" *American Whig Review* 12 (Nov. 1850): 536; Henry C. Carey, *The Past, The Present, and The Future* (Philadelphia, Pa., 1848), 113, 408; Carey, *The Slave Trade: Domestic and Foreign: Why It Exists, and How It May Be Extinguished* (London and Philadelphia, Pa., 1853), 173.
40. "British Policy Here and There: 'Free Trade,'" *American Whig Review* 12 (Nov. 1850): 529.
41. *London Spectator* (1833), in Colton, *Public Economy of the United States,* 402. "The United States are still colonies," according to Edward Gibbon Wakefield, *England and America; A Comparison of the Social and Political State of Both Nations* (New York, 1834), 255.

"Southern Planter" concluded that "[w]e are truly and literally now slaves of England."[42]

Protectionist polemics disclosed deep ambivalence about Britain. Whig Anglophobia of the antebellum decades, like the overheated rhetoric of the Revolutionary era, was closely linked to Anglophiliac envy and admiration as anxious, independence-minded Americans sought to demonstrate their mastery—and deny their servility. Certainly Whigs such as Carey, the son of Irish immigrants, genuinely loathed "murdering" Britain. But the underlying tone of protectionist rhetoric, particularly in its emphasis on British forcefulness and power, was much more positive. Britain was the great world power of the day, forceful, expansive, and civilized, the pattern for other nations anxious to achieve greatness: its "unbridled lust of wealth and power" bore more than a faint resemblance to America's imperial impulses in the age of "Manifest Destiny."[43] The secret of Britain's success, Whigs thought, was its government's ability to promote the nation's leading interests. The "mighty fabric of English greatness and wealth" was "the fruit of her labor, her manufacturing labor and skill, and the commerce based upon it," Nathaniel A. Ware wrote, and "these have been called into existence by wise policies and protections, and cherished up to the present point, when they are putting the whole world in requisition."[44]

Americans should ignore the siren call of free trade, protectionists warned, and instead follow Britain's example. "The gigantic power of England," wrote Hezekiah Niles, was "the result of centuries of care—of inexhaustible vigilance, and unbounded zeal—of a lofty national pride, and a just estimate of the domestic resources of the country."[45] Britain's greatness was a result of the nurturing hand of a protective state. In order to compete and so enjoy "true independence," every other nation in the modern world would have to follow its example, exercising "within its own limits, all the great branches of industry designed to satisfy the wants of man."[46] England, the Whig Review concluded, "is the great example of the fruits of protection; the strongest, richest, wisest, and just at this time, the most powerful monarchy on the globe": she has "by her example, and by cherishing the seeds of liberty, protecting and encouraging all rightful industry, whether of the hand

42. [Ware], "Southern Planter," Notes on Political Economy, 174.
43. Colton, Public Economy of the United States, 75.
44. [Ware], "Southern Planter," Notes on Political Economy, 171, 170.
45. Hezekiah Niles et al., Central Committee, New York convention, Memorial to the Senate of the U.S., Baltimore, July 4, 1832, Niles Weekly Register (Baltimore) 62 (July 28, 1832): 392.
46. Bowen, Principles of Political Economy, 26.

or of the head . . . made herself the patroness and protector of human liberty; and sending colonies into remote regions, carrying with them her laws and principles, has made herself the mother of future empires. . . . Such has been the policy of England, always protective, always patriotical."[47]

In emphasizing the role of the protective state in fostering British prosperity and power, Carey and other "national" or "historical" economists challenged the fundamental tenets of the "classical" economists of the Smith-Ricardo school. Doctrinaire free traders insisted that state interference *always* retarded economic development and that Britain rose to a preeminent position *despite* its mercantilist legacy; protectionists replied that Britain's progress to a dominant position as the "workshop of the world" could only be explained by the ongoing support of a protective state.[48] Controversy pivoted on the replicability of the British experience. Should developing nations embrace the new economic orthodoxy and integrate as rapidly as possible into the world trading system, or should they foster "infant" industries in protected home markets? Should they take the British at their theoretical word—ascending directly to "that commercial heaven of supposed equality, presumed reciprocal justice, and imaginary eternal right, they call 'free trade'"—or should they follow Britain's historical example?[49] The answers were clear to protectionist Whigs: if the new nation were to secure "true independence" it would have to become Britain's equal, capable of holding its own in a "strenuous rivalry for the commerce of the world."[50]

The antitheoretical, historical bias of protective economics led directly to the fuller elaboration of the national idea. Conceptualized in a temporal dimension, the "nation" had a corporate existence or life of its own, analogous to that of an individual and equally subject to the vagaries of fortune and circumstance. Rejecting the free traders' cosmopolitan conception of a single world market—an "absolute international communism" in which mercantilist nation-states progressively withered away—protectionists envisioned a crucial and widening role for "policy"—the exercise of political will—in the nation's unfolding history.[51] For free traders, enlightened statecraft meant

---

47. "The Future Policy of the Whigs," *American Whig Review* 7 (Apr. 1848): 337.
48. "The Democratic Review on Freedom of Trade," ibid., 13 (Mar. 1851): 233–47, at 237. For the other side of this exchange, see the critical review of Carey's *The Past, The Present, The and Future* in "Free Trade," *Democratic Review* 28 (Feb. 1851): 97–118.
49. "British Policy Here and There: 'Free Trade,'" *American Whig Review* 12 (Nov. 1850): 520.
50. "The Crisis of the Century: Alliances, European and American," ibid., 15 (Feb. 1852): 168.
51. Willard Phillips, *Propositions Concerning Protection and Free Trade* (1850; New York, 1968), 21.

the renunciation of state power and the promotion of private enterprise in a worldwide division of labor: the histories of peoples everywhere merged into a single world history. Protectionists reached the opposite conclusion. An increasingly interdependent global economy exposed *differences* among nations according to putatively universal standards of civilization and economic development. Indeed, nations in the modern sense could only be said to exist within Eurocentric conceptual frameworks generated by unequal and asymmetric commercial and diplomatic encounters with the rest of the world. If Enlightenment universalism enabled liberal free traders to look forward to the disappearance of nations at the end of history, Enlightenment historicism encouraged protectionists to look backward, to discover the keys to development of particular nations in their relations to other nations as well as in their distinctive histories.

Carey and his fellow protectionists understood that national histories did not necessarily follow a single, progressive trajectory. In their version of America's history, the new nation had prospered as long as it pursued a protective policy and resisted British commercial domination. "Resistance," the political will to counter British power, was the only guarantee of success in the continuing struggle to vindicate American independence. "The resistance of the United States put an end to the navigation laws," Carey wrote in 1848; "their resistance killed the right of search. Their resistance killed the corn laws. Their resistance will kill the colonial system, and give freedom to India and Ireland, to the people of England, and to themselves."[52] Yet the turn away from protection, culminating in the Walker Tariff of 1846, jeopardized the new nation's achievements and prospects. The failure to resist and thus to assume its proper role as savior of the benighted nations of the world would lead to underdevelopment and stagnation, even regression. India and Ireland exemplified the fate of weak and supine nations that submitted to Britain's free trade empire. Free trade did not diffuse the benefits of civilization to the far corners of the earth; to the contrary, wrote Carey, "a better system calculated to perpetrate barbarism never was devised."[53] The conditions that underwrote Britain's rise to the pinnacle of power and civilization worked to retard and reverse the progress of other peoples. As a result, he sadly concluded, "the people of Ireland were . . . passing rapidly toward barbarism."[54]

The Whig indictment of Britain's "grand siege against the independence of every nation on the face of the earth" failed to galvanize protectionist

52. Carey, *The Past, The Present, and The Future*, 443.
53. Ibid., 383.
54. Carey, *Slave Trade*, 179.

sentiment in the United States, much less effective resistance to Britain's dominant position in world trade. Partisan messages were confused and conflicted in the antebellum years: expansion-minded Democrats did not hesitate to pander to their party's traditional Anglophobia—thus securing the loyalty of Irish immigrants—and threaten war with Britain over territorial issues, even while embracing a political economy that, as Whigs charged, placed "the whole body of our agriculturists in the power of the *moneyed aristocracy of Britain.*"[55] Whigs might see themselves as true defenders of American independence, but their obsession with Britain as both threat and exemplar was sometimes indistinguishable from fawning Anglophilia. "Race for race—English, Irish, Scotch—they are of one blood with us," according to a writer in the *Whig Review:* "they are and will continue to be our friends and brothers, even though their government may sometimes mislead them, and introduce war between the two nations."[56] Straining to explicate a modern conception of the nation that combined notions of identity and difference, Whigs concluded that all great nations were equal, "rivals and competitors" in a dangerous and anarchic world.[57]

The broad historical and geopolitical analysis of Britain's place in the modern world served as a critical touchstone in the development of Whig nationalism. But the full development of the national idea depended on its application to conditions at home, at a time when an increasingly tenuous federal union seemed to be verging on collapse. Henry Carey's conception of "association," first laid out in his *The Past, The Present, and The Future* in 1848, provided the conceptual bridge between the Whig analysis of British free trade imperialism and a robust conception of American nationhood, grounded in American experience. Carey took his assault to the bastion of classical economic orthodoxy, insisting that its axioms were based on a fundamental misreading of history.

Protecting Hearth and Home

Classical economics earned its reputation as the "dismal science" because of the influential works of Malthus on population and Ricardo on rent. Free

---

55. "The Democratic Review on Freedom of Trade," *American Whig Review* 13 (Mar. 1851): 238, original emphasis.
56. "The Crisis of the Century: Alliances, European and American," ibid., 15 (Feb. 1852): 168–69.
57. [Bowen], Review of Phillips, *Propositions concerning Protection, North American Review* 72 (Jan. 1851): 421.

traders of the orthodox school optimistically looked forward to the dawning of a new era of peace and prosperity as mercantilist regimes were dismantled and a progressively more elaborate division of labor emerged in the world as a whole. But their confidence faltered when they turned inward to consider developments at home. Population growth inexorably outstripped the food supply; growing demand for food brought poor, marginal lands under cultivation, yielding progressively higher rents to proprietors of the best lands; and a surplus laboring population drove wages toward bare subsistence.[58] These so-called laws of political economy forecast a miserable future of class struggle as rentiers and capitalists consolidated their dominant positions and the laboring classes declined into barbarism. If the economists were right, the immanent contradictions of the capitalist system must lead to its collapse. "Ricardo-Malthusianism tends directly to what is commonly called Communism," Carey concluded, "and at that point will England arrive, under the system which looks to the consolidation of the land, the aggrandizement of the few, and the destruction of the physical, moral, intellectual, and political powers of the whole body of labourers, abroad and at home."[59]

Given the new nation's apparently inexhaustible land supply, American economists tended to discount Malthusian and Ricardian corollaries to Adam Smith's original teachings. Situated on the prosperous periphery of a rapidly expanding trading system, Americans could enthusiastically embrace free trade doctrines that promised vigorous competition for their staples without worrying about the ultimate fate of the mature or "stationary" economies of the Old World.[60] In his first writings as an economist, Carey hewed to free trade orthodoxy (despite the fact that he was the son of Mathew Carey, the most prominent protectionist of his generation): America enjoyed a special exemption from the new science's dismal implications because of

---

58. "With every step in the progress of population, which shall oblige a country to have recourse to land of a worse quality, to enable it to raise its supply of food, rent, on all the more fertile land, will rise" (David Ricardo, *On The Principles of Political Economy and Taxation,* (London, 1821), chap. 2, "Rent," § 5, Library of Economics and Liberty, Apr. 15, 2005 http://econlib.org/library/Ricardo/ricP2a.html). Also see Donald Winch, *Riches and Poverty: An Intellectual History of Political Economy in Britain, 1750–1834* (Cambridge, U.K., 1996).

59. Carey, *Slave Trade,* 281.

60. Drew R. McCoy, *The Elusive Republic: Political Economy in Jeffersonian America* (Chapel Hill, N.C., 1980), chap. 1; idem, "Jefferson and Madison on Malthus: Population Growth in Jeffersonian Political Economy," *Virginia Magazine of History and Biography* 88 (1980): 259–76; James Russell Gibson, "Americans versus Malthus: The Population Debate in the Early Republic" (Ph.D. diss., Clark University, 1982).

nature's extraordinary bounty.[61] Carey's great discovery, announced in *The Past, The Present, and The Future*, was that the "laws" Malthus and Ricardo had elaborated were based on faulty premises that were disproved by his own systematic historical research.

Most crucially, Carey asserted, "Mr. Ricardo's proposition" that human settlement moved from richer to poorer soils "is diametrically opposed to all the facts presented by the history of the United States: of England: and of the World." In fact, "man commences always with the poor soils," in pastoral and primitive agricultural economies of the uplands, "and proceeds onwards to the richer ones," in the river valleys.[62] Malthus's grim calculus was equally mistaken, for population growth made possible new forms of social cooperation and capital formation that enabled more advanced societies to unleash the productive potential of the most fertile lands:

> With the increase of population there arises a habit of union, tending to promote the wealth and to facilitate the acquisition of machinery to be used in aid of labour; and with each step in this progress, man acquires increased power over the materials of which the earth is composed, and increased power to determine for himself which to select for cultivation, as being most likely to promote the object of maintaining and improving his condition; and with every increase of this power he is enabled to obtain a larger return to his labour, and to consume more, while accumulating with still increased rapidity the machinery required for further improvement.[63]

Carey thus offered a more optimistic version of political economy, congenial to the progressive spirit of his fellow citizens, that seemed to resolve the new science's fundamental contradictions.

Carey's admiring disciple E. Peshine Smith believed that the publication of *The Past, The Present, and The Future* in 1848 marked "that year as a new era in the annals of Political Economy."[64] The book was a critical breakthrough for various reciprocally reinforcing reasons. First, it provided a theoretical justification for Carey's turn to protectionism, thus giving the

61. Henry C. Carey, *Principles of Political Economy*, 3 vols. (Philadelphia, Pa., 1837–40). Although Carey had already developed an elaborate rationale for limiting the settlement of new lands, he still believed with Ricardo that "in the infancy of society . . . superior soils alone are cultivated" (Ibid., 3:51).
62. Carey, *The Past, The Present, and The Future*, 56, 58.
63. Ibid., 56–57.
64. E. Peshine Smith, *A Manual of Political Economy*, intro. by Michael Hudson (1853; New York, 1974), 47. See also "Political Economists: Henry C. Carey," *American Whig Review* 12 (Oct. 1850): 376–87.

cause a powerful new impetus at a time when Democratic free traders dominated Congress and rolled back tariff protection. Protectionists of the elder Carey's generation had always been at a rhetorical disadvantage because their free trader opponents, the self-anointed "disciples of Adam Smith," had economic "science" on their side.[65] By distinguishing Smith from his successors and emphasizing the master's primary interest in fostering the home market, Carey gave protectionism a more legitimate, scientifically respectable lineage.

Most important, however, *The Past, The Present, and The Future* offered a compelling new narrative of American national history situated *within*— and not exempt from—the larger course of world history. The trajectory of American development, from poor to rich soils, was normal and normative, leading to progressively higher levels of social concentration and cooperation. The crucial point was that nationality was natural and that the continuing progress of civilization depended on the self-determination of all peoples. Carey's apotheosis of the nation enabled a new generation of protectionists to shake off the stigma of war-mongering power politics that peace-loving free traders had so successfully imputed to their neomercantilist predecessors. The cause of the American nation was the cause of humanity. And Americans who believed that by some divine dispensation "nature's nation" would enjoy a permanent exemption from Old World corruptions—and from history— were fatally deluded, oblivious to the "war of extermination" England was waging "against the labour of all other countries employed in any pursuit except that of raising raw produce to be sent to her own market."[66]

Carey and his followers depicted Britain as a monstrous aberration, a kind of antination that—like Napoleon's France—sought universal dominion, in the process fomenting war and promoting the degradation and enslavement of peoples all over the world—including its own people. Britain, Peshine

---

65. "The Infancy of American Manufactures: A Brief Chapter of Our National History," *American Whig Review* 1 (Jan. 1845): 53. Francis Bowen criticized fellow protectionist Willard Phillips for setting himself "in opposition to the doctrines of Adam Smith" and attempting to discredit

> his authority and that of the science which he established. . . . Whatever errors Adam Smith may have committed, he must be regarded as the founder of a science, which, for the last half century, in every civilized country on earth, has more directly affected and controlled the material interests and daily pursuits of men than any discovery or pure speculation that has been made since the revival of letters; and which is even now exerting an influence that can hardly be measured upon the legislation and economical polity of all nations that are not sunk in barbarism. [Bowen], Review of Phillips, *Propositions concerning Protection, North American Review* 72 (Jan. 1851): 399, 398.

66. Carey, *Slave Trade*, 216.

Smith wrote "has, in practice, regarded the nation collectively as a gigantic trader with the rest of the world, possessing a great stock of goods, not for use but for sale, endeavouring to produce them cheaply, so that it might undersell rival shopkeepers, and looking upon the wages paid to its own people as so much lost to the profits of the establishment." The "nation of shopkeepers" would be shopkeeper—and "workshop"—to the world, stifling the development of all other nations. But "the true conception of a State," Smith insisted, "is that of a Household, whose members have undivided interests."[67]

Carey's answer to British world domination or "centralization" was "concentration," the full flourishing of the associative impulse that led scattered individuals to come together to exploit more fertile soils and fulfill their human potential.[68] Americans were mistaken to think *they* were exceptional; to the contrary, it was Britain's exceptionalism—its quest for empire at the expense of the independence and welfare of all other nations—that threatened the progress of civilization everywhere. "Like Rome," Carey concluded, "England has desired to establish political centralization by aid of fleets and armies, but to this she has added commercial centralization, far more destructive in its effects, and far more rapid in its operation. . . . She needs, and must have new markets, as Rome needed new provinces, and for the same reason, the exhaustion of the old ones."[69]

Carey's conception of the nation developed in counterpoint to his horrific image of omnivorous Britain. Britain's insatiable appetite for cotton and other staple products exercised a powerful centrifugal force on American agriculture, scattering settlers across new lands, extending the regime of slave labor, and preempting the natural "concentration" of population in productive, civilized communities. Opposition to rapid expansion had been a familiar motif in Federalist and Whig ideology and still had a lingering aura of "aristocratic" nostalgia for village hierarchy—and cheap labor.[70] But Carey's analysis of the workings of the British-dominated global economy turned the conventional view of the beneficent effects of "free" land on its head: Americans could only become free and prosperous by resisting the pull of the frontier and turning "inward," thus "facilitating the growth of wealth and the preparation of the great machine of production." Concentration of settlement fostered social harmony, "a love of home and of quiet happiness, and a

---

67. Peshine Smith, *Manual of Political Economy,* 149.
68. Carey, *The Past, The Present, and The Future,* 289.
69. Carey, *Slave Trade,* 210–11.
70. Protectionist thought in Britain retained a strong Tory inflection through and beyond the Corn Laws repeal in 1846. See Anna Gambles, *Protection and Politics: Conservative Economic Discourse, 1815–1852* (Woodbridge, U.K., 1999).

desire for union," as well as a more equitable division of wealth; "centralization, on the contrary, looks outward, and tends to promote a love of war and discord, and a disrelish for home and its pursuits, preventing the growth of wealth, and retarding the preparation of the great machine."[71]

The exploitation and despoliation of frontier lands seemed to confirm the Ricardian hypothesis: of course, settlers chose the best lands first, stripped them of their fertility, and then moved on; as the supply of land diminished, latecomers were left with inferior, less productive lands. This resource stripping led to windfall profits, particularly for planters with slave labor, but left depleted soils in its wake, thus confirming—if temporarily postponing—the economists' gloomy predictions of surplus population and class conflict. But Carey's idea of the "great machine" suggested a more dynamic and optimistic conception of the relation between man and nature. The movement from poor to rich lands was both a broad cross-cultural historical description and a metaphor for the progress of civilization: humans improved nature, shaping it to their own ends, even as they developed their own productive capacities.

Human and natural history were inextricably linked in Carey's "great machine." "We are to regard man then as the lord," averred Carey's disciple Peshine Smith, "not the slave of Nature." But man was "no arbitrary lord," for he can only secure "freedom for that harmonious exercise of all his faculties, in which happiness consists, by means of the intelligence which enables him to apprehend the inevitable necessity that the physical laws *must* operate, and teaches him how to avoid opposing the irresistible, and how to make it work for him."[72] Insisting that they were Adam Smith's true heirs, Carey and Peshine Smith invoked the new science of soil chemistry to counter the scientific pretensions of "Ricardo-Malthusianism." "It is impossible to conjecture a limit to the increase of population," Smith thus concluded, "if man will but conform to the law which Nature exemplifies in all her processes, by which the soil regains whatever material of nutriment it has lent for the support of vegetable and animal life, and that with large interest, derived from the elements furnished by the atmosphere, and incorporated in the substance of the matter, which, on the extinction of its vitality, returns to the bosom of the earth."[73] Extensive, resource-stripping agriculture

---

71. Carey, *The Past, The Present, and The Future,* 289–90.

72. Peshine Smith, *Manual of Political Economy,* 17.

73. Ibid., 37. For an excellent discussion of the antebellum movement for agricultural reform, see Steven Stoll, *Larding the Lean Earth: Soil and Society in Nineteenth-Century America* (New York, 2001). On Peshine Smith's crucial contribution to the improvement literature, neglected by Stoll, see Michael Hudson's introduction to the reprint edition of Peshine Smith, *Manual of Political Economy.*

violated these fundamental laws: Americans exported nutrients to Europe, and Britain particularly, rather than recycling them and so improving yields; where they could, they invested their capital in slaves—the most degraded form of human labor—rather than in new technology.[74]

Agricultural improvement would increase crop yields, liberating capital and labor for other pursuits in a balanced, interdependent economy. By "placing the consumer by the side of the producer," as Jefferson had enjoined, wasteful transportation costs could be avoided and local exchange encouraged.[75] The reciprocal interests of consumers and producers were self-evident, as were the real, long-term interests of all social classes. Protectionist economists argued that workers would command a progressively larger share of the fruits of their labor as the wealth of the larger community increased.[76] The key to self- as well as social development was the freedom of choice that differentiated the free person from the slave, and this freedom was meaningless without a differentiated occupational structure. "Democracy is the practical recognition of the individuality of man," the *Whig Review* intoned, and "diversification of labor is the industrial means to secure to the laboring classes the benefits of Democracy."[77] There was a reciprocity between the natural distribution of talents in the community and the nation's interest: "NATIONS . . . should be complete and perfect, and should take care to have all the occupations well and ably exercised by their own citizens"; every nation "should fill out the circle of industry and make itself the complete and perfect representative of humanity."[78]

A community of interest was as natural to the nation as it was to the family, its microcosm. Conflict among sections of the country, sectors of the economy, and social classes was the unnatural result of an unbalanced economy unduly subject to domination and direction from abroad. Instead of fulfilling its enormous potential, the new nation "has raised food for the whole world, made its country a stock farm for every old and lazy empire, made its luckiest children the stewards of a foreigner, and the wearers of a

---

74. Peshine Smith, *Manual of Political Economy,* 220–21, 266–67; Carey, *Slave Trade,* 364, passim.
75. Carey, *The Past, The Present, and The Future,* 103.
76. Peshine Smith, *Manual of Political Economy,* 81, and the discussion in Hudson's introduction.
77. "The Tariff of 1846," *American Whig Review* 12 (Sept. 1850): 305.
78. "Short Chapters on Public Economy," ibid., 10 (Sept. 1849): 228. See also "The Influence of Manufactures, and the Protective System," ibid., 13 (Oct. 1851): "The real wealth of a nation consists in its industry; in its availing itself of its capital, skill, and labor, to the full development of all its natural endowments" (269).

foreign livery, and driven the rest back, and ever back, to the wilderness, 'to extend the area of freedom'": "from the hour of its freedom to this, it has not increased its nationality by a tittle, not solidified its national life by an atom, not attempted by any means to eradicate the provincial habitudes remaining even after the acquisition of liberty."[79]

The "progress of civilization," wrote Peshine Smith, depended on decentralized neighborhood, regional, and national development, conformable "to the order of Nature and to the natural inclinations of man."[80] Obsessed with Britain's supposedly unnatural interference in this natural process, Careyites tended to be oblivious to problems of "concentration" or unequal development *within* the nation—the equally obsessive concern of Southern sectionalists—and so to conflate the local and the national.[81] Instead, they lauded the beneficent effects of association and improvement for all parts of the country, making developments in the North normative and attributing Southerners' hostility to protection and continuing commitment to a staple export economy to the unenlightened self-interest and deficient patriotism of the planter class.

Union Betrayed

Henry Carey and his fellow Whigs hoped to strengthen the bonds of union between North and South. Their efforts to foster development of the home market under the aegis of protection attracted considerable support among Southerners concerned with sustaining land values, diversifying production, and promoting interregional economic ties. Protective nationalism did not disappear in the South even when the Whig party, its major vehicle, began to collapse. Carey sustained a wide-ranging correspondence with sympathetic Southerners well into the 1850s, and many of his major writings of the decade were designed to alleviate sectional tensions.[82] But Carey was not a

79. "British Policy Here and There: 'Free Trade,'" ibid., 12 (Nov. 1850): 530.
80. Peshine Smith, *Manual of Political Economy,* 61, 211.
81. Such imaginative identifications linked national citizens to their nations throughout the Western world. Alon Confino, *The Nation as Local Metaphor: Württemberg, Imperial Germany, and National Identity, 1871–1918* (Chapel Hill, N.C., 1997). On the local-national dynamic in the early republic, see David Waldstreicher, *In the Midst of Perpetual Fetes: The Making of American Nationalism, 1776–1820* (Chapel Hill, N.C., 1997).
82. George Winston Smith, *Henry C. Carey and American Sectional Conflict.* See Carey's correspondence in Henry C. Carey Papers, Edward Carey Gardiner Collection, Historical Society of Pennsylvania. We are indebted to Major L. Wilson's suggestive discussion of Whig and Democratic ideologies in *Space, Time, and Freedom: The Quest for Nationality and the Irrepressible Conflict, 1815–1861* (Westport, Conn., 1974).

compromiser in the classic mode. While Democrats desperately sought to sustain a national governing party by conciliating slaveholders, Carey and his colleagues offered an ambitious program for national development that would modernize the Southern economy and promote emancipation by rendering an increasingly archaic institution of slavery superfluous.

Carey's campaign seems bizarrely irrelevant in retrospect. In 1853, when he published *The Slave Trade: Domestic and Foreign: Why It Exists, and How It May Be Extinguished,* few Southerners could imagine a long-term transition from slavery to freedom that would not destroy their prosperity and devastate their cherished "civilization." Nor, given their long-standing commitment to the gospel of immediate action, would antislavery advocates in the North easily be persuaded to wait patiently for the logic of Carey's national history to unfold. But it would be a mistake to discount the significance of his project because he failed to offer a workable solution to the slavery problem. If, by the mid-1850s, Carey's nationalism could no longer compete with sectionalist sentiment in the South, it resonated widely and deeply in the North.

Southerners' refusal to consider seriously the offer of redemptive nationhood and gradual emancipation forced Carey to recognize fundamental sectional differences—and, through the medium of the new Republican party, make common cause with militant abolitionists in a war against the South and its "peculiar institution." In taking this fateful turn, however, Carey and his fellow Northerners did not accept the union's collapse with philosophic detachment and thus renounce the national idea. To the contrary, the mobilization of sectional sentiment to redeem the union was inspired by a widely shared vision of the nation's glorious future. "Disunionism," wrote Carey's disciple Stephen Colwell, "corrupts the minds of the young, and tends to extinguish patriotism and the sentiment of nationality in the heart of the youth of the country. *It is moral treason.*"[83]

All patriotic Northerners did not assent to the specific tenets and policy preferences of protective nationalism: the Republican party provided a big tent that covered a broad coalition of interests. But the bankruptcy of the historical alternative—a Democratic nationalism based on faith in limited government, territorial expansion, and the beneficent effects of free trade in world markets—gave rehabilitated Whiggery the historical initiative. Preservation of the union meant war, and success in war required the development of the modern, protective, war-making state protectionists had long advocated. Thus Whigs began to elaborate a conception of union and nation

---

83. [Stephen Colwell], *The South: A Letter from a Friend in the North, with Special Reference to the Effects of Disunion upon Slavery* (Philadelphia, Pa., 1856), 21, original emphasis.

that justified enormous sacrifice in meeting internal as well as external threats.

Earlier generations of American patriots had extolled the union as a model world order, a noble experiment in federal republicanism that sustained the liberties and rights of states and citizens. Nevertheless, the experiment's failure was obvious by the secession winter of 1860–61: a war to vindicate such a union was a self-defeating negation of its original purpose. For protection-minded Whigs, the union had taken on new national meanings—as the home of a free people fulfilling its genius by promoting the progress of civilization, as a great experiment, not in federalism but in republican self-government and national self-determination. A war to preserve this kind of union was morally imperative.

Carey's contribution was to give fullest expression to this emerging conception of union as nation. In *Slave Trade,* Carey defined the union as a moral community resisting the unrelenting assaults of British free trade imperialism, "the most gigantic system of slavery the world has yet seen."[84] British "centralization" fostered slavery—or equivalent systems of degraded, semiservile labor—by promoting export staple production around the world to fuel the machinery of its industrial dominion: "the tendency of the system is toward driving the whole people of the world into pursuits requiring little more than mere brute labour, and the lowest grade of intellect, to the destruction of commerce, both internal and external. The more this is carried into effect the more must the people of England and the world become brutalized and enslaved, and the greater must be the spread of intemperance and immorality."[85] Carey's comprehensive review of nations that embraced protection, including the United States under the tariffs of 1828 and 1842, showed that wherever British free trade imperialism "is resisted, slavery dies away, and freedom grows." It was during this period that "the Northern Slave States held conventions having in view the adoption of measures looking to the abolition of slavery."[86] But the turn away from protection in 1846 riveted the shackles of American slaves and slave owners alike. Southerners' celebrations of "King Cotton's" benign rule were cruelly misconceived, for as planters exhausted fertile soils as well as the lives of their laborers, they were unwittingly complicit in a despotic British regime that ultimately would enslave them too.[87]

---

84. Carey, *Slave Trade,* 364.
85. Ibid., 388.
86. Ibid., 375, 376.
87. As Henry C. Carey wrote in *Two Letters to a Cotton Planter of Tennessee* (New York, 1852), protection was "the true and only road to the emancipation of the planter from the tyranny of the spindle and the loom" (14).

Carey thus exonerated Southern slave owners from any moral responsibility for the "peculiar institution." Just as Jefferson had blamed King George III for the slave trade in his original draft of the Declaration of Independence, Carey indicted imperial Britain for imposing slavery on the benighted peoples of the world; and just as Jefferson challenged the good faith of Yankee hypocrites who professed concern for the slaves' well-being during the Missouri controversy (1819–21), Carey discounted the professions of British abolitionists of a later generation: What could be more hypocritical than the posturing of free traders who pretended to oppose slavery?[88] The difference was that where Jefferson sought to deflect responsibility for slavery, Carey challenged Southerners to rise to the challenge of British imperialism and make the choice for freedom—and the ultimate extermination of slavery and the slave trade—by embracing his idea of the progressive and protective nation-state.

In the Declaration, Jefferson did not call on his fellow planters to take any action to resolve the slavery problem.[89] But in the 1850s, Carey made clear, the onus was on planters to redeem themselves by eschewing free trade and throwing their support behind protection. It was a moment of truth for all Americans. "The history of the Union," he told President James Buchanan in a public letter in 1858, "is an enigma—our words having been those of civilization and freedom, while our tendencies, with only occasional intervals, have been in the direction of slavery and barbarism."[90] It was an enigma that could only be resolved by renewed commitment to the nation's progress, prosperity, and freedom.

Carey wanted immediate action. The commitment he demanded, however, was first to the nation, and then, through the nation, to the freedom and prosperity that inevitably would come to masters and slaves alike. The concentration of settlement, the improvement of the soil through proper manuring, rising land values, and a progressively more elaborate local and regional division of labor—all pointed toward freedom. "Our system," Carey told an admiring audience at a testimonial dinner in 1859, "is based upon the idea of elevating the laborer, by developing his various faculties, and thus fitting him for the position for which he was intended—that of master of nature, and

---

88. See Carey's contemptuous dismissal of "The affectionate and Christian Address . . . of the Women of England to their Sisters, the Women of the United States of America," excerpted in his *Slave Trade*, 6–7.
89. On the Declaration, see Onuf, *Jefferson's Empire*, 155–58.
90. Henry C. Carey, *Letters to the President on the Foreign and Domestic Policy of the Union and Its Effects as Exhibited in the Condition of the People and the State* (Philadelphia, Pa., 1858), 48.

master of himself." Carey's historical research convinced him "that men have everywhere become free as industry has become diversified—as the producer and the consumer have come together—as the powers of the earth have become developed—as agriculture has become a science—and as men have been more enabled to combine their exertions, each with every other."[91] The transition to freedom would not take long, Colwell assured Southerners: "in a well-arranged system of slave labor" slaves "would improve so rapidly, pay for their freedom so easily, and become fitted to enjoy it so quickly, that emancipation would come as fast, if not faster, than the wisest heads could prepare for it."[92] Slave owners would benefit both from the rising productivity of free labor and from the rising value of their lands. "In all countries of the world," Carey asserted, "man has become free as land has acquired value, and as its owners have been enriched."[93]

Southerners were defying the logic of history by refusing to support a protective regime that would gird the new nation against the assaults of British free trade imperialism. The history of the world stood at the crossroads of slavery and freedom. Carey and his fellow protective nationalists sought to explode the liberal myth that the dismantling of mercantilist nation-states and the spread of free trade would lead to peace and prosperity across the world. Britain "merely humbugs the nations with the phantom of free trade," disguising its "war of extermination . . . against the labour of all other countries" and quest for world dominion.[94] But nations that were wise enough to resist such entreaties were waging "a war for peace," building up their strength as nations not with "fleets and armies" but through the protection of precious natural and human resources.[95] By subverting and demoralizing nations and sapping them of their strength, free traders promoted "internal discord and foreign war." The real way to "peace, union, and brotherly kindness throughout the world" was through national development and self-determination.[96]

91. Carey's Remarks, *Testimonials to Henry C. Carey, Esq. Dinner at the La Pierre House, Philadelphia, Apr. 27, 1859* (Philadelphia, Pa., 1859), 8.

92. [Colwell], *The South: A Letter from a Friend in the North,* 13. See also [Stephen Colwell], *The Five Cotton States and New York; Or, Remarks upon the Social and Economical Aspects of the Southern Political Crisis* (n.p., Jan. 1861): "Slavery, as protected by the Constitution of the United States, has more friends in the Northern States than it has in all the world beside—friends who would march by the hundred thousand for its protection and defence as it exists under the Constitution" (6).

93. Carey, *Slave Trade,* 395.

94. "The President's Message, and the Report of the Secretary of Treasury," *American Whig Review* 7 (Apr. 1848): 391; Carey, *Slave Trade,* 216.

95. Carey, *Slave Trade,* 382.

96. Ibid., 409.

Because "peace and union" began at home, the failure of union meant war. Carey and like-minded Northerners were more than ready to fight. In Carey's case, the final failure of protectionist nationalism to heal the sectional breach in the 1850s led to the sudden displacement of belligerent rage from Britain, its long-term object, to the seceding states of the South. The logic of this displacement was straightforward: protectionists had long remarked on "the close and entangling, though tacit, alliance which . . . exists between the free traders of Great Britain and their subservient friends in America."[97] The consummation of this illicit union meant that the positions of Britain and the South had now converged: offered the chance to sustain union and nation, the planters instead aligned themselves with Britain, committing themselves to the spread of slavery and proclaiming the "peculiar institution" a positive good. Far from setting slavery on the road to extinction, Southerners now demanded that Northerners rally in support of the institution, thus submitting to the perpetual dominion of the "slave power." The South's betrayal turned the union inside out, taking Britain's historical place as the great counterrevolutionary power. Southerners had made themselves foreigners, enemies of the nation, a cancer to be purged: the nation could only realize its full potential by demolishing these traitors.

Blinded by Anglophobic rage and misplaced expectations that Southerners could ever embrace his idea of the nation, Carey suddenly found that his attitude toward the "slave power" differed very little from that of militant antislavery forces. Abolitionists moralized the slavery issue, tracing the evil scourge to slave owners' sinful natures—or the secular equivalent. Carey proceeded from the opposite premise, that slaveholding was a function of structural forces at work in British-dominated world markets. But because Carey and his colleagues moralized the nation, imputing moral value to the progressive fulfillment of the national idea, enemies of the nation were certainly traitors, arguably sinners. With that realization, the powerfully latent tendency to identify the nation with the North—its righteous remnant—became irresistible. Protective nationalism had always had a northern inflection, for Northern communities best exemplified the progress of civilization through association and concentration. Now it was clear that obdurate Southerners scorned the Northerners' example, declaring their independence from—and opposition to—the idea that the American nation was designed and destined to play a providential role in world history.

---

97. "The Crisis of the Century: Alliances, European and American," *American Whig Review* 15 (Feb. 1852): 169.

10
The South
and the Nation

"We have all the essential elements of a high national career," the Georgian Alexander H. Stephens boasted in March 1861, urging Virginia and other crucial border states to join the seceded cotton states in a slaveholding union. "The idea has been given out at the North, and even in the Border States, that we are too small and too weak to maintain a separate nationality," but "this is a great mistake." Even within its present circumscribed bounds, the new Confederacy was formidable enough to defy the world. "With such an area of territory—with such an amount of population—with a climate and soil unsurpassed by any other on the face of the earth—with such resources already at our command—with productions which control the commerce of the world—who can entertain any apprehensions as to our success, whether others join us or not?"[1] The South was destined to become a great nation. "The southern people," the Virginia senator Robert M. T. Hunter agreed, "have within themselves all the capacity of empire."[2]

---

1. Alexander H. Stephens, "Cornerstone Address," Mar. 21, 1861, in Jon L. Wakelyn, ed., *Southern Pamphlets on Secession, November 1860–April 1861* (Chapel Hill, N.C., 1996), 402–12, at 408.

2. Robert M. T. Hunter, *Speech . . . on the Resolution Proposing to Retrocede the Forts . . . Delivered in the Senate of the United States, January 11, 1861* (Washington, 1861), in Wakelyn, ed., *Southern Pamphlets on Secession,* 262–83, at 265. Our understanding of Southern nationalism is heavily indebted to Brian Schoen's brilliant dissertation, "The Fragile Fabric of Union: The Cotton South, Federal Politics, and the Atlantic World, 1783–1861" (Ph.D. diss., Virginia, 2004). The classic study of developing nationalist ideas is John McCardell, *The Idea of a Southern Nation: Southern Nationalists and Southern Nationalism, 1830–1860* (New York, 1979). See also Jesse T. Carpenter, *The South as a Conscious Minority, 1789–1861: A Study in Political Thought,* with a new intro. by John McCardell (1930; Columbia, S.C., 1990) and Rollin G. Osterweis, *Romanticism and Nationalism in the Old South* (1949; Baton Rouge, La., 1971).

As Southern secessionists embarked on their nation-making project, they jettisoned cherished principles of minimal government and strict constitutional construction. This ideological transformation followed a revolutionary script, proceeding from the premise that embattled Southerners had forged their collective identity as a distinctive people in an unending struggle with domineering and corrupt Northern enemies.[3] Southerners who had once insisted that "nationality" was a "fiction," that "the nation . . . is the mere aggregate of individuals," now insisted that vindication of their independence would make them "the freest, the happiest, and the most prosperous and powerful nation upon earth."[4] As they imagined themselves reenacting their forefathers' struggle against British tyranny, secessionists recognized that a state of war, not peace, was the normal condition of nations. "Nothing of national greatness or individual good has been achieved without sacrifice and sorrow," William Henry Trescot, a precocious South Carolina secessionist, wrote in 1850: "no nation has ever yet matured its political growth without the stern and scarring experience of civil war."[5]

An earlier generation of Southern economists had dismissed the threat of war when questioning the value of the union, insisting that powerful, centralized, neomercantilist governments provoked the very wars that constituted their leading justification. During his Carolina phase, the political scientist Francis Lieber continued to subscribe to classical free trade tenets, projecting a glorious, globalized future of market-driven interdependence. "In antiquity," he wrote, "history coursed in the narrow channel of single nations; in modern times history resembles our own broad ocean, where the flags of all nations meet."[6] After Lieber, despairing of the union's future, fled north, free trade ideas continued to dominate in the cotton-exporting South. But they were stripped of their progressive implications for world peace and prosperity: only "a few old fogies, who belong to a bygone world . . . are still

3. On the salience of revolutionary republican themes, see Michael F. Holt, *The Political Crisis of the 1850s* (New York, 1978) and George C. Rable, *The Confederate Republic: A Revolution against Politics* (Chapel Hill, N.C., 1994).

4. John C. Calhoun, *A Discourse on the Constitution and Government of the United States* [1851], in Ross M. Lence, ed., *Union and Liberty: The Political Philosophy of John C. Calhoun* (Indianapolis, Ind., 1992), 79–284, at 101; James McCord, "What Is Fair and Equal Reciprocity," *De Bow's Review* 15 (1853): 433–47, at 438; "The Non-Slaveholders of the South: Their Interest in the Present Controversy Identical with that of the Slaveholders," ibid., 30 (1861): 67–77, at 77.

5. William Henry Trescot, *The Position and Course of the South* (Charleston, S.C., 1850), in Wakelyn, ed., *Southern Pamphlets on Secession*, 14–32, at 27–28.

6. Francis Lieber, "Free Trade and Other Things," *De Bow's Review* 15 (1853): 53–65, at 61–62.

nodding and dreaming over the pages of Malthus and Adam Smith."[7] Instead, Southern nationalists emphasized the geopolitical significance of a *particular* trade relationship, between Southern cotton producers and English textile manufacturers—an exchange in which both partners enjoyed a virtual monopoly position that would be enhanced by the elimination of tariff barriers—over free trade in general, or in principle.

The apotheosis of "King Cotton" signaled the conceptual switch. The free trader Louisa McCord likened the cotton South to a "giant youth . . . governing the world by its vast produce," spinning "with the fine web of its cotton fibre, a network the destruction of which is the destruction of civilization."[8] McCord understood that this "network" was vulnerable to political interference—by Northern protectionists, or other heedless "foreigners"—but assumed that self-interest would keep the South's enemies at bay. Secessionists such as the North Carolinian Thomas L. Clingman imputed a more direct, irresistible power to cotton: "King Cotton governs two hemispheres," he told the U.S. Senate during the secession crisis in 1861, "and dominates on land and sea, and the kings of the east and the merchant princes of the west obey his bidding."[9] McCord's appeal to interest and her threat of civilizational apocalypse were staples of Southern rhetoric throughout the sectional crisis, implying but still suppressing Clingman's bald assertion of power. Southerners who had waged war against the idea of "sovereignty" now crowned their sovereign staple "king," anticipating with Trescot the day when the "South would be, in the maturity of her strength, the guardian of the world's commerce—the grave and impartial centre of that new balance of power."[10]

If economic advantages translated into political power, the exercise of that power was crucial to the full development of those advantages. This was the logic of Northern protectionists in the tariff debates, now deployed to promote a distinctively Southern sectional-national agenda. Nations were not withering away, as cosmopolitan liberals predicted, with the progress of civilization obliterating distance and difference. Quite to the contrary, Trescot argued, "national individuality seems to be the agent of Providence

7. Francis Lieber, "State Rights and State Remedies," ibid., 25 (1858): 697–703, at 699.
8. Louisa McCord, "Negro-Mania," *De Bow's Review* 12 (1852): 507–24, in her *Political and Social Essays*, ed. Richard C. Lounsbury (Charlottesville, Va., 1995), 222–44, at 240–41.
9. Thomas L. Clingman, *Speech on the State of the Union, Delivered in the Senate of the United States, February 4, 1861* (Washington, 1861), in Wakelyn, ed., *Southern Pamphlets on Secession,* 284–304, at 291.
10. Trescot, *Position and Course of the South,* in Wakelyn, ed., *Southern Pamphlets on Secession,* 24.

in the conduct of the world."[11] Civilization progressed *through* "the narrow channel of single nations," not as Lieber asserted, by overflowing those channels.[12] The "manifest destiny" of "great nations" was to promote the wealth and welfare of the world by exercising their superior powers and expanding to their "natural" limits. The moment had arrived, Trescot concluded, when Southerners must recognize their own role in world history.

> The Union has redeemed a continent to the christian world—it has fertilized a wilderness, and converted the rude force of nature into the beneficent action of a civilized agriculture. It has enriched the world's commerce with the untold wealth of a new and growing trade. It has spread over the vast territories of this new land the laws, the language, the literature of the Anglo-Saxon race. It has developed a population with whom liberty is identical with law, and in training thirty-three States to manhood, has fitted them for the responsibility of independent national life. It has given to history sublime names, which the world will not willingly let die—heroic actions which will light the eyes of a far-coming enthusiasm. It has achieved its destiny. Let us achieve ours.[13]

The South was destined to be a great nation, but fulfilling that destiny would require a massive exercise of will and power. Southerners expected that their aspirations to nationhood—like those of peoples everywhere seeking to throw off the shackles of despotism—would lead to war. The expectation of war in turn transformed all their other assumptions about politics and economics. Southern ideas about minimal government were predicated on peace: "a *peace government* with its limited powers, goes on quietly, to perform its peaceful functions, with its accustomed regard to constitutional restraints and vested rights."[14] But the threat of war brought forth a people's latent power. In 1851, a Carolina disunionist thus looked forward eagerly to "the crisis" when the "dormant" powers of the nation would be brought into play by "a *war government*, . . . when every energy must be strained, every resource put in requisition, and the concentrated force of the State, [would be] hurled like a stone from the hand of a giant."[15]

---

11. Ibid., 32
12. Lieber, "Free Trade and Other Things," *De Bow's Review* 15 (1853): 61.
13. Trescot, *Position and Course of the South,* in Wakelyn, ed., *Southern Pamphlets on Secession,* 32.
14. "South Carolina: Her Present Attitude and Future Action," *Southern Quarterly Review,* 4, n.s. (1851): 273–98, at 290, original emphasis.
15. Ibid., original emphasis.

"Thirty Years' War"

The political struggle between North and South that began with the nullification crisis and climaxed with the firing at Fort Sumter was, for some commentators, a "thirty years' war."[16] Three decades of "fighting" fostered sectionalist and then nationalist sentiment in South Carolina and throughout
the slaveholding South.[17] In the context of sectional polarization, limited
government and states' rights doctrines were directed increasingly at the
federal government, "a *foreign government* . . . to the slaveholding States."[18]
"The Federal *Government,* has no inherent strength, no feature of nationality," the militant editor J. D. B. De Bow argued in 1858, "for it is limited in
power, and has neither a people nor a territory" and lacks all necessary "elements of strength, cohesion and conservation."[19] By contrast, he subse-
quently noted, "each State [is] in itself a nation," with the "sovereign power"
to establish new governments.[20]

Southerners who "prize and guard State Rights," the Virginian George
Fitzhugh insisted, should seek to "preserve their separate nationality," making "each State independent of the rest of the world."[21] Cautious "coopera-
tionists" hesitated to take the plunge alone, urging instead that Southerners
"build up a new house" for a *single* "separate nationality."[22] The "sovereignty"
inherent in the people of each state would be fulfilled—and only could be
vindicated—by forging a new Southern nation. Through the alchemy of

---

16. *Richmond Semi-weekly Examiner,* Jan 6., 1860, in Dwight Lowell Dumond, ed., *South-
    ern Editorials on Secession* (New York, 1931), 5; David Christy, *Cotton is King,* 2nd ed.
    (New York, 1856), 27.
17. William W. Freehling emphasizes the retarded and incomplete development of proto-
    nationalist thought in *The Road to Disunion: Secessionists at Bay, 1776–1854* (New
    York, 1990). On South Carolina, see also William W. Freehling, *Prelude to Civil War: The
    Nullification Controversy in South Carolina, 1816–1836* (New York, 1965) and Manisha
    Sinha, *The Counterrevolution of Slavery: Politics and Ideology in Antebellum South
    Carolina* (Chapel Hill, N.C., 2000).
18. Jabez Lamar Monroe Curry, *The Perils and Duties of the South, . . . Speech Delivered in
    Talladega, Alabama, November 26, 1860* (Washington, 1860), in Wakelyn, ed., *Southern
    Pamphlets on Secession,* 35–54, at 47, original emphasis.
19. "State Rights and State Remedies," *De Bow's Review* 25 (1858): 697–703, at 698, origi-
    nal emphasis.
20. "The Union—North and South—Slave Trade and Territorial Questions—Disunion—
    Southern Confederacy," *De Bow's Review* 27 (1859): 561–72, at 561.
21. George Fitzhugh, *Sociology for the South: or, The Failure of Free Society* (1854; New
    York, 1965), 203.
22. *Florence Gazette* (Florence, Ala.), Nov. 28, 1860, and *New Orleans Bee,* Dec. 14, 1860,
    in Dumond, ed., *Southern Editorials on Secession,* 270, 335.

revolution, a "spontaneous uprising and upheaving of the people . . . irresistible as the mighty tide of the ocean," the disconnected parts of the old, failed union would be reconstituted into a powerful new whole "strong enough to maintain themselves against the world."[23]

The increasingly strained efforts of John C. Calhoun and other constitutional theorists to define a safe place for the South in the union pointed directly toward independent nationhood—and thus, inevitably, away from their original fealty to strict construction and limited government. The supposed transformation should not be overdrawn, particularly for Calhoun, who was always a "nationalist" in some sense.[24] In the wake of the tariff controversies, he concluded that the federal union did *not* constitute a nation. "With us," he wrote in his *Discourse on the Constitution and Government of the United States*, "the choice lies between a national, consolidated and irresponsible government of a dominant portion, or section of the country—and a federal, constitutional and responsible government."[25] Calhoun's condemnation of rule by the "dominant section" was predicated on the assumption that the "national" rights of the oppressed section were being violated, not on a rejection of the idea of the nation. His influential critique of majority rule did not reflect any solicitude for minorities in general and assuredly not for dissidents in South Carolina who jeopardized its vaunted unity and homogeneity.

Calhoun's theory of the "concurrent majority" proceeded from the illegitimate whole—a federal union that had been captured by Northerners hostile to the South's vital interests—to its constituent parts. The sovereign states were, of course, the source of legitimate authority, but the appropriate domain for the fulfillment of Calhoun's theory was a section with homogenous values and interests, a nation in embryo. Unlike Thomas Cooper and other antinational theorists, Calhoun did not begin with (or descend to) individual rights or interests. The contract theorists' notional "state of nature," in which "all men are born equal," was arrant nonsense; in fact, man is "born in the social and political state, . . . the one for which his Creator made him, and the only one in which he can preserve and perfect his race."[26]

23. *Nashville Union and American,* Apr. 20, 1861, ibid., 507; Rev. James Henley Thornwell, *The State of the Country* (New Orleans, La., 1861), in Wakelyn, ed., *Southern Pamphlets on Secession,* 157–78, at 175.

24. For a study of Calhoun focused on this theme, see John Niven, *John C. Calhoun and the Price of Union: A Biography* (Baton Rouge, La., 1988). The best work on Calhoun's political theory is James H. Read's excellent forthcoming study of Calhoun's political and constitutional thought.

25. Calhoun, *Discourse on the Constitution,* 189.

26. Calhoun, *A Disquisition on Government,* in Lence, ed., *Union and Liberty,* 3–78, at 44–45.

314 · Markets, Nations, and War

With "society being primary," Calhoun asked his fellow Southerners whether the federal government in fact served its "secondary and subordinate" function, "to preserve and protect society." The question was clearly rhetorical, for decades of intersectional strife had shown Southerners that the parts and the whole—sectionally distinct societies and a federal government with national pretensions—no longer stood in their proper relation. As Calhoun explained in his *Disquisition on Government* (1851),

> If the numerical majority were really the people; and if, to take its sense truly, were to take the sense of the people truly, a government so constituted would be a true and perfect model of a popular constitutional government; and every departure from it would detract from its excellence. But . . . the numerical majority, instead of being the people, is only a portion of them— such a government, instead of being a true and perfect model of the people's government, that is, a people self-governed, is but a government of a part, over a part—the major over the minor portion.[27]

Calhoun's doctrine should not be dismissed as reactionary and antidemocratic. Quite to the contrary, the great Carolinian was a forward-looking Southern nationalist—and was honored as such by the founders of the new Confederacy. His apotheosis of the "part," of the embryonic nation striving to fulfill its destiny by overthrowing the despotic rule of a "foreign" people, resonated with nationalist sentiments throughout the Western world, including the North. But Calhoun had nothing useful to say about how to manage or reconcile diverse interests or to secure the rights of minorities *within* the modern nation-state.

As Calhoun saw it, the great mistake of his Northern foes was "to confound the numerical majority with the people." For his part, Calhoun had no doubt that the "people" of South Carolina—and, by extension, of the South as a whole—had an irreducible sectional and incipiently national identity.[28] Majority rule was the legitimate mode for making decisions within a national community, but when the majority ruled within a federal system, the inevitable result was to "divide" the union "into two hostile parts, waging, under the forms of law, incessant hostilities against each other." The "concurrent majority" would solve this problem "by giving to each interest, or portion, the power of self-protection."[29] In other words, the South would gain the

27. Ibid., 25.
28. Ibid., 24.
29. Ibid., 37.

benefits of national self-determination while continuing to enjoy collective security within a binational (or, perhaps, multinational) continental union.

Calhoun's theoretical works were directed at federal, not at republican or constitutional questions. But even when Calhoun addressed the character of the union and proposed remedies to secure Southern interests, his fundamental commitment to Southern nationhood left little conceptual space for constructive, innovative thinking. His broad generalizations and abstract formulations have entranced political theorists, but they amount to little more than a high-sounding gloss on a long litany of Southern grievances. Calhoun's great contribution to the cause of Southern nationalism was to provide a rhetorical high ground, to reconcile a proto-nationalist agenda with continuing, although contingent devotion to an idealized union. This was clearly not the "union as it was," or even the union as it supposedly *once* was, for Calhoun's "concurrent majority" jettisoned any pretense of fealty to a strictly construed federal Constitution. Nor could Calhoun expect that Northerners would rally to his proposal. If, as McCord claimed, "the Northern States prosper by us and through us" and a hopelessly corrupt union enriched Northern politicians, why would they be willing to renegotiate the federal alliance?[30] Why would Northerners forfeit the "vast millions of tribute" they exacted from the South?[31]

The nationalist answer to these questions was that the seceding South would give their erstwhile Northern brethren no choice. Southerners would declare what was barely concealed in Calhoun's doctrine: the South was an independent nation, prepared to vindicate its claims before the whole world. No compromise was possible. A history of intersectional struggle had shown that the North would never accommodate the South within the union. To the contrary, as a sympathetic writer in the *Democratic Review* asserted, "*all the concessions of the South have been rendered without an equivalent.*"[32] It was therefore highly unlikely that Northerners, clinging to notions of national greatness and the perpetuity of the union, would let Southerners leave the union without a bloody civil war. On the eve of war, timorous Southerners held back, warning that disunion would mean "fraternal strife, civil and servile war, murder, arson, pillage, robbery, and fire and blood through long

30. "Letter to the Duchess of Sutherland from a Lady of South Carolina," *Charleston Mercury*, Aug. 10, 1853, in Louisa McCord, *Political and Social Essays*, 350–60, at 364.

31. John H. Reagan, *State of the Union. Speech . . . Delivered in the House of Representatives, Jan. 15, 1861* (Washington, 1861), in Wakelyn, ed., *Southern Pamphlets on Secession*, 143–56, at 150.

32. [A. B. Johnson], "The Philosophy of the American Union; Or, The Principles of its Cohesiveness," *Democratic Review* 28 (1851): 15–23, at 22, original emphasis.

and cruel years."[33] But their more militant fellow Southerners had been preparing for just such a war for decades.

Pretending to perpetuate the union, Calhoun's constitutional theorizing justified its destruction. The Carolinian's original premise was in fact his ultimate point: "a State, as a party to the constitutional compact, has the right to secede."[34] Subscribing to the tenets of Madisonian compact theory, most antebellum commentators on the Constitution agreed. The major caveat, that secession would destroy the union, made it all the more appealing to Southern nationalists. Because the Constitution did not explicitly provide for its own dissolution, a writer in the *Democratic Review* acknowledged, "the right of a state to secede from the Union" might not be "constitutional" in a strict sense. But "the right of secession is nevertheless perfect, being among the 'inalienable rights' referred to in the Declaration of Independence; and with which it says, we are endowed by our Creator."[35] Southerners welcomed a move from 1787 to 1776—from the federal Constitution to the Declaration of Independence—that lifted them out of the fog of constitutional interpretation and into the clear air of John Locke's right of revolution. By focusing on the earlier break with Britain, they could affirm their fealty to foundational American principles even while demolishing the superstructure of the union the founders had constructed.

By emphasizing the original authority of sovereign states, compact theorists progressively subverted the distinction between the federal Constitution and the Articles of Confederation and interpreted both as treaties.[36] The ambiguity of Madison's formulation in *The Federalist*—the new regime was "partly national and partly federal"—was thus banished and "states" could be recast as "nations."[37] As the sectional crisis deepened, "federal" and

---

33. *North Carolina Standard* (Raleigh), July 11, 1860, in Dumond, ed., *Southern Editorials on Secession*, 143.

34. Calhoun, *Discourse on the Constitution*, 212.

35. [Johnson], "Philosophy of the American Union," 20.

36. "Considered and treated as a league or treaty between *separate States* or *Nations*," George Fitzhugh concluded, the Constitution "may yet have a long and useful existence" (Fitzhugh, *Cannibals All! or, Slaves Without Masters* [1857], ed. C. Vann Woodward [Cambridge, Mass., 1960], 248, original emphasis). On the tendency to see the federal Constitution as a treaty, see Andrew C. Lenner, *The Federal Principle in American Politics, 1790–1833* (Madison, Wisc., 2000).

37. Jacob E. Cooke, ed., *The Federalist* (Middletown, Conn., 1961), no. 39 (Madison), 257. "How strange," wrote Calhoun, "after all these admission[s], is the conclusion that the government is partly federal and partly national! It is the constitution which determines the character of the government. It is impossible to conceive how the constitution can be *exclusively* federal (as it is admitted, and has been clearly proved to be) and the government *partly* federal and *partly* national" (Calhoun, *Discourse on the Constitution*, 109).

"international" became indistinguishable and Southerners reflexively called Northerners—and the federal government they supposedly dominated— "foreign." Southerners were thus prepared to invoke the first law of nature— and nations—"the rule of self-preservation."[38] "The right to change a government, or to utterly abolish it, and to establish a new government," a New Orleans editorialist explained, "is the inherent right of a free people."[39] "All communities," a colleague added, possessed "the indestructible right . . . to provide for their own safety and happiness."[40] Secessionists did not doubt that the slave states, separately or collectively, constituted such a "community."

Secessionists burnished their patriotic credentials by invoking the Spirit of 1776. Southerners cast off "the yoke" of a union dominated by Northerners, just as their ancestors had cast off "the yoke of King George III, and for causes immeasurably stronger."[41] The "long train of abuses" recorded in Thomas Jefferson's Declaration paled in comparison to "the wrongs" Southerners had endured. "What was the *actual* grievance then?" a writer in the *Southern Quarterly Review* asked in 1851. Patriots "'augured misgovernment at a distance,'" but Southerners had in fact experienced "tenfold greater evil than the most far-seeing politicians of that day anticipated from British tyranny."[42] This long history of grievances gave rise to Southerners' collective identity as a distinct people with the "revolutionary right" to change their government in order to secure their "freedom, property, and safety."[43]

The union established by the founding fathers had ceased to exist, giving way instead to the despotic rule of one section, the North, over its subjugated Southern provinces. By seceding, the slave states exercised "that first law of nature and of nations, the right of self-government," Hunter told the Senate, thus signaling their intention to make war, if necessary, in order to vindicate their rights.[44] Southern independence would thus make explicit—and force

38. Curry, *Perils and Duties of the South*, in Wakelyn, ed., *Southern Pamphlets on Secession*, 46.
39. *New Orleans Daily Crescent*, Nov. 13, 1860, in Dumond, ed., *Southern Editorials on Secession*, 236.
40. *Daily Picayune* (New Orleans, La.) Jan. 15, 1861, ibid., 400.
41. Rev. Benjamin Morgan Palmer, *The South: Her Peril and Her Duty* (New Orleans, La., 1860), in Wakelyn, ed., *Southern Pamphlets on Secession*, 63–77, at 73.
42. "South Carolina: Her Present Attitude and Future Action," *Southern Quarterly Review* 4 (1851): 295, original emphasis.
43. Judah P. Benjamin, *The Right of Secession* (Washington, 1861), in Wakelyn, ed., *Southern Pamphlets on Secession*, 101–14, at 108.
44. Hunter, *Speech . . . on the Resolution Proposing to Retrocede the Forts*, in Wakelyn, ed., *Southern Pamphlets on Secession*, 282.

the world to recognize—an ongoing state of intersectional conflict that the union could no longer contain or conceal. Disunionists had long railed against the perverse and unnatural consequences of a union that enabled a hostile, "foreign" section to expropriate the wealth and interfere with the domestic institutions of the South. "No one in the South," William Gilmore Simms asserted in 1850, "can blind himself to the fact that we have no worse enemies *without,* than those which assail us from within."[45]

Southern nationalists turned the founding fathers' union, a pact to secure the independence of the weak and vulnerable new American republics, inside out. Unlike the founders, Southerners no longer saw foreign powers—their allies in a burgeoning export trade that promoted the prosperity and progress of the civilized world—as serious external threats; nor, as beneficiaries of "King Cotton"'s rule, did they see themselves as weak and vulnerable. What was therefore most unnatural about the antebellum union was not, as Calhoun argued, that a powerful (Northern) majority tyrannized over a (Southern) minority, but, rather, it was that the most prosperous and powerful section of the union—a section with the population and resources of a great nation—should be dominated by a section whose *only* comparative advantage was sheer numbers. Northern domination was a function of the federal constitutional regime, not of its advanced economic development or superior institutions.

The fundamental premise of secessionist thought was that the South constituted a distinctive region with superior natural and human resources. The discrepancy between this assumed superiority and a perceived loss of mastery over the machinery of federal governance helps explain Southerners' increasingly belligerent posturing during successive crises of the union. The honor of the South—and of individual Southerners—was called into question by their supposedly pusillanimous submission to "the most corrupt Government on the face of the earth."[46] Unionism in the secessionist South was even worse than loyalism in the Revolution, for Britain had commanded extraordinary advantages over its rebellious colonists in 1776. In 1861, however, the North's continuing domination was solely a function of Southern

45. William Gilmore Simms, "The Southern Convention" (1850), *Southern Quarterly Review,* 2, n.s. (Sept. 1850): 199–208, 231–32, excerpted in John Caldwell Simms, ed., *The Simms Reader: Selections from the Writings of William Gilmore Simms* (Charlottesville, Va., 2001), 317–26, at 323.

46. Alfred Pike, *State or Province? Bond or Free?* (Little Rock, Ark., 1861), in Wakelyn, ed., *Southern Pamphlets on Secession,* 326–48, at 347.

submission and the willingness of ambitious politicians to sell out their fellow Southerners for personal advancement (Carolinians thought Virginians were particularly prone to these temptations).[47]

Southerners called for a peaceful end to the union, but few believed war could be avoided. Rev. James Henley Thornwell, one of region's most eminent theologians, enjoined North and South "to part in peace." "A course like this," he exclaimed, would be "heroic, sublime, glorious, . . . something altogether unexampled in the history of the world." No great nation had ever consented to its own dismemberment, and it would be "the wonder and astonishment of the nations" if "two great people" should agree to "divide our common inheritance, adjust our common obligations, and, preserving, as a sacred treasure, our common principles, let each set up for himself, and let the Lord bless us both."[48]

Thornwell underscored the obstacles to such an outcome: nations were "great" precisely because they possessed the power and will to claim what was rightfully theirs, and it was highly unlikely that either side would be more willing to conciliate the other—and therefore forfeit its share of the "common inheritance"—as an independent, sovereign power than it had been as a member of the same union. The only plausible alternative to war, Hunter explained, was "the establishment of some league" that might "secure many of the benefits of this Government and this Union," while leaving "each section free to follow the law of its own genius."[49] The Mississippi senator Jefferson Davis also thought "that two Confederacies could be so organized as to answer jointly many of the ends of the our present Union," by forging an alliance that would be "close" enough "to give them a united power in time of war against any foreign nation"—but not too close to jeopardize their distinctive interests and institutions.[50] In other words, the North should capitulate to Southern demands, recognizing that its determination

---

47. "Virginia has given five Presidents to the United States," a Carolinian wrote in 1851. "Joy to South-Carolina, that she has never given one. He who administers power, can never be jealous of that power. He who feeds from the public treasury cannot be expected to care much by what means it is filled" ("South Carolina: Her Present Attitude and Future Action," *Southern Quarterly Review* 4 [1851]: 276).

48. Thornwell, *State of the Country*, in Wakelyn, ed., *Southern Pamphlets on Secession*, 157–78, at 177–78.

49. Hunter, *Speech . . . on the Resolution Proposing to Retrocede the Forts*, in Wakelyn, ed., *Southern Pamphlets on Secession*, 280.

50. Jefferson Davis, *Remarks on the Special Message on Affairs in South Carolina* (Baltimore, Md., 1861), in Wakelyn, ed., *Southern Pamphlets on Secession*, 115–42, at 133.

to preserve or reconstruct the union by force would lead to a devastating war that would blast the prospects of both "great peoples."

Southern advocates of peaceful disunion invoked the threat of war, confident that fellow Southerners would rally to the cause when the final crisis arrived. Perhaps Northerners, calculating the value of the union, would then recognize the South's legitimate interests. But, warned Davis, "if in contempt of reason and reliance upon force, you say we shall not go, but shall remain as subjects to you, then, gentlemen of the North, a war is to be inaugurated the like of which men have not seen."[51] There were innumerable causes of conflict between South and North, as the history of intersectional conflict demonstrated, and all would be exacerbated with the union's collapse. A cautious New Orleans editorialist asked secessionist readers to consider the consequences: "Will the North, after the South has seceded, be any more willing to grant its just demands, than while it was an integral part of the Republic, with acknowledged rights and common interest?" Would "the arts of diplomacy out of the Union" lead to concessions by the North "which could not be gained in it?"[52]

Of course, a new Southern Confederacy would not secede quietly, leaving the North in full possession of the Western territories. The South would "either relinquish all pretension, all claim, all right to participate equally in the national property, public domain, improvements of all kinds, army, navy and appurtenances, etc., or prepare herself to vindicate her demands for her share by a resort to force."[53] But if the South sought to enforce its claims, it was absurd to expect "that all or any one of these things will be yielded by the North."[54] Conflicts would flare over boundaries—would the Confederacy embrace all fifteen slave states?—and over control of strategically critical positions. Inevitably, "the two Confederacies, the Northern and the Southern, would meet as rivals in foreign courts and in foreign markets," another unionist writer warned, involving "themselves in endless and most injurious complications in their intercourse with foreign powers."[55]

A swelling chorus of Southern voices anticipated the coming bloodbath. Unionists took the rhetorical lead in cataloguing the horrors of war—and thus in a perverse way escalating the crisis—but secessionists did not blanch

---

51. Ibid., 140.
52. *Daily Picayune* (New Orleans, La.), Oct. 31, 1860, in Dumond, ed., *Southern Editorials on Secession*, 200.
53. *Daily True Delta* (New Orleans, La.), Dec. 9, 1860, ibid., 313.
54. *The Review* (Charlottesville, Va.), Jan. 25, 1861, ibid., 418.
55. *North Carolina Standard* (Raleigh, N.C.), Dec. 1, 1860, ibid., 284–85.

at the prospect. "When I contemplate the dissolution of these States," Rev. George H. Clark of Savannah told his parishioners, "my heart trembles, and the blood thrills through my veins." "The destruction of such a nation," the unleashing of the awesome, terrible power of a great people—or, rather, of two great peoples—in violent conflict, would "be no common calamity" in the annals of human history.[56] The apocalyptic language of disunionists and unionists alike constituted a kind of perverse paean to the American nation, "the greatest and best government under the sun," fulfilling its manifest destiny in massive slaughter rather than in territorial expansion.[57] The Americans might "astonish" the world by peacefully resolving their differences, as Thornwell hopefully suggested, but they were more likely to astonish the world—as they would in fact—by the savagery of their civil war. "Nations die a terrible death," a unionist writer warned, and once kindled, "the fires of civil war . . . will burn until all is consumed that is perishable, and the land become a waste over which shall brood the silence of another and hopeless desolation."[58]

Southern nationalists welcomed the onset of war, exulting in the carnage that would mark the passage to nationhood. The idea that the South would soon fulfill its destiny as a great nation followed a straightforward logic: if North and South together constituted a great nation—"one of the greatest, if not the very greatest, upon the face of the globe"—under the union, each separate section had sufficient resources of its own to secure a leading position among the civilized nations.[59] The spread eagle rhetoric of "manifest destiny," emphasizing the expansive genius of the "Anglo-Saxon race" and its "free institutions," continued to strike resonant chords throughout the collapsing union.[60] On the eve of Civil War, Americans no longer shared the founders' fears of descending into a Hobbesian war of all against all. Disunion blasted the patriots' dream that "this beautiful land should be forever

56. Rev. George H. Clark, *A Sermon, Delivered in St. John's Church, Savannah, On Fast Day, Nov. 28, 1860* (Savannah, 1860), in Wakelyn, ed., *Southern Pamphlets on Secession*, 55–62, at 61.
57. *Daily Herald* (Wilmington, N.C.), Nov. 9, 1860, in Dumond, ed., *Southern Editorials on Secession*, 226.
58. *Daily Picayune* (New Orleans, La.), Nov. 4, 1860, ibid., 218.
59. *New Orleans Daily Crescent*, Dec. 17, 1860, ibid., 340.
60. The struggle over the westward expansion of slavery, predicated on sectionalized versions of national greatness, thus provides the central narrative line in histories of the coming of the Civil War. The definitive study is Michael A. Morrison, *Slavery and the American West: The Eclipse of Manifest Destiny and the Coming of the Civil War* (Chapel Hill, N.C., 1997).

one country, for one great, united, prosperous people." Instead, "one kindred people" would "become two hostile nations."[61]

The secession crisis marked the culmination of a generation of nationalist thinking throughout the antebellum union. The idea of the great, expansive nation was normative everywhere, even—and especially—in the South, where the identification of constitution, union, and nation had been under assault for more than a generation. Struggling to hold the balance between polarizing extremes, border state unionists also embraced the great nation idea, both in their continuing fealty to the union—although not, significantly, to an increasingly dysfunctional federal constitutional regime—and in celebrating the power and prospects of their *own* embryonic, if poorly defined, region. Unionists from Virginia, Kentucky, and other border slave states cautioned against following the lead of secessionists in the cotton South who agitated for reopening the slave trade and demolishing the tattered remnants of protection. "Do you want free trade and direct taxation?" asked the Kentuckian Robert J. Breckinridge. "Do you want some millions more of African cannibals thrown amongst you broadcast throughout the whole slave States? Do you want to begin a war which shall end when you have taken possession of the whole Southern part of this continent down to the isthmus of Darien?"[62] Why should the border states submit to the rule of their hotheaded neighbors to the South? Occupying "an area larger than all Western Europe, and finer than any of equal extent upon the globe, embracing a population inferior to none on earth," the border states were "sufficiently numerous at present to constitute a great nation" by themselves.[63] The Virginian William Cabell Rives agreed. The border states possessed "more varied and complete elements for a prosperous and self-sufficing national existence than any separate aggregation of States of our glorious Union," and they should use this immense power to determine the union's destiny.[64]

The argument that the border states (including a range of free states to the north) potentially constituted a great nation was an artifact of the sectional crisis, not the result of a sense of self-conscious sectional identity emerging

---

61. Richard Keith Call, *Letter to John S. Littell* (Philadelphia, Pa., 1861), in Wakelyn, ed., *Southern Pamphlets on Secession*, 179–94, at 181.
62. Dr. Robert J. Breckinridge, *Discourse Delivered on the Day of National Humiliation, January 4, 1861, at Lexington, Kentucky* (Baltimore, Md., 1861), in Wakelyn, ed., *Southern Pamphlets on Secession*, 247–61, at 258.
63. Ibid., 259.
64. William Cabell Rives, *Speech on the Proceedings of the Peace Conference and the State of the Union, Delivered in Richmond, Virginia, Mar. 8, 1861* (Richmond, 1861), in Wakelyn, ed., *Southern Pamphlets on Secession*, 349–72, at 368.

out of the polarization of federal politics. Secessionist agitation in the border slave states showed that definition of incipient section-nations was highly contingent.[65] As the secession crisis deepened, Americans recognized that the union would collapse and that separate nations would fill the vacuum of power, but they could not anticipate the shape those nations would take. Paradoxically, border state agitation accelerated the rush to the precipice: belligerent bluster about their own immense power—the chimerical idea that the border states could or should act like a nation—was matched by a nearly universal determination to resist any effort by the incoming Lincoln administration to secure the survival of the constitutional union by force.

In other words, the crisis could only be resolved if "union" and "nation" were distinguished and dissevered and Republicans capitulated completely on controverted questions of constitutional interpretation and amendment. However moderate or conciliatory the professions of its border state sponsors, a peace conference to negotiate a new constitutional settlement—or super-treaty—between section-nations would be a victory for the insurgent South. The national idea would be sectionalized and the constitutional union cherished by Northern nationalists jettisoned. Border state unionists thus unwittingly collaborated with cotton South radicals in elaborating a mature conception of Southern nationhood. Endorsing an interpretation of the Constitution that would protect the slave states from the interference of a "foreign" federal government and resisting coercive measures to secure the union, many border state "unionists" prepared to join in a region-wide mobilization against "black Republican" tyranny.

Secessionists recognized that the vaunted "power" of the border states could only come into play within an enlarged Southern Confederacy. As long as they remained in a union dominated by Northerners, their ability to shape policy and protect their vital interests would be radically diminished. Disconnected from the cotton South, border state breeders would no longer enjoy their "flourishing monopoly of the production and sale of slave labor." Was it reasonable to expect the Southern Confederacy to "perpetuate this tariff, this protection, this monopoly, for the special advantage of States which sought the alliance of its enemies?" As an independent power, the Confederacy could look elsewhere, a secessionist writer warned, reopening a "free trade" in cheaper foreign slaves. Impoverished and impotent, the border states would be "ground into atoms" in the inevitable conflict between South and North, "this nether and this upper millstone." Unable to

---

65. Charles B. Dew, *Apostles of Disunion: Southern Secession Commissioners and the Causes of the Civil War* (Charlottesville, Va., 2001).

get rid of a growing surplus of now worthless slaves, they would come to see, too late, that "the fate of St. Domingo and Jamaica" was "prophetic of their own."[66]

Border state bluster would not make the incoming Republican administration retreat from its fundamental commitments—to contain the spread of slavery and to preserve the existing union—or deny itself the fruits of the long-anticipated electoral victory. But it did underscore the critical geopolitical significance of expanding the Southern Confederacy to its "natural" limits, to include not only the "frontier" slave states to the north but perhaps even the grain-producing, "free" states of the West whose prosperity depended on Southern markets.[67] A more inclusive Confederacy would have to accommodate the diverse range of slaveholders' interests, muting secessionists' original emphasis on "increasing the profits of the cotton culture" through free trade "and diminishing the value of the labor employed in it" by reopening the slave trade. In other words, secessionists had to articulate and implement a more capacious conception of a "civilized," slave-based Southern nation capable of defending its interests and enforcing its will in a world of potentially hostile nations. The Southern nation would be defined by a peculiarly civilized form of slavery, not by the uncivilized practice of the foreign slave trade; it would also be defined by the standard of all great nations, the capacity to develop and expand, to "speedily become, as, from her natural advantages, she always deserved to be, 'magnificently rich and gloriously independent.'"[68]

National Economy

Southern nationalists abandoned the liberal cosmopolitanism of an earlier generation of free traders. Outside of the union, independent Southerners

---

66. *Daily Delta* (New Orleans, La.), Jan. 30, 1861, in Dumond, ed., *Southern Editorials on Secession,* 432.

67. On the harmony of interests between South and West, pivoting on cotton and trade through the Mississippi, see Christy, *Cotton is King* and the discussion in Schoen, "Fragile Fabric of Union," chap. 5, "Bridges to the West and the World." In his famous "Cornerstone Address," Alexander H. Stephens predicted that "the great States of the northwest shall gravitate this way as well as Tennessee, Kentucky, Missouri, Arkansas, & c. Should they do so, our doors are wide open to them, *but not until they are ready to assimilate with us in principle*" ("Cornerstone Address," in Wakelyn, ed., *Southern Pamphlets on Secession,* 410, emphasis in original).

68. Hon. J. H. Lumpkin, "Industrial Regeneration of the South," *De Bow's Review* 12 (1852): 41–50, at 42.

would enjoy the benefits of direct relations with the rest of the world, the free traders' great desideratum. But independence could only be secured by re-creating the powerful and protective nation-state that free traders had once sought to abolish. Preparing for war, militant Southerners now embraced the nation-building logic of National Republicans who had driven Southern opponents of the tariff to "calculate the value of our union." The free-trade millennium was thus indefinitely postponed. As the collapse of the American union and the emergence of two powerful nations in its place made clear, the nation-state was not about to wither away.

Southern nationalists built on a political economic foundation. The tariff controversies taught Southerners to think of the union as a vast redistributive system, a political machine for transforming Southern wealth into Northern prosperity. The advanced state of Northern manufactures and internal improvements, Southern writers long insisted, was the adventitious result of an arbitrary and unequal regime of federal taxation and expenditure, not of any inherent, "natural" advantages the North might possess. Thus "the wages of Southern labor and the profits of Southern capital" were, according to a typical complaint, "swept northward by this current of Federal taxation and disbursement."[69] Free traders sought to curtail the powers of an intrusive, neomercantilist federal state, convinced that unencumbered market relations were the best guarantee of world peace and prosperity.

Yet by focusing on the ways Northerners supposedly exploited their dominant position in the union, Southern free trade rhetoric also pointed in the opposite direction, toward nationhood. That the South did not get its just rewards from the cotton trade—that, as George McDuffie claimed, the profits from forty of every one hundred bales were diverted northward—was a political problem, requiring a national solution. Southern nationalists resented the redistribution of their wealth through political means but, unlike doctrinaire free traders, were not opposed to an activist government that promoted the genuine interests of the Southern people. If the vindication of Southern rights *in the union* required radical limitations on the powers of the federal state, the fulfillment of the South's destiny as a separate, civilized people depended on domesticating national power, aligning economy and society with a legitimate and effective government capable of vindicating Southern independence on the battlefield.

---

69. [M. R. H. Garnett], "A Citizen of Virginia," in *The Union, Past and Future: How It Works and How to Save It* (Washington, D.C., 1850), 16. "Such is the Union to the Northern States," William Gilmore Simms concluded; "It is their place of pleasant pasturage. There they feed and fatten free of charge" (Simms, "Southern Convention," in Simms, ed., *Simms Reader*, 319.

Southern nationalists envisioned a new relationship between the South and the world. They emphasized the inherently adversarial character of trade relations, eschewing the free traders' rosy view of complementarity and reciprocal benefit. Southerners believed that their cotton production propped up the national and world economies, even civilization itself. Northern prosperity was contingent on the South's continuing good will, the Carolina senator James Henry Hammond told his Northern colleagues in 1858. "You are our factors. You fetch and carry for us. One hundred and fifty million dollars of our money passes annually through your hands. Much of it sticks; all of it assists to keep your machinery together and in motion. Suppose we were to discharge you; suppose we were to take our business out of your hands;— we should consign you to anarchy and poverty."[70]

Fellow Southerners, nursing their long-standing sense of sectional grievance, usually reversed Hammond's formulation, emphasizing instead the "vast millions of tribute" they paid their Northern masters and imagining that "we of the South are *almost* reduced to the condition of overseers of Northern capitalists."[71] But all agreed that the South possessed ample power to master the world, if only she would "awake from her ignoble slumber, and act for herself."[72] "We have the right to protect ourselves," the editor De Bow proclaimed, and "we should demand the power. If the poor boon of justice is denied us, the craven only is content with less, and the South is thus to be vanquished; Southern chivalry is a vagary of the wildest romance; Southern manhood a dream; and the truth and justice of our cause will be our damning shame."[73]

The secession crisis created many nationalists, suddenly waking from their slumbers and determined to vindicate their manhood. Invoking the geopolitical logic of "King Cotton," Northerners' pusillanimity and their patriotic eagerness to fight, most Southerners did not probe deeply into the implications of Southern nationhood. In the event of war, they predicted, "a million of militia" would rise up in arms, thus constituting "the most effective

70. James Henry Hammond, "Speech on the Admission of Kansas, under the Lecompton Constitution, Delivered in the Senate of the United States, Mar. 4, 1858" (The Mudsill Speech), excerpted in Paul Finkelman, ed., *Defending Slavery: Proslavery Thought in the Old South. A Brief History with Documents* (Boston, 2003), 80–88, at 88.
71. Reagan, *State of the Union*, in Wakelyn, ed., *Southern Pamphlets on Secession*, 150, emphasis added.
72. *Vicksburg Daily Whig*, Jan. 6, 1860, in Dumond, ed., *Southern Editorials on Secession*, 16.
73. "Our Country—Its Hopes and Fears," *De Bow's Review* 29 (1860): 83–86, at 86.

military force in the world."[74] While the machinery of world civilization jolted to a catastrophic halt, planters would switch from cotton to foodstuffs, redeploying slave labor to secure the subsistence and survival of the Southern nation. The "dispersion" of the Southern population "over a mighty space" and its "active and independent habits" and "warlike" character guaranteed the failure of any Northern invasion.[75]

Yet these sanguine—and sanguinary—predictions barely concealed fundamental anxieties. If, as the Alabaman Jabez Lamar Monroe Curry claimed, "the South has more elements of strength and wealth, more ability to sustain herself as a separate government than any country of equal size in the world," those elements remained merely potential until the new nation acted.[76] The challenge to Southern manhood was thus also a challenge to Southern nationhood. "Are we prepared for separate nationality?" asked William Gregg, a prominent advocate of Southern manufactures.

> There is no dependence in man, and nations are equally as unreliable. The nation that may be our friend and great customer to-day, may make war on us to-morrow. Hence the necessity of the South becoming more self-reliant, by the encouragement of direct Southern commerce, and, as far as possible, diversified home industry. It is not necessary that we should have any intermediate agents in exchanging our cotton for the articles of Southern consumption, but it is absolutely necessary that we should make, within ourselves, all the prime necessaries of life, in order to secure independence.[77]

The South had every prospect of *becoming* a great nation, but it was not one yet. It was not enough simply to assert a wish to be free and independent of—and in—the larger world. It was necessary for the new nation to develop its resources fully, not relying on the good will of trading partners who were friends today but might be enemies tomorrow. Gregg's image of the Southern nation thus reversed the free traders' conception of the region's relation to the world: the South was no longer seen as a part of a larger

---

74. Curry, *Perils and Duties of the South,* in Wakelyn, ed., *Southern Pamphlets on Secession,* 52. "At any time," Hammond boasted, "the South can raise, equip, and maintain in the field, a larger army than any Power of the earth can send against her" (Hammond, "Speech on the Admission of Kansas," in Finkelman, ed., *Defending Slavery,* 83).

75. "The Future of Our Confederation," *De Bow's Review* 31 (1861): 35–41, at 36.

76. Curry, *Perils and Duties of the South,* in Wakelyn, ed., *Southern Pamphlets on Secession,* 51.

77. William Gregg, "Southern Patronage to Southern Imports and Domestic Industry," *De Bow's Review* 29 (1860): 77–83, at 78–79.

whole—a world market within which Southerners participated to their own and others' advantage—but rather as a self-contained and "self-reliant" whole or nation. In effect, Southern nationalists turned the free traders' world outside in, domesticating an international division of labor that made Southerners vulnerable to foreign domination.

Advocates of commercial independence gathered in Nashville in 1850 and filled the columns of *De Bow's Review* and other journals with calls for regional economic development that prepared the way toward nationhood. "Political independence is not worth a fig without commercial independence," Fitzhugh wrote in *Sociology for the South* (1854). Breaking from the union and diverting federal revenues to the South would not end the region's dependency, for it would continue to pay "tribute" to "the centres of trade, of capital, and of mechanical and artistic skill" in "England and the North." Only by developing its own resources could the South rise above the degraded level of "conquered provinces."[78] "A Citizen of Virginia" urged planters to invest their profits in a more balanced and diversified economy, thus giving rise to "a higher system of civilization than the world has ever yet known."[79] Southerners naturally were reluctant to invest in the future—and forgo present profits—as long as "King Cotton" reigned supreme. But the threat of war, disunion's inevitable concomitant, focused attention on the liabilities of unbalanced development in an interdependent world economy. Forward-looking Southerners thus called for radical change in the region's political economy: paradoxically, these visionaries recognized, the South would have to become more like the North in order to secure its "separate nationality."[80]

Alienation from the union and agitation for sectional economic development were closely linked throughout the 1850s. Radicals were confident that the South, "like every other separate nation, . . . would establish for itself all those industrial interests indispensable to its independence." To foster "domestic enterprise," a separate national government might even embrace "a policy of national protection"—an astonishing reversal of the South's long-standing commitment to free trade.[81] Given the prosperous state of the Southern economy—and widespread attachment to the union—the prospects for achieving nationhood remained frustratingly ambiguous in the years leading up to the secession crisis.

78. Fitzhugh, *Sociology for the South,* 18.
79. [Garnett], "Citizen of Virginia," in *The Union, Past and Future,* 20.
80. Joseph J. Persky, *The Burden of Dependency: Colonial Themes in Southern Economic Thought* (Baltimore, Md., 1992).
81. Review of *The North and the South,* a pamphlet republished from the editorials of the *New York Tribune, Southern Quarterly Review* 11 (1855): 1–45, at 32.

Secession would be the moment of truth when Southerners became conscious of their new national identity and recognized the need for developing a balanced, self-sufficient, and independent sectional economy. But that recognition might come too late. Could Southerners build a nation in the midst of wartime destruction? Fearing the South's prospective failure, "a Remedial School" of national economists thus called for preparedness, urging Southerners to copy "the industrial improvements of the North." These reformers "have studied the resources of the South and found that it possesses every attribute necessary to an independent and prosperous empire"; by the mid-1850s, their efforts to promote education, internal improvement, and manufacturing had begun to pay dividends.[82]

The key to national power was the development of manufactures. "King Cotton" diplomacy might buy time for Southern development and cotton profits might underwrite its costs, but the new nation could only prosper if it threw off the shackles of economic dependency. The South "must resort to the same means by which power has been accumulated at the North," a writer in *De Bow's Review* urged in 1851. "We hold the raw material," he explained, "and if we will but go into its manufacture, we can control the world." Manufacturing enterprises "will increase our population," in turn promoting "rail-roads and other internal improvements" that "will prove our surest defence either against foreign aggression or domestic revolt."[83]

Sounding very much like Henry Carey, their Northern Whig counterpart, advocates of Southern manufacturing emphasized the multiplier effects of intensive development. Fitzhugh thus dismissed neophysiocratic arguments for the superiority of agriculture—arguments that lingered on in the apotheosis of "King Cotton"—perversely concluding that luxuriant soil was a curse, not a blessing. "Holland and Massachusetts," he concluded, "are two of the richest, happiest, and most highly civilized States in the world, because they farm very little. . . . Ireland, the East and West Indies, and our Southern States, are poor and ignorant countries with rich soils."[84] Celebrating

---

82. Ibid., 44.
83. E. Steadman, "Extension of Cotton and Wool Factories at the South," *De Bow's Review* 11 (1851): 315–19, at 319.
84. Fitzhugh, *Sociology for the South*, 157. For an astute analysis of Fitzhugh's political economy, emphasizing its similarity to Carey's, see Woodward's introduction to Fitzhugh's *Cannibals All!* esp. at xvii–xviii, and Harvey Wish, *George Fitzhugh, Propagandist of the Old South* (1943; Gloucester, Mass., 1962). Eugene Genovese dismisses the resemblance between Fitzhugh and the national economists as superficial, emphasizing instead Southerners' conservative attachment to "old regimes everywhere" (Eugene D. Genovese, *The World the Slaveholders Made: Two Essays in Interpretation* [New York, 1969], 118–244, at 166–67, 172–73).

intensive, neighborhood development, the Hon. J. H. Lumpkin also struck Careyite chords. It was "impossible," he told readers of *De Bow's Review,* to exaggerate "the effect of a manufacturing establishment of any sort in fostering the various branches of trade and business, in producing comfort, refinement and intelligence, and in stimulating the growth and populousness of the surrounding country."[85] "Civilization consists in producing the comforts and luxuries of life," De Bow concluded, and "the measure of national civilization is its industrial skill."[86]

Southern nationalists ran far ahead of Southern opinion generally. McCord and other patriotic Southerners denounced Fitzhugh's heresies, remaining true to their free trade faith until the onset of war. Given its natural monopoly, a free trade in cotton obviously worked to the South's advantage. But Fitzhugh's economics were shaped by his precocious nationalism, not by the free trade axioms that had led an earlier generation of Southerners to question the value of the union. Like Carey, Fitzhugh emphasized the pernicious effects of an "international free trade" that "centralize[d] wealth in a few large cities," impoverishing the agricultural hinterland and, worst of all, "rob[bing] men of their nationality, and impair[ing] their patriotism by teaching them to ape foreign manners, affect foreign dress and opinions, and despise what is domestic."[87] "We must become national," Fitzhugh enjoined, by rejecting the free traders' "cosmopolitanism" and building up "centers of trade, of thought, and fashion at home."[88]

Again like Carey, Fitzhugh linked home and home market:

Towns and villages are breaks that arrest and prevent the exhausting drain of agriculture, aided by rivers and roads. They consume the crops of the neighborhood, its wood and timber, and thus not only furnish a home market, but manures to replenish the lands. They afford respectable occupations, in the mechanic arts, commerce, manufactures, and the professions, for the energetic young men of the neighborhood. They sustain good schools, which a sparse country neighborhood never can. They furnish places and opportunities for association and rational enjoyment to the neighborhood around. They support good ministers and churches, and thus furnish religious consolation

---

85. Hon. J. H. Lumpkin, "Industrial Regeneration of the South," *De Bow's Review* 12 (1852): 41–50, at 48.
86. "State Rights and State Remedies," ibid., 25 (1858): 697–703, at 700.
87. Fitzhugh, *Cannibals All!* 57–58.
88. Ibid., 59. "We are no cosmopolite philanthropists," Fitzhugh wrote in *Sociology for the South,* 122.

and instruction to many who have not the means to visit distant places of worship.—Rivers and roads, without towns, are mere facilities offered to agriculture to carry off the crops, to exhaust the soil, and to remove the inhabitants, rich and poor.[89]

Fitzhugh and Carey both juxtaposed "association," the intimate, reciprocal, and enriching bonds of home and neighborhood, to the deracinated, impersonal, and impoverishing long-distance exchange relations free trade fostered. Their idealized image of the neighborhood was the protectionists' classic antidote to the free traders' cosmopolitanism. It also helped nationalists everywhere forge powerful, affective connections between home and home market, family and nation.[90]

That Fitzhugh's and Carey's conceptions of home and nation should be so similar is not surprising. Great nations necessarily took on a common form through the legal and political processes of mutual recognition, by commercial exchanges that brought the world's products to every home, and by participating in the progress of Christian "civilization." But the most powerful impetus toward convergence was war, for the prospect of violent conflict forced nation-states to turn inward, mobilizing their resources and straining their capacities to the limit. In wartime, cosmopolitan visions of a single, harmonious, interdependent world dissolved, and national distinctions were thrown into sharp relief; with hearth and home under siege, all patriots became protectionists.

Yet even as the outward form of nations converged, nationalists cherished the distinctive personality, the vital "genius" that animated their nationality and justified its preeminent place in the world. Carey and fellow Northern Whig economists persisted in identifying union and nation because they could not imagine that the archaic institution of slavery could possibly make a difference among forward-looking Americans as they ascended to the next stage of civilization and development. But for Southerners such as Fitzhugh who had lost faith in the union, slavery made all the difference. With three billion dollars in slave property on the eve of the war, Southern slaveholders obviously had a material interest in the institution.[91]

---

89. Ibid., 136.
90. On the resonance of *Heimat*, or home, in German nationalist thought, see Alon Confino, *The Nation as Local Metaphor: Württemberg, Imperial Germany, and National identity, 1871–1918* (Chapel Hill, N.C., 1997).
91. James L. Huston makes this point in *Calculating the Value of the Union: Slavery, Property Rights, and the Economic Origins of the Civil War* (Chapel Hill, N.C., 2003), 27–29.

Fitzhugh insisted that slavery was not the archaic institution portrayed by abolitionists, surviving only because selfish slaveholders were unwilling to sacrifice their property and power. To the contrary, slavery as practiced in the South was a progressive, benevolent institution that put Southerners in the moral vanguard of Western civilization. The South was happily free of the social pathologies that afflicted the industrial North: "all is peace, quiet, plenty and contentment." [92] Northern capitalists espoused "free" labor doctrines, all the while exploiting an increasingly immiserated—and potentially revolutionary—working class. By contrast, enlightened planters assumed the rightful responsibilities of social and racial superiority, sacrificing the profits that pauperized free labor afforded their Northern counterparts. "Slavery is a blessing to the negro," Fitzhugh concluded, but it is "too costly, too humane and merciful an institution for France, England or New England," where labor was so cheap it could barely "support human life." [93]

Fitzhugh was convinced that he had caught exponents of free labor in a fundamental contradiction. Northern advocates of a protective tariff were only halfway protectionists, jettisoning protection at home, where it was "Every man for himself and Devil take the hindmost." [94] Northern protectionists were opposed to "international free trade" but not to "social free trade" in the home market, thus sanctioning, at least implicitly, a "terrible . . . war" of rich against the poor that rends "the bosom of society." [95] In Southern society, the protective principle—the animating principle of modern nationhood—was most fully and coherently expressed. The North was divided against itself; Britain, as the great Tory Benjamin Disraeli acknowledged, suffered from a still more advanced case of the social pathologies of free society and had become "two nations." [96]

Yet if Southerners practiced protection at home, most remained theoretically committed to free trade precepts. "The world is divided between two philosophies," Fitzhugh wrote in Sociology for the South. Paradoxically, "the philosophy of free trade and universal liberty—the philosophy adapted to promote the interests of the strong, the wealthy and the wise . . . prevails in the slaveholding States of the South," while the appeal of "socialism," or the protection of the "weak, the poor and the ignorant," prevails in free society.

---

92. Fitzhugh, Sociology for the South, 253.
93. Ibid., 278.
94. Ibid., 10.
95. Fitzhugh, Cannibals All! 57; Fitzhugh, Sociology for the South, 12, 22.
96. Benjamin Disraeli, Sybil: or, The Two Nations (1853), ed. Sheila M. Smith (New York, 1981).

Each section thus cherished "theories at war with existing institutions. The people of the North and of Europe are pro-slavery men in the abstract; those of the South are theoretical abolitionists."[97] Fitzhugh called for a transvaluation of values, the same realignment of institutions and ideology advocated by disunionists who argued for a new Southern Confederacy. When Southerners discarded the maxims of free trade and minimal government, they could fulfill their destiny as a free people. "Government is the life of a nation," he concluded, and "strict construction will destroy any nation, for action is necessary to national conservation."[98] *Government* was simply another word for *protection,* and the protective principle was institutionalized in racial slavery.

Slavery was the foundational institution and animating principle of Southern nationhood. Southerners faced a choice between fulfilling their national destiny (Fitzhugh remained unclear about whether this would be in the states separately or in a new union) and submitting to the regressive, anarchic tendencies of unbridled capitalism in an international free market that dissolved all national differences. "There is no middle ground—not an inch of ground of any sort, between the doctrines which we hold" and those of William Lloyd Garrison and the radical abolitionists. "If slavery, either white or black, be wrong in principle, or practice then is Mr. Garrison right—then is all human government wrong."[99]

Slavery and Civilization

Southern political economists cleared the way for Southern nationhood by demonstrating that the federal union was *not* a nation. As Southerners invoked the right of secession and contemplated disunion, they rediscovered and relocated the national idea. Few followed the precocious Fitzhugh to the anticosmopolitan, nationalist extreme, embracing protection and denouncing British free trade imperialism. Nevertheless, Fitzhugh anticipated the totalizing logic of nationhood, linking political and economic interests in the larger world to the defense of a distinctive form of family and social life, built on the foundation of racial slavery, that guaranteed the region's peace and

---

97. Fitzhugh, *Sociology of the South,* 80.
98. Fitzhugh, *Cannibals All!* 249.
99. Ibid., 254. Fitzhugh extolled the "separate nationality" of the slave states in *Sociology for the South* (1854) and still hoped "to cling" to the union "as long as honor permits" in *Cannibals All!* (1857), 234.

prosperity. Proslavery and sectional-nationalism thus were intimately, inextricably linked.

Southerners came to terms with the institution of slavery long before they discovered their new national identity, but the logic of proslavery moved in a nationalist direction. The defense of the "peculiar institution" constituted an increasingly self-confident defense of the South as a whole that transcended the particular interests of the slaveholding classes. Southern nationalists did not see themselves as benighted defenders of an archaic institution, isolated from the progress of Christian civilization. Instead, the movement for separate nationhood—and for membership in the family of great nations—was a bid for universal recognition of the South's civility.[100]

Provincial Southerners had been obsessed with their relation to the metropole and its progress since the first British settlements.[101] For Southern colonists, the transit through the stages of historical development from barbarism to civilization was complicated by the movement across space, to the margins of the civilized world. The development of slave-based plantation agriculture meant that "barbarous" peoples would be exploited, not displaced. It became increasingly clear—to Southerners at least—that the prosperity of the civilized world depended on the continuing exploitation of darker-skinned peoples and that humanity as a whole therefore could not aspire to the highest levels of civilization. During the Revolutionary years, Jefferson and a few other enlightened Southerners had mistakenly seen slavery as a cancer to be excised by emancipating and expelling enslaved Africans and thus enabling the white republic to fulfill its moral and political promise.[102] But the increasingly sectionalized debate over slavery led Southerners to question both the utility and morality of colonization. Although "the two races" were "so widely separated from each other by the impress of nature," Chancellor William Harper concluded, they "must remain together in the same country."[103]

---

100. The literature on proslavery is voluminous. For a good introduction, see the documents and commentary in Finkelman, ed., *Defending Slavery*. See also Drew Gilpin Faust, *A Sacred Circle: The Dilemma of the Intellectual in the Old South, 1840–1860* (Baltimore, Md., 1977), 112–31, and Kenneth S. Greenberg, *Masters and Statesmen: The Political Culture of American Slavery* (Baltimore, Md., 1985), 85–103.

101. Joyce E. Chaplin, *An Anxious Pursuit: Agricultural Innovation and Modernity in the Lower South, 1730–1815* (Chapel Hill, N.C., 1993), 23–65.

102. Ari Helo and Peter Onuf, "Jefferson, Morality, and the Problem of Slavery," *William and Mary Quarterly* 60 (2003): 583–614.

103. "[Chancellor William] Harper on Slavery," in *The Pro-Slavery Argument; as Maintained by the Most Distinguished Writers of the Southern States* (1852; New York, 1968), 1–98, at 88–89. For an excellent analysis of Harper's work, see Schoen, "Fragile Fabric of Union," 255–62.

The great challenge for civilized lighter-skinned peoples was not to escape the presence of their darker-skinned cousins—the hypocritical impulse of the slave's so-called abolitionist friends—but instead to raise them up from barbarism by imparting the gifts of the Christian gospel and imposing a regime of disciplined labor. "The enslavement of inferior races," McCord wrote in the *Southern Quarterly Review* in 1856, "is an efficient and perhaps the sole available means for" their "physical improvement and . . . moral, social, and religious amelioration."[104] The alternative to enslavement was extermination. As civilized peoples advanced, she explained, "inferior races have invariably disappeared"; this "universal rule of nature" has only been "arrested . . . in the Southern United States" where, "instead of extermination," the "negro" has "met protection."[105] Slavery thus should not be seen as an archaic survival in the civilized world—a barbarous, despotic form of rule at odds with the spirit of the age—but rather as the triumph of restraint, bridling the primitive impulse to destroy "natural" enemies.

According to jurists, restraints on war making measured the progress of civilization. By this measure, Southerners were arguably *more,* not less, "civilized" than their Northern or European critics. As Southerners recognized and celebrated the centrality of slavery to their way of life, they jettisoned free traders' fantasies about the coming millennium of peace and prosperity, acknowledging that war was the normal condition of nations—and races. The triumph of Southern civilization was to secure a lasting peace in the war between the races that promoted the best interests of both and gave the fullest scope to their moral development. "Christian morality is the natural morality in slave society," Fitzhugh insisted, for only where natural (racial) inequalities are recognized is it "natural for men to love one another" and so rise above the "competitive and antagonistic" relations of free society. A state of war characterized social relations within states as well as among them—except in the South, the most civilized society on Earth.[106]

When proslavery Southerners charged their critics with hypocrisy they did not mean to reduce all beneficiaries of slavery in the commercial system of the civilized world, direct and indirect, to the same sordid level of self-interest. To the contrary, they insisted that slave owners, under the

---

104. [Louisa McCord], "Slavery and Freedom," *Southern Quarterly Review* 1 (1856): 62–95, at 87.

105. Louisa McCord, *Political and Social Essays,* 407. On McCord, see Eugene D. Genovese, *A Consuming Fire: The Fall of the Confederacy in the Mind of the White Christian South* (Athens, Ga., 1998), 111–12.

106. Fitzhugh, *Cannibals All!* 218–19.

benevolent regime that was emerging in the South, were the real philan-thropists: *emancipation*, they agreed, was simply another word for *extermi-nation*. The sorry history of persecuted free blacks in the North and the steady descent into barbarism of postemancipation societies in the French and British West Indies gave the lie to the abolitionists' "swindling philan-thropy." [107] Slavery was "a perfect labor system" that secured "harmony, good order, and permanent prosperity in society," while preventing "the collision" between capital and labor, the war of all against all that threatened to reduce all combatants, black and white, to a state of barbarism.[108]

Not surprisingly, proslavery arguments had to overcome significant re-sistance. But resistance had its uses. The abolitionists' war against the South had the happy, unintended effect of convincing "all Southern men of the moral right, the civil, social and political benefit of slavery." [109] "Until within a comparatively recent period," a writer in *De Bow's Review* noted in 1860, "there were but few persons at the South who defended negro slavery as right and proper in itself," but now "it would be difficult to find a Southern man who even doubts the proposition." [110] Antislavery agitation had a *"na-tionalizing* influence," another writer remarked, emphasizing

> the necessity it has produced and the influence it is exerting, to make us a
> separate people [by creating] discordant divisions between the South and
> the world *without,* and the most complete affinity in laws, opinions and
> interests, *within.* It has *sectionalized* our prejudices—the first essence of
> national character and patriotism, and the resolving agent in popular disinte-
> gration. The deduction to be drawn is, that the South *will be forced upon* a
> separate government—a government based not on slavery as a *principle*
> alone, though that will be a sufficient reason, but on slavery as a *fixed fact.*[111]

Southerners sensed—and anxious abolitionists feared—that the tide of world opinion was turning in their favor. Inspiring this view was a new racial

---

107. Ibid., 185.
108. "Our Country—Its Hopes and Fears," *De Bow's Review* 29 (1860): 84; [Louisa Mc-Cord], "Slavery and Freedom," 86–87.
109. *Daily Picayune* (New Orleans, La.), Nov. 4, 1860, in Dumond, ed., *Southern Editori-als on Secession,* 217.
110. A. Roane, "The South—In the Union or Out of It," Washington, May 1860, *De Bow's Review* 29 (1860): 448–65, at 456.
111. "The Destinies of the South," Review of Message of Governor John H. Means to the Carolina Legislature, Nov. 1852, *Southern Quarterly Review* 7 (1853): 178–205, at 187, original emphasis.

"science" that vindicated their assumptions about white supremacy and the emerging conviction that the great challenge, or "burden," of European imperial powers in the mid-nineteenth century was to govern darker-skinned peoples of the tropics for their own and the world's benefit.[112] "Enlightened English minds" were already entertaining doubts about emancipation, the *Southern Quarterly Review* reported in 1851. A decade later, on the eve of the war, a secessionist editor exulted in the progress of proslavery: "no sentiment on earth—not even the new born glories of Christianity—ever gained ground with such rapidity as the rightfulness of African slavery."[113]

Slavery defined the emergent Southern nation. In the most extravagant formulations, the institution and the embryo nation became indistinguishable. "Slavery, and its tendency to expansion, has become a power of itself, inherent, massive and moving"; it is "full of life, vigour and pliability; capable of self-creating power and preservation."[114] Slave labor power was the source of Southern wealth and military strength, "the very substratum, of every individual or national necessity," the single great interest that bound Southerners together, slaveholders and nonslaveholders alike. The South "knows the blessings she enjoys from her labor system, and those who would trifle with this, her sacred right, will arouse a spirit at which, in pallid horror, they will recoil!"[115] "Servitude underlies and supports our material interests," but it was also something far greater, "a providential trust."[116] "For all that we are," Trescot proclaimed, "we believe ourselves, under God, indebted to the institution of slavery—for a national existence, a well ordered liberty, a prosperous agriculture, an exulting commerce, a free people, and a firm government."[117] "Divine Providence" did not bestow its blessings on the master class alone, but it "has rescued more than three millions of human beings from the hardships of a savage state" and "brought them within the blessings covenanted to believers in Christ."[118]

Slavery defined the providential role of the new Southern nation in world history. "We of the South are about to inaugurate a new civilization," De Bow

112. On racial science in the antebellum decades, see William Stanton, *The Leopard's Spots: Scientific Attitudes toward Race in America, 1815–59* (Chicago, 1960).

113. "South Carolina: Her Present Attitude and Future Action," *Southern Quarterly Review* 4 (1851): 297; *Daily Constitutionalist* (Augusta, Ga.), Dec. 1, 1860, in Dumond, ed., *Southern Editorials on Secession*, 280.

114. "Destinies of the South," *Southern Quarterly Review* 7 (1853): 203, 191.

115. "Our Country—Its Hopes and Fears," *De Bow's Review* 29 (1860): 84.

116. Palmer, *The South*, in Wakelyn, ed., *Southern Pamphlets on Secession*, 68.

117. Trescot, *Position and Course of the South*, in Wakelyn, ed., *Southern Pamphlets on Secession*, 16.

118. [Garnett], "Citizen of Virginia," in *The Union, Past and Future*, 27.

announced in July 1861: "We shall have new and original thought; negro slavery will be its great controlling and distinctive element."[119] "Slavery" in these exalted formulations constituted the foundation of Southern nationhood and defined the national character of the Southern people. "Slavery" taught Southern whites to think of themselves as a people, or "race," in juxtaposition both to the black nation in their midst and to the promiscuously mixed society of the North and its seething population of immigrant laborers.[120] Yet if the institution of slavery guaranteed the unity and racial homogeneity of the Southern people, it also brought blacks and whites together. Blacks collectively constituted a distinct nation whose safety and welfare was secured by slavery, but blacks individually were incorporated into plantation families.[121] In the idealized image of the Southern family, the microcosm of the new Southern nation, potential enemies were transformed into productive laborers and loyal, loving children. The nation that slavery created was prepared, even belligerently eager, to mobilize unprecedented and irresistible power in defense of its "sacred right" to determine its own destiny.

Confederate Nation

What sort of "nation" did the secessionists create? The usual answer is that the Confederacy was no nation at all, a radically imperfect political experiment that was bound to fail. Historians have emphasized the "emergent social frictions" and "internal contradictions" that led to defeat on the battlefield and the evanescent regime's "disintegration."[122] In the long trajectory of modern Western history, they assume, the failure of the slaveholders' republic was

---

119. "Future of Our Confederation," *De Bow's Review* 31 (1861): at 41.
120. We are indebted here to David Moltke-Hansen, "The Rise of Southern Ethnicity," unpublished paper in the authors' possession. James M. McPherson emphasizes the ethnic dimension of Confederate nationalism in his *Is Blood Thicker Than Water? Crises of Nationalism in the Modern World* (Toronto, 1998). For an excellent analysis of the complexities of racial and ethnic thinking in Southern nationalism, see Robert B. Bonner, "Roundheaded Cavaliers? The Context and Limits of a Confederate Racial Project," *Civil War History* 48 (2002): 34–59.
121. "Though divided into families, and domesticated with white families," wrote Richard Keith Call, Southern slaves constituted "*a distinct nation of near 4,000,000 of people, and constitutes a part of the American people*" (*Letter to John S. Littell*, in Wakelyn, ed., *Southern Pamphlets on Secession*, 187).
122. Drew Gilpin Faust, *The Creation of Confederate Nationalism: Ideology and Identity in the Civil War South* (Baton Rouge, La., 1988), 84. See also William W. Freehling, *The South against the South: How Anti-Confederate Southerners Shaped the Course of the Civil War* (New York, 2001).

inevitable: it could not possibly survive in an increasingly liberal world committed to slavery's demise; nor, in the long run, could it possibly command the loyalty of its nonslaveholding majority. After all, slavery was, in the words of the Republican party platform, a "relic of barbarism," and the future lay with "free trade and universal liberty."[123] The civilized nations of Europe refused to recognize the Confederacy in its brief time, and historians have been reluctant to recognize it ever since: the Confederacy was not "civilized," nor was it a "nation."[124]

But the judgment of history—*our* judgment—is necessarily ahistorical. God is always on the side of history's winners, making the contingent seem inevitable and providing an inspirational myth of origins or—for "Americans" who survived the Civil War—of redemption in a "new birth of freedom." Yet during the long years of slaughter that constituted the Confederacy's brief life, God apparently could not make up His mind about the war's outcome—or, perhaps, He took advantage of a rare opportunity to chastise Southerners, or Northerners, or Americans generally for their sins, yet another mark of divine interest, if not favor, in His people's fate. Christian faith valorized conflicting conceptions of nationality, and thus justified war.

Southerners did not betray any religious scruples about their own "high mission" on the eve of the war. In the South, "Christ is acknowledged as the common bond of union," De Bow proclaimed, a unity he imputed to God's providential design in instituting slavery.[125] There was no contradiction between slavery and Christianity. To the contrary, "Christian morality can be practiced only in slave society." Slavery brought the gospel to barbarous Africans while promoting the faith among whites: "the South adheres to Christianity," De Bow explained, "*because* the institution of slavery accords with the injunctions and morality of the Bible."[126] Pious Southerners drew inspiration from proslavery's fusion of slavery and nationality, exulting in a Christianizing and civilizing mission that transcended mere material interest. Christian reformers were transforming slavery into a benevolent and

---

123. We repeat Fitzhugh's ironic formulation here (*Sociology for the South,* 80).
124. On the "valuative aspect of nationalism" and the resulting compulsion "to deny that the Southern movement represented a full nationalism," see David M. Potter's influential essay "The Historian's Use of Nationalism and Vice Versa," in Don E. Fehrenbacher, ed., *History and American Society: Essays of David M. Potter* (New York, 1973), 60–108, at 73, 95. Of course, it was hardly foreordained that the European powers would not recognize the Confederacy. See Howard Jones's excellent study *Union in Peril: The Crisis over British Intervention in the Civil War* (Chapel Hill, N.C., 1992).
125. "Our Country—Its Hopes and Fears," *De Bow's Review* 29 (1860): 84.
126. "Future of Our Confederation," ibid., 31 (1861): 38, original emphasis.

civilized institution: perhaps the term *slavery*, evoking as it did the unbridled despotism of a more barbarous age, would have to be jettisoned.[127]

Dedicated to restoring the union but divided on the future of slavery, Northerners had to overcome an apparent piety deficit. Abraham Lincoln's great, belated achievement, eloquently articulated in his Gettysburg Address and sealed by his martyrdom, was to forge an enduring link between restoration of the union and God's providential design for humanity, resolving "that the dead shall not have died in vain; that the nation, shall, under God, have a new birth of freedom; and that Governments of the people, by the people, and for the people, shall not perish from the earth."[128] But most Confederates never doubted, until the last months of the war, that God would reward their heroic sacrifices, that His providential purposes would be served by the triumph of the slaveholding republic. "The whole world should unite in sustaining" slavery, one secessionist exhorted, "and give every encouragement in raising it to a still higher degree of civilization, intelligence, and respectability, and a still higher degree of usefulness to mankind."[129] By what other means could "inferior" races be saved from destruction? How else could they contribute to the prosperity of the civilized world while sharing in its material and spiritual benefits?

Slavery, Southerners were convinced, was the only answer. Slavery was "interwoven with our entire social fabric," and its destruction would "dissolve society" and "ruin our commercial and political prospects for the future."[130] But the resulting devastation would not be confined to the South,

---

127. Henry Hughes suggested the term *warranteeism* in his *Treatise on Sociology, Theoretical and Practical* (Philadelphia, Pa., 1854): "Warranteeism is a public obligation of the warrantor and the warrantee, to labor and do other civil duties, for the reciprocal benefit of, (1), the State, (2), the Warrantee [the slave], and, (3), the Warrantor [the master]" (66–67). See the discussion in Bertram Wyatt-Brown, "Modernizing Southern Slavery: The Proslavery Argument Reinterpreted," in J. Morgan Kousser and James McPherson, eds., *Region, Race, and Reconstruction: Essays in Honor of C. Vann Woodward* (New York, 1982), 27–49. Proslavery polemicists achieved the same rhetorical end by calling "free" workers "white slaves." See, for instance, Louisa McCord, "Negro and White Slavery—Wherein Do They Differ?" *Southern Quarterly Review* (July 1851), in her *Political and Social Essays*, 187–202, at 199.
128. Lincoln, Gettysburg Address (newspaper version), Nov. 19, 1863, in Roy P. Basler, ed., *The Collected Works of Abraham Lincoln*, 9 vols. (New Brunswick, N.J., 1953), 7:20–21. See the discussion in Garry Wills, *Lincoln at Gettysburg: The Words That Remade America* (New York, 1992). On Lincoln's successful efforts to overcome the piety deficit, see Richard J. Carwardine, *Lincoln: Profiles in Power* (Edinburgh, 2003), 220–26.
129. Call, *Letter to John S. Littell*, in Wakelyn, ed., *Southern Pamphlets on Secession*, 188.
130. Palmer, *The South*, in Wakelyn, ed., *Southern Pamphlets on Secession*, 68; Reagan, *State of the Union*, in Wakelyn, ed., *Southern Pamphlets on Secession*, 146–47.

or even be felt most severely there. "Strike now a blow at this system of labor and the world itself totters at the stroke." [131] By ending slavery, the Texan John H. Reagan warned, "you strike down all the investments made in the manufacture of cotton goods; you bankrupt your capitalists; you beggar your operatives; you bankrupt Great Britain; you beggar millions there; you inaugurate starvation and famine in Great Britain to an extent ten-fold beyond that which will be suffered here." [132] "If we fail," the Reverend J. Henry Smith of North Carolina told his fellow Confederates in 1862, "the progress of civilization will be thrown back a century." [133]

The Civil War tested Southerners' faith in their new nation. That the war lasted as long as it did demonstrated the extent and depth of their patriotic commitments. [134] Confederates launched an extraordinary nation-building project—the consolidation of power in a modern, war-making state—that called into question long cherished precepts of limited government and individual liberties (for whites). [135] Slavery was their new nation's vital principle, as secessionists boldly and unashamedly proclaimed—to the eternal embarrassment of neo-Confederate advocates of the "lost cause" who identify instead with the states' rights and strict construction principles that antiprotectionists once deployed against Henry Clay's American System. Slavery was much more than a system of labor to Confederates: it defined their role in world history and brought them closer to God. Without slavery, Southerners would not have constituted a distinct race or people; they would not have possessed the wealth and power to assert and vindicate their claims to national independence; they could not have believed themselves to be a civilized, Christian nation.

---

131. Palmer, *The South,* in Wakelyn, ed., *Southern Pamphlets on Secession,* 70.
132. Reagan, *State of the Union,* in Wakelyn, ed., *Southern Pamphlets on Secession,* 149.
133. J. Henry Smith as quoted in Genovese, *Consuming Fire,* 102. Genovese's recent books offer a sympathetic account of faithful Southerners' commitments to Southern nationhood. See Eugene D. Genovese, *The Slaveholders' Dilemma: Freedom and Progress in Southern Conservative Thought, 1820–1860* (Columbia, S.C., 1992) and *The Southern Tradition: The Achievement and Limitations of an American Conservatism* (Cambridge, Mass., 1994).
134. Our understanding of the Confederate nation is indebted to Gary W. Gallagher, *The Confederate War* (Cambridge, Mass., 1997). See also Emory M. Thomas, *The Confederate Nation: 1861–1865* (New York, 1979) and Rable, *Confederate Republic.*
135. On state building in the Civil War North and South, see Richard Franklin Bensel, *Yankee Leviathan: The Origins of Central State Authority in America, 1859–1877* (New York, 1990).

Epilogue
"Rivers of Blood"

In 1816, Thomas Jefferson excoriated Napoleon for the "rivers of blood" that had so recently run through Europe. A few years later, he foresaw that "rivers of blood must yet flow" for Europe to achieve the republican institutions and liberal practices necessary for peaceful relations.[1] This rhetorical figure was familiar to Jefferson's classically read contemporaries. In Virgil's *Aeneid* (book 6, lines 86–87), the Sybilline prophetess says to Rome's founder: *"bella, horrida bella, et Thybrim multo spumantem sanguine cerno"* ("Wars, horrid wars, and I see the Tiber foaming with much blood.")

The spilling of blood has a familiar, honored place in history; human societies seem always to have gone to war with other societies, and societies have often violently torn themselves apart. Major wars have been such a striking feature of the modern world that historians often use them to mark off periods within the modern era. The Italian wars brought the Renaissance to the heart of Europe; the Thirty Years' War set the stage for early modern ways of thinking; mid-eighteenth-century wars did the same for the Enlightenment as a transitional moment; the Peace of Vienna marked the arrival of a fully realized modernity. Nor was this the end of it. World War I more or less coincided with modernist movements in literature and the arts and the end of the Cold War with the postmodern movement. Whatever the causal relation between major war and the advent of new ways of thinking,

---

1. Thomas Jefferson to Benjamin Austin, Jan. 9, 1816, in Andrew A. Lipscomb and Albert Ellery Bergh, eds., *The Writings of Thomas Jefferson* (Washington, D.C., 1903–4), 14:387–93, at 389; Jefferson to John Adams, Sept. 4, 1823, in Lester Cappon, ed., *The Adams-Jefferson Letters: The Complete Correspondence between Thomas Jefferson and Abigail and John Adams,* 2 vols. (Chapel Hill, N.C., 1959), 2:596.

we conjecture that successive periods in the span of five centuries signal distinctive ways of thinking about the purpose and conduct of war.

Of course, social disruption, material destruction, and loss of human life are constant features of every war, including every modern war. Nevertheless, modern wars became better defined and better institutionalized over time. Wars in the Renaissance ran the gamut from imperial struggle across the Mediterranean to wars of religion, peasant uprisings, princely feuds, and brigandage; beyond the death and destruction they rained on Europe, they resembled each other only in idiosyncratic ways. Early modern war was regularized by law and given its proper place in the natural order of things. Ostensibly undertaken for limited objectives, early modern wars were one of several ways in which the crowned heads of Europe ordered their relations.

Enlightenment thinkers gradually took war out of nature and put it into history, but they did so without giving up the early modern model of war limited in both its objectives and its conduct. As Europe took its place in a world of civilizations, it did so not as an empire but as a society of nations. Civilized nations might indeed have imperial relations with the rest of the world. Nevertheless, common values, set practices, and rules of conduct constituted the bulk of Europe as a public order validated by nature *and* a civil society validated by history. Relations within this society were open as to content, volume, and tenor; in important respects, it was a liberal society.

Such a society accelerated the movement of goods and ideas, and it helped to make the nations of Europe increasingly prosperous. A multiplicity of nations also fostered competition and rivalries. Relations among nations could be, and often were, hostile. Issues of honor and other provocations could result in war. While prosperity, competition, and the diffusion of technology undoubtedly made war deadlier, war making could bring many consequences, not all of them to be feared. A civilization taking the form of a liberal society, and not an empire, meant a public order that still took war for granted.

If these nations were civilized by Enlightenment standards, they were not yet entirely modern. What made them modern—a way of thinking that starts with the properties of wholes—also made war modern in a quite specific sense. Nations function as wholes only when they are peaceful societies, and the first task of the state is to guarantee peace internally. As wholes, nations (here meaning nation-states) also engage in relations with other nations— peaceful relations or war, by their choice. Liberal international society does not preclude war if any nation's ends—the common good of its members— make it the best choice in uncertain circumstances. And if any nation is justified in this choice, then all are.

In a minimally regulated liberal society, nations choose war and pay costs because they can—and because, in a world of nations, they must. If this sounds Hobbesian, it is because we supply a schematic state of nature—an early modern expository device or, as we say today, a thought experiment—with modern nations and project unintended consequences that no liberal could countenance. Romantic nationalism, social Darwinism, the total state: all these a fully modern way of thinking made possible, and all of them contribute to an imaginative reconstruction of the Hobbesian state of nature.

The Hobbesian war of all against all is *not* a civil war because the state of nature is an uncivil state of affairs. Modern nations embrace war at least in part *because* they are modern nations, and their wars are *always* civil wars because they are also members of a civil society. In this respect, the wars arising from the French Revolution represent a transition, since the wars so significantly contributed to making the belligerents into modern nations. Arguably, the first fully modern war was the Civil War fought within the boundaries of the United States. Its belligerents were already modern nations, and there would have been no war had they not been modern nations.

"Modern times are distinguished from earlier ages by the existence, at one and the same time, of many nations and great governments related to one another in close intercourse. Peace is their normal condition; war is the exception. The ultimate object of all modern war is a renewed state of peace." These are the words of Francis Lieber, the Prussian expatriate and citizen of the United States, and they appear in the first formally promulgated "instructions" for the conduct of war, in this case the conduct of Union forces in the Civil War:

> Ever since the formation and coexistence of modern nations, and ever since wars have become great national wars, war has come to be acknowledged not to be its own end, but the means to obtain great ends of state, or to consist in defense against wrong; and no conventional restriction of the modes adopted to injure the enemy is any longer admitted; but the law of war imposes many limitations and restrictions on principles of justice, faith, and honor.[2]

Lieber's code drew on the international law of war for use in a "rebellion" because "humanity induces the adoption of the rules of regular war toward rebels"; "in no way whatever" does it "imply a partial or complete acknowledgment of their government, if they have set up one, or of them, as an

---

2. General Orders, No. 100 ("Instructions for the Government of Armies of the United States in the Field"), War Department, Washington, Apr. 24, 1863, Section I, §§ 29, 30, rpt. in Richard Shelly Hartigan, *Lieber's Code and the Law of War* (Chicago, 1983), 50–51. On the drafting, adoption, and legal status of these instructions, see Frank Friedel, *Francis Lieber: Nineteenth-Century Liberal* (1947; Gloucester, Mass., 1980), chap. 14.

independent or sovereign power. Neutrals have no right to make the adoption of the rules of war by the assailed government toward rebels the ground of their own acknowledgment of the revolted people as an independent power."[3] Early in the hostilities, the union had acknowledged a legal condition of war, thereby making the Confederacy a belligerent power and inducing other powers to declare their neutrality.[4] The union had little choice in this matter; the Confederacy had a government, control over territory, and impressive military successes; it *was* a modern nation. Fought by two nations, the Civil War could only be a modern war, its conduct reflecting the normative requirements of liberal international society. Even by the terms of Lieber's code, it could not be construed as a "civil war," meaning "war between two or more portions of a country or state, each contending for the mastery of the whole, and each claiming to be the legitimate government"— a war that might not be the business of other states.[5]

Lieber's code was the first of its kind. The United States Army continued its use for decades after the Civil War came to a close. Soon translated into German and French, it was also used by the Prussian army in the Franco-Prussian War. At professional meetings beginning in the 1870s, legal scholars drafted model treaties codifying the customary law of war based on Lieber's code and eventuating in The Hague Conventions of 1899 and 1907. Thus was launched a movement to codify the whole of international law, and not just the law of war, in order to identify gaps to be filled and enhance the law's effectiveness. Under the auspices of the United Nations, this emblematically modern project is still underway. Meanwhile the progressive development of the law of war has ensured its relevance for rebellions and even civil wars as Lieber defined them.

In one respect, Lieber's code reflected the sentiments of the time but failed the test of history. Consider these confident assertions: "The more vigorously wars are pursued the better it is for humanity. Sharp wars are brief."[6] Experience with modern war suggests something else. Some wars are sharp

---

3. General Orders, No. 100, X, § 152, 70. "The term rebellion is applied to an insurrection of large extent, and is usually a war between the legitimate government of a country and portions of provinces of the same who seek to throw off their allegiance to it and set up a government of their own" (§ 151, 70).
4. See Quincy Wright, "The American Civil War, 1861–65," in Richard A. Falk, ed., *The International Law of Civil War* (Baltimore, Md., 1971), 30–108, at 42–94, for an overview.
5. General Orders, No. 100, X, § 150, 70.
6. Ibid., I, § 29, 50.

and brief, some are as shapeless as they are lingering. Other wars become more intense as they lengthen, some less so. And some wars are striking for their intensity, duration and cost to belligerent combatants and civilians. Even if they are relatively infrequent, wars of the last sort—wars approaching the condition of total war—are the exemplary instance of "great national wars" fought for "great ends."

By any standard, the Civil War was a "sharp" war but hardly "brief" for a conflict of such unrelenting ferocity. Its intensity called into question the relation among military necessity, the available means for conducting war, and needless suffering, which in turn prompted the adoption of Lieber's code at what turned out to be the war's halfway point.[7] By then not just the fate of the union but the future of slavery defined the war's "great ends," even as it exacted an ever-greater toll in lives. When the war ended two years later, more than six hundred thousand combatants had lost their lives. In a land of thirty-four million people, where more than one-tenth of these people had gone to war and millions more were directly affected by the war's conduct, many rivers had indeed flowed with blood.

The Civil War is the prototype for a certain kind of war—intense, unremitting, protracted, deadly—that has periodically wracked the modern world. Before the Civil War, there were none like it; even the most important wars had been shapeless, shifting affairs. After the Civil War, there were none like it until World Wars I and II. Fought by modern nations and framed by the modern law of war, pursued by means that increasingly obliterated the distinction between civilians and combatants, these wars reflect the modern propensity to look for wholes having properties of their own. Beyond their global reach, the magnitude of destruction, the lives lost, the most salient properties of these wars were the unconditional ends of the belligerents and the lengths to which they went in pursuit of those ends.

After World War II, Winston Churchill asked "the nations of the Continent, between whom the rivers of blood have flowed, to forget the feuds of

---

7. According to Lieber's Code, "military necessity, as understood by modern civilized nations, consists in the necessity of those measures which are indispensable for securing the ends of the war, and which are lawful according to the modern law and usages of war." It followed that "military necessity admits of all direct destruction of life or limb of armed enemies, and of other persons whose destruction is incidentally unavoidable in the armed contests of the war." But "men who take up arms against one another in public war do not cease on this account to be moral beings, responsible to one another and to God," and "military necessity" therefore "does not admit of cruelty—that is, the infliction of suffering for the sake of suffering or for revenge, nor of maiming or wounding except in fight, nor of torture to extort confessions" (Ibid., I, 48).

a thousand years."[8] Yet the nations who fought these wars were not just European, their relations defined not by ancient feuds but entirely modern hopes, fears, and plans.[9] Even the trope is wrong. What we remember is this: burning cities, fields of rubble, human bones and ashes, twisted metal, mushroom clouds—the bloodless images of modernity gone mad.

If we moderns did not invest ourselves in wholes defined by their properties, and thus invest nations with a vitality bodies never before possessed, then these wars could not have happened. If we had not gradually constructed the modern world into another whole whose properties make it a liberal society, then these wars would not have been civil wars. If we do not see them as civil, it is because we have succumbed to the peculiarly liberal myth that the modern world is just a Hobbesian place, a whole with no properties of its own, dominated by the hostile relations of its parts. If, in times of peace, we still doubt the existence of an international society that has the telltale properties of a liberal world, it is because successive world wars have challenged the premises of a civil society.

By convention, the long stalemate following World War II is called the Cold War; we might call it the world civil war that never happened. Two modern nations—the United States and the Soviet Union—confronted each other in righteous indignation and paralyzing fear, the former a product of their co-constituting identities and the latter an acknowledgment of the mass destruction that each could inflict on the other. Any war the so-called superpowers might directly engage in would likely be too sharp, too brief, and too costly even for the greatest of ends; instead, they sponsored, financed, and frequently participated in messy, bloody, indecisive proxy wars. Many of these wars were ostensibly civil wars within nations; most were conducted on the fringes of the liberal world by decidedly uncivil means. When finally the Soviet Union collapsed from the cost of competing with the United States while resisting integration in the liberal world economy, the Cold War ended in 1989 with an astonishing lack of bloodshed.

---

8. Winston S. Churchill, "A New Parliament," Radio Broadcast, Feb. 14, 1948, in Robert Rhodes James, ed., *Winston S. Churchill: His Complete Speeches, 1897–1963*, 8 vols. (New York, 1974), 7:7590–93, at 7591.

9. According to Ernst Nolte, *Der europäische Bürgerkrieg, 1917–1945: Nationalsozialismus und Bolschewismus* (Frankfurt, 1987), a titanic contest between modern ideologies whose champions were Germany and the Soviet Union, and not some ancient feud, made World War II a European civil war. While this claim is perhaps an attempt to vindicate Nazi policies, as many of Nolte's critics aver, we note here its stunning disregard of the war's global dimensions and the ends of other participants—not least the liberal societies whose ends took for granted a liberal world of many nations.

The end of the Cold War prompted a striking variety of conjectures about the future of the modern world. Some writers see the dominant position of the United States as subject to eventual challenge as other nations join forces or join the world economy. Thus the European Union could in due course spawn a European nation whose identity is shaped by the overbearing American "other," just as a modernizing China could finally realize its vast potential. In this view, the world remains a Hobbesian place. Such a world cannot change because it is a whole that has no properties of its own enabling it to change, and it will not change as long as there are modern nations pursuing their inevitably incompatible ends. In John J. Mearsheimer's recent, influential exposition of this point of view, great powers are destined to fight great wars, and China's rapid rise tells us where to expect the next such war.[10]

A second, related conjecture about the future of the modern world is no less bleak in its implications. Some writers emphasize that the most powerful modern nations have always been empires. Indeed, "Thomas Jefferson cherished an imperial vision for the new American nation."[11] Westward expansion fulfilled this vision even as it exacerbated tensions in the federal union and fueled the rise of two nations. After the Civil War, reconstruction meant the forcible incorporation of the South into a continental nation-empire equipped with what amounted to a renovated Constitution and progressively centralizing federal government. By the end of the nineteenth century, the United States had become an empire with extensive overseas dependencies; all of the great powers were empires, even if all of them were not modern nations. After two world civil wars had disrupted existing imperial arrangements, the United States and the Soviet Union emerged as competing empires, and the collapse of the Soviet Union was in the first instance the collapse of an unsustainable empire. Today the United States stands alone, an imperial colossus.[12]

In this view, the modern world is a relatively safe place as long as the United States assumes its imperial responsibility and imposes its will, and eventually its republican institutions and liberal practices, on local despots, fractious peoples, and upstart powers with regional ambitions. The model for this kind of empire is nineteenth-century Britain, which effectively gave the modern world a long peace, sheltered the United States as a nascent empire, and underwrote liberal prosperity. In recent years, the government of

---

10. John J. Mearsheimer, *The Tragedy of Great Power Politics* (New York, 2001).

11. Peter S. Onuf, *Jefferson's Empire: The Language of American Nationhood* (Charlottesville, Va., 2000), 2.

12. See Niall Ferguson, *Colossus: The Price of America's Empire* (New York, 2004), for a striking elaboration of this assertion.

the United States has adopted this model in all but name. Mesmerized by sharp, brief wars of conquest, the nation nevertheless pays insufficient attention to the magnitude, complexity, and cost of its imperial commitments. Even if it did, the fate of the British empire suggests that the uneven development of the liberal world economy, the transiency of empires, and the persistence of nations can only mean that world civil wars will someday resume.

A third conjecture about the fate of modernity takes the end of the Cold War to be "the end of history." Francis Fukuyama popularized this phrase in tribute to G. W. F. Hegel, who, at least in Alexandre Kojève's account, realized that world history had ended with Napoleon's triumph at Jena in 1806.[13] It is perhaps surprising that Fukuyama gave so much attention to Hegel, and so little to Adam Smith, since, for Fukuyama, the end of history in 1989 meant the triumph of "the worldwide liberal revolution." Fukuyama's revolution is ideological: "there is now no ideology with pretensions to universality that is in a position to challenge liberal democracy, and no universal principle of legitimacy other than the sovereignty of the people."[14] Evidently liberal democracies can live in peace and prosper forever; liberal ideology simultaneously vindicates nations pursuing their sovereign destinies and global markets operating without national interference.

That national interests and international markets smoothly fit together in a liberal world is, of course, an article of faith, not just for Fukuyama but for most liberal economists after Smith, the governments of many advanced industrial nations, and large segments of the informed public in these nations. Faith's reward has been two centuries of accelerating material prosperity, occasionally but only temporarily deflected by war and depression. After 1989, with transportation and communications networks knitting the world's economies evermore tightly together, circuits of capital and production increasingly "globalized." To many commentators, globalization is the direct material consequence of liberalism's ideological triumph, and cultural homogenization is one of its most obvious results.

Not everyone thinks that these developments are desirable. National markets, old industries and their workforces, local crafts and customs all suffer. Activists have found a cause and taken to the streets. In direct opposition to Fukuyama's claim that the end of history ratifies popular sovereignty, some writers on the left see in globalization the arrival of a totalizing order that

---

13. "Kojève was of course aware that there had been many bloody wars and revolutions in the years since 1806, but these he regarded as essentially 'an alignment of the provinces'" (Francis Fukuyama, *The End of History and the Last Man* [New York, 1992], 66).

14. Ibid., chap. 4, 39, 45.

betrays "the multitude." As Michael Hardt and Antonio Negri have remonstrated, this too is empire, a new form of domination, one that "operates on all registers of the social order." Such an empire has no territorial limits; "although the practice of Empire is continually bathed in blood, the concept of Empire is always dedicated to peace—a perpetual and universal peace outside history."[15]

Underlying this dark view of history's end, or at least its suspension, is the rise of functionally segmented bureaucracies reaching across all borders and managing every conceivable human need and desire. Deeply implicated in the production, distribution, and consumption of goods and services, managerial and professional elites occupy every department and stratify every zone of modern life. They do much of their work in organizational settings that distance them from nations or markets. They are infrequently accountable to their nominal employers, whether public or private. They operate modernity's complex machinery, including its war and peace machines. They worry about the challenges unleashed by modernity's successes—global warming, environmental degradation, aging infrastructure, aging populations—just as they worry about its failures—poverty, malnutrition, and the disruptive effects of war. It is hardly surprising that observers have such different reactions to a phenomenon so pervasive and yet so elusive, so alien to liberal ideas about civil society and yet so readily integrating the daily reality of a liberal world that is simultaneously a society of nations, a far-flung market economy, and a global civil society.

There is one last conjecture about the future of the modern world to consider, one that differs in kind from the others. It starts not with a liberal world composed of nations, empires, markets, or managerial elites in various combinations but, rather, it begins with worlds set part by virtue of being civilizations. Forced by modernity into an unprecedented degree and range of contact—political, economic, and especially cultural—these are worlds in collision. In Samuel P. Huntington's famous formulation, the future promises a "clash of civilizations." The liberal West's "universalist pretensions increasingly bring it into conflict with other civilizations, most seriously with Islam and China"; furthermore, "the balance of power among civilizations is shifting" against the West. Because "[n]ation states remain the principal actors in world affairs," wars remain an important agent in effecting the great shifts already underway.[16]

---

15. Michael Hardt and Antonio Negri, *Empire* (Cambridge, Mass., 2000), xv.
16. Samuel P. Huntington, *The Clash of Nations and the Remaking of World Order* (New York, 1996), 20–21.

Nevertheless, Huntington claimed that the clash is ultimately about cultural practices and preferences and that the appropriate response of the liberal West is to reaffirm its unique civilizational identity. In other words, the threat is not war but, as Huntington asserted in a later polemic, the more insidious dangers brought on by globalization, such as immigration and multiculturalism.[17] If Western civilization is embodied in a society of nations, it would seem then that the hope for the future is an unapologetic reassertion of a national identity crafted long ago and tested by history. Of course, Huntington is hardly alone raising these alarms, nor is the United States the first liberal country where they have stirred debate. A British politician, Enoch Powell, is still remembered for a speech he made in 1968 decrying the flood of immigrants. "As I look ahead," Powell said, "I am filled with foreboding. Like the Roman, I seem to see 'the River Tiber foaming with much blood.'"[18]

Powell went on to say, although rather obliquely, that Britain might condemn itself to repeat the experience of the United States. "The tragic and intractable phenomenon which we watch with horror on the other side of the Atlantic but which is there interwoven with the history and existence of the States itself, is coming upon us here by our own volition and our own neglect."[19] If in quoting Virgil, Powell had the American Civil War in mind, he need not have worried, for Britain is no more likely than the United States to spawn two nations in this day and age. If he was thinking of the long and troubled history of race relations in the United States, then many nations in today's world can learn from one nation's experience. As Abraham Lincoln said of the bloodbath at Gettysburg, "These dead shall not have died in vain."[20]

---

17. Samuel P. Huntington, *Who Are We? The Challenges to America's National Identity* (New York, 2004).
18. Enoch Powell, "To the Annual General Meeting of the West Midlands Area Conservative Political Centre," Speech, Birmingham, Apr. 20, 1968, in Rex Collins, ed., *Reflections of a Statesman: The Writings and Speeches of Enoch Powell* (London, 1991), 373–79, at 379.
19. Ibid.
20. Lincoln, Gettysburg Address (final text), Nov. 19, 1863, in Roy Basler, ed., *The Collected Works of Abraham Lincoln*, 9 vols. (New Brunswick, N.J., 1953–55), 7:23.

Index